ALL THAT'S HOLY

[A YOUNG GUY, AN OLD CAR,
and the
SEARCH FOR GOD IN AMERICA]

Tom Levinson

Foreword by Harvey Cox

JOSSEY-BASS
A Wiley Imprint
www.josseybass.com

Published by Jossey-Bass

A Wiley Imprint

989 Market Street, San Francisco, CA 94103-1741
www.josseybass.com

Jossey-Bass books and products are available through most bookstores. To contact Jossey-Bass directly call our Customer Care Department within the U.S. at 800-956-7739, outside the U.S. at 317-572-3986 or fax 317-572-4002.

Jossey-Bass also publishes its books in a variety of electronic formats. Some content that appears in print may not be available in electronic books.

Library of Congress Cataloging-in-Publication Data

Levinson, Tom, date
   All that's holy: A young guy, an old car, and the search for God in America / Tom Levinson; foreword by Harvey Cox.—1st ed.
    p. cm.
   ISBN 0-7879-6166-3 (alk. paper)
   1. United States—Religion. 2. Levinson, Tom, date—Travel—United States. 3. United States—Description and travel. I. Title.
   BL2525.L483   2003
   200'.973'090511—dc21   2003010512

Printed in the United States of America
FIRST EDITION
HB Printing   10 9 8 7 6 5 4 3 2 1

CONTENTS

Foreword by Harvey Cox   ix

Part One
Pilgrimage   1

Part Two
Where Are You?   33

Part Three
Preponderance of the Small   111

Part Four
Death and Texas   199

Part Five
All That's Holy   265

Epilogue   299

Acknowledgments   307

The Author   309

For my parents
and
For my wife

FOREWORD

"Who was that young man you were just talking to? You were going on and on, and you're not normally like that. And he just listened and nodded. Seemed like a nice young fella' though."

I can imagine this conversation, or one much like it, having taken place numerous times after Tom Levinson finished his coffee or beer, sauntered out the door and chugged away in his 1994 Nissan Altima. How did he pull it off?

I've found over many years that there are three types of people who want to talk to me about God and religion. The first type I can already detect in a dim light at fifty paces. They're the ones I see coming and cross the street to avoid. Then there is the person who thinks, because I have spent many years teaching religion and theology, that somehow I must know The Answer. Since I do not, those conversations are often very short. But there is a third type, the person who somehow manages to convey to me that he or she really wants to know me and hear my personal views on what is, after all, the most vital and fascinating range of questions imaginable. Tom Levinson is that third kind of person. NO wonder the people he talked with all over America were so willing to open up. And no wonder that the result is the best introduction to what is really going on in the multicolored religious lives of our dappled population you can lay hands on today.

I think I know why Tom Levinson got so many fabulous stories out of so many different people. I was once his teacher, and I know he is not only a Type Three. He is the kind of guy who would put anyone at ease. I am not surprised that people—from heavily robed Moslem women to evangelical preachers—trusted him so quickly. I am just glad he was putting his affableness to good use and not trying to sell them Florida real estate or shares in a Ponzi scheme, because I think if he had been he could have made a pile of money. Putting people at ease so they talk about their faith is not easy to do. Most sociologists of religion I know cannot manage it. That is why they retreat so quickly to graphs and statistics. Most theologians don't even try. They stay mired in the textbook versions of what any given religion is. That is so much tidier. But if there is one thing I have learned in my years of teaching, there is often a big gap between what the textbook says about Christianity or Hinduism or Islam or Judaism and what any given Christian, Hindu, Muslim, or Jew actually believes and does.

It is true, of course, that your average Main Street practitioner of a religion may not know much about its history—or worse, may know it wrong. This is where Levinson's book is also wonderfully helpful. He did, after all, graduate from Divinity School, and as one of his teachers I can testify that he did really pick up a thing or two there. In fact I always saw him as a young man with a voracious inquisitiveness and a huge generosity of spirit. In a school that had its share of Hindus and Buddhists as well as Jews and many different varieties of Christians, everyone liked him. I hope I am not divulging any secrets to reveal that he did seem to spend a good deal of time in the snack bar schmoozing with other students and faculty. Maybe he was in training for the pilgrimage-cum-research journey he catalogs in this absorbing book. But he also passed many hours in the library and plunged into a wide variety of courses. Consequently, when he set out on his quest he had not only honed his conversational skills, he had also packed away enough history and theology to be able to fill in the cracks his informants left open so the reader gets the full picture.

Almost two hundred years ago an inquisitive young French nobleman named Alexis de Tocqueville also set out on a tour of America. He had not come here to study religion in particular. He wanted to find out more about the peculiar brand of democracy that was emerging in this new nation. But what he found, and what he wrote about so eloquently, was religion. In fact, Tocqueville came to believe that without its religion, America's democracy would falter. The values and sense of belonging, the practice in moral argument and institution building Americans derive from their religious groups were, he believed, the sine qua non of the country's democratic ethos. He called them "habits of the heart."

In the years since, Tocqueville and others have sought to grasp the peculiar interpenetration of faith and culture and society that makes America what it is. Today their task is even more difficult. The mosaic of American religious life is more many-faceted now than anything the young French noble could have dreamed of. Still, they try, but few have the gift Levinson has for leading readers into this complex and captivating tangle and actually enabling us to enjoy the plunge.

Reading this book brought to mind other writers who have the knack of getting people to talk, listening well, and writing engagingly. One, of course, is Studs Terkel. He talked to people about their work lives, also terribly basic to who people are. But it just may be that the faith that keeps people going through employment and unemployment, from teen years to the assisted living facility, in "sickness and in health," is even more basic, and that is what *All That's Holy* is about.

This engrossing book about the soul of America comes at an opportune moment. Not many years back some scholars were declaring religion was in decline, faith was no longer needed in an era of science and maybe even God was dead. But as the twenty-first century begins religion is back in a very big way. For bane or for blessing it is an unavoidable subject, not just in America, but all over the world. After Tom Levinson has caught his breath maybe he will want to set off on a wider pilgrimage. The whole world could be his parish, and I warrant that—if this book is any indication—what he comes back with will benefit, inform, and inspire us just as much as he has in these pages.

Cambridge, Massachusetts   HARVEY COX
June, 2003

"Tom coughed delicately.
'For a fella that don't preach no more—'
he began.
'Oh, I'm a talker!' said Casy. 'No gettin' away
from that. But I ain't preachin'.
Preachin' is tellin' folks stuff. I'm askin' 'em.
That ain't preachin', is it?'"

John Steinbeck, *The Grapes of Wrath*

"*The Torah is not in Heaven.*"

The Talmud

PART ONE

[Pilgrimage]

[1]

Pilgrimage isn't something that runs in my family. Skinny legs, noses round at the tip, an affinity for John Hughes movies, yes; those seem to be part of the Levinson family's genetic predisposition. But pilgrimage? Not really, unless you count my Russian forebears' trudging overland to Hamburg before their transatlantic trip to Ellis Island in the late 1880s, or if you grant me—and this I know is a stretch—the forty-year trek from Egypt to the land of milk and honey a few millennia ago.

I think that's why, when the idea for a pilgrimage first arrived, it seemed more like personal whim than religious wonder. I didn't see a bright light, couldn't hear the clap of thunder, never felt the hand of God on my heart. All I got was a whisper from within that curled up the corners of my mouth. It was on the cusp of a mid-afternoon nap on a muggy August afternoon in 1998, a few weeks before my second and final year at Harvard Divinity School began, when the prospect of a homemade, highway pilgrimage appeared before me. The pilgrimage would take the form of a road trip through America. I would talk to people about religion, hear about their faiths, traveling not so much from place to place as from person to person, less to speak than to listen. Learning of their paths, I would pave my own. Hearing their testimonies, I would learn to speak mine. I didn't end up leaving that day, or that month. In fact, it took me a whole year to pull the trip together. But within minutes that afternoon, the flight of fancy became a calling, and the only question I could ask of the whim was, When? I happened to be a pilgrim who, for a host of reasons, didn't need much prodding to be on my way.

Had everything worked according to plan, divinity school should have answered all of my questions about religion. Lectures would have clarified how America could be at once a Christian country and among the most wildly pluralistic cultures ever assembled. Professors would have explained the gulf between the religiosity of America and the secularity of my family. Classmates would have communicated the rationale behind their faith in a way that helped me understand my own. My education, however, didn't come prepackaged. I thought that just by showing up I'd receive the enlightenment I sought, as though it were part of the tuition. But bright lights don't just arrive. One has to search for them. I enrolled at Harvard Divinity School hungry to learn about religion, only to graduate with an increased appetite, as though divinity school were a form of metaphysical Chinese take-out. An hour after finishing, I was ready to eat again.

Of course, had my educational interests proceeded a bit more predictably, I never would have found myself studying religion in the first place. I am Jewish, a born and bred, fourth-generation New Yorker who grew up a Christmas Tree decorating, Judaism heckling, doubting Thomas. We weren't antireligious as much as we didn't believe the subject merited serious attention. Judaism, and in a larger sense religion in general, was viewed in a few ways: as a hobby some families chose; as a relic others stashed, dusting it off for special occasions; and as a leg iron that other people spent entire lifetimes dragging around, clinking at their sides. For us, religion was an antique, though for my older brother, older sister, and me, being Jewish acquired a rosy tint at semiannual intervals, because we got school days off for High Holidays, and spent a fun evening once a year with cousins at the kids' table on Passover. I didn't know that the American colonies had been founded as a New Zion; that the Puritan Pilgrims had cast themselves as "a city on a hill"; that America, like no other place in the history of the world, found religious traditions and personal faiths bumping off of, seeping through, and etching into one another; that 95 percent of Americans believe in God; or that the First Amendment to the U.S. Constitution endowed my Jewish family not simply with the freedom to practice religion but with the historically unprecedented opportunity to ignore it.

Growing up I traveled an adolescent orbit on which God was no more than a figure of speech: "God damn" was my expletive of choice as a nine-year-old Little Leaguer when a ground ball rolled through my legs, and "God knows" was my expression of adolescent exasperation. But before I paint myself as an utterly godless youth, let me confess that I spent the Wednesday afternoons of my preteen years at Hebrew school. Technically, the decision to go was mine, but let's face it, Upper East Side peer pressure brought me there more than any familial obligation or ancestral tug. (Of course, it's true that a desire for belonging has initiated more than one spiritual journey.) To this day I remain convinced that during my four

years of Hebrew school, Omar, the guy who ran the deli next door, recognized me better than the rabbi. Playing hooky, stuffing my face with
Slim Jims and Doritos, was as much an activity as coloring in Abraham
and Jacob in our "My Favorite Patriarch" workbook series. My Bar Mitzvah came, I danced with a pretty girl, and I didn't step into a temple again
until the end of high school, five years later.

It was then that I entered my own spiritual puberty. Friends recommended that I take an elective class on the history of religion, and because
I had already had the teacher for American history a couple of years earlier, I signed up. I saw the teacher, Mr. De Vito, as a quasi shaman-in-
training, though in reality he was a husband, father, alumnus of Union
Theological Seminary, and Marlboro-smoking homeowner in northern
New Jersey. He adorned the walls of his classroom with pictures of religious images from around the world: the gathering of the Muslim faithful at the Ka'aba in Mecca, a portrait of Gandhi, a watercolor print of a
Native American tribal chief. We read from the Gospel of Luke and the
Bhagavad Gita and the story of the Buddha's enlightenment, and under
Mr. De Vito's tutelage, religion's wise, curious, worldly side emerged. To
me it didn't matter whether the people we learned about were historical
facts, inventions of the faithful, or amalgams of an interpreter, because
each of them had a personal story. Before the Buddha was an enlightened
teacher, he was a prince suffering through a spiritual crisis; the warrior
Arjuna, the main man in the Hindu *Gita,* froze as he approached the
battlefield, only to learn over the course of this metaphysical paralysis the
spiritual purpose of his life; and Jesus—I honestly never even knew him
to be a Jew before the class—seemed consistently ambivalent about the
rigor and requirements of his calling. These guys didn't always know they
were going to be prophets. Most of them didn't even want to be prophets.
They were struggling, and the circumstances of their lives demanded that
they uncover spiritual truths that, though canonical for us today, were far
cloudier for them in the moment. I liked this. I relished that they had
doubts, that they changed, and that they cared deeply about those changes.
For the first time, I noticed I had something in common with the faithful.
Religion, I realized then, was located at the individual level as much as, if
not more than, in brittle canon or pious theology.

I entered college and wound up, to my surprise, a religion major. My
senior year, as friends bought pinstriped suits to wear to interviews with
investment banks and consulting firms, I sent out applications to divinity schools. The future bankers smiled admiringly (or was it patroniz-
ingly?) when I described earnestly (or was it smugly?) my plans over plastic
cups of foam-crowned beer in the late spring. I was heading to Harvard

Divinity School, I said, because after majoring in religion, I still yearned to learn more about faith, to understand better why it meant so much to so many when it hadn't meant a thing to me growing up. I didn't give any thought to what I would *do* with this degree. In some respects taking the road less traveled was an end in itself. My distinctness signaled my chosenness. The choice made me a kind of celebrity of the spirit, your friendly neighborhood Deepak Chopra. Other people make plans, I told myself around that time; you have a path. The groundwork for a pilgrimage was being laid even then—though to where and for what I wouldn't know until I returned.

In the aftermath of that initial August afternoon, I pocketed the pilgrimage idea, concealing it the way you smother a newspaper under your jacket during a downpour: in protecting the thing, you can't help but hide it. In early November I called a college playwriting teacher of mine, both because I knew that in her creative life she had been moved to action by whims, and because I suspected that if my idea seemed excessively flaky, or perhaps too conventionally iconoclastic—like the pilgrim's equivalent of a navel piercing—she'd let me know right away, and the flicker of a dream she'd snuffed out would be a mercy killing.

I spent a couple of minutes weaving my way through an explanation before she cut me off. "Oh, *Tom,*" I heard her say, and for an instant I could not tell if the gate was swinging open or slamming shut. "You know what you're doing, don't you?" she asked, pausing for rhetorical effect. "You're leaning toward a quest, a moral quest, and that's not something you have to understand in order to start. Go. Get the feel of listening to people talk. Learn how to be silent. Then talk to anybody. Talk to a toad. Just start. But Tom: understand that, even now, you've already begun."

Her advice ran counter to one of the unbreakable commandments of my youth, a Manhattan-based injunction that in my mind's eye was inscribed not on stone tablets but on Formica countertops: "Thou shalt not talk to strangers." This commandment came with corollaries: accepting rides from strangers was prohibited, eye contact with them was a no-no, and taking food from people you didn't know was out of the question, although Halloween did provide one sanctioned annual respite from our usual state of vigilance. These rules were essentially nonnegotiable. They had been conceived, I assumed, with my best interests in mind, and they existed, I trusted, for my own good. But when the whim arrived, it came accompanied by the impulse to break this commandment.

I felt ready for everything that pilgrimage offers: adventure, transformation, insight, a community found in spontaneity and forged in conversation. But at the time, I overlooked much of what a pilgrim leaves behind.

○

We live in an awe-filled age, smack dab in the midst of world-transforming religious ferment. What's happened in the few years since I traveled around America has only magnified this sense. But even before the catastrophe of September 11 initiated a long run of religion hogging the national spotlight, as the abuses of pedophiliac Catholic priests surfaced, as Muslims and Hindus in India and Kashmir slaughtered each other, and as the numbing, incessant carnage in Israel and the Palestinian territories precipitated a global rash of antisemitic violence, seismic rumblings were altering America's religious, political, and cultural landscape. Established religious authorities and age-old spiritual certainties had broken down. Meanwhile, new orthodoxies ballooned in size and influence. Amid the frenzy of the technology boom and the fear of the impending Y2K, the second half of 1999 was a golden, anxious time. Here people stockpiled for the End of Days. There people splurged as though there were no tomorrow. It was a moment in our shared history when, despite the exterior sheen of invention and possibility, there sat under our collective hood an unpredictable engine. By all apparently measurable scorecards—economic, military, court of world opinion, soft cultural influence—America was winning. Yet within, America felt fractious.

I looked around, heard the voices of people talking, read the papers, and sensed that in profound ways Americans viewed their country as a *pluribus* without an accompanying *unum*. At such a time, talking to strangers seemed like a contribution I could make to the culture—if not as an antidote, then as an offering. The stories of strangers, I believed, could teach me about religion, and about community. I anchored my belief in the core conviction that people wanted to talk, needed to connect, and in the hypothesis that our rapidly fraying public life could be revitalized if strangers could come to be trusted, not feared. There was insight in that thesis, because in the immediate aftermath and subsequent commemorations of September 11, people questioned their faith and groped for understanding, all the while clinging to one another. But there was irony also, because instinctively I assumed that the best way to form community was by tying together a string of strangers rather than neighbors. Like religion itself, pilgrimage is a process of transformation. And like religion, pilgrimage can offer immersion or escape. Sometimes, it can do both.

○

My lease ran out at the end of June, but I wasn't going to leave until the beginning of August, so my girlfriend Liz, who shared an apartment in Boston's South End with a roommate, generously okayed a month of

co-residence. On her way to begin medical school in Chicago that fall, Liz
spent the summer directing a nonprofit sailing program on the Charles
River for Boston-area kids. Late at night, in the weeks before I set out, we
sat in the muggy darkness of her room, drafting the questions I would ask
the people I met on the road. I scrawled out the notes of our conversations on the unlined pages of a notebook, cramming them with chicken-
scratched questions about faith and spirituality, tradition, and memory.
Though I sought her unspoken assurance that strangers would receive me,
Liz forced me to confront a series of questions I thought I could just as
soon neglect, questions more about me than about them. Liz wanted to
know if I realized that my trip would be easier for me because I'm a man,
a white man, a tall, not unattractive white man with straight teeth and no
visible scars. She wanted to know, wanted me to know: Was it my educational pedigree that granted me the right to say hello to strangers, to
"make a contribution to the culture"? Had my personal ignorance about
organized religion emboldened me to inquire into areas where most people are taught early on not to dig? Did I realize that my sense of calling
was indirectly spurred by my sense of privilege? Was it my relative freedom from economic hardship that had anointed me as the one to drive
and ask? After all, didn't my folks have my education covered? I didn't
have to get a job to chip away at my debt right away; in fact, my debt had
been pretty well taken care of. I had taken out loans, borrowed federal
money, but it was my dad, who makes a good living as a financial plan-
ner, who was paying it off. When classmates and friends griped about
their financial predicaments, I nodded but stayed silent. Did any of them
know I had grown up on the corner of Eighty-Eighth Street and Park Avenue, that my brother and sister and I thought our family wasn't poor but
wasn't rich either, because our doormen weren't the ones who wore white
gloves like the ones a few blocks south? Had the scarlet *P* for Privilege
seemed too shameful, the implication being that the where and how of my
upbringing could compromise me, my theological rigor, my status as a pilgrim? These weren't intended as make-you-feel-guilty questions, she said,
but as questions whose answers would make me a better pilgrim, more
attuned to the way people might see me before they actually saw me.
While I tried to welcome these questions, I didn't see their explicit relevance to my trip. After all, I was the interviewer, not the subject, and though
conversation was my destination, I envisioned myself as a chronicler of
it more than a partner in it. I answered Liz's questions haltingly, stutter-
steppingly. To tell the truth, they made me antsy. Now, with the trajectory
of my travels and the arc of our relationship intimately familiar to me, I

understand why. At the time, my eyelids grew heavy when her interrogational high beam turned toward me. Inevitably, I'd turn on my own internal hazards, pull over for the evening, and wake up anew to anxiousness.

By the end of July 1999, I was impatient to get started and, at the same time, strangely impatient to return. I thought I could hear what I needed to before Thanksgiving. My 1994 black Nissan Altima, the one missing both hubcaps on the passenger's side and in desperate need of a wash, would be my mobile classroom. Conversation would be my curriculum, and strangers would be my subjects. Almost everybody believed in this plan, I think—with one exception: a friend of mine's girlfriend, who at a party that summer asked where I was planning to go.

"Out West, Southwest, Texas, Midwest, Deep South, Near South, and Northeast." I can still see the "you've *got* to be joking" look on her face.

"Sounds like a life's work," she said.

"I'll be back by Thanksgiving."

As it turned out, both of us were right.

[2]

The night before I left, Liz gave me a going away gift: a small shopping bag of supplies that was half medicine chest, half pantry. She dumped the contents onto her bed, picked up each item, and narrated its functions as though together they formed the pieces of a slide show. There was a travel toothbrush, a deck of cards, pens, markers, a piece of orange oaktag, pocket notebooks, Wet Naps, and two big packs of regular-flavored Chex Mix. "The oaktag and marker," she said, "you should use in case of a breakdown. And you never know when you're gonna want to play cards with somebody." Then she started in on the medical supplies, among them a box of Band-Aids, a package of Neosporin, fifty yards of gauze, and a roll of adhesive tape. She apologized for failing to include a splint. She conceived of hypothetical mishaps and asked me to envision possible forms of self-care. In the event of a minor accident, I was to wrap my wound in the gauze; however, if some foreign object—she cited a highway sign and my car's emergency brake as examples—protruded from the wound, I had to wrap the bandage differently. I said, "Thank you, that is so sweet," and meant it, but was thinking at the same time, "Whoa! It's gonna be mostly highway driving, Sweetie. No need for the crash course on survival medicine." Liz prepared for worst-case scenarios. I assumed the ideal would come to pass.

Late that evening, I packed my car's trunk with a duffle bag of clothes, a packing box of books, a laundry basket of notebooks, and a small satchel filled with my recording equipment and a Pentax K-1000 camera, the old-school manual kind. I didn't bring a laptop, but a few days before my departure I splurged on a cell phone, largely because I would be un-reachable otherwise. (In the summer of 1999, cell phones had not reached saturation point in the culture; they were still flashy and annoying, not just commonplace and annoying, as they have since become.)

I had a handful of addresses printed neatly into my notebook, and un-derneath them, a few dozen phone numbers prefaced by a few dozen area codes. These belonged to friends and contacts. This was my network of way stations. To keep costs low I would call every one of these names that I could—friends, friends of friends, acquaintances of friends, relatives of acquaintances, though definitely not acquaintances of acquaintances, be-cause a pilgrim ought to know his limits—bartering the hospitality they provided with accounts of the people I met and my most sincere appreci-ation. From their apartments and railroad flats and condos and houses, I planned to make discreet, radial trips, leaving early in the morning, re-turning after nightfall, crashing on futons and floors and beneath wed-ding-present quilts on guest-room beds.

On one of those notebook pages I had written a to-do list. There were three things on it, three scheduled or anticipated events between that first Monday morning in August and my trip's projected finish. I needed to re-turn to Boston in mid-August for a graduation-related event, assist Liz with her move out to Chicago to start medical school at the beginning of September, and visit Washington, D.C., in early November for the birth of my sister Lynn's first baby.

In the morning Liz and I kissed goodbye. Once she roller-bladed into the distance, and after I double-checked her apartment, I opened my car door, eased into the driver's seat, confirmed that the side mirrors were in the right places, and affectionately petted the provisions riding shotgun alongside me: a thermos of water, an apple, and a bag of Chex Mix.

I planned my groundbreaking interview on the road to take place in midtown Manhattan. I read that an Evangelical Christian revival was tak-ing place at Madison Square Garden, and I loved the prospect of fusing the familiarity of the Garden with the relative foreignness of a soul-saving crusade. I slid the key into the ignition on the right side of the wheel and held it there, soaking in the moment, the last before the trip began. With a deep breath I turned the key toward the right, only to hear a conspicuous lack of sound. No automatic revving, no engine grumbling. Nothing but a quiet Boston street on an unseasonably crisp Monday morning. Assuming I'd done something wrong, I turned the key again.

Hard to believe: I had driven the damn thing twelve hours earlier, and here the Nissan had died. Frozen in my seat, I wondered what ancient diviners might have augured when, on the night before beginning a trip on foot, the traveler misplaced his sandals.

AAA arrived about the same time as Liz, kind enough to leave work to answer my distress signal, was helping me with my first attempt with jumper cables. For Christmas a couple of years ago, my mom had bought me a set of jumper cables. *Eddie Bauer jumper cables.* Even then I felt gracious but embarrassed. They came in a circular, black canvas pouch, with that Eddie Bauer signature emblazoned on the front in white. When the tow truck guy from AAA stepped down from his cab, I turned the pouch over so the Eddie Bauer insignia faced the bottom of the trunk.

"That whatcha been usin'?" he asked. The question hit me as though he had laughed at my physique in the locker room. With one hand he pointed to the flimsy designer cables in Liz's grasp while with his other he held his own set coiled like a snake up his forearm. Had he not been wearing a tank top, and had his arms not been covered from wrist to elbow with tattoos, he might have looked like a Hasidic Jew preparing for prayer. "Ya can't start a car with something that small," he said.

We watched him attach metal clamp to aluminum frame, wire to source. We heard the car retrieve its customary hum. I thanked the driver with an obsequious sort of gratefulness as he climbed back into his cab. By now my separation from Liz felt like a syndicated rerun: I kissed her goodbye again, hopped into the front seat, and put the car into drive. No sooner was the car resuscitated than it wheezed and stopped, like some narcoleptic dog. The tow truck, three blocks down the avenue, almost out of eyesight and definitely out of earshot, was no longer an option.

I slumped in the driver's seat. "What the f——?" I began, before Liz shushed me. In place of mourning, we lumbered into action, this time using her cables and her car in an effort to give my car new life. It was then we noticed, under the hood, right near the base of the windshield, a bare, gray, pinky-long chicken-bone. Both of us gulped at what seemed like a foreboding omen. With the cables again in place, Liz took a moment to choreograph an ad hoc dance routine she named the Chicken Dance, something she offered to the gods of vehicular mercy. To a pedestrian passing by, the dance would have straddled the hop in a Native

American circle and the shake of a Chubby Checker twist. I laughed as the car purred for a moment—fifteen seconds, maybe—making a turn left, even, before sighing again into inaction. We tried four or five more times. Liz apologized before breaking the news that she had to get back to work.

"Great pilgrimage, Tommy," I muttered to myself as she rolled away. "Really, top of the line."

I made a second, bashful call to AAA. At least the cell phone worked. The operator told me the wait would be about an hour, so I popped open the trunk and then the box of books, picking the Hebrew Bible from the top.

The whole year I had been reading the Torah—the five books of Moses—every *Shabbat* with Liz and some friends. (In the Jewish tradition, Shabbat, or Sabbath, begins at Friday sundown and ends at Saturday sundown.) The Torah is broken down into fifty-four portions, one for each Saturday of the year, give or take a couple of weeks in which two portions are read and a few weeks set aside for the major holidays. I had missed the previous Saturday's portion, so I read it there on the curbside.

Near the beginning of Deuteronomy, the whole community of Israel is poised to cross the Jordan. Their old leader Moses is speaking. He has already learned that he won't be making it across the river, so his words have the melancholy feel of a farewell. When your kids and their kids, who'll be born across the Jordan, dismiss our deliverance from slavery as a folk tale, Moses says, as some kind of scriptural urban myth, shake your head and tell them that you were there to see the whole thing. "Hear this, O Israel," Moses says, his message reaching a crescendo, "you must befriend the stranger, for you were strangers in the land of Egypt." Though I was waylaid at the starting line, the recognition that Moses had my back was a consolation. My mission to talk to strangers was a *mitzvah,* something one is commanded to do.

The second tow truck arrived. "I was gonna be starting a drive across the country this morning," I said to the driver as we rode in his mountain-fragrance-scented cab.

"You heading south?" he asked without turning his head from the street.

"Eventually," I said.

He chuckled. "Watch out you don't get saved too quick." A theme for the day, I gathered.

The Mobil service station behind Fenway Park fixed the car's ignition and changed the battery, and had me on the westbound Massachusetts Turnpike by late afternoon. The phone rang, with Liz on the other end.

"I got some of the kids in the program doing the Chicken Dance for you," she said.

"It definitely helped. Thank you. But they can stop now. I'm on my way."

[3]

Two days into my journey, having missed the revival, after more than a dozen hours spent putting distance between the Nissan and the familiar terrain of the East Coast, I found myself on a highway somewhere in south-central Ohio. The sun was high, my windows were down, the left lane was clear: the entire setting could have been in the *Pilgrimage for Dummies* manual. Everything ought to have been fine. It wasn't. It is amazing that two days could inspire so much self-doubt. But at the time, I couldn't imagine why *anybody* would want to talk to me.

The highway felt like a vacuum. I couldn't get off, I didn't want to slow down, and as one gas tank and then another emptied, I grew impatient with my reticence. Whatever my hypothesis about contact and conversation and the remaking of American community had been (and how depressing it seemed that after two slow-motion days I was speaking of my pilgrimage in the past tense), I feared I was merely windmill chasing. What if this journey had been only a whim after all, and my first days on the road were merely a preamble of missteps to come? In daydreaming and sugarcoating, had I hatched a pilgrimage from some stale, adolescent, Jack Kerouac fantasy? Or worse, had I simply purchased my identity as a pilgrim?

In the nervous days before I left, after those evenings of conversation with Liz, I sought a way to authenticate myself as a pilgrim. In the process, I followed in the footsteps of many proud Americans who seek to be what they are not yet: I pulled out my wallet. I visited the audio-video store on Newbury Street near the Boston Common and invested in a Sony mini-disk player-recorder and microphone that would capture radio-quality sound. Of course! I will create radio programs of these interviews. I am Charles Kuralt, only hipper. Then I walked over to the Copy Cop on Boylston Street near Fairfield and went straight to the desk where business cards are designed. When I returned the following day, the store's clerk, a woman about my age, pulled from beneath the counter a rectangular box of five hundred cards that cost fifty bucks. Impatiently, I reached for the box. I wanted to insert a few in my wallet, then unsheathe one in front of the store's mirror, flashing it like a police badge, this verification of my calling. But before handing over the box, the clerk snuck a peak at the side of the box, where a sample card had been stapled.

In raised black ink, at the center of the white card, in a typeface I saw as stylized *and* basic, a sort of everytype, I had designed the card to read as follows:

GOD IS:

AN ORAL HISTORY OF FAITH IN AMERICA

Beneath that claim was another, in raised, gray ink: Tom Levinson, *Project Director*. I had chosen to call myself project director, not freelance pilgrim, not stalling member of the workforce, not Quixote 2000. Underneath my name and the italics was the address of the nonprofit organization of a friend who had agreed to sponsor my project, enabling me to apply to foundations for grant money. During July I had written a proposal and sent it to a couple of small foundations, but I wasn't expecting a windfall. My dad offered me a small chunk of money for the trip. To me it was a loan; to him it functioned like an investment. I was a growth stock, and he believed there was at least a chance, hangnail-thin but visible nonetheless, that my pilgrimage would spawn some kind of cottage industry, with me as full-time writer-religious road tripper, or documentary journalist and token Jew for the 700 Club. Such a rationale made my economic dependence palatable.

"*Cool*," the clerk said. As soon as the word left her mouth, I blushed. The Copy Cop lady believed in me. Her small, reflex reaction had suddenly vindicated the plan and my project. "God bless you, Copy Cop!" I wanted to shout.

I shook my head at the memory. The cards were in my wallet as I drove through southwestern Ohio, thinking about how to explain my premature return to family, friends, and self without being branded an armchair visionary and a roadside wallflower. I half-expected that by virtue of naming a road trip a pilgrimage, the world would welcome me without my needing to introduce myself. And so I drove as though expecting some kind of signal—not exactly the burning bush variety, not a command, but a suggestion, an exit off the interstate that looked like an invitation.

I found myself twenty miles north of Dayton, Ohio, when I resolved to quit whining, stop waiting, and just choose an exit. As the signs for Dayton drew nearer, then arrived, I signaled, changed lanes, then left the highway. The off-ramp split in two and I chose the route the car in front of me had not. That road spat me out at a red light. Utterly uninformed about where to go, who to see, and what to hear, I was guided by the exit, the off-ramp, and the road to an answer.

The street signs informed me I was at the corner of Fifth and Keowee. Opposite me, on the other side of the red light, lime green Arabic script ran from right to left across the pediment of a white-stuccoed corner store. That's cool, I thought. Maybe I'm supposed to pull over. No, dummy, I heard, not maybe. Of *course* you're supposed to go in. I parked the car in front of a ramshackle two-story house with its front door wide open, packed the recording equipment and camera in a small, canvas bag, and walked to the storefront. The door had vertical bars and opaque glass, and before opening it I caught in the reflection a cloudy glimpse of my clueless face.

The store stretched long and narrow like a train car. A whiff of spices, heavy like a Middle Eastern potpourri, evoked the atmosphere of an East Jerusalem market. A mechanical grinding sound—occasionally punctured by the screech of a saw—came from a room at the back of the store. The noise halted when an aproned man stepped from the room to the register at the counter. I could see he carried a package wrapped in white paper, held together by masking tape. When he looked up to speak to his customer, I ducked into a side aisle, where I picked up bottles of imported artichoke hearts, canned cherries, and green olives, turning them upside down, blowing off dust—procrastinating, basically. I seemed fourteen again, at the dance in the school cafeteria, nestled between coy and cowardly. The lone customer soon left. With a deep breath I tried to look nonchalant as I walked the thirty feet up the carpeted aisle to the counter.

I waved to the man behind the register—it was less a wave than a "how," the way the native chief is portrayed greeting the Pilgrim spokesman in Thanksgiving reenactments—before saying anything. When I did open my mouth, I came up with, "How's it going?"

"Hi," the young man behind the counter said. He had short, dense black hair, thick black eyebrows, a slightly beaked nose, and a goatee that hadn't quite filled in yet. Light from the windows in the back room lent a soft glow to the counter lined with cigarettes, phone cards, and Chiclets.

Okay, he said hi. Now you, Tommy. "I'm a, I'm, uh,"—there was a good start, promising, professional. "Here's the thing. I've been working on a project where I've been recording talks with Muslims all over the country." This, of course, was a fiction, or as I preferred to see it, a prediction. "And I just got into Dayton and I pulled off the highway and there I was, with Arabic right in front of me. And so I'm wondering if you maybe might have any time to talk." I paused to collect my breath.

"Well, it's Thursday, you know, so it's going to be very busy," he said. In Islam Friday is the set day for rest and prayer, so Muslims do much of their shopping and preparation on Thursdays. I hadn't thought of this. Nodding, I was about to thank him for his courtesy and leave him my card before backpedaling and making a swift pivot out the door. "But if you do not mind the crowd, then yes," he said, sounding flattered, "I would love to."

I introduced myself to Hayder Almosawi. Born in Iraq, Hayder moved to southern Ohio as a teenager with his brothers in 1992, after the first Gulf War.

I had just finished setting up the equipment on the front counter when a swell of customers entered the store. Indian men wearing pleated slacks and golf shirts; light-skinned women in loose-fitting ensembles of silk pants, tops, and head coverings of the same color; and African American men wearing dashiki prints, knit headpieces, and sandals crammed the space near the counter. I felt bashful and hoped that Hayder would proceed with his commerce without thinking of me. But, ambassadorial in the way he greeted customers, Hayder kept introducing people to me in his halting, Middle Eastern accent. "Brother," he said, looking toward a man at the left of the counter, "please, won't you talk to this friend." "Sister," he said, raising his hand to ask the question, "if you have just one moment, here is Tom." He reminded me a little of my grandma Ruth, who at a restaurant has been known to introduce her grandchildren to the maître d', waiters, and occasionally the coat-check staff. As I met more of Hayder's customers, I realized that I had stumbled upon a global sampling of Muslims—natives of Bangladesh, Syria, Uzbekistan, and Dayton—who converged at the market at 5th and Keowee every Thursday afternoon.

Roxanne Masni overheard me introducing my road trip in a nutshell to a Pakistani physician. Roxanne wore a cream-colored, body-length *hijab*. Her wardrobe matched her skin tone. Once the physician left, I pointed down to the microphone and asked if she might have a moment. She nodded. "I'm gonna just give you a few minutes, cause I've got a baby in the car."

Roxanne came from an Indian background, but while many relatives were Hindu and Sikh, her immediate family, living in New Jersey, was Christian. She had worked as a nurse at a local hospital, where many other staff members were Muslims. Contact with them, and her own self-initiated comparative study of Christianity, Islam, and Judaism, had led her to convert to Islam years earlier. Now she taught at the Dayton Islamic School. I would have butted in to ask about this comparative process— what about Christianity had raised questions and what about Islam had answered them—but Roxanne seemed in such a hurry that I worried she might simply leave if I interrupted her. After a few minutes speaking, she paused.

"Is it difficult to be a Muslim in America?" I asked her.

"No," she said. "Because if you go back and read, everything that's in the Bible is in Islam. All the prophets stress exactly the same thing. The covering of the hair, modesty, pork is forbidden—it's all in there. Some people look at Muslims as strange people, all covered up. But if they go back and read their Bible, they'll see the very same thing. In the New Testament, Corinthians talks about women covering the hair, and the modesty, and the dress. Everything's the same. It's just that in Christianity it's gone away over the generations.

"No man makes me cover my hair," she continued. "I cover *my* hair on *my* own. This"—she cradled the fabric covering her head with her hand—"comes from Allah. This is why my hair is covered. No man told me to dress the way I'm dressing."

Now we were rolling. Roxanne made her points forcefully, with none of the quiet deference I expected from a woman in traditional Muslim dress. She spoke with a quick, no-nonsense cadence, as though dictating a letter to a skilled shorthand secretary.

"Excuse me," Hayder said, "if I could interrupt you for a second. If you don't mind."

"No, that's okay," Roxanne said. "I'm gonna go." No, I thought to myself, you *can't* go. Somebody bar the door! But once Hayder started to speak, she remained at the counter to hear what the young shopkeeper had to say.

"There was an Indonesian lady," he said, "she was an exotic dancer. Then she converted to Islam." (I admit, for a moment the thought crossed my mind: Will *she* be in today?) "She chose to get covered. People asked her, 'How come you go from exotic dancer to covered Muslim lady?' She said, 'You know, being a Muslim is wonderful. Being naked and an exotic dancer, it's old-fashioned. A long time ago, before the prophets, ladies and men were all naked. But being covered, where no one can see your body, this is a new fashion.'"

"So the covering is an innovation?" I asked, redirecting the question to Roxanne. "Do you see it that way?"

She nodded. "Modesty's a very, very big part of Islam. Men have a code of dress, too, and a code of conduct. And both have codes of punishment. Men and women are each responsible for our own actions. I'm not going to care about what my husband looks at. He's responsible to God for how he behaves, and I'm responsible to God for how I behave," she said in the kind of finger-wagging tone often reserved for the sets of daytime talk shows. "There's a lot of negative, not truthful things about the way the roles of men and women are perceived in Islam. In the Koran, the roles are equal but different."

As Roxanne spoke I felt a surge of gratitude to both the independent, stereotype-razing perspective she offered of Islam and the highway for leading me to her and Hayder. Islam, before and after the events of September

11, has frequently been represented by images of women cloaked from head to toe. The only visible parts of their bodies are their eyes, peering from narrow slits in their veils. Under yards of seemingly shapeless fabric, the women appear to lack not solely physical shapes but individual identities. They glide like specters, shrouded, as if they live in a state of perpetual mourning: the implication, of course, is that they mourn for themselves. These pictures function mainly as the synonyms for Islamic extremism and women's subservience.

Roxanne Masni transformed my notion of what it is to be a Muslim woman. The veil I assumed to be a commonly understood symbol of subjugation became an emblem of her independence. To be covered was not demeaning but elevating, not a humiliation but an honor. "This is a shield for me," she said, again touching her head covering. She moved her hand back and forth to her head with the compulsive sincerity of teenaged Jewish boys I had observed in an Orthodox Jewish *yeshiva* (school), fidgeting incessantly with their yarmulkes. "This is honor.

"You have to understand," Roxanne continued, "this is religion. To understand Islam, you have to know the religion, and not mistake it for the culture. As converts, we practice the religion and leave the culture out. We try the pure form. My husband is Egyptian. If I know Koran and Hadith, the teachings of the Prophet, and my husband is behaving a certain way and he says, '*That's* part of Islam,' I can say, 'No, it's not.' *That's* only a part of culture."

While I received Roxanne's empowered attitude with enthusiasm, I felt stumped by a few questions that her perspective raised. First, I didn't know if this was Roxanne's opinion or widely acknowledged fact. The Koran called for modesty, but did it specify with any particularity the type of wardrobe that constituted modesty? Second, I wondered whether other converts, both in Islam and other religious traditions, lay claim to a proprietary perspective unavailable to people born into the faith. And what did the "pure form" of a religion, one trimmed of cultural fat and anachronistic, traditional bone, look like? Was such a thing even possible? I wasn't sure.

The Hadith Roxanne mentioned is a collection of hundreds of traditions, also known as *Sunna,* recounting the behavior and words of the Prophet Muhammad, his colleagues, and the earliest Muslim adherents. Muhammad was a seventh-century Arabian merchant, already a middle-aged man when he received the first in what became a twenty-three-year series of revelations. What he heard in these revelations would come to be the complete text of the Koran. While the Koran is Islam's sacred scripture and its immutable text, Hadith constitutes a more elastic recounting of the

Prophet's customs, actions, and lessons. An individual Sunna describes not only what the Prophet preached and practiced, but how. The Hadith, compiled over the two centuries after the Prophet's death, reverentially describes the ho-hum every day of the Prophet—how he walked and talked, how he ate a meal, and how he clipped his nails. The Prophet's life serves as a blueprint for all Muslims, and through Hadith the ideal life became at once historical reality and instruction manual. Interestingly, Hadith is derived from a root meaning "being new." When I asked Roxanne if she saw her covering as "an innovation," she nodded "yes," adding that the etiquette of modesty in dress extended to men as well as women. Both Hadith and the traditions it spawned cloak inheritance as invention, tradition as novelty. Certainly, to dress with a mindful, explicit conservatism is a statement of defiance in America; what might seem hopelessly old-fashioned actually constitutes a vanguard of discretion. I wondered if orthodox believers in other traditions feel the same way.

Roxanne said she had to go. I thanked her. She thanked me. Hayder thanked Roxanne. Roxanne thanked Hayder. We were a chorus of courtesy. As Hayder and I watched the door close behind Roxanne, I glanced over at the mini-disk recorder to confirm it was running. *Yes!* At the very least, even if I was to pack in the pilgrimage then and there, even if no one else spoke with me, I still would have witnessed fifteen iconoclastic, redefining minutes of religion in America. I nodded at Roxanne's points, although what I ended up wanting to say as a reply amounted to a most American expression of emancipation: "You go, girl!"

Still, in the hours spent driving after I left the Almosawis' market, I wondered if Roxanne's form of empowered orthodoxy had been facilitated by her having been born outside Islam's traditional borders. She understood her choices as expressions of a pure form of Islam. But as I thought about them and the rationale behind them, they seemed to be products of her Americanness. After all, had she been born in Saudi Arabia or Iran, where hijab is not an option but an obligation for a woman, Roxanne probably would have been compelled to adopt the customs and the logic behind them offered by the native culture. As an American, she had the advantage of approaching Islam as a student, curious and critical, not as an internal reformer perceived as a troublemaker. Her path seemed a typically American, consumer-bred approach to religion: survey the options, compare and contrast, select what works best for you, then personalize it so that your theology fits your ideology. Like many other satisfied consumers, Roxanne had made a conscious decision to be identified outwardly with a recognizable "brand." Clothing was a personal choice and, simultaneously, a religious declaration.

"She pretty much said whatever I have to say," Hayder said. "That was excellent."

Roxanne's departure sapped some of the energy from our conversation. Not certain how initially to proceed with Hayder in his now-quiet store, I thought I would try to impress him with my Arabic. "*Kiif haalak?*" I said, Arabic for "How are you?" Arabic is a gender-based language, like Spanish and French and Hebrew, and my hope in that moment was that I had remembered to use the masculine form. "I don't know too much more, I'm afraid." He laughed. From the back room, the groaning of a saw made us pause. The shop doubled as a *halal* butchery, where meats are prepared in accordance with Islamic dietary regulations, much the same as Judaism's kosher prescriptions.

Two customers asked for Hayder's help and he excused himself for a moment. I watched his interactions: every time someone asked him "*Kiif haalak?*" or offered some similar greeting in Arabic, he responded with something like a curtsy of the shoulder. When women approached the register, his head momentarily lowered, a subtle sort of bow. I asked him about Islamic protocols and the traditional etiquette of conversation.

"More than twenty *suras* in the Koran speak of it," he said. "How you should speak to people, the level of your voice. When I speak to you, I can't speak with a loud voice when I'm close to you. When you speak with a very loud voice, you do not show respect. You have to speak nicely and properly. Also, the Koran tells you how to walk: you don't keep lifting your head to look at people. This is not a good way. Try to keep your eyes down, not lifting them from the floor. That will win respect from people looking at you. Maybe here people wouldn't understand, but in Muslim countries they do. If I see a lady, looking at her is not nice."

I thought about how I try to make as much eye contact as possible, having inherited, I suppose, the American esteem for eye-to-eye cordiality. I had budgeted in precisely these moments of recognition with strangers as a fertile ground for finding people to interview. Hayder said the Koran preaches a radically different kind of protocol, in which respect is shown through restraint, not directness. The details of the daily world conspire to widen the gulf of misunderstanding between Islamic cultures and America, I thought. Muslim mores seem dogmatic to the U.S. observer, just as American informality appears licentious and explicitly un-Prophetic to the Islamic world. Roxanne's decision to cover herself came from Hadith, and she found strength and pride in what I assumed was a symbol of second-class citizenship. I wrote a note to myself: interpretation should always be available for reinterpretation.

Hayder and I chatted for another hour or so. He seemed content about life in Dayton. He and his brothers had attended Ohio public schools, worked at fast food restaurants like McDonald's and Cracker Barrel, and saved enough money to buy this market. They enjoyed a flourishing business, a close-knit local community of Muslims, and American citizenship. His Islam was very clearly connected to, but distinct from, Roxanne's. Behind the counter, he wore a polo shirt, pants, and brown shoes. Unlike Roxanne, Hayder presented no visible shorthand for his Muslim identity. He was an American shopkeeper, a merchant, and his store operated like a community center. When a young woman with teased blond hair and cut-off jean shorts came in, chomping on chewing gum, looking for cigarettes and a phone card, Hayder greeted her enthusiastically. Though the Koran might legislate them, there were no dress codes to enter Hayder's store. For the American convert, being religious in America means outing oneself and one's faith; for the Iraqi immigrant, being religious in America becomes, in part, a process of blending in.

Before I departed, Hayder filled my backpack with mangoes and homemade baklava. I protested in vain, thinking his offerings way too generous, but my twenty-something self-sufficiency was trumped by his old-school hospitality. I handed him my card. He looked at it and smiled. I told him to feel free to call me, that I'd be on the road a few months more. I walked outside and inhaled the early evening air. I started my car and it hummed. I left the Almosawi brothers' halal market at the corner of Fifth and Keowee, a pilgrim back in business.

[4]

Early the next morning I pushed open the door to the main public library in Covington, Kentucky, a curiously funky, disheveled town across the Ohio River from Cincinnati. In Covington I saw run-down abandoned lots and refurbished Victorian brownstones, oversized Confederate flags hanging from second-story windows and swanky wine bars, all in what seemed to be unusually close proximity to one another. I was in an early experimental phase of my trip, and while the highway and off-ramp had with providence (or dumb luck) led me to Hayder's shop, I wondered if accessing the religious lay of the land in a structured, studious way might yield a more predictably eye-opening day in the field. Perhaps this is also to say that I fully recognized the fickleness of the previous day's discovery, and aware of the old saying that fortune favors the prepared, I thought it wise to do some homework. So I headed to the local library and asked the librarian on duty for something on the community's religious history. After a short search, the librarian handed me a call number and sent me to the stacks to look for *The German Churches of Covington: A History of the German People and Churches of Covington, Kentucky.* Enjoying a catchy title and a breezy read as much as the next guy, I pulled the dusty volume from the shelf.

French and Spanish Catholics were responsible for much of the early colonizing of the New World, especially today's Northeast and Southeast; each culture was as intent as English Protestants on staking a claim to material gain and religious prominence in the late sixteenth and seventeenth centuries. Two centuries later, in the first part of the 1800s, the total number of Catholics in the United States remained small. Yet it was then that the immigration tides of German and Irish Catholics were beginning to flow; within a generation these millions of immigrants would transform American Catholicism and the face of American cities. German Catholics followed the American frontier's expansion westward, and by 1840, with dioceses already formed in Bardstown, Kentucky, and Cincinnati, two hundred Germans a day streamed into Covington. It seemed from my cursory research that the community's first priest, Father Ferdinand Kuhr, was a real catch. But he saw Covington as the Catholic boondocks. In an 1844 letter to a friend back in Austria, he wrote that upon his arrival he "met with families who possessed so little knowledge of churchly matters that one could not attribute a name to them. I myself carpentered an altar that at the present time serves as high altar in the new church. I made the remaining objects necessary for spiritual services or sought to borrow them."

That afternoon in Covington I met a contemporary incarnation of the town's Catholic self-sufficiency, a twenty-six-year old named Maureen Scowby. A native of Milwaukee, a city that like Cincinnati was an early magnet for German Catholics, Maureen worked with the Catholic Volunteer Corps (CVC). The CVC is a community of young Catholics committed to living simply, intentionally, and in close contact with the poor, in imitation of the ministry of Jesus. Maureen, a skinny woman with chestnut brown hair that curled into ringlets like the segments of a Slinky, had the afternoon off the day we spoke. She rolled her white T-shirt, emblazoned with a logo from a community benefit for homeless kids, in cuffs over her pale white shoulders. Maureen was a colleague of an acquaintance, and we sat and spoke on a back porch in the muggy afternoon. Each of us drank a beer.

"I was raised Roman Catholic and went to Catholic school," Maureen told me. "When you grow up that way, certain beliefs get to be engrained in you. The Catholics very much believe, you know, 'We are the true faith.' It wasn't until high school or college when I started thinking about how most of the world doesn't believe in Christ. That was kind of a startling reality to stumble upon. Clearly, most people believe in something other than I do. And I remember thinking, can all those people really be wrong?"

Maureen took a sip from her beer. "It's been in the past five years that, because of one of my community members who's very interested in Eastern religion and philosophy, I've kind of broadened my perspective. You know, spirituality can include reincarnation and the whole idea of the spirit world, and I never really learned that for myself until recently. My struggle with that stuff got me to look at different things and say, Why not? Why can't it be like that? Because someone's been telling me for the last however many years that I have to think a certain way when I don't?

"In college I came to this point when all of a sudden I was like, this is garbage. Women can't be priests. There's all this repression in the Church. This is bullshit. I was very angry, and nothing was making sense. I couldn't even go in a church cause I felt so ostracized by the teachings and the structure. Coming into the volunteer year, I still felt that separation from the Church."

Though we only met that day, Maureen's perspective sounded surprisingly familiar to me. While I knew a lot of disenchanted Catholics in college, and recognized in Maureen's grievances with Church dogma and politics their own struggles, it wasn't their shared gripes that rang a bell. It was more that I deduced that Catholicism had been as feebly presented to Maureen as Judaism had been to me. In her high school awakening to the breadth of religious life, in her open antagonism to the religious tradition of her youth, in her willingness to mine other spiritual traditions for their treasures, Maureen reminded me of me. She seemed like she might be as comfortable talking about Melrose Place as the Via Dolorosa, and this too alerted me to the fact that we shared both early religious disenchantment and popular cultural fluency. Yet despite all of the features that irked and enraged her about the Catholic Church, she nevertheless had made the conscious choice to join the CVC. She appeared to feel at ease with her choice.

"It almost seems," I said, "that you took a leap of faith to enter this community. Did you ignore the things that you couldn't stand, or just learn to live with them?"

Maureen nodded, and picked at the sopping wet label on her beer bottle. "I just realized that I couldn't separate myself, and who I was, from my tradition of being raised Catholic. And I've come to think of it as not any better or worse than anybody else's tradition. It just happens that it's the tradition I was raised in. I think I really kind of came to terms with what that meant for me. It didn't mean that I had to embrace all the tenets or beliefs of the Church. It was okay that I didn't do that. I didn't have to leave the Church, either. But where at one point I felt like, oh, I've *got* to leave the Church, it's so terrible, and I'd ask friends, 'How can you stay in the Church?' I think I came to the point where I felt like, this is my tradition. This is how I was raised. My dad's Irish, and my mom's Czechoslovakian, and their families have been, like, Catholic forever. And that's my tradition, for generation upon generation. I guess people would call me a Cafeteria Catholic, because I kind of pick and choose what I want."

Cafeteria Catholic was a new phrase for me, and I liked it a lot. I assumed, though, that people used it as an epithet, not as a compliment. To many devoted believers, a Cafeteria Catholic was the religious equivalent of freeze-dried coffee. To them, the individual faith that makes demands on the religious tradition reeks of watered-down, liberal arrogance. For Maureen, this was simply part of the personal contract she had drawn up with the Catholic Church. Yet who had given her the opportunity to draft such a contract? I had a hard time grasping the relative ease with which she balanced her antagonism to the institutional Church and her immersion in the life of the Catholic community. Part of me was confused, and part of me was envious. I guess I aspired to the ambivalent clarity Maureen professed, and I had no idea whether I might be able to have it at some later date.

At the core of Catholic history is a series of interpretations—about canon, orthodoxy, and the borders of the faith and its God—that suggests that Maureen's Cafeteria Catholicism was at once iconoclastic, and somehow also an inheritance from her tradition. Ecumenical councils have long been a part of Church history, from early events like the one at Nicaea in 325, called to settle theological disputes, to the one at Carthage in 397, convened to determine what was, and was not, scripture. While these gatherings rigidly defined the acceptable and the heretical, they also revealed the breadth of possible interpretations within the tradition.

The Second Vatican Council, which took place in the 1960s, had an analogously broad impact on the Church. The mission of that meeting was to "update" the Catholic purpose in the world, and while the Church remained a hierarchical institution in the wake of Vatican II, as that council came to be known, individual Catholics were given new power and privileges in relation to the Church itself. It's almost as though organized Catholicism came to the conclusion that, as in the children's song, the Church is the people. Mass could be conducted in peoples' own languages, not just Latin. Catholicism recognized the validity and relevance of other religious traditions. Vatican II placed increased emphasis on the teachings of scripture and the ministry of Jesus. In each of these ways, Vatican II explicitly encouraged Maureen's own search. I figured that the Catholic Volunteer Corps was itself a direct descendant of Vatican II, and its sweeping reinterpretation of the role of laypeople in the life of the Church.

Maureen said she felt a pull to participate in the CVC because she grew up in a "very comfortable" white, middle-class community in Milwaukee, where "people did not have any idea of what was going on outside of the suburbs. They were all closed in their little houses. And that just made me feel suffocated. That's something I struggle with every day still. I definitely have ideas about what kind of lifestyle is right, and what kind of lifestyle is not right. However, I think at one point in my life, driving through a rich neighborhood, I'd be like, 'These people are wrong for doing this. They are wrong for having this house. They are wrong for having that Lexus. They are just spending their money while people don't have anything to eat.'" Just then an ice cream truck circled the block, seducing customers with a repetitive loop of "Home on the Range." The song, rippled by the humid air and the truck's speaker system, played with the muffled quality of a Depression-era record player. "But I've gotten away from that finger-pointing thing. I think there are certain things that I'm uncomfortable with. I have this whole theory about comfortability. I don't ever want to be comfortable, because I think as soon as you become comfortable, you become complacent. When you become complacent, you start forgetting about everyone who's not in that position."

Maureen's community was not a monastic order. It didn't demand chastity or require lifelong fidelity. But the CVC sounded a little like a co-educational set of training wheels for young people looking to learn about and live life as devoted, albeit iconoclastic Catholics. They weren't cloistered in a traditional sense, the way monks and nuns are in monasteries and convents, but Catholics like Maureen Scowby remove themselves from their home communities to discover a more authentic religious experience amid the poor, the stranger, and the other. Maureen stamped the Church of her youth as parochial, a kind of cloister of the suburbs, even as she reconciled it with her new appreciation of the tradition. Did she feel she had to leave to find comfort for herself? Was she fated to a life of spiritual complacency if she remained? Had these questions been pushing me toward the road, too?

As it turns out, Maureen was a lot like Father Ferdinand Kuhr, Covington's first priest. She borrowed from disparate sources to ensure a space for her own spiritual sustenance, and carpentered her own, individual kind of altar. But as she constructed a faith that worked for her—"I kind of have come full circle," she told me—I wondered if a full circle could include equal measures of renunciation and return.

[5]

I drove west out of southern Ohio and watched night spread slowly over the horizon before me. The end of my first week on the road bled into the start of my second. I passed through Missouri, making it as far west as Kansas City before I turned north, skirting the eastern edge of Nebraska as I headed toward Iowa. Though lacking an itinerary, I found that I didn't really need one. Unanticipated clues popped up for me, pointing me down a road, toward a street, and sometimes even into a driveway, strangely, especially when I felt most stymied by my uncertainty.

Without a doubt a story lurked behind the short-circuiting neon and fraying polyester comforters at the roadside motel I stopped at in Des Moines. The owners burned incense at the check-in desk, hung a gaudy deity-of-the-month calendar above their computer monitor, and parked a gleaming Mercedes-Benz, with a bumper sticker that read "I Love Krishna," beside the pickup trucks and Pintos outside the front office. Within the past three decades, since immigration restrictions were repealed in the mid-1960s, people from South and East Asia—among them Hindus and Muslims and Buddhists and Sikhs—have moved to America and built communities in big cities, small towns, and locales in between. The Hindus who run this motel are part of that movement, I thought. I spent the night there, hopeful that come morning I would learn the story about what brought these Hindus from India to Iowa. But when I entered the office in the morning and rang the bell on the counter, a sleepy-eyed Indian woman wearing a casual *sari* covered by a zip-up sweatshirt shuffled out, took the room key from my hand, and promptly returned to the television in the room behind the office. If she had a few minutes to talk, I didn't know, because I never asked.

Demoralized by my lack of gumption, I was about to leave the motel when I spotted the front page of the *Des Moines Register* open in front of me. A lead story highlighted a Trappist monastery near Dubuque that was celebrating its 150th anniversary. Trappist monks spend most of their lives in silence, committing themselves to routines of prayer and manual labor, so I took a few minutes to deliberate about the prospects of a potentially fruitless trip to find tight-lipped Trappists. In the end, though, I figured the breadcrumb provided by the *Des Moines Register* couldn't lead me wrong. I checked my map and from the motel parking lot started on my way to New Melleray Abbey in Peosta, Iowa.

A few blocks into the drive I spotted a man crowned in an orange turban opening the front door of the India Starr restaurant. I pulled over and peeked inside.

"I was hoping to speak—" I started to say, but he cut me off.

"We're closed right now. Come back at lunch."

I held off on the trip to the monastery and returned in the late morning to the Indian restaurant nestled in a Des Moines strip mall for their $5.99 buffet lunch. While there I chatted with the proprietor, a Sikh from India's Punjab region named Porbindar Singh. Porbindar, a tall young man with close-cropped black hair, excellent posture, and a passion for the Russian novels of Gogol and Tolstoy, told me to call him by his nickname, "Baba." Sikhism, a religious community founded in the early sixteenth century in India, is a tradition born of India's religious pluralism, a fusion of Hindu spirituality and Islamic mysticism. Baba said that open practice of the Sikh faith still sometimes provokes hostile reactions among members of different religions in India. Though Sikhs were a tiny minority in the United States, Baba expressed a confidence that they enjoyed legal protection in America in ways they lacked in India. Punjabi Sikhs planted roots in Des Moines and raised money in the hopes of opening a community center. Baba refused money for lunch, so I made a ten-dollar contribution toward the progress of the Sikh Center of Des Moines, and resumed my drive.

When I pulled into the parking lot at the New Melleray Abbey a few hours later, I noticed a bent and shriveled man, draped in a brown robe, leaning against the banister that led to the front door. The robe offered no sense of the shape of this body. I couldn't gauge whether he wore his thick leather belt buckled at waist-level or chest-high.

I introduced myself and extended my hand. "Brother Gus," he said, doing the same. The words creaked from his mouth as though they had aged a decade in a cellar before appearing. We shook hands. I was amazed at the size of his hand and the strength of his grip. He was the size of a ball boy but shook hands like a power forward.

Brother Gus staffed the monastery's gift shop, a brightly lit, carpeted space that sold thin volumes on Catholic spirituality next to homemade jam.

"Do you have a last name?" I asked as we sat on opposite sides of the cash register. "Or are you just Brother Gus?"

"N-A-V-E," he said, spelling out his family name. "It's a German name. It's also the center of the church," he added, giggling. Raised a Catholic in Crete, Nebraska, he worked on a farm during Depression times, milking cows. Perhaps, I thought, that accounts for the strong grip. As a teenager he read a book called *The Story of a Soul*, written by a late nineteenth-century nun who died young. After reading the book, he started to pray for an answer about whether he should become a monk. He was eighty-seven years old when we spoke and had lived and worked at the monastery since he turned twenty-four. Clearly the answer he received had been "Yes."

When we started talking, I peppered Brother Gus with questions, assuming that the key to a successful interview lay in securing the most answers, as though relevance was measured in quantity. Often, though, Brother Gus answered my questions with only one word, and at a certain point in our conversation I concluded that the less I talked, the more he might. Maybe my questions were like so many gnats buzzing around his wrinkled head. One doesn't approach a conversation with a monk, a person nourished by silence, as though it were a press conference.

So Gus gazed at a point past the desk. Ten seconds went by. Then ten more, and then half a minute. It felt nice to sit there quietly in his presence. I noticed that amid the hush, gestures and tics and twitches gained volume. Brother Gus shifted gingerly in his chair. I placed my pen behind my ear and heard the slight scratch of the plastic Bic against my skin. I allowed the silence between my questions and his replies to condense and settle like dew.

"I had a beautiful dream last night," Brother Gus said. I sat at attention. "I was walking, walking different places, but I was always in the presence of God." He laughed for a moment. His torso bristled as though he had coughed. "I never had a dream like that, so I've been trying to do it today." Again he laughed, this time to the point of near exertion. The silent-treatment strategy was paying off. Just keep your mouth shut, I told myself. I was almost giggling with satisfaction.

But alas, as we sat together in the gift shop, the monk's train of thought was punctured by the entrance of a middle-aged woman and her twenty-something son.

"I hope we're not interrupting," she seemed to yell as she walked through the doorway, "but we have to get our shopping done." She was chipper and polite and bustling, and as she headed for the homemade jam aisle, I felt seized by an impulse to pick her up and carry her out of the gift shop, then close and lock the door behind her so Brother Gus and I could have some uninterrupted quiet time. "Don't you *knock*?" I wanted to say. "*We were having a moment in here.*"

"Perhaps we won't have much quiet now," Gus said.

"No, perhaps not," I replied.

We didn't get much time together, because once the customers left, the phone in the gift shop rang. The monk who drove Brother Gus to see his doctor for his semiannual pacemaker checkup was ready to leave.

I offered my hand to Brother Gus and, shaking it with his right hand, he reached out his left hand for mine, and we stood there for a moment, arms crossed like an *X*, my long fingers in his long fingers.

"I also had wanted to give you a hug," he said.

So I bent forward, tucking my chin into the coarse brown robe draped loosely over his angular shoulder. I felt on my back the grip of those hands that had milked cows sixty years earlier. For a few seconds we held each other in a warm, unbalanced, gangly embrace in the empty gift shop. In that moment I believed I gripped bones and prayers. I wished him good luck. He wished me God's blessings.

In the way his small, wrinkled head peeked out from his brown hood, in the way he spoke, with the plodding pacing of homemade pasta being cranked through a grinder, and in the way he called a remote cloister "home," Brother Gus came to remind me more than a little bit of the ancient Yoda in the movie *Star Wars*. There I sat, in the Dagoba System of Peosta, Iowa, listening to this man who might have been almost ninety or, like Yoda, more than nine hundred, share thoughts hewn from a lifetime of prayer. And our meeting happened because of a headline.

From Peosta I drove east into Illinois, tracing a Nissan-shaped shadow across cornfields and asphalt. I had planned to follow Interstate 90 until I reached upstate New York and from there travel the small local roads to Palmyra, the hometown of Joseph Smith and the birthplace of Mormonism. Toledo, Ohio, was both on the route and the home of a friend from divinity school named Mark Russell, so I called him, while I was still in Iowa, to ask about spending the night at his house. He hadn't expected to be home, but as it turned out, he and his girlfriend of however many years had broken up two days earlier, and instead of sticking around Boston to linger amid the messy aftermath, he chose retrenchment in Toledo. I expressed my condolences and pumped my fist. I had a place to sleep in Toledo on Friday night.

Upon waking on Saturday morning and stumbling into the Russells' kitchen, Mark and I saw no sign of his parents save for a symbol of their affection: breakfast. They had left on the table a plateful of prodigiously large cinnamon buns, a carton of orange juice, and a behemoth *New York Times*, one of the Sunday editions in which the sections arrive on Saturday. Had the Russells been around while we ate breakfast, we would have talked about my trip, who I'd seen, what I'd heard. Then I'd have downshifted to talk about Toledo, home of the Mud Hens, the Detroit Tigers' Triple A franchise, and when I came up with something so superficially arcane to the outside world but so germane, so elemental to the lifelong Toledoite, I would be showered, I imagined, with rice, paraded with garlands, and offered doubles, maybe even triples, on the cinnamon buns. Had all that transpired, I likely would have missed the article that altered my itinerary once again.

The Dalai Lama was in New York, and I read that he was slated to speak in the Meadow in Central Park the next day at 11 A.M.

Too bad, I thought. If I weren't in Toledo—in fact, if I were anywhere on the Eastern seaboard—I'd be there. I started my drive toward the Mormons of Palmyra around noon. But an hour later, with the prospect of the Dalai Lama still in my head, I pulled over to a rest stop a stone's throw west of Cleveland, cradled the tattered road atlas in my lap, and calculated the miles still to drive to make it to New York for the talk by His Holiness. The drive, depending on traffic conditions, would take anywhere from eight to ten hours. I called Liz to ask her advice. She wasn't home. I left a message describing my quandary. The decision was not that hard to make. And so it was that a friend's untimely breakup led me to an unexpected date with the Dalai Lama the following morning. I'd just have to find Mormons elsewhere.

That Sunday, at 10:50 A.M., the southern end of Central Park was dead quiet. I walked to the Meadow, the grassy clearing near 65th Street, to find answers, but the vast green lawn looked untouched under a chalky white sky. I moved quickly to the Summer Stage, a concert venue a quarter mile away. That scene struck me as equally disheartening, though at least there I found company, a handful of equally oblivious nomads who stared out at an empty stage for a missing Dalai Lama. Had I read the paper wrong? Not possible, I thought. The monk had to be somewhere. A young guy leaned against the railing, his back facing me, a black backpack with thin straps slung over both shoulders. I nudged him on the side of his arm.

"Any Lama sightings?" I asked.

"Nah, man. Unh-unh."

"You're waiting on him, too?" I asked. He nodded. "You wanna look around?"

He shrugged. "Why not?"

I introduced myself. "I'm Tom."

"Pleased to meet you. My name is Elvis."

The day started muggy, and as we trudged through the Park's intestinal pathways, deliberating at every fork, waiting for the Spirit to guide us, we built up a sweat. I had on a T-shirt and shorts. Elvis Miranda, in his late twenties, was outfitted less appropriately. He wore a long-sleeved black shirt, white jean shorts that hung below his knees, white tube socks that stretched almost as high as the hem of his shorts, and black walking shoes. With the exception of the space stretching between the top of his calves and the bottom of his knee, his whole body was covered. Beads of sweat perched above his upper lip like Christmas lights. Black hair, gelled and matted to his head, fell limp and frizzy in kinky curls around his neck. Elvis, several inches shorter than me, walked with a little swagger, but once our walk turned into a forced march, the swagger turned herky-jerky as he worked to keep pace.

In uneven breaths Elvis told me that he had done some background reading on "the Dolly," as he called him. He shared that he had been in and out of a drug rehabilitation place for a year. He had been introduced to Buddhist teaching in part as a structured response to deal with his addictions. Elvis had circled the date on his calendar weeks before, studied up, arrived early, and found only empty space. I had learned of the event haphazardly, chosen to come spontaneously, arrived on time, and found Elvis. I got the sense that neither one of us necessarily expected to find the Dalai Lama with ease. A recovering addict and a peripatetic pilgrim share a perverse affection for obstacles and digressions. For both of us, the event marked the first time we would hear the Dalai Lama in person.

Arguably one of the three or four most notable spiritual leaders of our time, the Dalai Lama is a Tibetan monk, discovered at the tender age of two to be the spiritual leader of Tibetan Buddhism. The Dalai Lama—an honorific title meaning "Ocean of Wisdom"—is at once religious guru and political figure, the exiled leader of a Tibetan Buddhist community displaced by the Chinese Communist government for the past four decades. He has played a central role, through his travels, his speeches, and his writings, in introducing an accessible Buddhism to a Western audience.

Neither Elvis nor I had a clue where to go. We decided to head west toward the Delacorte Theater, where Shakespeare in the Park takes place. On the way we crossed paths with a pack of thirty or so people. One in their midst wore a turban, a visual cue I interpreted as a divine signal that, finally, we were walking on the straight path.

"Are y'all heading for the Lama?" I asked anyone and everyone in the group.

"No," a woman said. "My husband's leading a tour. I missed it last year 'cause of my bad back. We're heading for Bethesda Fountain. Feel free to join us if you like." Unsolicited chiropractic conditions exist to throw pilgrims off their scent.

"No, thanks," I said on behalf of the two of us, Elvis and me. The king and I backtracked over ground wet and sludgy from a downpour the previous night. Twenty minutes had passed since we began our zigzag, and we appeared no closer to enlightenment about His Holiness's whereabouts. Then it dawned on me that we were enacting some kind of parable. "Of course," I consoled myself, "of course." We played the feature roles in the premier production of the Central Park Sutra, one of the Buddha's lesser known but seminal teachings. My friend Steve, a Zen-practicing Jew, had delivered words of cautionary wisdom when I visited him before leaving Boston a few weeks earlier. He told me, "The only finding we have is in the looking," and I considered his maxim to be an illustrative caption for the scene.

"Maybe this march of ours is metaphoric," I said.

Elvis wheezed an acknowledgment.

At the Delacorte Theater, people sat in a line on blankets. I stepped to the counter to ask about the Dalai Lama's whereabouts.

"He's up at Ninety-Seventh and Fifth, in the East Meadow."

"The *East* Meadow?" I said, sputtering the word. "Shit." I must have looked like I needed oxygen and a sponge bath.

"Now what would the Dalai Lama have to say about that?" asked the far-too-cheeky young woman, no doubt a college drama major interning for the summer.

I struggled in that moment for a clever comeback. But in that moment, winded, all I could muster was, "Keep marching, wuss."

We turned around once again, by this time twenty minutes late with twenty blocks still to go. Once we hit Eighty-Sixth Street, though, we found ourselves among a parade of people who pushed strollers and toted plastic bags filled high with Snapples and bagels and squeeze bottles. In August 1999, the Sermon on the East Meadow was unofficially catered by a consortium of uptown Korean marketers. I overheard people saying that estimates of the crowd ranged from sixty to seventy thousand people. I didn't believe that the Dalai Lama could attract the same number of fans as the band U2 until I saw that south of Ninety-Sixth Street, two blocks from the main seating area, people had already parked themselves. Elvis and I slithered past ringing cell phones, clamoring toddlers, and burning incense, eventually locating a patch of asphalt on the bike and jogging path. We considered ourselves lucky to find what amounted to nosebleed seats.

"The Dolly" was hard to hear. Partly due to an insufficiently powerful speaker system, partly due to neighbors who interpreted the occasion as a picnic, I caught, maybe, every fifth word the Dalai Lama offered. Elvis sat cross-legged, a finger plugging each ear, his head bowed low, down to his lap almost. I clicked pictures of people straining to hear, their hands cupping their ears. I heard three words in a procession: "love, compassion, forgiveness." Then there was a break in which the speakers offered only dead air. Then, "patience." I strained successfully to hear his parting words: "Be nice to one another." Elvis and I had enacted the Central Park Sutra and received static for our efforts.

As it turns out, the Dalai Lama did not say anything in his speech that day that he hadn't said or written before. While well-received and perhaps, momentarily, spine-tingling, the Sermon on the East Meadow was part of a longer speaking tour. It was not a seminal or singular experience for me or Elvis in our seats. As the event dispersed, I thought about similar gatherings—ancient, canonized, unamplified gatherings like Jesus' Sermon on the Mount or Moses' farewell sermon to the people at the end of Deuteronomy—and about how, in truth, almost everybody probably couldn't hear a thing. Some folks took their kids to the Jordan River for a drink of water, others stood on line at the loaves and fishes stand, while still others concentrated with all their might to take in every last word. In the end, people wound up relying on word of mouth. The speaker's injunction to remember what was said amounted, in all likelihood, to a recognition that folks in the bleachers needed some help to know what went down. This struck me then as an important point: most of us don't find ourselves within earshot of Moses. And in the absence of front row seats and first-rate speaker systems, we need to be in earshot of one another.

I neglected to tell Elvis that this, the northern end of the park, was my old stomping grounds, where my dad, brother, and I used to throw a football together, and where, as occasionally delinquent eighth graders, my friends and I shared wine coolers purchased at those same Korean markets. I wanted to hear about Elvis and his background, but I kept up my guard through our sojourn so he wouldn't know anything personal about me and mine. I presumed this reserve to be the pilgrim's appropriate demeanor.

The morning spent looking for the Dalai Lama seemed to me like a thematic postscript for the previous twenty-four hours. On my drive to New York the previous evening, the sky had turned overcast in Cleveland. The sun had broken through near State College, Pennsylvania, then ducked back inside the clouds. Soon, traffic had slowed, and drivers had tapped their brakes to rubberneck the sky above, looking bruised like a boxer's eye, half-yellow, half-purple. Then, with great flair, a biblical kind of rain had fallen. Its claps of thunder had interrupted the radio's AM frequencies and forced me and my car to an interstate crawl of thirty miles per hour. For three hours, torrents of rain had pounded my car, coating the windshield with an opaque film. I had felt like I was driving blindfolded. But once the skies cleared and the stars returned over the rural western half of New Jersey, the Nissan had snaked through traffic as if wearing a siren. I had eaten no dinner. I'd felt a fever coming on. I'd stopped for a break only once. In short, I had driven like a man chasing something.

Something had happened that night during my return to the City, some sort of fatigue-bred possession in which, after two weeks of looking for someone, I'd finally felt like I was heading toward something. Instead of depending on fate—the page a newspaper opened to or the street a highway exit dumped me on—I'd taken direct aim on where I wanted to end up. Of course, the events of the past few days—finding Hayder Almosawi and Baba Singh, meeting Brother Gus, making it back to Manhattan to hear "the Dolly," heading to the wrong spot and finding Elvis Miranda— had revealed that all of these chance encounters can have meaning. Indeed, in the months that lay ahead, I would come to find many stories and people without even looking for them. But if I chose to see the positive signs, then I had to acknowledge the negative omens. On the way from Toledo to New York, once I knew where I wanted to go and how long the trip would last, the sky had opened up, darkening my way. The sun had shone when I appeared clueless; the deluge had struck when I felt clued in.

PART TWO

[Where Are You?]

[6]

I returned to Boston as scheduled and pulled up to the curb in front of Liz's three-story walk-up. I turned off the engine, then immediately turned it back on, just to show the corner where the car had broken down two weeks earlier, where Liz had first unveiled her chicken dance, that the Nissan still lived. We spent the next days living amid cardboard boxes, preparing for Liz's move to Chicago. We folded towels in tall piles, peeled posters from walls, and wrapped glasses in newspaper. Liz recruited a few other people for the moving day itself, strong young bucks who coached in her sailing program. One afternoon in particular, we worked in the kitchen, packing silverware and ceramic bowls. We used a stack of week-old newspapers for packing material. A few hours into the day's efforts, surveying the apartment, I calculated that we wrapped and stored and stashed at a brisk pace. The young guys—they looked like *Dawson's Creek* extras—seemed perfectly capable of lugging the heaviest boxes down the three flights of stairs to Liz's car themselves. So I'd bundle a handful of knives, then check out some of the outdated headlines on our packing material.

"Tom," Liz said, her voice beckoning me to focus. I had been lassoed, softly but firmly, back to task. I wrapped more utensils, stowed them in the packing box, then moved on to the frying pans. While securing one of the pans for travel, I noticed a Yankees box score from a few days earlier. I couldn't stop myself. As soon as my eyes lowered, her voice rose, and once again I heard the sweaty reprimand, "*Tom!*"—this time louder, more assertive, yet somehow also sadder. It was as though she had been waiting for my attention span to wane.

I attributed Liz's antsiness that day to the stress of a move away from family and friends, into a new life and professional path. Moving is an admittedly terrible process, something I had done just about every year since the beginning of college, steeling myself to its apparently annual inevitability. But in the eight months we'd been together, I had never seen Liz so agitated.

The setting in her kitchen, dusty, muggy, sweaty, was a far cry from where and when we had met, at a Christmas party the previous December, one of those curious events that felt to me like kids playing dress-up in their parents' house. The young women wore black dresses and strings of pearls. The young men wore oxford shirts with seasonally appropriate bow ties. I noticed Liz as soon as the door opened for her. She walked in wearing black velvet pants, a vintage fur coat, and funky tortoise-shell glasses. She smiled at the host, who helped her with her coat, and suddenly something chemical and inexplicable took place. It was as though the lights dimmed on everything except her. I had had a few drinks, but this reaction transcended whatever light buzz I felt at the time. She hugged the friend who had invited me to the party, and stuck out her hand for me to shake.

"No bow tie?" she asked me. I had on a plaid shirt, baggy corduroys, and black boots.

I shrugged. "I don't know how to tie one."

I admit, I saw her dark blond hair at this super-WASPy Christmas event and made the mistaken assumption that she wasn't Jewish, so when she said she'd come from a little *latke*-making party at her place, I politely corrected her on the pronunciation. (She called the potato pancakes "lotkeys," not "lot-kuhs," as I had been taught.) She protested, said she was a tribe member, too; that she had grown up saying "lot-key," not "lot-kuh"; and that if I had any other questions, I could raise them then and there. I was smitten instantly. We talked for hours that night, and months later we admitted to one another that we'd started to fall in love at the Christmas party in Beacon Hill.

Of course, all of that was a long way from the less glamorous moving party in the South End in late August. When not packing (and occasionally shirking), I looked for possible interview subjects, and through the wife of a colleague I learned about Sokha Diep, a Cambodian Buddhist who lived a forty-minute drive north of Boston. I called Sokha (pronounced "*so*-kah") at her office, and we arranged to meet late on a Monday afternoon at her home.

Sokha and her husband, Tony, lived in a one-family house on a quiet street in the one-time industrial boomtown of Lowell, Massachusetts. Sokha and I sat at her kitchen table while Tony, who had the afternoon

off, lounged in the next room, watching television. A slow-simmering kettle of curried fish exhaled its scent in steam. She spoke and multitasked
with the sort of adroitness I imagine congresswomen possess, shuffling
from kettle to table with short, efficient steps. She stood no more than five
feet tall, even with the black-and-white-striped scarf, accented with yellow flowers, wrapped tautly around her head like a swimming cap.

Sokha, thirty-four, arrived in the United States as a sixteen-year-old refugee in 1981. Like many of the refugees fleeing Cambodia's murderous
Khmer Rouge regime, her immigration was sponsored by a church group.
She learned English in high school, eventually attending community college near her home in New England. Sokha worked at a hospital in Lowell as a cultural mediator around health care issues. She translated doctors'
questions and diagnoses from English to Khmer, the Cambodian language;
advised Cambodian patients how best to synthesize traditional medicines
with Western care; and advocated for her Cambodian patients in the hospital system.

I asked Sokha what her name meant in her native language.

"Diep is half Cambodian, half Vietnamese," she said. "Long time ago,
Vietnamese invade my country. They move down, integrate. Like in the
United States, they're all mixed. *Sokha* means 'Live forever, happy, healthy
forever, no obstacles.' But it's not that way." She giggled, a machine-gun
type of giggle that could puncture an inflated balloon. She seemed to me
one of those indefatigably cheery people, able to present a sweet side even
when burdened with dark thoughts.

In 1975, when the Khmer Rouge asserted control over Cambodian political and public life, Sokha Diep was ten years old. The regime set out
on a campaign to re-create Cambodian society into a classless, history-
less, religionless utopia. The ruling leaders reset the Cambodian national calendar to year zero; disbanded all institutions, among them banks,
schools, and Buddhist temples; and shepherded the population into rural
fields to work and, frequently, to be slaughtered. In its barbarous ambition, the Khmer Rouge aspired to purify the Cambodian people, and part
of that purification process was the draining of both Buddhist teaching
and animistic, or more magical, folk practices from the population.

Sokha and her fellow Cambodians' experiences seem a testament to the
first of the Four Noble Truths that mark the core of the Buddha's teachings. The basic principle that links Buddhists worldwide, the First Noble
Truth, says, in essence, "Suffering exists." From that single foundation, the
Buddha, a one-time prince and historical Indian teacher who found enlightenment through renunciation and meditation in the sixth century
B.C.E., developed the next three Noble Truths. They posit that desire is the

cause of suffering; that if one eliminates the cause of suffering, one can do away with suffering itself; and that there's actually a bona fide, detailed way to achieve that end of suffering. This fourth Truth unveiled the existence of the Eightfold Path, which asserts that through right intention, right action, and right speech, among other forms of proper conduct, suffering can cease and *nirvana* can be reached. Nirvana is not heaven; it's not even really a place. It is, rather, the state in which the suffering caused by desire ceases. Buddhism teaches that this isn't an article of faith; in fact, there are no articles of faith. Buddhism stresses practice over belief. Buddhists are called to encounter and understand these teachings for themselves.

Three major strains of Buddhism emerged over time from the Buddha's original teachings. One strain, *Theravada,* views itself as the traditional practice, that which sticks closest to the original teachings of the Buddha. It is practiced mostly in south Asia, in places like Burma and Thailand. A second strain, *Mahayana,* emerged as a reform movement in response to *Theravada*. It is practiced in China and Japan and other northern Asian countries. The third strain, a much smaller variety, is *Vajrayana,* the Buddhism practiced in Tibet and Nepal and Mongolia, by the Dalai Lama, and poorly heard by me and Elvis Miranda in Central Park.

The traditions differ with regard to how enlightenment is achieved: one says by chanting, another says by meditation, and still another, like Zen, says that the bewilderment caused by a *koan,* a Zen riddle, can spark an instant of insight. Theravada teaches that monks have a head start toward enlightenment, because they don't have to worry about the grind of the everyday, while Mahayana disagrees, stressing that householders and laypeople have the same opportunity to recognize nirvana as Buddhist monks and nuns. Theravada asserts that we're all on our own, and each person is responsible for his or her own enlightenment. Mahayana looks at enlightenment differently, teaching that an enlightened one, or *bodhisattva,* can help all sentient beings—birds and bees as well as people—reach nirvana, and in fact holds off on individual enlightenment until a collective one can be reached. Vajrayana, expanding on Mahayana, stresses that enlightenment is more easily accessible to the masses than either of the other traditions allows and that through meditation practices, enlightenment can happen quickly. Before the Khmer Rouge declared the practice of Buddhism a crime punishable by death, Cambodians typically practiced the traditional Theravada version.

I asked Sokha how she and her husband had met.

"Met?" she asked as her hands, the color of varnished wood, darted up from her lap to cover her mouth. "Oh, funny. He believe in Chinese fortune-teller. He looking for wife. So he went to Chinatown in New York, and he met this Chinese fortune-teller, this Chinese guy." Sokha dipped her head, a gesture informing me that she found this method not altogether authoritative. "The Chinese guy take chopstick that has some certain word written on it and put it in a can, and he shake, shake, shake." Sokha, imitating the diviner, moved her hands as if mixing a drink served in a coconut. "Whatever chopstick falls on to the ground, then they pick that and read your future. So they said, 'If you looking for wife, then you come up this way.' He came to Lowell because a lot of Cambodians live in Lowell."

In the years following the Khmer Rouge's defeat by the Vietnamese government in 1979, Lowell had become a magnet for Cambodian Buddhist refugees, in part because of the presence in nearby Providence, Rhode Island, of Cambodian Buddhism's most revered monk.

"So the fortune-teller was right?"

"Yeah," she said, smiling with a concession, "the fortune-teller was right. Cambodians usually hang their children's pictures on the wall. My mom hung my picture on the wall. He saw my picture and he fell in love with the picture. He said, 'Who's that girl?' She said, 'Oh, that's my daughter. She come back every summer.' So he wait for me. We married since '95."

I knew that families in many Asian cultures hung pictures of living family members on their walls, but I wasn't aware whether pictures of grandparents and great-grandparents were visible, too.

Sokha told me they were. "It's partly a decoration thing. If you put them in an album, sometimes you go years without seeing them. But also it's tradition. You want to see them every day, even though they're gone. On the wall you see the pictures, and you say, 'Oh, it's time for ancestors.'" Sokha said that at regular intervals funerals are held for deceased ancestors, months and even years after their deaths. "We do it so the ancestors don't get mad at us. We have a ceremony for them. We cook food, give it to people, and when the people eat the food, they believe it will feed the dead ancestors, too." Ancestors with full stomachs make for happy ancestors, Sokha said. Happy ancestors protect, while neglected ancestors imperil, the living. She paused for a moment. "I used to believe that. I still am Buddhist, but I believe only certain things. Not everything, because now I know better." She sat still, resting her arms, fleshy and smooth like a newborn's legs, on the table. "I still know the way they taught me, but now, do I follow or not? Am I flexible a little or not?"

"Is it since you've been in the United States—" I began to ask.

"Mm-hmm."

"That you've started to pick and choose?"

"Yep, pick and choose." Her clipped, high-pitched voice neatly turned the sentence into what sounded like one long German word: *yuhpicken-choose.* "For example, when I get sick I go to the doctor. I get medicine. I don't go to the monk to get blessing water. But I still follow the traditional healing: coining, cupping, pinching to make myself feel better." The coining and cupping Sokha mentioned were methods of acupressure, parts of an ancient Cambodian healing tradition. Practices like these were common among the patient community Sokha counseled in her work. Many Cambodians clung to these practices because they were tradition, but also because they had sustained them during their years of persecution in their homeland.

"But I don't believe in fortune-teller," Sokha said, "and I don't believe in witchcraft either: you know, the spiritual healer who goes into a trance and channels. Dead people come and tell them to do this and this and this, and then you go and do it. I don't believe in that anymore after I learn about scientific way in the United States.

"But I remember when I came to the refugee camp," she continued. "We went to the forest to cut some trees to make a hut we could stay in. That night I got very sick. I almost died. How come I get sick? It not the food; everyone eat the same thing. My aunt said I must have cut some certain tree that I was not supposed to cut because the spirits live in there. So she prepared this offering of a certain food to the spirit, so the spirit would calm down and forgive me. She got chicken, candles, incense, and then she brought it to the place where I cut the tree. The next day, my fever was gone. Everything back to normal. So that made me even more of a believer. Next time I want to cut down even a small tree, I have to ask for permission." It sounded as though, when Sokha lived among Cambodians, when the belief system and the religious structure were homogenously Buddhist, she believed in the traditional healing practices and, consequently, benefited physically from that faith. The ritual, functioning essentially as a placebo effect, worked because Sokha believed it would.

"Looking back on that now," I asked, "do you see what she told you as—"

Again Sokha anticipated my curiosity. "I don't know," she said. "I'm kind of confused. You know? Do I believe in that or not? Like right now, I am on chemo." She tugged at the front of her scarf, snug over her shaved scalp. Sokha had lung cancer. She had learned of her cancer two years before we met. An aggressive chemotherapy regimen seemed to be working, with moderate success. She had lost all of her hair. She and Tony had postponed raising a family. My colleague's wife, the one who introduced me to Sokha, alerted me of this, but I hadn't known how forthcoming Sokha would be about it.

"I'm really sorry," I said. The question of how illness begins, and how to react once it presents, was of more than passing cultural or pertinent professional interest to Sokha. Her life depended on the responses she made to these questions.

"Thanks. Sometimes I get very sick from the chemo. My friend, she's very Buddhist, she come and tell me to meditate, to pray to Buddha for help. And when I see my mom, she tell me to pray to Jesus, because she converted. She's a Christian." Sokha shrugged. "I don't know what's going to help. For me, I think it's only one God anyway, because they all believe in the good path. One path only. So I say, 'Which one do I pray to?' My friend said, 'Pray to both, it can't hurt.' I have to believe, so I do that."

I suspected, however, that praying to both might not double her rate of remission. Here in the United States, Sokha had options about how to respond spiritually and medically to her illness. I thought it possible, and disheartening, that multiple options might in fact dilute the prospect of beneficial effects. The recovery that came from making a poultry offering to a tree's bruised spirit had taken place overnight, but Sokha did not doubt the efficacy of her prayers then the way she did now. Sokha worked as a cultural mediator, so she spent her days straddling traditions. In some respects it made sense that despite her level of expertise, she remained unsure about which course of action to take. But if the experience of the ritual in the refugee camp had any kind of predictive value, the efficacy of Sokha's prayers depended not so much on to whom she prayed, but on what result she believed those prayers would have.

Sokha's mom apparently moved between traditions, too. I was curious whether she had chosen Christianity at the expense of Buddhism, leaving her heritage and its legacy in the dust, or whether she had sculpted her own fusion of Buddhism and Christianity—a Buddhianity, perhaps—from her own sadness and the family's struggles.

"My mom," Sokha said, "she doesn't believe in ancestors anymore. My father, he disappeared during the war. We don't know if he die or live. But we assumed he die, right? 'Cause he never returned to hometown. Everyone came back to look for their family. But not him." Sokha's father, then, was one of the victims of Cambodia's Killing Fields. "So my sister and brother, we thinking during the new year we want to prepare a special meal, and we believe his spirit will come and eat that food. My mom, she wouldn't participate with us because she doesn't believe in Buddhism anymore. She just ignore. She go to the temple with my grandparents, and when they pray, my mom, she just sit there. She not against it; she just don't do it."

Sokha said her mom wasn't "against it, she just don't do it." But I felt saddened and a little wary of the spiritual rift I perceived in her family now. I gathered that Sokha's mother's trust in Buddhism was a victim of the Khmer Rouge regime as well. For some reason I felt an impulse to push Sokha on this point: your mom must have made a blanket rejection of her former tradition if she said no to you, I thought while sitting across from her. I figured this had to be at the root of her conversion. I shuddered at the thought of how terrible that moment must have been, when she and her siblings called over to their mom's house, inviting her over for a ritual that honors and "feeds" the memory of their father, only to hear her regret to inform them of her planned absence. When Sokha's mom replaced Christianity with Buddhism, she effectively purged herself of the past, her ancestors, and their bequests on her present. America permits this kind of substitution, no doubt, just as it endorses Cafeteria Catholicism. The country encourages selection in the religious life the same way it fosters competition in the market. But the kind of selection that operated in Maureen Scowby's brand of Catholicism was not in play here.

I felt I was beginning to understand why. People arrive in America shrouded and scarred. America preaches the virtues of resurrection, of playing it one day at a time, of not looking back lest you turn into salt. For Sokha, along with Hayder Almosawi and Baba Singh, as with the Pilgrims and my own ancestors, fleeing a tsar's edict or the threat of a pogrom, America seduces and saves with its promise of newness. When an immigrant arrives here, having fled a war-torn or famine-ravaged homeland, oftentimes it is their memories from which they seek refuge.

"Do you offer food to your father now?" I asked.

"Every new year's," Sokha answered, smiling. "And for the ancestors, too. I remember every day we'd go to the temple in Cambodia. Every day, my mom prepare food, and then we go off to the temple to pray. I don't go every day here, cause I'm working. In Cambodia, my father work, he support whole family. We could afford to do that. Here, God, you cannot afford. You don't have time. You got to go to work. Go to work, come back," she panted as though having sprinted up flights of stairs. "Here, the tradition kind of fade away. It's not followed strictly here anymore like it was before. A lot of elders isolated, sad, and depressed here in United States.

"Here, the way of life has become Western. The children don't understand tradition. Parents too busy, working, working, working. They don't take time to explain. And grandparents, how can they explain when they don't speak English? The children understand English only. So they lost all the language; not just the culture, but the language, too. I feel very sad for my people. Very sad. There are monks who teach the traditional culture, but nobody goes to learn."

"Do kids with Cambodian parents in America, do they know what happened, or why they're here?" I asked.

"They know, but they don't know. I grew up in Cambodia. I was sixteen when I came here. I went through the war. Children here, they never been through the war. I work with Cambodian teenagers. When I tell them, 'Your parents went through a lot,' they listen but they don't take it serious. Maybe a few children do, but most children, like, 'Ugh, I don't want to hear it.'" She giggled again.

"Yeah, that sounds familiar." I offered this point not as consolation, although maybe it might have been, but as an acknowledgment of familiarity. As a kid, I was clueless about how we had gotten to New York City, what my ancestors were chasing after or hightailing it from.

"Do you believe in reincarnation?" I asked her.

"Yeah, I do," Sokha said. She covered her mouth again, as though she was thirteen years old and had burped in front of a boy she liked. "It's strange." She sounded apologetic. "But sometime I say to myself: 'I try to do good things in this life, why I get sick? Why I have cancer?' I don't understand. I say, 'Maybe in my past life, I do bad things.' So this life I better do good things, so when I reborn, I don't have this kind of disease. I still say that to myself. Then I accept it, and I'm not afraid to die. Whatever come, I take it."

I thanked Sokha for her time, wished her a full recovery, and drove along the edges of the rusting, weathered city. In an earlier time, another wave of immigrants had settled in Lowell to make their American lives. But the factories were now empty, their windows shattered, the smokestacks idle. Other ways of life had died here too.

[7]

The scent of my next destination hit me before I caught sight of it. A slow stream of coiled smoke from incense offerings slithered out a street-level open window. I made eye contact with a thin man wrapped in a robe. This robe, the light orange color of white socks after they've been washed in hot water with a red shirt, had the translucent thickness of tissue. He was young, about my age, with a five o'clock shadow for hair and a vertical streak of yellow dye in the center of his forehead. He stood on the top level of steps leading to an elegant brownstone's entrance on Commonwealth Avenue in Boston's high-end Beacon Hill neighborhood.

"How're you doing?" I asked, looking up at him from the bottom of the steps.

"Fine," he answered. I wondered aloud if there was somebody available to talk, because I wanted to learn a bit about the Hare Krishna community. "I think there is," he said, a noncommittal affirmation.

He motioned me up the steps and into a hardwood hallway. I asked whether I should remove my flip-flops. "Up to you," he said. He spoke with the soft, hesitant tone of someone talking to a librarian. I decided to take them off, slipping them into an empty cubbyhole of a shoe shelf next to aged, beat-up running sneakers and embroidered slippers with threadbare weavings.

In the midday, the house felt like early evening. Painted portraits of mustachioed teachers and garish, gray-skinned deities adorned parts of the dim room's walls. My bare feet tingled against the cold hardwood floor. I cracked my toes. This man and I stood next to each other in the quiet hallway.

"I'm Tom," I said, holding out my hand. His hand met mine and he told me his name.

It's not that I didn't hear him the first time, or that I didn't catch the name in its entirety the second time. He could have repeated it ten more times and still I'd have waved my personal white flag. In that instant, post introduction, I uttered a silent prayer: may I never have to call roll for a gathering of Hare Krishnas. I asked him to spell the name, and he did. Put together, the letters became Kisna Duaipayana Das. He told me that the name harkened back to an author of the Vedas—the encyclopedic corpus of Hindu sacred revelation and the accompanying traditions—who chose to live as a hermit five millennia ago.

"Every devotee at the end says *Das*," Kisna said, "because *Das* means servant. *Kisna Duaipayana* is the great devotee who wrote down the Vedas. So *das* means I'm the servant devoted to that person."

Kisna and I sat on floor pillows. I have to admit I was trying to impress him, albeit discreetly. I wanted to display my yogi-like discipline by remaining in one cross-legged position throughout our interview. I hoped he might remember me with a wistful admiration as the guy who sat without shifting.

"Is the name you take as an initiate a description of you?" I asked.

"I'm not a massive crowd person. I'm more content to be solitary or in smaller group situations. Kisna Duaipayana was like that. He was writing, he was a devotee, but he wasn't with so many other people. Everyone has different qualities. That's what makes spiritual life nice. Everyone in this temple's certainly different." Fifteen devotees lived in the house, he told me, both men and women, from the ages of eighteen to sixty-one. "People do a variety of things. Some might distribute books. Others might do a Food for Life program—where we cook vegetarian meals and feed people who don't have much income. Other people might be writing or teaching Krishna consciousness. Some people will chant 'Hare Krishna' all the time. They don't seem to do anything else. But that's also preaching. When someone comes to the temple and they hear the chanting, they'll ask about the chanting, and they'll get spiritual benefit from hearing it. The ways of expressing Krishna consciousness are almost unlimited."

I requested a sample of the mantra.

Kisna began a spoken-word version. "It goes 'Hare Krishna, Hare Krishna, Krishna Krishna, Hare Hare. Hare Ram, Hare Ram, Ram Ram, Hare Hare.' One reason why this is called the Hare Krishna movement is because people would always see devotees on the street chanting this mantra. The mantra is made up of names of God: *Hare* signifies God's energies; *Krishna* signifies the all-attractive person; *Ram* means one who takes away all inauspicious things, all bad qualities. So by chanting *Hare* and *Krishna* and *Ram,* then we associate with God through his name." Kisna started chanting, then stopped himself. "It's very hard. Many people would say, 'Can you show me God?' They want to see God face to face. But we are taught that if you chant the names of God in that way, you can associate with God, and through that, ultimately see Krishna. Everyone has a relationship with Krishna." In the young monk's words I heard that the Hindu God is accessed through language.

"Did you feel that experience the first time you chanted?" I asked, adjusting my seating position as casually as I could.

"No, I can't say it was immediate. Krishna wants to see if you want to know him, if you have some determination. For example, if you show a coach that you want to be on the team, you really give it your all, then they see you're serious and they show you their mercy by letting you be on the team. It's the same thing with Krishna. Krishna knows the sincere will always try their hardest, and Krishna will recognize that and then reciprocate by giving you some advancement in spiritual life."

The Hare Krishna movement began in the middle of the 1960s, a time in American culture when both the breadth of spiritual diversity and the availability of countercultural lifestyle choices dramatically increased. Two generations earlier an Indian teacher predicted that a prophet would arise to spread Krishna worship throughout the world. That prophet turned out to be a charismatic Indian ascetic named Srila Prabhupada, a teacher who took a steamer from India to New York, arriving in 1965 with no money and only a drum. He made his way up to Central Park, where he began to play his drum and sing the mantra. Within a couple of weeks, he found a room where he prepared free meals for the spiritually curious. They in turn brought friends.

His appeal as a teacher and the apparent simplicity of his lifestyle served as a powerful fundraising device, because within a few years, brownstones like the one in Boston, as well as a London mansion owned by devotee George Harrison, were donated to the movement. In the process, Prabhupada developed a well-structured administrative hierarchy for this free-spirited, hippie magnet of a community. A seemingly contradictory feature like this one points to others in the tradition: though many of the people he attracted were drug-exploring, free-sex-enjoying hippies, Prabhupada stressed a strict moral code devoid of drugs, alcohol, sex, and attachment to material possessions. The movement demanded a renunciant, ascetic lifestyle, but its members often practiced in settings like Beacon Hill, where affluence surrounded them. And though it seemed a radical expression of the counterculture, Hare Krishna was in fact an extension of a long line of Hindu Krishna worship. What seemed carnivalesque to Westerners—from the believers' Indian uniforms to their public chanting—was part of everyday Indian life.

Kisna had grown up Catholic in Albany. Now twenty-seven, he related that when his brother became addicted to drugs, Kisna felt the impetus to search for something more spiritually meaningful than the world in which he had been brought up. "My exposure to Krishna consciousness came through alternative music," he said. "There were some punk rock bands that were devotees. And they were trying to teach Krishna consciousness to younger people through the music. One band had been on a major heavy metal label. It turns out that the lead singer, through his own personal process, came to Krishna consciousness, and he transformed the whole band into devotees of Krishna. They call their music straight-edged. You know, from living straight: no drugs."

When speaking, Kisna sounded like the kid in my high school English class who didn't talk much, and I assumed my classmate was bored or stoned. When he did speak, his words, though cautious, were purposeful. Contemplative sometimes disguises itself as spacey. Kisna seemed an incidental sage: he knew his stuff without an obvious air of knowing.

"I have a question on the practical level," I said. I had been wondering about his and his community's interactions with the rest of the neighborhood. Did neighbors avoid them? Like them? Visit them? "Do you ever hit the 7-Eleven on the corner in your wardrobe now? And if you do, how does the community react to you?"

Kisna smiled, seeming happy I asked. "Devotees do that lots. I go to the store to get things sometimes. I don't think that much about it. If you go to India, nobody would think anything of wearing *doti*, this kind of clothing. The only reason we stand out here is because most Americans don't live like this. So for a devotee, it's about just being who you are. The longtime residents here, who grew up seeing devotees in the '70s chant 'Hare Krishna' for many hours, are very familiar with it. They don't think much about it. And sometimes we'll be out walking and we'll hear a neighbor chanting 'Hare Krishna.' Some people even sing and dance, 'Hare Krishna, Hare Krishna.' But very few will give a real negative reaction."

When Kisna told me of his neighbors' sharing in the mantra, part of me assumed the neighbor's chant stunk of parody. Wasn't he getting that they were teasing? My first encounter with the Hare Krishna movement came through their hilariously unflattering depiction in the movie *Airplane*. The hero, Ted Stryker, is hustling through the airport near the movie's beginning, trying to get to the gate on time to make the plane with his estranged love Elaine aboard, when he is approached by two saffron-robed men, smiling like mannequins, who offer him a flower. He shakes his head no; they persist. He shakes his head again; they press on. He punches them in the mouth. Kisna, however, enjoyed people's acknowledgment of the mantra, even if it was sometimes stereotyped and comical. To him, a satirical serenade isn't a stereotype; it's a spiritual practice. Every time someone utters the words "Hare" and "Krishna" and "Ram," regardless of their intent (although, as he pointed out, a sincere intention obviously helps), every instance in which a neighbor clangs together imaginary hand cymbals, despite their possibly sardonic tone, impromptu sermons are preached.

"Do you have a favorite meal?" I asked.

He looked surprised at the question. "I don't know. There's a lot of variety in temple foods. Growing up in America, we have particular attractions to things like pizza and stuff like that."

"Are you still able to eat pizza?" I wasn't sure. When somebody joins a movement like this, and in the process renounces a former life and switches worlds so completely, do former practices, likes and dislikes, persist? Or is everything just wiped clean?

"Yeah, yeah." He made it seem like this was obvious. "We make it." As he said this the expression on his face changed. He had remembered something. The last time his mom and dad visited from Albany, the devotees on kitchen duty happened to have prepared, alongside rice and Indian lentils, homemade pizza. Kisna's parents are still Catholic, and though they visit, their stays are typically brief, their entries into the world of Krishna consciousness cursory. But pizza, he said, had made a visible difference in their time here. With pizza on their plates, they felt a bit more at home, its familiarity an anchor to their own world in a place that could not help but seem alien to them.

"Do you ever order out?" I asked, continuing along the same line of questioning. I rearranged my legs, uncrossing and extending them outward. I knew Kisna had noticed.

"No," Kisna shook his head, smiling. "We make everything here so that it's all fresh. In Krishna consciousness, eating becomes a spiritual activity for a devotee. Anything in a devotee's life can be a spiritual activity; not just chanting or going to certain services. If we have a computer, it can become spiritual if we use it in Krishna consciousness. If we're writing up the philosophy of Krishna consciousness, to keep track of the congregation, or mailing things out about festivals, then it becomes spiritual activity."

Kisna pointed out that even in the life of a modern-day renunciant, the spiritual life need not avoid the everyday or cloister the initiated to maintain its importance. A corner store like 7-Eleven could be an ad hoc classroom on religious pluralism; pizza could be an effective, edible textbook.

"When I look at you, and around this place, certain connections come to mind. That," I pointed to the beaded necklace Kisna was wearing, "certainly resembles a rosary. The paintings look like icons, and with the statues and the incense and the smells, this space really has the feel of a Catholic church." I paused to craft my question. "Was there a sense when you were beginning in this community and this tradition that it was familiar to you?"

Kisna rubbed his long, slender fingers together. "I think many younger people, when they're growing up, tag along to the church service without understanding what the philosophy and the real practices are." From my own experience, I could say amen to that. "For me, church was the hour where I had to go somewhere before doing what I wanted to do. But when I came to Krishna consciousness, I was actually able to see Christianity in a whole different way. The teachings of Jesus Christ opened up for me. Then if I went to church with my parents, and they read from the Bible, I would think, 'Hey, that sounds familiar.' Like something that Srila Prabhupada said, or something from *Bhagavad Gita*. I found a lot of similarities."

"Do you see yourself as more of a Christian now that you're a devotee of Krishna than you were when you were a Catholic growing up?"

"Yeah," Kisna said. "It's kind of a far out thing. Some people think that when you leave one practice and take up another, you're totally rejecting the first practice. But actually, Krishna consciousness helps me see it in a whole new way. Some people wonder why Catholic priests live as they do. Now I can see. They're trying to focus on spiritual life. Now I also see why Jesus Christ said that one can't enter the kingdom of God if one thinks that material possessions are everything. Yes, I was brought up in a Catholic family, but it wasn't until I was exposed to Krishna consciousness that everything fell into place. I don't see this as opposed to Christianity, even if a Catholic may. Devotion to Krishna isn't a sectarian movement. You know, we may look a certain way, and we may chant Hare Krishna, but we believe everyone is worshiping the same God."

I appreciated Kisna's sentiment. From the outside, his newfound faith may seem to have supplanted and edited out his Catholic upbringing. In truth, Krishna worship has clarified Catholicism for him. I didn't anticipate his return to Catholicism anytime soon, but for Kisna, departure from home and family and faith had brought him understanding and, eventually, a measure of reconciliation with the faith he had left behind. I wondered if I might find the same.

[8]

A few days later, on the first Friday evening in September, the sun set in front of us. Liz drove, I sat shotgun, and six hours into our drive to move her to Chicago, we looked for an exit off the interstate. She signaled right, pressed the brakes along the bend of the off-ramp, and in the dimming light followed a quiet country highway for less than a mile before she turned onto a back road of dust and gravel. On our left was a dark orchard of trees; on our right, a cornfield primed for harvesting. (As I sketch the romance of the scene, I feel obliged to draw its melodramatic side as well. We agreed that if at any point in this off-road search for a place to celebrate Shabbat the trail we blazed spooked us excessively—if some dude in a hockey mask started trailing us on a Harley, for example—we were permitted to postpone candle-lighting until we reached whatever Holiday Inn Express or Motel 6 we camped at for the night.) Liz's family's 1984 grocery grabber station wagon rumbled over a grassy lane that separated segments of the cornfield from one another, until we reached a bucolic, secure place to stop. She shifted the car to park, turned the ignition off, kept the lights on, and popped the hatchback. We lay a sheet on that part of the wagon's floor not covered by moving boxes, and on top of it arranged two votive candles, a loaf of *challah* (braided egg bread) purchased the prior day in Boston, and a bottle of Manischewitz Concord grape wine. We recited the blessings over the lighting of the candles, the drinking of the fruit of the vine, and the eating of the bread from the earth, though not so loudly that any gremlins would awake from their slumber. I took a picture of her there. She was almost beaming, wearing one of my long-sleeved shirts, with a chunk of challah in her small hands, her blond hair pulled back, the maroon car at her side, the lavender sky behind her head. The event came to be known as Cornfield Shabbat, and the picture remained, even after the months that followed—a treasure to me and a reminder of who we were.

After five hundred miles more and another evening on the road, we caught our first look at the ivory minarets of a mosque on the edge of the freeway. The slender spires pierced the blue sky like silos. A white dome, bookended by the minarets and crowned by a short spire, appeared taut and inflated like the profile of a woman who's thirty-nine weeks pregnant.

We drove closer and noticed that the building beneath the dome was octagonal, with a large window set into each wall. The front doors rose massively, designed in arabesque detail. Both the door and the windows were peaked by a tapered curve, pointed at the top, like a candle's flame.

With Liz along for the ride, I had returned to the fateful greater Toledo area, this time as destination, not springboard. It was my friend Mark Russell who told me about the Islamic Center of Greater Toledo and showed me how to drive there. It was a four-hour straight shot from Toledo to Chicago, so Liz agreed to accompany me for a Sunday morning at the mosque. The Toledo mosque, though technically located in Perrysburg, Ohio, is one of the largest, both in physical size and membership, in the country.

Toledo may be a Triple A baseball town, but it has a major league Islamic pedigree. Detroit was the initial magnet for Muslims in the region, because the Ford Motor Company at the start of the century hired anyone willing to endure the conditions of its River Rouge plant. For immigrant Muslims, as well as for blacks migrating north, this meant steady work and decent pay. The first Muslims who settled in Toledo came from Syria and Lebanon. Mostly single men, they worked in the factories that had opened south of Detroit, and they assimilated, many of them marrying local American women, raising families, and creating mosques that functioned more as social centers than worship spaces.

The *imam,* or spiritual leader, of the Islamic Center of Greater Toledo is Farooq abo-Elzahab, an Egyptian-born American who led the mosque in Cedar Rapids, Iowa, for seven years before receiving the call from Toledo in 1998. (Cedar Rapids is also in America's Muslim major leagues: the small Iowa city is reputed to be home to one of the first mosques—if not the very first—in America.) He succeeded a prominent imam who led the Islamic Center for a generation. Imam Farooq brought his wife and four children to this community of almost five hundred families, where Muslims from South Asia and North Africa mingle with those raised in the western hemisphere. As in Dayton to the south, the range of flesh tones and wardrobe was remarkable: Egyptians and Pakistanis and Russians, in T-shirts, saris, and hijab.

The day we visited—a bright, seasonally cool morning—Imam Farooq wore a short-sleeved white button-down shirt with a black and gray patterned tie. He was short, a bit stocky, and looked like a local insurance agent might. His black hair, cut close to his scalp, pointed down to his forehead in a widow's peak, and he had a well-trimmed beard. By the time we arrived, Imam Farooq had only fifteen minutes to talk before he led the late morning prayers. Muslims pray five times daily—it is one of the five pillars of the faith—and among the roles played by the imam, one is worship leader. I told Liz I'd like to speak to the imam on my own. She stayed outside, striking up a conversation, I'd soon find out, with a few of the mosque's members.

"I was trained my whole life to become imam," Imam Farooq said once we sat down together in his office. The walls, painted white, were adorned with plaques of service and framed *suras*, passages from the Koran, inscribed in Arabic. "Even when I was in school, I functioned as the imam. In my small village, when I was maybe sixteen, I was imam." He came from a long line of religious authorities, many of whom had memorized the Koran. "They taught me the Koran by heart. My grandfather was a great scholar, a great *khari*." A khari functioned as a reciter of the Koran. "I inherited many books from him. I was five or six when I began studying. I finished the Koran when I was twelve."

"Memorizing?" I asked.

He nodded, his eyes lowered. Though he recounted the accomplishment with pride, it nearly made him blush. I think I had memorized most of the collected works of Hall and Oates by the time I was twelve.

"The whole Koran?" I asked, just to be sure.

"The whole Koran, yes."

"How did he teach you?"

"Everyday there is a page or a portion in the Koran that I had to write with ink, the old fashioned way, on a plate. I would spend sometimes two hours, sometimes half the day memorizing, and when I felt sure, I would go to my grandfather and close the Koran and recite to him. If I didn't recite it correctly, then he would ask me to go back and study further. That was old-fashioned, I know. I used to think, why me? Every child is having fun outside and I have to stay home most of the day and study. I felt my freedom was very limited. But after growing up, and after graduating, I realized my grandfather had a very good vision about the future. Maybe I didn't realize it at the time, but I was very thankful." The imam attended the famous Egyptian seminary al-Azhar in the late sixties. His English enunciation, while precise and fluent, occasionally reflected that it was a second language: when the imam said "1967," he pronounced it, "nineteen sickesty-seven."

"Are you trying to teach the same way your grandfather taught? Through memorizing?" I asked.

"Of course, we are trying to teach some, though not the whole Koran. Some parents hire a teacher to do that, to teach their children two hours or more every day, to try to finish the Koran. Some kids have one quarter of the Koran, or one-fifth, or one-tenth. But this generation is totally different from ours. We were devoted to the Koran. Nowadays, everyone would like to be a doctor, or a lawyer, a businessman or computer scientist. We are trying at least to teach them some, so they can have a Koranic vision for their life."

"What is a Koranic vision?"

"Koranic vision is very, very, very important, not only for the children, but for the whole community, the *umaa*, the Muslim nation. A Koranic vision gives them a sense of the meaning of life, how to fulfill their obligations, and how to please God."

I asked him if a Koranic vision and American culture overlapped.

The imam shook his head no. "In ways, perhaps, but American culture and the Koranic vision are totally different, of course. American culture has a misunderstanding of freedom, and it has side effects on the practice of religion. A child says it's okay if I do not go to mosque, it's okay if I don't pray, it's okay because it's up to me. It is not easy for my child to continue his prayer *and* be honest, *and* sincere, and, and, and,"—his *ands* were not a stutterer's repetition, but a laundry list of reputable characteristics—"and then go outside to see a different picture, where children believe freedom means they can do whatever they want. If we just forget about this and let them have a good time, these little mistakes might in time grow bigger and bigger.

"So if you are a good Muslim first, then you can be a good American," I asked.

"Of course. You can be good citizen, good worker, good lawyer, good congressman, whatever. That is why we see corrupt people in politics, because they do not implement their religion in their life. You see, there are people who say they are Muslims, but it's not necessarily the practice of every Muslim to be Islamic. Because Islam is a way of life. The prayer and fasting and all the obligations of Islam exist to teach us how to implement Islam in our life. Maybe you see someone who says he is a Muslim. He says, 'I go to the Islamic Center.' But his behavior, his practice, his conduct is disastrous: he cheat, he lie, he doesn't care about human life. So his behavior is not Islamic even if he claims he is a Muslim." I understood what he was getting at. If you cheated on your wife or stole from your employees or beat your kids, you might be a Jew, but you weren't *Jewish*. The imam stressed the praxis of Muslim identity: *acting* Muslim mattered more than simply *being* Muslim.

The precedence Imam Farooq placed on praxis is magnified in Islamic worship. Islam's five pillars of faith bind all believers together in a community of shared practice and aspiration. The first pillar, the foundation of the faith and the only one that hinges on belief, is the *shahadah*, or

Muslim creed. "There is no god but Allah, and Muhammad is the Prophet of God" emphasizes the oneness of the Divine and the central place of the prophet Muhammad. The other four pillars include fasting during the month of Ramadan; praying (*salat*) five times daily; practicing *zakat*, or charity; and performing a *hajj*, the pilgrimage to Mecca, if physically and financially well enough to get there and back.

Still, despite his reservations about American culture's impact on young Muslims, Imam Farooq articulated an enthusiasm about the strengths America has instilled in his community. One of these is America's religious diversity. "In America," the imam said, "I've seen many things, and I've come to discover that all of us are not to hate each other. We need to learn that if one person has good things to give, or if I have good things to teach, we can both learn from each other. We have to deal with these kinds of differences. I am not going to come to your services and tell you that you are wrong. No, that is very insulting. I can be there, very attentive, very respectful, even though I disagree with you. So disagreement or agreement does not affect our listening or respecting our differences." The imam, and the Islamic Center, played prominent roles in the area's ongoing interfaith dialogues. And in a larger sense, they played equally leading parts on the national stage as leaders of what Imam Farooq called "Progressive Islam." The imam relished visits from elementary school groups and elderly visitors from a local church. He attended dinners at nearby temples, spoke in high schools, and invited people into the mosque.

"Do you feel as though you have learned much from your contact with other faiths, and with American culture?" I asked.

"Of course. And I learned the value of my religion, too. There, back in Egypt, I took my Islam for granted. Everyone was Muslim. No one was there to say, 'Why you are doing this? Why you are doing that?' No one was there to ask, 'Why do you pray?' or 'Why do you think your God is one?' People take it as faith. Some years ago it was forbidden for a kid to ask, 'What is God?' But here you can raise any question mark. Here you can ask about anything." In pointing to the American willingness to permit and even encourage questions, the imam expressed considerably less ambivalence about America's impact on Islam than about the differing perceptions of freedom.

Imam Farooq had to run. Even as he and I spoke, though, I had a sense that there was no shortage of willing conversationalists around. I heard Liz's voice in the next room, going back and forth with several male voices: one older, with an Indian-sounding accent; the others higher-pitched, midwestern, freckled with "ums" and "likes." The imam excused himself and I followed him out, parking myself on a sofa in a sitting room with Liz.

Several other sofas surrounded a central coffee table. Nasr, Rafae, and Aseeb occupied them.

Nasr, a man of sixty-something, was born in India but for the past thirty-two years had run a Volvo, Saab, and Volkswagen dealership in the area. Nasr wore eyeglasses with huge frames and thick lenses, and when he smiled, which was often, his eyes crinkled up and he suddenly appeared more than a little like Mr. Magoo. Nasr loved America. He reminded me of an old Jewish businessman who regales country club staff about how he made it big in the pickle business.

Rafae, sixteen, and Aseeb, fourteen, were friends and the children of Pakistani immigrants. Both boys chose a style I will alliteratively call Mellow Mosque Mode, which included well-worn T-shirts, shorts, and flip-flops. I had assumed the culture inside a mosque to be necessarily more formal and decorous. Apparently not. Rafae and Aseeb attended different high schools but knew one another from their time at the mosque's Sunday school. Rafae, the older, had hangdog eyes and ruffled hair that lent the impression he had woken up within the last twenty minutes; Aseeb, on the other hand, wore gel in his well-groomed hair. A v-neck, red and blue jersey hung loosely from his thin neck.

I was curious to explore, without explicitly alluding to the perspective of the imam, how these three understood the relationship between American culture and the Koranic vision. I asked the teenagers, "Does being Muslim demand a certain different kind of behavior, in the culture, in your schools, with your friends?"

"That's a really tough question," Rafae said. "I have different beliefs than my parents, and my parents have different beliefs than their parents. But then again, they grew up in Pakistan. If I tell my parents I'm going to a party, they ask me fifty questions about it. 'Who's going? Where can we reach you? When are you coming back? Who are you gonna be with? What speed were you going?'" His tone, a pretty reasonable facsimile of frantic parental worry, made me and Nasr laugh. "I'm sure someday I'm gonna ask my kids some questions, too, but not to that extent. They just don't want me to deviate from the path too much." His parents sounded like protective parents, not necessarily Muslim protective parents.

"We have to follow the basic rules," Aseeb said, "like no drinking, and not much interaction with girls. You just have to find the middle area, something that's good for living here, but still good for our culture."

"Everyone has to make Islam true for themselves," Rafae added. "My dad wants me to understand my roots, so he'll try to get me to read a book about it. But I'll take one look at the book and run away. I'm like, oh no, another learning book. He says, 'But I want you to understand your roots.' I'm like, 'I don't wanna understand it.'" Nasr giggled.

Aseeb and Rafae's parents were, like Baba Singh in Des Moines and Hayder in Dayton, part of the generation-long surge of immigrants who arrived in the United States after restrictive immigration policies eased in the mid-1960s. Professionals from South Asia and the Middle East composed a significant portion of this influx (though people moved across the border from countries in Latin America, too). They arrived with modern, marketable skills—in fields such as medicine and engineering—and a sentiment for the places they had left behind. Islam began its meteoric growth in America at precisely this time. Statistics show that at the end of World War II, 52 mosques were up and running; by the end of the century, more than 1,200 mosques had been established. In addition to gaining immigrants arriving from abroad, Islam grew an indigenous American strain as well: the black Muslim movement, spearheaded by the Nation of Islam, came into national prominence in the early and mid-1960s. In fertile American soil, Islam sprouted with the same gusto as did technology stocks on the Nasdaq market in 1999.

The surge in the number of mosques reflects two oppositional trends within the Islamic tradition in America. The first trend, responsible in part for keeping the number low, was the tendency toward assimilation exhibited by the Syrian and Lebanese Muslims who came at the start of the century; the second trend, represented in a later inclination toward cultural and religious identification, emerged over the century's second half. Some communities, like the Islamic Center of Greater Toledo, emphasized a shared Islam, attracting hundreds, sometimes thousands, of Muslims from many different countries and cultures. The Islamic Center of Greater Toledo, like many other mosques founded around the same time, expanded and plucked features from America's churches and synagogues, like Sunday schools and women's auxiliary groups, to build community and foster Muslim learning. Other communities stressed a more particular brand of Islam: storefront mosques cropped up next to Afghani-owned auto garages and Pakistani halal restaurants. These communities retained the specific ritual mores and linguistic familiarity that marked public worship space in their home countries. They cultivated an atmosphere where they could preserve and express their religious, cultural, and national particularity.

"I think this community is different than any other community in the United States," Nasr said. "Our imam, who just retired, was here for nearly twenty years. He was most knowledgeable. He tried to get us to question certain things. He wanted to bring us back to Islam." Nasr removed his glasses, squinted at the standard halogen bulb above our heads, and tinkered with the wide frames. "See, in the last 1,400 years, people got culture. In India, Muslims are different than in Pakistan. In Malaysia, more different. And in Africa, there are completely different things added into the religion. So we're trying to shed all of that. We're just going back to the Koran, to pure Islam." The sense that such a thing as a *pure Islam* existed, as though the Prophet and the Koran emerged from a cultural vacuum and not in a specific time and place, marked an assumption of Nasr's shared by Roxanne Masni in Dayton.

"See," he continued, "the problem with most Muslim countries is the vast majority of the people are uneducated. In this country, when you meet Muslims, they are educated, and so they are looking at things with a different eye. In the old country, if the farmer has ten children and nine of them are smart, they will leave the village and go and find some job. The most stupid one will stay home, and he'll become imam. With no education, no nothing, he would come out and tell you and me how to live our lives. I remember listening to one imam in India say you must beat your wife once a week. He said it's Islamic. How is that Islamic? In Koran, the woman is given completely equal rights in every way. But this from an imam who's preaching from his own damn book. Our imam was criticized by most traditional Muslims for being too liberal. But the thing is, he was trying to take us back to Koran."

"So he was criticized as liberal for returning you to the source?" I asked.

"Yes," Nasr said. "People don't know the source. They haven't read it. It's written in Arabic. But in India, for example, they don't speak Arabic; they speak Hindi or Urdu. So these people teach from the Koran and think they're the expert. But how can you be the expert when you can't read and understand it? In this country they're so lucky to have the Koran in English so they can read it." He wagged a finger at Rafae, then Aseeb. "These kids will learn the real Islam, and spiritually they will be deeper than anybody that comes from the old country. In the old country they've just been listening to some gobbledygook from somebody and believing it."

Rafae was nodding. Pointing to Nasr, he said, "He's mostly right. I'm not trying to talk bad about them, but the people I saw over there in Pakistan are kind of like sheep. Whatever the imam tells them to do, they do. Here, if somebody tells us to do something, we think and ask questions. If we think it's right, then we'll do it. If we don't think it's right, then we won't. But we're definitely gonna question it."

A middle-aged man walked through the room, telling Rafae and Aseeb that the time had come to pray.

"In a minute," Rafae said.

"*This* is the American way," Nasr said, the enthusiastic certainty in his voice rivaling that of a boardwalk barker. "Questions. That's what we'd really like to see our children learn here. Questioning. Other places, they don't allow questions. But that's the best way." As Imam Farooq had said earlier, any question mark could be raised.

Aseeb shook his head. "But questions are really what my parents get most mad about," he said. "When they were growing up in Pakistan, things were different. They never saw anything like that before."

"People are afraid to ask questions, and that's what our imam did here," Nasr said. "He used to say, 'God gave you a brain, you use it.' Islam is very beautiful. Very simple. It's very easy to follow, but some of these guys make it such a problem for everybody. Like making women wear hijab. Where the hell is headgear in the Koran? All it says in the Koran is 'modestly dressed'." Nasr glanced at Liz, in pants, sneakers, and a long-sleeved shirt, and declared her to be attired Islamically. To me, she looked like an ad for Urban Outfitters; to him, she was Miss Crescent Moon on a pin-up calendar of respectfully dressed women.

Rafae and Aseeb were smiling, but in that way teenaged boys do, straining not to show any teeth. The same man who had walked through earlier repeated his circuit, reminding Rafae and Aseeb through a slightly clenched jaw that the prayer had started. Already tardy, they rose in unison, apologized together, shook our hands good-bye, and began their gangly moves down the hallway. Liz and I were looking at each other, exchanging smiles, when Aseeb turned around. "He's a lot older than us," he said, nodding at Nasr, who also stood up and began to follow the boys out. "He's figured out a lot of stuff already. He's got his own way. We're only teenagers. We're just trying to follow the guidelines, and still find our own way."

In a now empty room, Liz and I sat together on a couch. I wanted to talk for a few more minutes with the imam, so we waited around. Down the hall we heard the sounds of the midday prayer under way. Teenagers in T-shirts and stout old women in hijab bent and kneeled to the floor in separate rooms. Nasr's philosophy, as I thought about it, sounded on the one hand eminently reasonable, yet on the other, an extreme Islamic perspective I had not heard before. When he described the former imam's decision to return to the Koran, choosing a calculated rejection of culture in favor of a unifying return to the value system of the Koran, the former imam positioned himself as something of an Islamic iconoclast. His favored approach: upon entering America, check your nation-state, its language, its culture, and its heritage at the door, and find in the scriptural sources your sustenance as a Muslim. But do not cast out the old merely to substitute Koran unthinkingly in its place. No, question! Question everything, from the traditions you practiced as a child to those the Koran impresses upon you now. In that questioning, Nasr suggested, you become most Muslim.

What struck me as especially fascinating in our conversation with Nasr and Aseeb and Rafae was their description of America as a place where the foundational vision and the dominant impulse lay in inquiry, or rational skepticism. Nasr had said, "This is the American Way." Yet in leaving behind their Indianness and Pakistaniness, hadn't these Muslims, whether young or old, absorbed the cultural paradigm in which they lived and learned and worked and thrived? The return to the Koran, the retrieval and re-creation of a Koranic vision for the *umaa* in Toledo, was in fact fueled by these Muslims' very cultural Americanness. What they claimed to be pure Islam was, in fact, American Islam. In Dayton, Roxanne Masni asserted that she had left culture behind. Nasr might have told her no, that she was lugging culture at her side. Regardless, I saw that in the choice she made to return to tradition, and in the choice Nasr made to restore a pure, original Islam, both superimposed American culture on Muslim life. I'm not sure if they saw that—that in shedding one culture they had attired themselves in another, perhaps far more attractive culture. This can be difficult to see from inside. I didn't realize that my own ridicule of religion and mistrust of the religious were functions of the implicitly secular culture in which I was brought up, until I started studying religion, and learned how crucial a role geography plays in determining one's belief system.

Still, as in any motley, vibrant community, gurgles of dissent rippled toward the surface of the Islamic Center of Greater Toledo. Not everybody at this mosque bought into the progressive vision. Liz wound up speaking with a few women in traditional garb. Their dress *was* a part of Islam, they told her, not merely cultural detritus they had not yet flung overboard. Attempts to convince them otherwise both disrespected their particular religious perspective and attempted to impose a kind of popular Americanizing orthodoxy on all those who chose not to wear Levis. These women still watched their kids play basketball on the court outside the mosque, still slurped from cans of Coke as they cheered in the stands, but they drew the line somewhere between the cultural ubiquity of soda and their specific inheritance of the teaching of the Prophet. If they found their needs weren't being met, if they were somehow made to feel wrong at the Islamic Center for their retention of traditional dress, they would respond with another quintessentially American course of action. They'd up and move, starting Second Islamic in some cornfield or opening Mosque of the Holy Koran in what had been an abandoned lot. Others—the likeminded, the curious, the people who lived a shorter car ride to wherever they inevitably opened their doors—would follow. As the community expands over time, many will remain but others will diverge, and the cycle of departure and creation will recur. At each step in this process, the dissident voices, in their inquiry, will unwittingly affirm the vision of the Islamic Center. A new mosque is conceived from a question, a new community hatched from a dissatisfaction, perhaps ideological, perhaps prosaic. And so the number of mosques, the choices for Islamic community, expand.

Another gurgle: most Muslim parents who arrived sometime during the past thirty-five years want their children to absorb something of their homeland and their heritage. The children, while they might intuitively get that this knowledge is important, and why its transmission is essential, uncover in their Americanness the opportunity to decide what from their past they want to carry with them. When Rafae resists with a soft rebelliousness his father's attempts to ground him in the Pakistani, he doesn't really say no. He says, "Not yet." This ability to pick and choose, as Sokha Diep called it, reflects the Muslim's entry on the American spiritual buffet line. Maureen Scowby, our Covington, Kentucky, Cafeteria Catholic, had arrived already, and called first dibs on the Jell-O. The Muslims of Toledo revealed that America also creates Mess Hall Muslims— the Islamic equivalent to Cafeteria Catholics.

It didn't take long for the prayer to finish. The imam strode back to his office with a young man wearing a navy polo shirt tucked neatly into saggy, off-white jeans at his side. He introduced me to his son, Said (pronounced "sa-*yeed*"). Said attended public school in the area, played sports, and prayed during lunch period, sometimes even in the locker room. "I set my schedule so I always have time for prayer." Said aspired to become a physician and enrolled in college classes as a sixteen-year-old to get a head start. I asked the imam how Islam contributed to Said's educational motivation.

"One of the things mandatory in Islam is to seek knowledge. As a matter of fact, the first Koranic verse, as it was revealed to the prophet Muhammad more than fourteen hundred years ago, was an invitation to read and to seek knowledge. It says in Arabic, *Ikkra*: read, try to comprehend, try to realize, and try to investigate. Islam does not respect ignorance at all. Islam tries to make man more ambitious, wants him to look for something more."

The imam continued: "The life of the Prophet isn't just a story to be narrated for certain times and forgotten after that. We have to take the episodes and relate them to our lives. Muhammad lived twenty-three years as a prophet, and during this time the entire Koran was revealed. His life is very rich in the matter of example, because he was not an angel; he was a human. He had a family, he had parents, he had a wife: not just one, but more than one. He had relatives and cousins, so on and so forth. He had some people who loved him, some people who were against him. He traveled. He worked as a businessman, sometimes rich, sometimes not. Sometimes sick, sometimes healthy." The variability that Imam Farooq emphasized about the life of the Prophet underscored that the Prophet, too, came from a particular place and lived in particular times, which changed over the course of his twenty-three-year series of revelations.

And yet, Imam Farooq continued, stressing the universality of the Prophet's message, "Islam is not an old fashioned religion, just related to the desert and camels and Bedouins. No. When we quote things from the Prophet, we can apply these stories to our lives today. It's like the Prophet is living with us right now and telling us about everything. When we consider how the Prophet sees America and corruption and the threat of nuclear war, we can find it easy to find some kind of relation between the life of the Prophet and our lives as Muslims nowadays. Our role is to teach and show a good model for Muslims, not only by my conduct, but also by teaching about the prophet Muhammad, our great model. And this will bridge the gap in cultures. Some people are from India, some are from Pakistan. They have respect for this imam or that scholar. But that is not enough. No, the only model for the whole Islamic nation is the prophet Muhammad, and the Koran is the only factor that can unify them, because Koran is the same all over the world."

I learned only after we left that the Islamic Center of Greater Toledo boasted a membership of thirty different nationalities, an incredible melting pot of perspectives. Nasr had described the imam who preceded Imam Farooq as a visionary, who understood that a community this varied could reliably find commonality only in the members' shared points of origin, the Prophet Muhammad and the Koran. The *pluribus* of this microcosmic *umaa* was a feature of, but subordinate to, its *unum,* which found in its shared beginning a way to pave over all of the myriad cultural deposits of the past fourteen hundred years.

"Some people mistake Islam for what they see on TV," Imam Farooq said. "They think all Muslims are terrorists or all Muslims are Arabs. But Arabs make up only 18 percent of Muslims. The rest of them are in countries like America or India or Indonesia or China. In India there are nearly 150 million Muslims, and Muslims are a *minority.*"

I asked him how he understood terrorists who claimed to defend and uphold Islam through their use of violence. "The terrorists are liars, of course. Consider the source. The terrorist is killing innocent people, destroying life and the living. So how can you trust him as a source about Islam? No." The imam's eyes began to bulge. "Those people are fully ignorant about Islam. Like someone who is all the time in a bar drinking, do you think that he would be good to speak about Christianity? If I want to know about Christianity, I can go to the church and ask the minister. But I don't go to the man who is sitting in the bar twenty-four hours a day with naked women and ask him about Christianity."

That I considered this one possible source for interviews, I decided not to inform Imam Farooq. Liz and I thanked him and his son.

"Come back whenever you can," Imam Farooq said. I promised I would.

Said saw Rafae and Aseeb in the common area where we had sat and gave them a "Wussup?" American Islam, I thought, is flourishing in Toledo.

[9]

By five o'clock that afternoon, we hit the Chicago Skyway and saw the city's long lakeshore skyline against the bright blue sky. Liz almost bounced off the windshield with excitement. Stories about her childhood in Chicago started spilling out—soccer games on the Midway, how house music came to be all the rage in the mid-1980s, the Filipino kid she first kissed—stories I had maybe heard before but lacked the visual aid to appreciate adequately. We stopped off on the South Side, in the neighborhood of Hyde Park, where she had grown up and which was home to the University of Chicago. We ordered a stuffed spinach pizza from Eduardo's on Fifty-Seventh Street and tore through it once it was ready. We arrived at her brother's place on the North Side twenty minutes later, as we put the car to bed for the evening, covering her earthly possessions with the same sheet we had used as a backseat tablecloth the previous Friday evening. Then we headed upstairs to sleep.

We enjoyed a productive day of apartment hunting the next morning. Our prompt and efficient discovery earned me leave to continue my own exploration the following day. I took the commuter rail an hour west to Dupage, to meet my friend Soren. Soren's grandfather, Wallace Johnson, was ninety-two years old and a retired Evangelical minister who lived in a Rockford, Illinois, nursing home. I met Soren during a stay in Jerusalem, at which point he was enrolled in seminary, considering a ministerial career in the footsteps of his grandfather. I remember how he at first struck me as white bread. He was tall, soft-spoken, clean-cut and gracious, prone to wearing short-sleeved, button-down shirts like Mormon missionaries. Underneath this exterior, though, was a person of deep faith whose earnestness never approached self-satisfaction, whose love of gospel music led him to sing in an otherwise all-black gospel choir in college, and who worked at an East Jerusalem pediatric hospital, dressing up on Christmas as a guitar-playing Santa. Soren credited his grandfather Wallace with making faith an essential part of his life, and I was glad when Soren invited me to meet him.

Soren met me at the train station, then brought me to World Relief, an Evangelical-run relief organization that aids recent refugees, where he worked for the summer. All day long, arrivals from the world's microcosmic exoduses stepped into World Relief's Dupage, Illinois, quarters. The office, housed in a low brick building in a suburban office park, buzzed with a polyglot anxiousness. With doleful eyes, wearing borrowed clothes, refugees from Somalia, Bosnia, Pakistan, and Guatemala—children, parents, grandparents—trudged across the office's industrial carpet to a staff member who spoke their native tongue. They filled out questionnaires that asked for their names and their ages and a description of the conditions from which they had fled. I shook hands with a Kosovar couple, Vosfi and Ina Mustafa. They smiled and looked down. Unknowingly, bashfully, I mimicked their gestures. Vosfi, the husband, spoke a little bit of English, so after a few minutes of halting conversation, I asked if his family was Muslim or Christian.

"Muslim," he said. Then he raised his hand, as though asking permission to offer another thought out loud. "Muslims, Christians, all God, One." As he made this point, he shaped his flat, outstretched hands into a pyramid, one angled against the other, each hand a different approach up the same mountain.

"How are you liking Illinois?" I asked. Vosfi nodded vigorously. He didn't quite understand my question, I thought. "Do you like it here?" Again, he nodded. "How come?"

"No bombs," he said.

Soren gave me a quick tour of the office. Behind the cubicles and water cooler was a warehouse crowded with orderly piles of donated goods. In one section of the glum, gymnasium-like space lay a collection of dinette sets, old lamps, and end tables; in another, unwrapped Christian-themed toys sat like a Christmas morning bounty without a tree to cover them. The people who arrived there with nothing left with a few items from each stash to begin their new lives.

I met a few of Soren's colleagues. One, a twenty-year-old with a square face, spiked black hair, and three earrings in his left ear, lit up when Soren introduced me as his friend from New York.

"Ohh," he said, wobbling backward, as though starstruck. "That's a real city."

"George is from a real city of his own," Soren said.

"Where's that?" I asked.

"Sarajevo."

The conversation paused. Hearing someone comes from Sarajevo felt then like meeting a resident of Hiroshima. Of course, after September 11, presenting myself as a New Yorker generated, at least for a time, an analogous automatic gasp in a conversation. Aware that a perverse kind of fame rises from tragedy's ashes, I wasn't quite sure, meeting George, whether to offer my sympathies or ask to see photographs. In the open-air space of a casual conversation, I considered my measured reply. Then: "I hear it's a wonderful place."

"Was," George Pejovic said, correcting me.

"Was," I said. "Right, was."

I asked Soren if we could delay our trip to Rockford for an hour. He nodded. I asked George if he could talk for an hour or so. He nodded, too.

"Sarajevo was great growing up," he told me after I had set up my recording equipment. "We had snow for three months a year, so you could go skiing. We had the Olympics in 1984. It was really cool. I *loved* that city. But now I don't want to go back. Too much has changed." George's English was excellent, his command of American colloquy appropriate for someone just emerging out of teendom. It figures: he spent his last two years of high school as an exchange student in Seattle before moving to Illinois and working for the past year and a half at World Relief. Still, the Serbian accent remained, and words sometimes rolled heavily from the roof of his mouth.

"Do you enjoy working here?" I asked.

"Yeah, I do. You're happy when you do something for somebody. You just get a satisfaction out of it. The people that arrive here, they are coming for a fresh start. I don't especially like working with people, though. I prefer working with computers. Computers do what you tell them to do, and they don't ask questions. People are more complicated. They never do what they're supposed to, and it takes a lot of time just to convince people what is good for them. Over and over, I have to tell them not to put all their money under their pillow, because maybe somebody will steal it, or maybe the house will burn down. I tell them they need to use checks. But they always want to pay for everything with cash." He shrugged at the newcomers' learning curve. "It takes a while to explain everything."

As we spoke, I saw that on the one hand George had acclimated almost completely to the life of an American twenty-year-old. He loved computers and studied them in school. He played guitar, both rock and blues, and said he focused especially on the music of the Beatles and Nirvana. On the other hand, his work life revolved around a daily recognition of his past, and the traumas still inflicted by it on the refugees who walked into his cubicle. His mother also served on the World Relief staff.

"Did you grow up in a particular religious tradition?"

"My parents were atheists. So am I. My grandparents are religious— you know, Orthodox—but I don't practice any of that, and neither did my parents." A majority of present-day Serbia's population, Sarajevo included, is Eastern Orthodox. The tradition stretches back to the fourth century, when the Emperor Constantine converted to Christianity and made the once-despised religion the imperial faith, lending it new credibility in areas like the Balkans, east of Rome. Eastern Orthodoxy represents Christianity's second largest subcommunity, after Catholicism. It stretches through the former Eastern Bloc, the Balkans, and much of Russia. "Nobody ever spoke about religion," George said. "We weren't forbidden to talk about it, but they didn't force us to believe any one way. Their approach was to say, 'This is the way we believe. You choose whatever you want to believe.' That's how I grew up. So the chances were really high that I'd be atheist." The atheist in the Evangelical office: there's a new one. I assumed that the antireligiousness of Communism had a major impact on the religious perspective of George's parents and their generation. I wondered if his grandparents tried to ground him in their Orthodox tradition, maybe as a private expression of defiance of the Communist regime. Had they tried to smuggle little bits of tradition to him, as though making a trade on the black market? Had they communicated anger or sadness in watching their faith seem to expire in their own time? He shook his head. Religion simply wasn't discussed, he said. The same, he told me, held true for many in his generation and for their parents as well.

My eyes got squinty and I cocked my head to the right, as if stumped by a seemingly easy clue in a crossword puzzle. Because I thought the roots of the war in the Balkans were religious and ethnic difference, I assumed that the subject would be addressed more passionately.

George shifted in his seat. He believed that a lethal fusion of an extended economic downturn, devious, opportunistic political leaders, and the scapegoating campaigns they led amounted to the main contributing factors. "People just use religion as an excuse. Because doesn't every religion say, Thou shall not kill? And treat people like they treat you? If they didn't have religion, they'd all have to wear blue or red shirts to know who's fighting who."

George was paid to smooth the transition for those who hobbled in speaking only Serbo-Croat. He assuaged their mundane fears and translated what it took to get by from English into an understandable idiom. As in Hayder Almosawi's case, the twenty-year-old, the next generation, played the role of ambassador and gate opener. I asked if he spoke about Sarajevo with those who had just arrived from that part of the world.

"If someone is a Muslim, I'll definitely avoid it. And even if someone is a Serb, I try to avoid it, because I don't want them saying bad things about Muslims. I don't want to get into that. I had good friends who were Muslims. There's no use talking about it. You try to get on with life. This war left huge scars on people. There's rarely a family that did not lose a member. A lot of people just want to forget it."

Who could find fault in this? George's father was killed during the war. A noncombatant, he stayed in Sarajevo to finish construction on a dam after his wife and children had moved away, because the city had become too dangerous. One night, men knocked on his door, abducted him from the family's apartment, and brought him to a makeshift prison camp. For four years George's family searched for his father, tracking down clues of his whereabouts. They eventually uncovered that he had been killed the night of his abduction. Every day George Pejovic did remarkable, necessary work, which when set against the context of his loss, made his encounters with his one-time home all the more harrowing, and in many ways, all the more heroic.

In George's words I thought I heard the logic that underscored why settling refugees amounted to a quintessentially Christian Evangelical project. As an Evangelical, one's life changed forever as a result of the personal encounter with Jesus Christ. The conversion experience signaled a rebirth in Christ, while at the same time it demanded a dramatic turning away from whatever one had been beforehand. The commitment to start over and the inclination to leave behind linked the Evangelical conversion and the refugee's arrival in America. Both Christ and America, at least in their own mythic self-conceptions, promised a refuge where the past could be left behind, once and for all.

George admitted with a subtle tone of self-defeat that his mother had grown to be more of a believer since learning of her husband's death. She was not religious, but believing in an afterlife "made life easier for her." George acknowledged the function, but resisted the effect. "It would be easier if I thought, I'm gonna see my dad again," he admitted. "For me to say no, he's gone forever, it's much harder."

I said, "It makes a lot of sense when you say how things seem easier when you say you'll see your dad or relatives or friends in another place, like in heaven. I guess what I'm wondering is why is it important for you, as an atheist, to resist that?"

"I never thought about it like that. I always thought of all religions as related, so if you refuse one, you refuse all." George had not yet allowed himself to indulge in the possibility that he could sample pieces of spiritual life without gorging on the whole. He understood that he had received his atheism, the conscientious disbelief in the wisdom or order or logic of a God above, as an inheritance from his parents. To his thinking, his was an orthodox atheism, a monolithic repudiation of the rigid dogmas and meaningless rituals and age-old hatreds he saw in organized religions.

George's sentiment made me think of Maureen Scowby. A Cafeteria Catholic like Maureen declared what I'll call religious free agency. I think the free agent analogy is useful because, the way I understand it, the days before free agency in sports constituted an era of indentured servitude, when the bosses made the rules and the players submitted to them. Free agency brought with it an empowered new age of fluidity, in which players were able and willing to sign a new contract with any new team they chose, to move to other cities and to look out for themselves. But what accompanied that newfound freedom was a new brand of uncertainty, because the make-up and structure and personality of a team changed year to year. Maureen chose to re-sign with her former team—let's call them the Roman Candles. But the contract she drafted to remain with the Candles stipulated her right to reject, and actively struggle against, any institutional policies in which she did not believe. Like many other contemporary believers, Maureen had shifted the weight of power in that contract from institution to individual. Amid the American smorgasbord of spiritual options, the Church needed to maintain and attract believers. Otherwise, they could go somewhere else.

George Pejovic saw himself bound to atheism. Accepting an article or two of faith—whether Eastern Orthodox or Muslim or Catholic—was for him a sign of resignation, a failure, in some ways, of endurance. Though employed by Midwestern Evangelicals, though a guitar-playing, computer-tinkering American guy, he had not quite immersed himself in America's egalitarian religious landscape, had not yet announced his spiritual free agency from his own past. For this I both admired and sympathized with him.

I played with these thoughts while in the front seat of Soren's mom's shiny green pickup truck on the drive out to see his grandfather Wallace. The smorgasbord metaphor felt both appropriate and timely, given that Pastor Johnson was the son of Swedish immigrants. We reached Rockford by late afternoon. Wallace lived in a two-room apartment on the ground floor of a nursing home. It was the kind of place where Wallace didn't feel the need to lock his door when out to dinner, though that kind of trip seldom happened these days, because of his difficulties in getting around. He rose to greet Soren and me at the door upon our arrival, and together we positioned him back down into his well-worn brown recliner. Feeling the papery skin above his elbow, I flashed back to the texture of my own grandpa's arm in the weeks before he died. A pit settled in my stomach.

Soren felt about Wallace the way I felt about my grandpa Arthur, who had been a model for me. He had been a graceful, elegant, charming, and generous man who, when I was small, would wade with a smile in a chilly pool while I deliberated whether to step off the diving board. As I grew, he came to watch my plays and baseball games. He was supporting and loving, and it had been four months since he died in his sleep on a Friday in April. I eulogized him at his funeral two days later.

A few weeks before his death, on a day when he drifted in and out of sleep, he received a letter I wrote to him, a letter in which I thanked him for who he had been to me, congratulated him (I still wondered whether that was the right word) on a life well lived, and shared with him my plans for this trip. The letter had been Liz's suggestion, and she helped me navigate my way through several drafts. She had a knack for gauging difficult emotional scenarios and offering deft responses to them. I intended the letter to be a prologue to a longer conversation about where he was and how he was feeling in those days as he lay dying. I feared, correctly, that no one was engaging him in this conversation.

My grandfather was not a philosophical man, nor did he seem introspective in any significant way. He wasn't much of a storyteller, and he wasn't out front on his political views or upfront with regard to his internal emotional landscape. So who really knew what he was feeling then? Tended to by Jamaican home care workers, unable to discern waking hallucinations from sleeping dreams, he must have known his time approached. My grandmother, his wife Ruth, bless her heart, a New York Jew from her high heel shoes to her salon-styled hair, chirped desperately optimistic pleas at him: "Perk up, Artie," she'd say, and "Snap out of it, Sweetheart." I couldn't gauge if she expected him to improve, or chose not to acknowledge his decline. My family struggled to confront head-on his impending death, and in the absence of acknowledgment, I sensed that I needed to step up, open up the conversation, and just hope he lived long enough to offer a reply. He didn't.

In the three or four years preceding his death, however, I had begun to ask more questions of him and the age in which he had lived. My family seemed content to delegate this process of exploration to me. My dad, when I discussed writing Arthur the letter, suggested that I was the only one among our family who "could pull something like this off." I assumed this responsibility, secretly relished it, I think, because I recognized that through it I had access to something deep and otherwise hidden.

In a way, writing that letter began my pilgrimage. In it, I began a conversation about deep things, about living and dying, about memory and wisdom, about faith and its absence. In it, I invited him to share his fear with me—though whether I was truly prepared to hear his unvarnished reply I can't say for sure. I expressed how this pilgrimage idea scared me. Liz suggested that I tap into the fear he had by acknowledging my own. "Do you think there's a way I can use this fear to my benefit?" I wrote him. "Do you think it's okay to be afraid?" In Wallace Johnson's apartment, with the touch of the back of his elbow lingering on the tips of my fingers, I remembered that I never got an answer.

Soren asked his grandfather if he could bring him anything from the kitchen, and I snapped out of my reminiscence. Wallace asked him to repeat the question. The air conditioning blew cool air at full tilt, and the appliance chugged like a model train.

A large-print Bible, the size of a large family's photo album, sat open on Pastor Johnson's side table. Soren told me that his grandfather was nearly blind, so I wasn't surprised to see a hand-held magnifying glass by his Bible. As I set up the microphone on his coffee table, Wallace combed his hair, silver save for some vestiges of black near his temples, back from his forehead with a wavering hand. His words emerged slowly from his mouth, which was bookended by crescent-shaped wrinkles.

He began his ministerial career in a northern Minnesota church, building the church membership and, subsequently with those people, the church itself. "From those early days," he said, "in my ministry and preaching and seminary work, through my own reading and meditating on the Word of God, I've been developing my own theology, as it were. It's on the Evangelical side. Do you know what that is, Tom?"

I wiggled my hand, an expression of "sort of," only to realize he couldn't see the gesture. I asked him to tell me.

The Evangelical movement is said to have begun in the 1730s, with the conversion of an Englishman named John Wesley, eventually the founder of the Protestant denomination known as Methodism. Shortly after his conversion, Wesley journeyed to the American colony of Georgia as a missionary. In his visit, the First Great Awakening and, with it, the Evangelical impulse in America was born. A direct reaction to the Age of Reason, when the Enlightenment sensibility catapulted rationality over faith and mind over soul, the Evangelical movement rejected these modernizing tendencies, stressing instead the infallibility of the Bible, the inherent sinfulness of humankind, and the individual's need for a personal relationship with God. In the wake of Wesley's visit, religious revivals swept the colonial American countryside, calling for individual conversions, a strict personal morality, and the corresponding reshaping of cultural morality. A new preaching style was born, an emotional, fist-clenching, brow-wiping style that would, in time, give us Jimmy Swaggart. The Evangelical movement during the First Great Awakening molded new generations of empowered believers, who believed that salvation was a choice they made. They believed that public, political life could be transformed in much the same way individual souls were. The religious spirit of the First Great Awakening was a fuse that helped light the American Revolution.

I was thinking about this, mulling over Wallace Johnson's faith and its historical precedents, all the while trying to formulate another question, when I heard this: "ye-ah." He pronounced the syllables distinctly, and in his cracked voice the word made him sound like he was clearing his throat. How close this old man is to Brother Gus, I said to myself. Old people need time to formulate their responses. Old people require a moment longer to open their mouths. In Wallace's "ye-ah," I detected traces of the Swedish heritage Soren had told me about.

"When God created us," Wallace said, "he created something wonderful. I can't get over the marvels of the human life and body, soul and spirit, the inner light. 'We are fearfully, wonderfully made': that's the way the Psalms put it. But of the needs of our lives—and we have many of them, from food to clothing to shelter—we need an inner experience of some kind. There's a longing for God, a longing for peace, a longing for inner rest. There are many things that disturb these longings. But we are created with these desires. And I suppose you would call those religious desires." Through sunken, glassy eyes, Pastor Johnson stared toward me. "I don't know if this is helping you at all, Tom," he said.

"It is," I told him. "Does the desire for inner rest increase as you grow older?"

"It's constant. I feel it every day. And have all the way through life. You know, Tom, so many of our Lord's invitations to us are offered in those spaces where we need him." The rumble of the air conditioning in Pastor Johnson's ground floor one-bedroom seemed to block out the noise from the street and the hallway. In the pauses between his words there grew an almost palpable drama, as though Soren and I waited to be told a secret. "These are words spoken by the Lord Jesus himself: 'Come unto me all ye that labor and are heavy-laden and I will give you rest. Take my yoke upon you and learn of me, for I am meek and lowly of heart, and ye shall find rest unto your souls. For my yoke is easy, my burden is light.' This is the Lord Jesus speaking to men, about this matter of religion, and what he can do for those that come to him. These words, as all, should be pondered. The Word of God should be pondered." Wallace paused. In the moment of quiet, I wondered if these words would have offered any solace to my grandfather. "I don't know if this helps any, Tom."

"It does," I said. I took a deep breath. Shivers radiated from my neck down my arms. I bit my lip. Was I getting choked up? I told Wallace he had earned his dinner, and he smiled.

"*Voh-shogut*," he said. Soren, quiet through our hour-long conversation, laughed. "That's a Swedish idiom," Wallace said. "*Voh-shogut*—it means, 'You're welcome.' That's not a literal translation, that's an idiom translation."

"What's the literal translation?" I asked.

"*Voh-shogut* means 'Be so good.' The phrase is so often used when the hostess is passing food around the table. *Voh-shogut*: help yourself; it's for you. It can be used as a thanksgiving, too, when you say thank-you: *Duksemekye*. Then the reply is '*Voh-shogut*.' You're welcome."

I nodded my head. "For your time, and for allowing me the opportunity to listen to you and speak with you, *Duksemekye*. That's where my Swedish runs out," I said, an admission Wallace and Soren surely felt was unnecessary. They giggled in unison.

"We also have an expression," the pastor said, "*Comeyen*. That means 'Come again.' The door will always be open to you, Tom. I wish you lived closer. I wish I could follow you in your spiritual pilgrimage, and watch you grow and develop through the years."

Now I clearly felt like crying. "Well, I'll tell you, I believe in a way you will."

"Oh, I don't know." He sighed. "We long to be of help to one another. It's not always easy to be the help we want to be, and to do it in such a way that we know it." Again he paused. By this time spoiled, I expected more wisdom. "Listen," he said, "where shall we go for supper tonight?"

Soren suggested the Swedish Pancake House.

"Closed," Wallace said. After considering our other options in Rockford, we quickly reached consensus. We escorted Wallace out of his apartment and he strolled down the hallway, pushing his walker past nurses who smiled and offered a "Good evening, Pastor Johnson." Soren drove us to Applebee's, a few minutes from his grandfather's nursing home. Wallace sat in front with Soren. I sat in the open-air flatbed, holding on to the sides as Soren curled around a bend in the mall driveway.

When the food arrived, Wallace announced that he would say grace. We bowed our heads. "We thank you for this food, O Lord. We ask you to bless it. We thank you for Tom's presence. We thank you for letting us be together. We thank you, O Lord. Amen."

Chicken strips have a different flavor after being blessed. As I dunked them in sweet and sour sauce, I knew to be gentle. As I chewed, I tried not to bite too hard. Applebee's is no church. A plate of chicken fingers and French fries isn't communion. Still, I couldn't shake the feeling that that night, we together were part of a congregation.

The sun had not yet set over the Applebee's parking lot when we emerged from dinner. Soren guided Wallace toward the truck, stopping at the driver's side to unlock the doors. I led Pastor Johnson to the passenger side. I held his walker and, gripping his hand, assisted him as he slumped into the front seat. When we returned to Wallace's nursing home and led him back, his arms in ours, to his open door and large-type Bible, I think I saw clearly that we would not meet each other again. His "*Comeyen,*" his invitation for me to return, was hospitality tinged with nostalgia, a prayer of the dying. It was a prayer, I imagined, uttered in the souls of George Pejovic's grandparents, and mine, as well.

[10]

The following afternoon I learned that Arnold Wolf had made Liz cry at her Bat Mitzvah. He wasn't some boy with braces and a cowlick who Liz had a crush on, who spurned her on this coming-of-age day by choosing Debbie or Sonji in her place. Nor was he one of her older brother's friends, tweed-blazered and corduroy elbow-patched, silently, mercilessly heckling from the twelfth pew. No. Arnold Wolf shared the bimah, the pulpit, the stage, with Liz. He was her rabbi, who scolded her for Hebrew mispronunciation as she stood in front of the Torah scrolls and her family for the first time. We bumped into him at the corner of Fifty-Seventh Street and South Blackstone, blocks from where she grew up, and literally across the street from the apartment she would rent that year and the next. Our meeting ended up cordial enough, with the three of us smiling at news of family, the temple, and the old neighborhood.

"That was easy," I said as we walked away.

She agreed. "You know, we do have a bit of a history, but I'm aware that he knows a lot and has a lot to offer." She paused. I watched a thought cross her mind as though I was stopped at a railroad crossing, following a rumbling freighter. "You know, he'd actually be someone you should talk to. He's pretty fascinating."

"Yeah?"

"Totally." She started to tell me about her childhood rabbi, his iconoclastic support of a Palestinian state a generation before such a notion achieved any sort of widespread audience, his rigorous intellectual approach to the Torah, and his life outside the pulpit.

"Talking with him would be cool with you?" I asked.

"Of course," she said.

On our way to Harold's Chicken Shack, a neighborhood place that serves fried chicken with hot sauce and white bread through a protective Plexiglas window, Liz didn't mention her rite of trauma, so I assumed the temporary drama of revisiting it had subsided. It sounded like it was over. I was, naturally, willing to hear more about it. As long as my asking didn't prompt her to talk all the way through lunch about it, I would have been poised for more. There was a limit, of course, and that day, for some reason, I felt edgily close to the limit on my historical crisis hotline.

I reminded myself how much I love to listen, how during the first month of my drive I had come to view listening, and my role as drive-thru witness, as a sort of calling. Still, on the way to Harold's, stimulated by the potential interview of Arnold Wolf, the ache of my gnawing appetite, and the patter of Liz's feet against the pavement, the possibility dawned on me that I listened when I was good and ready. On this pilgrimage, folks had spoken when I asked them to. After leaving them, caressed by quiet, or its automotive surrogates, FM radio and the blaze of wind through the window, I enjoyed what felt like a reprieve. In those moments I didn't question how my calling might be more than a little self-serving, meticulously scheduled so as not to put a dent in my personal space and private time. Might it be that I listened when listening felt good, and then at other times rolled my neck and inhaled strategically, as though I were a parent about to smack his baby who suddenly remembered to count to ten? Why did I feel that my patience was tested when my girlfriend prepared to unfurl the past in the space between us? Why did the eloquent silence of a Harold's fried chicken lunch, as though I ate not with Liz but Brother Gus, hold more appeal than a trip down memory lane? Low blood sugar didn't tell the whole story.

In other people's testimonies, I homed in. Had I heard the story of the young woman brought to tears by her rabbi *during* her Bat Mitzvah in the course of an interview, I would have made a beeline to that memory, hungry—predatory, almost—for a fuller picture of that very specific sadness. Somehow a stranger recounting this moment helped illustrate my own teenage revulsion to organized religion, when it seemed that all rabbis fit the oversized mold of the one who met me the day before my Bar Mitzvah (at least in my revisionist memory that's when he met me) with encrusted remnants of a lunchtime egg salad sandwich caked in the corner of his mouth, winking to me about how much he looked forward to my participation in confirmation classes in the years to come. The very thought of these classes used to send involuntary shudders through me, bringing me near tears when I felt I had signed on to Judaism for any longer than my Bar Mitzvah party might last. To hear a stranger tell this story, to encounter the unanticipated and see myself in her story, well, there's gold in dem dar hills, methinks. But to hear Liz tell this story, well, that might take too long, might divert me from the strange, the other, and the head-scratchingly familiar in our midst. Liz would be around for a long time, I reasoned. Because her history and mine would flow into each other like streams of snowmelt dumping into a river, I didn't feel compelled to learn hers by rote so early in the game. We'll have more than enough time together. That is what I told myself.

Two mornings later, I walked to Temple K.A.M. Isaiah and my appointment with Rabbi Wolf. His office was a street-level room off the hallway to an extraordinarily beautiful sanctuary, made in the Byzantine style, a circular space rimmed by a second-story balcony and with, in the manner of other Reform synagogues, a *bimah* on a stage in front of the congregation. Outside light struck his office's smoky-paned windows, seeping rather than flooding through light-brown Venetian blinds to shade the room as if the rabbi's desk sat below a tree in bloom. Several walls were lined with bookshelves, so jam-packed that the books seemed to need elbows. Another wall, the one in which the windows were set, featured two framed pictures, one below the other. On top was a photographic portrait of an old man whose devious grin lifted his shaggy white mustache and beard. I recognized the man to be Martin Buber, twentieth-century Jewish sage, mystic, intellectual, and author, and not without his devious side. I remembered reading how, during lectures as he grew older, he stationed a photograph of a naked woman next to his notes on the lectern. He intended the picture as a "just in case," which is to say, if his interest in his subject matter flagged, he needed only to glance over at the photo to stoke the fire in his words. Below Buber was a charcoal sketch of a man in prayer, wearing phylacteries and a shawl, the prayer book held close to his face. In a corner of the office leaned a metal sign, the insignia of the Chicago White Sox. The rabbi might have made my girlfriend cry, but my opportunistic side said, let's play ball.

Arnold Wolf was born March 19, 1924, on the North Side of Chicago. He was almost exactly fifty years older than I.

"Hey, I'm a Pisces, too," I said. "We're a week apart. I'm March 12."

"You know what they say about Pisces?" he asked.

"We're sensitive."

"Sensitive. Also depressed, intuitive, creative, but sometimes," he searched for the word, "not exactly duplicitous, but privatized. I don't believe in any of that, but it's uncanny how accurate it is. The fact is, my whole family is exactly what they're supposed to be according to their signs."

I don't know what he looked like in 1949 when he was my age, but as a seventy-five-year-old, Arnold Wolf had a crusty, gnomish quality. His voice, so deep and scratchy it sounded as though wrapped in burlap, gave one the impression that he had just risen above ground after an extended stay in a subterranean burrow. A squat, at this point, barrel-bellied man, he wore a salt-and-pepper goatee, a signature uniform for an older Jew on the political left. He nibbled on a piece of pastry from an open drawer at his right hand. I wondered if different drawers had different meals in them. He had a nearly larger-than-life reputation, both within the Reform movement, where he was renowned as one of its political and intellectual luminaries, and in Hyde Park, where as he walked down the street he routinely sang in so booming and guttural a voice that a microphone seemed to have been placed at the mouth of a stomachache sufferer.

"I have to ask you a question first and foremost," I said. "I don't mean to start off so seriously, but I feel I need to get this straight, just sort of for my own understanding." I sounded incredibly somber, as though I had arrived to perform the joyless task of avenging my lady's honor. "You grew up on the North Side, so how in the world did you become a White Sox fan?"

The rabbi understood the gravity of my tone. The North Side, after all, is Cub territory, while the South Side seemed to me reserved for Sox fans. "As a kid, I went to Wrigley Field every Sunday when they had double-headers, with my cousin. But at sixteen, I came to the University of Chicago, and I had a conversion experience. From there I never looked back. From that time on I was never anything but a Sox fan, and my kids were never anything but Sox fans. I don't hate the Cubs, but the Cubs are like an alien tribe."

"Who did it?" I asked.

"My granduncle was rabbi of this congregation, and a huge Sox fan. Those were the days when rabbis didn't work hard, and the games were all during the day. He must've gone to see them twice a week. That's what I thought rabbis did. Later, it turned out things had changed, and the games were at night. I really got screwed by my own illusions. He had no children, so he took me to Sox games. He was sort of the chaplain of the team. He had a free pass, that I remember."

"So your uncle must have been around for 1919?" That was the year the White Sox allegedly threw the World Series to the Cincinnati Reds, the bleak autumn of "Say it ain't so, Joe."

"Oh yeah. He was here from the turn of the century."

"So he was able to get over the betrayal?"

"Well, he would never tell me what he thought about the Black Sox, although they were certainly in his consciousness, and in mine, too, in a strange way, even though I wasn't alive. There was also a Jewish angle, because it was probably Rothstein, a Jewish fixer, who bought them off. It was a dark moment." The rabbi rubbed his wide fingers along the sloped ridge of his goatee. "I'm very conscious that people have an evil inclination, and one of the ways I learn it is from sports; another way is from psychoanalysis; and another from Judaism. But they all converge, and together they tell you that you can't count on people just doing the right thing—including yourself. You can be hopeful, but not foolish."

"Does that seem to you like a distinctly Jewish perspective?" I asked.

"Well, I get it from Judaism, but I think somebody like Martin Luther King got it from Christianity. He had a very dark side, and he knew the depths of human evil, but he didn't let it stop him. He still had a messianic side that said, 'That's not the last act, there's hope for redemption.' But even now, I think maybe Jews and Christians are a little different. For Christians, the world has been redeemed. And they have the problem that, if it's been redeemed, how come it's so bad? For Jews, the world has not been redeemed, and the problem is, if it's this bad, how could it ever be redeemed?"

I asked the rabbi when he knew he wanted to be a rabbi.

"I remember when I was a little kid, people would ask what I wanted to be and I'd say, a rabbi. And they would laugh and I would laugh. My friends didn't believe me, because I was a jokester and, to some extent, mildly delinquent. And they would laugh when I said rabbi. But after a while, I think they knew it wasn't exactly a joke. I think it's a Pisces way. Although I certainly didn't behave in a puritanical way, I was sort of there for them, and I was intuitive, and pastoral, so I could bring people out of themselves, sometimes. I think they thought that was sort of a sign."

The rabbi's words hit me the way scents freeze other people, smelling salts of recognition. "I think I get that occasionally, too," I said, making what felt oddly like an admission to Rabbi Wolf. "Late at night, and a number of beers into the evening, I'll hear somebody call out, 'Rabbi!' across the bar. I'll turn around, and invariably it's me they're shouting at."

In fact, during divinity school, the school's chaplain heard me preach a few sermons for a class she taught, and declared to me that God had told her I needed to become a rabbi. Acquaintances from New York, learning I attended divinity school, assumed it was rabbinic seminary and, when they saw me, asked when I'd be ready to Bar Mitzvah their kids. The talk made me antsy and flattered. Though I recognized that he may have been a jerk at some point or another, Rabbi Wolf illustrated that all of our autobiographical villains can eventually tunnel through to daylight.

Was this what Liz would want from our conversation, my seeing myself in the rabbi's story? I couldn't tell if I had somehow sold out her sadness. I concluded that she would not have recommended I pursue the conversation if she hadn't found peace both in the memory and the prospect that he, a born teacher, could help me.

Arnold Wolf had been a rabbi for fifty years. He told me his parents met in this congregation. He held several different posts, leading a few different communities, before returning here to his origins.

"What does it mean to you to be a rabbi?" I asked, adding, "and have you been one?"

"In principle, the answer's easy: a rabbi is a teacher and nothing else. If I understand what the word *rabbi* means in Judaism, I think that's pretty close. The "nothing else" is what I've emphasized. Not a spiritual teacher, and not an administrator, and not a fundraiser. Just a teacher. But a teacher is a hard job, cause you're teaching all the time. Not just in a class. Maybe not even mostly in a class. Here, at a cocktail party, on television, wherever, it's all teaching. It's not a priest—we don't have any privileges or sacraments. We don't have any responsibilities that other Jews don't have. The only thing we've got is some knowledge, and we have to get more and pass it around. I suppose some would say exemplar, but I have a problem with that. I don't want people to be like me, I want them to be like what we're both striving for.

"The young rabbis are more like you than like me," he said. Like me? I thought. Did the rabbi actually see me as a potential rabbi? I worried I might be blushing. "They don't come from an embedded family or community experience. They come intellectually seeking or personally feeling out. There's a plus and a minus to that: the plus is that they're unencumbered, and in a way more sincere; but the bad thing is, there is no memory of being in community. They have to sort of invent a memory, and create a family. Whereas I'm trailed by literal family, and by more than that: by generations."

"Are the members of the community responsible for that memory in the same way the rabbi is?" I asked.

"Absolutely. That's one of the things I've stood for. The congregation has to make big decisions. It has to make serious commitments."

Reform Judaism, however, at least in my extended circle, was notorious for demanding little and receiving less from its adherents. Certainly this was a shame at a contemporary level, but in a deeper sense, the "whatever" approach to Judaism that the Reform movement seemed to inspire represented a profound dereliction of historical responsibility. A creation of Enlightenment-influenced Jews, the Reform movement was a revolution when it began in the first part of the nineteenth century in Germany. Taking advantage of their newfound citizenship in Western European countries, these Jews embarked on the historical project of modernizing the religious sphere. This required a dramatic transformation of liturgy and worship space, and also of law and observance. These reformers, following the lead of Protestant believers in Western European countries, privatized religion, made *halachah,* the ritual observance of *mitzvot,* or commandments, effectively optional, and instilled in Jews the sense that they were individuals, not exclusively community.

The individual, private ethos of Reform Judaism contrasted with the communal sense of identity and responsibility I noted in the Torah portions over the previous few weeks from the middle of Deuteronomy. Whether in the command to "open your hand to the poor and needy kinsman in your land" or the injunction to return the ox that wanders from your neighbor's field, I gleaned that one's accountability to others is a nonnegotiable matter of paramount importance in Judaism. "In the text the last couple of weeks," I said, "the portions are so suffused with the sense that you have to make a promise to be part of the community, you have to be willing to commit up front to what you're gonna do." The rabbi nodded his assent at my reading. "I mean, is it because we're Americans, because we're moderns, that we don't do that?"

"Mm-hmm," he answered. "That's right. We want to keep our options open, and Judaism is partly about closing options. There are certain things you can't do. And there are certain things you're intended, if not obligated, to do. When I suggest here more Jewish study, people agree and they try; or more Sabbath observance, absolutely; but if I take some of the more remote obligations—family purity, for example—they wouldn't know how to hear that." Admittedly, in my reading I had glossed over those parts, too. "So you start where some progress can be made. People are doing more than they think they're doing. They're all much better Jews than they think they are. Are they good enough? I don't know. But they're better than they think."

"Is good enough a pertinent question?"

"I don't know how you could answer it. My answer is the following: it's not how many *mitzvot* you observe. It's are you going in or going out? Are you doing more or doing less? Are you caring more or caring less? It's the same thing in a marriage. Or study. You can say that about everything, I guess. It's the direction that's important, not the accomplishment." Wasn't this one more way of paraphrasing my friend Steve's line that fit my wandering with Elvis so well—that the only finding is in the looking?

The rabbi paused. He waited a beat. "I saw a handicapped kid do a Bar Mitzvah, against all odds. And I thought, whatever I do in my life will never be as accomplished as what he did. That would be like my trying to be on the White Sox. You can't say he should've done more. He only read three verses. But his three verses, he was sweating *blood* for them." My mouth quivered at its corners. I wasn't ready to feel tugged emotionally so quickly.

Through eyes like black olives, Arnold Wolf looked at me and blinked. When he did, the grid of wrinkles on his forehead compressed, as if a map of Chicago had been folded to display only the downtown Loop. "From your perspective, in your life, how would you describe Judaism?" I asked. With some people, to hear detailed answers you must ask detailed questions. Not so with Arnold Wolf. I peppered the rabbi with these general questions because I found that his answers flashed with particular insight.

"I don't think Judaism is a religion," he said. "Jews are a community, a civilization, which *has* a religion, or *is* religious, but it's not a religion, the way Lutherans are, for example. It's not about doing religion; it's about doing everything in a certain religious way. So it's about what you eat, and who you sleep with, and doing your politics a certain way.

"A Jew is a Jew no matter whether he believes in God or does the commandments. But if you want to do the Jewish thing authentically, then it seems to me that you have to grab its religious, adjectival nature. I mean, what does it mean to do politics religious*ly*? Jewish*ly*?" He stressed the adverb ending of each word. I heard the echo of Imam Farooq's commitment to instilling in his community a Koranic vision, to ensure that Muslims acted Islamically. "It's not so easy to say. A Christian, especially a Protestant, goes in one by one. Jews don't go in one by one. They go in together. The hardest thing for a convert to Judaism to understand is that all Jews are relatives. I say to them, 'That doesn't just mean the good guys; it's not just Einstein and Marx. It's Meir Kehane, Netanyahu, Michael Milken, and all the bastards that are Jewish. They are now your brothers.' 'Well how can they be my brothers? I don't know them.' 'Yeah, they're now your brothers. And you are now responsible for them, and that's no fun.'"

"The exhortation that we are responsible for each other, where does that come from?" I asked.

"I would almost say everywhere. It says in the Talmud, 'All Jews are responsible for each other.' But already in the Bible, it's a community that goes up or down, and a few people can destroy it, and maybe a few people can save it, but basically the community is exiled, not the individual; the community is redeemed, not the individual, or not *only* the individual." Amen, I thought. And yet if this was so, how could Reform Judaism veer so profoundly to its accommodation of the individual above the collective? And if this was so, did my very individual pilgrimage represent a rejection of Jewish values, some sort of unintended abdication of larger responsibility? I thought that I was heading in, not out, and that I moved in the right direction. But did Judaism? Was it possible to distill the tradition to answer that question? And if it felt right to me, then did the tradition's answer, should it arrive, even matter?

The rabbi stopped talking. He breathed heavily. He dipped again into the snack drawer, broke off a piece of the cracker, and deposited it in his mouth. For some reason it didn't feel like the time to ask the question.

I looked around his office. "I think your picture of Buber is fantastic," I told him.

"The photograph was taken by a former mistress of his when they were both about eighty years old. They had known each other for sixty years." The rabbi sighed. I got up from my chair and moved toward the picture. I could see it in Buber's crinkled eyes. They were the eyes of a preening octogenarian recalling what it was to be a teenaged flirt. Or maybe it was the secret smile of the octogenarian who savors this kind of flirtatiousness, knows it's worth more than, or as much as, the teenaged brand.

Buber's *I and Thou* is a classic of twentieth-century theology. Though it took me some time to get through it, his thinking blew me away. Reader's Digesting seminal spiritual philosophy in a sentence or two seems irreverent, but what the hell? This bullet-pointing of the relevant Buber for this conversation goes out to the CliffsNotes enthusiasts out there: (1) People are defined only in existence to one another. (2) "In the beginning," he writes, "is the relation." (3) "I require a You to become; becoming I, I say You. All actual life is encounter. (4) "Through every single You the basic word addresses the eternal You."

That is to say: I am because you are, and you are no different; in our contact and connections with others, we locate ourselves, and in the finding, approach an understanding of God. *Yes*, Martin, sing it, brother. Skimming through his book as I traveled, I understood how Buber's visions were like the tread on my tires. I carried the book wherever I went for a month my first year of divinity school, feverishly underlining on the subway, mentally noting interactions as Buberian each time they felt reciprocal, in every instance when I had seen the other and the other had seen me.

One small example: on a soaking February afternoon in Cambridge, just down the street from the divinity school, walking home, holding an umbrella, a feeling of Buberosity in a moment of picayune proportions nearly overwhelmed me. Umbrellas seemed to pass me, not people. Underneath these mobile shelters we remained dry, and I thanked the umbrella for that. I distinctly remember saying that aloud: "Thank you, umbrella." But I felt how protection was a cloister of comfort, one that in shielding couldn't help but hide us. As the rhythm of rain plinking on pavement vibrated through my boots, the thought coursed through me that each time footsteps approached I *had* to peek out from under my umbrella, to see what hid beneath those other umbrellas. Awninged torsos and thudding feet glided past me on Oxford Street—one, two, three, four—every street another two cocooned pedestrians walking the other way. Then, near Prentiss Street, an umbrella tilted backward, lifting like a veil, to reveal a middle-aged woman with frizzy hair whose eyes met mine. The only thing we could do in the space between surprise and bashfulness was smile, shrugging off the weather in a glance. I can't explain why, and I don't know how, but what filled me, what snaked through me, what touched core and edges, skin and bones, was joy. We had crossed paths. Buber teaches us that we are always crossing paths.

On rush-hour sidewalks and in steam-pressed bus aisles the encounter with the stranger feels impossible, because there are just so many of them and only one of you. But when you pass me, or I pass you, on a sidewalk, up a staircase, in an elevator, a force stronger than ourselves—modern insecurity, urban anonymity—keeps us from one another. We need one another, but we act as though we don't, or won't. But when the glance is shared—if by some freak, dumb luck or some conscious, intentional effort the gaze is held and contact is reciprocated—you feel—well, I can't speak for you, so I'll go on what I know—that this bubble has been punctured, these personal walls have been razed, if only momentarily. The moment of passing is an *event*, each moment a new opportunity—like saying your name in a public gathering or saying "here" when called for attendance— to reject, defer, or forge connectedness: I can't, I could, I have. This is today and forever at stake in every passing. Arnold Wolf was walking from his house to some local store when we spotted him. In that moment of recognition, from the shudder of recollection, came an encounter.

"When he was an old man," Wolf said about Buber, "I took my sons to visit him." This was when Buber, who had fled his native Germany in 1938 to settle in what was then Palestine to teach at the newly formed Hebrew University, lived in Jerusalem. "He didn't talk to me, he talked to them. And he said to them, 'What would you like to know?' And my older son, who never shuts up, was silent. He couldn't think of anything. And my younger son, who was about seven, said, 'Please tell us how the telephones work in Jerusalem.' I could've killed him. You know, he could've asked, 'When will the Messiah come?' But *How do the telephones work?*" as if to say, could there be any more useless request. "For thirty minutes,

Buber showed them how the telephone worked. He made a call with them, he made a call to them. He showed them the dial." Arnold Wolf swallowed, shaking his round head from side to side. "And in a way, that said more than if he had talked about religion. If that's what this little boy wanted to know, *that* was going to be their dialogue." The rabbi inhaled. "*Amazing.*"

I asked the rabbi if he had a particular passage, or a handful of particular verses or passages or characters, that touched him most substantively, to his very core.

He grinned. "I tell ya." The Chicago accent was unavoidable. "It used to be the prophets, maybe Isaiah in particular. But not now. It's too poetic for me; it's too gorgeous. I like the nitty-gritty stuff now. I don't like Genesis as much as I like, say, the nineteenth chapter of Leviticus: the holiness chapter. That's stuff to do, and it gets to me now. Some of it is pretty clear, some of it isn't. The gorgeous passages are too gorgeous for me. And I've never been less poetic than now. I'm more and more prosaic. I think that may be common as you get older. I used to speak beautifully. I don't speak beautifully anymore, and I don't want to. Because then people would say, 'You speak beautifully'; now they say, 'I hear you. I know what you meant.' And that's much better. At least now it is."

[11]

Maybe Martin Buber would have hung up the walking stick, taken off his sandals, put the car up on blocks, and stayed with his love. I don't know. But I was scheduled for a flight back to Boston the next morning, so I kept to my internal itinerary. I said good-bye to Liz with her apartment cluttered but her new life in her old home in order, reclaimed the Nissan in Boston, and again drove south. I reached Washington, D.C., that night and spent the following morning with a garrulous hippie convert to the ascetic Indian tradition of Jainism in Shepherdstown, West Virginia, and part of the afternoon with a reserved Hindu motel operator in Petersburg, Virginia. Still, it wasn't until I hit the verdant green backdrop of western Virginia late the next morning that I felt my trip had recommenced, after the domestic immersion of moving Liz to Chicago.

Liberty University sits on the top of a hill in Lynchburg, Virginia. This position, though perhaps due to convenience or the availability of inexpensive real estate, did not slip past my Pilgrim-conversant side. Certainly one could make a case that Liberty, founded by the Reverend Jerry Falwell as an institution of higher learning for the devotedly high-minded, is a descendent of the Pilgrim aspiration to be like a city on a hill.

As I pulled into the campus, part of me thirsted for the chance to rework the caricature of Fundamentalist Christians painted by media and a few of their pharisaic spokesmen, like Reverend Falwell, and to present in its place a revised, nuanced, lifelike tapestry of voices. But another, nagging part savored others' pigeonholing of them and aspired to leave Liberty validating the stereotype rather than redrafting it. A wave of outsider machismo surged through me and I wanted to declare, nonchalantly, that I did not belong there. If I'd had a hat that said "Unsaved," I would have worn it.

Next door to a darkened, locked snack shop was the Student Activity Office. A couple of friendly college-age people staffed the air-conditioned office. A bowl of chocolates rested on top of the desk. I asked if I might nab one. They asked if I needed help finding somebody.

"Well," I said, sensing a suitable space for an introduction, "actually I do." I told them I was a writer and recent divinity school graduate working on a project about faith in America. "And I wanted to see what's happening here at Liberty."

Robert, a twenty-two-year-old senior, seemed excited. He wore ankle socks and Nike running sneakers. Stubble covered his chiseled jaw. Hannah, a twenty-year-old sophomore, was an American-born Korean woman who worked at the Gap. I admit I expected a different sort of scene, with a choir maybe, and mini-Bibles where the chocolates were. Instead, I wondered whether I had stumbled into the casting call for the 700 Club's version of MTV's *Real World* series.

Robert and I began to talk about the class he had recently finished on the historical Jesus. The professor had challenged the students to discard their suppositions about Jesus as the risen Lord and instead to look at him in the context of the time and place and culture in which he had lived. Robert acknowledged that much of the gung ho faith he'd come to Liberty with as an eighteen-year-old four years before had faded. This is it, I thought, a kid who comes to Liberty sure of his faith and leaves groping for answers. I didn't waste any time: I asked him if he wanted to be interviewed. He apologized. He worked at the Outback Steakhouse and his shift started in half an hour. I turned to Hannah and asked her the same question. I was the first Jew she'd ever met, it turned out, and she confided that she was uncertain of her life's path, that though she waited for the Lord to speak to her, prayed for his voice and his message to arrive, she heard nothing. This would do fine, too: the young woman waiting for God's instructions like a customer holding a "now serving" number in a delicatessen who grows nervously impatient. She demurred, saying she was too bashful.

That's when Jeff Paul appeared out of central casting.

"I overheard you say that you're looking for somebody to interview," he said. I nodded. "Well, I would love to offer you my testimony. I'll be in my office if you want to hear it." Jeff, a twenty-eight-year-old Liberty alumnus now working in the Office of Student Activities, had an accent that screamed South Jersey and Philadelphia to me. He was losing his sandy blond hair. He wore a Liberty University polo shirt tucked snugly into khaki pants. I looked back at Hannah and Robert with pleading eyes and tried them once more. Couldn't Robert skip work and this month's rent to chat with me for an hour? Wouldn't Hannah muster the courage to sit with me? No dice. With the same sort of pit in my stomach I had at middle school dances when girls I liked had better things to do than dance with me and one I didn't bother with could think of nothing she'd rather do, I knocked on Jeff Paul's door, fully expecting the party line, the Falwell mission statement. He thanked me for giving him the chance to testify.

"One of the things I appreciate about this school," Jeff said once I'd turned on the recorder, "is that because there are so many different religions here, it really causes you to think about where your faith is." I wondered if by "so many different religions" he meant Baptists, Methodists, and Pentecostals. "You have to ask yourself if your faith is a result of how you were brought up, or is it truly your own faith? The Bible says it needs to be a *personal* faith—not what your parents told you, but a personal walk on a daily basis."

Incorporating the personal walk in an academic setting was the inspiration behind Liberty University's founding in 1971. Falwell had already gained national prominence as the Fundamentalist pastor of Thomas Road Baptist Church in Lynchburg when he began fundraising to establish a Christian university. It would be a kind of denominational descendant of the major Catholic universities throughout the United States. Jeff Paul valued the diversity of the student body, and while I made light of it, the school was, it should be said, designed for Christians by Christians. Students committed to attend chapel three times a week. Robert, the student who couldn't stay to talk at length with me, alluded to a kind of ideological pledge of allegiance that faculty members were contractually bound to sign. In signing, they made binding declarations to the dictates of Evangelical faith. Robert hadn't seen it, but he referred to the document as though it were a piece of common knowledge at the school.

Because I'd had such negligible contact with Evangelical Christians in my life, sentiments that might seem canned or trite to others were not to me. That's not to say that testimonies like Jeff Paul's might not grow wearisome relatively rapidly; instead, I mean this as an admission that such pronouncements, because they were novel to me, felt not flimsy but weighty. I learned that the Jesus in Jeff's life died for Jeff. The historical context of Jesus' life—the child born in a backwater garrison of an imperial power at or near its zenith, the Jew who approached other Jews with visions of religious as well as social reform—had filtered through the Reformation and the Enlightenment and American Individualism to produce a Jesus who lived—more importantly, died, or most importantly, rose again—for those who believe in precisely this version of his story.

Jeff's ideas, and this branch of Protestantism, represent potent forces in contemporary American life. Liberty University in particular is a leading organizer of these forces, and it is Fundamentalists like Reverend Falwell who can claim much of the credit for the meteoric growth of Evangelical Christianity over the past half-century. Fundamentalism entered the American culture in 1910 with the publication of a series of pamphlets called *The Fundamentals*. At the time, conservative Christians faced a dizzying array of cultural and religious hurdles. Darwin's theories of creation and evolution had swept the Western world and punctured the belief that an omnipotent God had created the Earth in six days.

Immigrants and a new way of reading the Bible crossed the Atlantic Ocean around this time, too. Millions of people from southern and eastern Europe flooded the country, changing the demographic complexion of the American population. Meanwhile, German biblical criticism, which asserted that people, not God, had written, redacted, and edited the Bible, transformed the way people related to the scriptures with a tectonic, not to mention Teutonic impact. Threatened by these sea changes and aiming to foment a counterinsurgency, a pair of wealthy brothers published *The Fundamentals* and sent three million copies to pastors, evangelists, students, YMCAs, and YWCAs. The pamphlets stressed the evils of the modern, secular, liberal world. The Bible did not merely represent or allude to God's Word; it *was* God's Word, the literal account of creation and revelation. Protestant Fundamentalism declared that the scriptures were not subject to analysis, interpretation, or critique. Government was to be a servant of faith, the public sphere was to revert to being an explicitly religious space, and religious orthodoxy was the only way to know God. Fundamentalism spawned radio and TV evangelism and the political power of the Christian Right, and that first publication may have marked the advent of one of the true milestones of the twentieth century: direct mail.

"Let me share a story with you," Jeff said. "Right now I'm taking a class called Evangelism. Evangelism is basically about how I share my faith with you. It's not an easy thing to do, because I'm not a very bold person. It's hard for me to go up to somebody on the street, start talking to them, and then all of a sudden start witnessing to them about Jesus Christ. But if I believe that unsaved people are going to hell, then I should be out there witnessing. It's a sin for me *not* to go do it. But I struggle with it. Anyhow, two years ago, I brought fifty kids to New York City and our job was to go out witnessing every day."

"You'd have kids on the street?" I asked. "Had they ever been to New York?"

"No," Jeff answered.

I laughed, in my own form of arrogance, my too-smug rebuff at the naïveté of the testimony-wielding tourists. "They would just walk up to people?" I asked, my eyebrows arched to the ceiling.

"Listen. We did this. I sent all these kids out in pairs to share the Gospel with strangers. I was with this fifteen-year-old kid from North Carolina. We were walking through the park and I said to him, 'Are you nervous?' He said, 'Yeah.' I said, 'Me, too.' So I said, 'Listen, why don't we stop and pray.' So we did. I said, 'God, we ask you to give us the words you want us to say. Help us not to be nervous. Help us to find a person that you want us to talk to.' And after we looked up, in two different directions we saw two guys sittin' on benches. So we decided, let's go to the one on the left. Next thing I know, I'm sitting down on that bench and I'm talking to this guy. He was in his thirties, wore a short-sleeved shirt, and had a beer in his hand. Middle of the day. Just sitting there.

"One of the awesome things about when you share the Gospel is that God gives you the words to say. I find out this guy was homeless. His wife just left him, he had lost his job, and he was a drunk. He shared all this with me, and I shared my faith with him. About my personal walk with Jesus Christ, and how Jesus Christ never leaves you or forsakes you. I shared with him how God brings fulfillment into your life. And this guy started to cry. He said, 'You know, Jeff, you couldn't come to me at a better time in my life. I really need something right now.' He told me his name was John. And I said, 'You know, John, I just prayed that God would send me to the person he wanted me to talk to. And I believe that person was you.' I said, 'Would you like to have the same faith I have?' And he said, 'Yes.' And so I said, 'All we have to do is pray together, and say, 'God, I'm a sinner. And I know that Jesus Christ died on the cross, and I want him to come into my heart, and be my personal savior. And I want to have a personal walk with him.' And we prayed together. Meanwhile, this guy's just got tears flowing out of his eyes. When we were done, he had a big smile on his face, and he said, 'Thank you so much, because I really and truly needed that.'"

A humbling irony hit me right then. If you substituted me for Jeff, and his faith in the answers for my faith in the questions, his meeting with a stranger was not unlike my own. What dawned on me as I listened to Jeff was the evangelical impulse of my trip. I too had endured the timid anxiousness before opening a door, had enlisted an analogous spirit to guide me toward people who seemed to expect my arrival, had experienced a similar bewildered gratefulness at destinations unplanned and conversations unimagined. I guessed that Jeff's feeling at these coincidences wasn't bewilderment but validation. And I supposed that my understanding of my essentially improvised route fell somewhere between those two emotions, imbuing me with a bewildering sense of validation. Because, like Jeff, part of my pitch, part of my message, was, "Would you like to have this same faith that I have?" My faith in words, Jeff's, in the Word. So I needed to hold the judgment here.

A direct descendant of the American conviction about its own chosenness, Protestant Fundamentalism blurs the biblical truth that all people are created in God's image, instead aspiring to re-create the world in its own image. Jeff Paul, for example, understood his faith as a template for others to imitate. Ideally, eventually, the whole world would worship the same God in the same way. Perhaps, I thought, that accounted for the bumper stickers that seemed to surround my Nissan on the nation's highways. I read, "Jesus died for me," "I've got a friend in Jesus," and my personal favorite, "My boss is a Jewish carpenter." Each of these messages signaled how people tried to put personal signatures on their faith, even using their car as a tool for evangelism, but also how prepackaged the personal expression of this faith can be. The abundance of what I will call *bumper psalms*—adhesive odes to Jesus, which line entire aisles at the Christian stores in malls all around the country—illuminated an irony in the Evangelical faith of Jeff Paul. While personal and individualistic, it was not correspondingly individual.

"Now, about this evangelism class," Jeff said. "One of the things we have to do is witness to one person every week. And like I said, that's very hard for me. So I prayed to God. I said, 'God, I'm not a very bold person. You're going to have to send somebody to me.'" Jeff snapped his fingers, like *voila*. "Now here you are. God couldn't make it any easier for me. He sends somebody to me so I don't have to go out and do something that I'm not real comfortable with. That's why I said I've got to be interviewed by you. Basically, you are an answer to my prayer."

"Okay." Something had come to my mind, and I considered the question, wondering whether it was too bold or impudent, or even rude, to ask. But I wanted to hear his answer. "When Jesus went to the cross, did he have you in mind?"

"Uhh," Jeff said, stumbling out loud for a moment. I sought not a reply about how Jeff saw Jesus, but whether Jesus saw Jeff, whether Jesus understood his own agony through the prism of the salvation of the guy I sat across from. From my historically sensitive, contextually conscious perspective, the proposition seemed almost ludicrous. Jeff nodded his head before answering, "Yeah. He had me in mind when he was on the cross. And he had you in mind."

"He had *me* in mind?" I asked, incredulous. Jeff was really upping the ante.

"Yes. He had you in mind. But you don't have to understand it. That's just the awesome thing about faith, that you don't need to know." No, I thought, that's not the awesome thing about faith. I understood the need for a leap of faith in one's religious life, whether about the particulars of God—the details of the Trinity, Yahweh's dispensation of the Torah to Moses—or about the very existential generalities about God. But if I needed to make a leap in my religious life, I wanted it to be on a human, earthly scale, not the kind of cosmic leap made by astronauts on the lunar surface. Faith should not require a waving of the intellect's white flag. The awesome thing I hoped for in faith—*my* faith—was that my belief could be rooted in my pursuit of knowledge, not my abdication of it.

"My view is this," Jeff continued. "What if my belief was wrong? What have I lost? I've been a good person. I've lost nothing. But if all those other people are wrong, they're going to hell." Jeff smiled as though let in on a secret. "I'll take *my* chances. You and me are the same. We both sin, we both make mistakes, we both try to live a moral life. But there's one difference: my personal walk. That's the only difference between you and me. And because of that, I believe I'm going to heaven. Because you don't, I don't believe you're going to heaven."

I was listening, patiently I believed, but if the truth be told, I had started to feel more than a little irritated. "Just so I have it straight," I said, seeking clarification, "there are six billion people on the Earth. And there are, I don't know, let's say, a couple billion Christians."

"A small percentage," Jeff said.

"Is the sense you have that the other four billion are fated to go to hell because they don't believe precisely the same thing?"

Jeff waited, then nodded. "Yeah," he said, sounding considerate, if not apologetic.

"So how does that affect your conversations with people who aren't Christians? Like us—we're having a nice conversation. I'm Jewish, so I don't accept Jesus as my savior. I think he was a phenomenally good and extraordinary man, but I don't see him as God. How does that affect the way you and I are going to interact?"

"It would cause me to have—" again, Jeff paused, this time earnestly seeking the right words for the occasion, "concern for you. And to pray for you."

At that point I was perched on the edge of my seat, excited—not quite panting, but expectant. "Can I ask you something?" I asked. "If you were to pray for me, how would it go?"

"See, one of the awesome things about God is that he puts it in everybody's mind to want to know him. And he put that desire in you. You're searching for the answer. I would just say, 'God, help him to find the truth. Help him to find what he is searching for.' Because you're searching, and I know what you're searching for is him. And I want you to have the same faith I have, because I know the fulfillment it has brought in my life. And it would do the same for you. I have a personal walk with Jesus Christ. You could have the same thing. And it would end your search."

Ugh. My mind raced. My first instinct was frustration: Why would I possibly want the same thing? If it's supposed to be such a personal walk, then why would I want to superimpose my path onto yours? That doesn't make any sense. It wasn't the tenets of the doctrine that annoyed me, but the deferential fealty to the doctrine itself, the intensity as much as the ingredients. My second instinct was, I was pissed off: I don't think so, my friend. I do not believe that God is leading me in the direction of your faith, toward your answers. I do not believe that, not right now, not when I walk out of this room, and certainly not upon reflection. My third instinct was ambivalence: How come I'm nodding yes to what he just said? I could have walked out of his office in exasperation, but I stayed seated. Perhaps because, amid the bluster, Jeff was right. Not about his path—I cannot substantiate that; but about me and my path, I can say yes. Jeff articulated something about me that no one I had spoken to had as of yet. Maybe other people believed that such reflections about my search were obvious, unnecessary, or tangential to their own spoken spiritual autobiographies. Some assumed I was a scholar; others figured I was a nomad; a few suspected I might have arrived on the coattails of providence. But nobody had spoken so directly of me back to me, pinpointing the why of my trip beneath its what. "You're searching," Jeff said, "searching for answers and fulfillment." And this was true. Jeff had at once confirmed my portrait of the Fundamentalist frame of mind, and pinpointed my trip's umbilical connection to it. My fourth instinct was consideration: How can this guy be right and wrong in the same breath, observant and obtuse, knowing and nauseating all at once? Where, oh, where was Martin Buber when I needed him?

[12]

On the narrow country highway that led me from Lynchburg, Virginia, south to Durham, North Carolina, I made a wrong turn and had to pull into a strip mall to reverse course. On my way in, I spotted an old man playing the role of human billboard at the parking lot's entrance. He was dark-skinned and small, and he stood a little hunched over with an orange sign made of oaktag dangling from his neck. With only a cursory glance, the man might have seemed a lamppost or a slumping sign. But as I steered the car around, I caught a long glimpse of him. Sensing my gaze, he raised his head from his torso, like a curious turtle, and smiled. The line of three or four cars waiting to make a left turn ahead of me moved slowly, and when, moments later, I peeked up at him again, he was still looking in my direction. So I waved to him—we were no more than twenty yards away from each other, an easy baseball toss—and he waved back.

"How you doing?" I yelled.

"Good, good, fine," he said, "and you?"

I stuck my arm out the window, pointing my thumb upward, or maybe my gently clenched fist out, just some simple indication that I was feeling all right. A momentary encounter with someone I didn't know and would not see again. As I rolled into my left-hand turn toward Durham, I was wiping moisture from my glassy eyes onto the sleeve of my shirt. The human billboard's smile had brought me to tears.

I was heading south to spend the weekend with my college roommate, Mark Rambler, then in law school at Duke University. I had two interviews planned in the area, one with Larry Goodwyn in Durham on Monday, the other with Harvey Lee Green in Raleigh on Tuesday. Larry Goodwyn was a professor, a connection through a close friend of Liz's; Harvey Lee Green was a convicted murderer who had experienced a conversion and become a born-again Christian while on death row.

Mark lived with his fiancée, Steph Snow, also a friend of mine from college. I arrived at their apartment after dark on Friday, and after our initial embraces, I asked them if they wanted to "do a little Shabbat." They agreed with an enthusiastic curiosity. Shaking off cobwebs that had been collecting since his own Bar Mitzvah, Mark accompanied me through the prayers over candle lighting, a bottle of eight-dollar red wine I'd bought in West Virginia, and hamburger rolls from their cabinet. With my mouth full, I admitted to Steph, a liberal Protestant, that this was not the ideal Shabbat table, because Shabbat really means Manischewitz—also known as four-dollar wine—and the braided bread called challah that Liz and I had eaten in the cornfield. Still we succeeded, to whatever degree unconventionally, in remembering and observing the ritual prescribed in the Fourth Commandment: "Observe the Sabbath day to keep it holy." We spoke about Shabbat, how in our weekly pause we commemorate the imperfect satisfaction with creation that God expressed at the end of the sixth day—that the world, while not perfect, was "exceedingly good"—and the Exodus from Egypt. I mentioned that Rosh Hashanah, the Jewish New Year, was on Sunday. Mark said he hadn't planned on going to services, but when I suggested we attend together, they agreed without any prodding. Rosh Hashanah, like Shabbat, is a day on which work traditionally was forbidden. In deference to the tradition, I hadn't pursued or conducted any interviews on Saturdays over the course of the trip, and this particular Saturday and Sunday became, in effect, a mandatory slowdown.

Worried that we were late, we scurried into the Reform Sunday morning Rosh Hashanah service at the Hillel Center at Duke. There were plenty of good seats still available. Although the pews were filled almost entirely by college students, the scene was instantly familiar: as with every High Holiday I had ever attended, the service had already started and the well-groomed crowd was late arriving. The service plodded along, as young women with shimmering hair distracted young men trying not to be caught staring at them. The sermon, something New Agey and disappointingly inconsequential, felt like a forfeiture of the liturgy's drama. I wriggled in my seat, almost angry that the rabbi was squandering one of the two times all year when the congregants were sitting ducks to learn something new about the tradition.

In the scripture for the morning of Rosh Hashanah, everyone hears Abraham say, "*Hineni*," which is Hebrew for "Here I am." Three times the phrase is repeated in Genesis 22, an undisputedly climactic moment in the Torah. "Abraham," a voice says, and Abraham replies, "Hineni." Told by the voice to sacrifice his son Isaac, for whom he and his wife Sarah have waited nearly the length of their lifetimes, Abraham wordlessly accedes. The morning after the command, he, his son, and two young servants embark on a journey that leads them, one verse and two days later, to Mount Moriah. On this third day Abraham leaves the servants behind, loading Isaac with wood for the burnt offering. He carries only a knife and a torch in his own hands as together they ascend.

Isaac looks up. "Father?"

"Hineni," Abraham answers.

Isaac says, "I see the wood and the fire, but where's the lamb to sacrifice?" Is he a smart kid or a dumb kid, apprehensive or clueless?

Abraham replied, "God'll take care of that." Is he trusting his soul or out of his mind, devoted or delusional?

On the mountaintop, after they have built a stone altar, the father binds his son and places him on the firewood the boy had carried. Abraham raises his knife, only to hear the voice call him once more by name.

"Hineni," Abraham says. The voice belongs to an angelic messenger, who shows Abraham a ram trapped in a thicket, a substitute offering in place of Isaac. The tradition teaches that this moment offers proof of Abraham's faith, but I wondered if today Abraham might live on the same cellblock as Harvey Lee Green, the death row inmate I planned to meet two days later. Regardless, each time I heard "Hineni," the story's unanswered dysfunctional traumas faded away and I felt a lump form in my throat. I couldn't help but whisper, so low it must have sounded like a breath, here *I* am.

During the service, a clean-shaven, hair-gelled twenty-year-old in horn-rimmed glasses and a royal blue oxford shirt walked to the *bimah,* the Jewish altar, and exhaled into the *shofar,* a ram's horn trumpeted during the Rosh Hashanah service to announce the arrival of the New Year. The young man's cheeks blushed from the exertion of blowing for nearly a minute, the sound he made more like a struggling animal than a musical instrument. He blew little blips, and then a long blast of a final note lasting half a minute, his face inflating like a bellows. The effort was so prodigious that when he finished, he ripped the shofar from his mouth and strode like a conqueror back down the aisle toward his seat. I gave him an "Amen!"—an excited, church-folk kind of amen. My praise made the glistening, quiet congregants giggle.

At least Mark, sitting next to me, understood. He went "mmm," a trademark sound of his, and I knew what *he* meant. In his "mmm" was a bittersweet recognition, an appreciation of how I had been moved, and an apology that the congregation hadn't better understood. I knew what Joe Pesci's character felt in *Goodfellas,* because I envisioned myself standing and asking, in all seriousness, "What, do I make you laugh? Am I some kind of a clown, here to amuse you?" I wanted amens to rise from the pews, Reform Jews turning into Southern Baptists. I wanted over-the-top sentimentality, a movie scene, a vocal, visible acknowledgment of our connection. What I got was the flipping of hair.

I had been seized by the need to say amen so often already in my journey. The throwaway banter in drive-thru lines and at tollbooth windows struck me as a series of existentially significant, Buberian events. Teary-eyed at tiny things, like the smile from the human billboard, I could be moved in a moment. Sitting in a pew, sitting in my car—it didn't really matter.

Yet in the days before my arrival in Durham, encountering scenes that transformed the ho-hum into a benediction, I found myself in my front seat, tears forming in my eyes, deriving inadequate commiseration from my companions, an open road atlas and empty soda bottles. People had revealed themselves to me, and for their offerings I felt grateful. Still, in my interviews up to that point, I often felt something missing—not so much from them as from me.

"Hineni," I was saying. But where was I? I had gone on the road asking people to tell their stories, yet I was revealing precious little of my own. Too often in response to others' confessions, I held back, telling only enough to get by. I said I was from New York, but not that I'd grown up on the Upper East Side of Manhattan, which I thought might put people off. I acknowledged that I had just graduated from divinity school, but didn't mention that the school was Harvard. Such disclosure, I feared, might make people nod knowingly, as though they had me all figured out, or smile, kind of giddily, as if my pedigree denoted celebrity.

What I thought I had shared thus far was the core belief in everybody's somebodyness that fueled my journey. The same conviction had been at the root of my volunteering in a Massachusetts prison while in divinity school. Somehow this same belief also accounted for the anxiousness I felt soliciting other people's stories without disclosing many chapters of my own. I feared, I think, that although I traveled to hear others' stories, my own story might not be enough to keep people in their seats. I worried that the folks I was talking to would cut me off: "I thought you came to listen to my story. I don't want to spend half my day listening to you." Deep down, I wondered, do I mistrust them? Or me?

For thousands of miles, as I asked Muslims and Buddhists and Baptists what "Here I am" meant to them, I mumbled "Hineni" under my breath, not quite loudly enough to be heard. Yet "Hineni" was intended as an audible declaration, not a tentative request. I seemed to be stuck between my desire to be a somebody and my desire to be an anybody.

In the beginning of my trip, the ability to look and sound like anybody felt like a head start, though when people actually treated me just like anybody, making me peripheral, unimportant, I felt an impulse to rush to someplace where I was somebody. I wanted to be a stranger, but only if guaranteed that it was a preface to being known.

What occurred to me was that maybe, *maybe*, I am hiding. But what would I have been hiding from? The question, when it came, felt at once rhetorical and accusatory, as though I didn't need and shouldn't have to answer it. Hiding? Please. Hiding implied fear, and while I might have felt anxious off and on, I was feeling strong and connected, as though part of a very big thing. In fact, it sometimes seemed as though I had taken a clarity drug, some uningested Ecstasy equivalent. Walking down the street I saw faces and not just figures; moments, not just movement. Everyone appeared a possible subject, all strangers capable of being known. The more I spoke to people, the more specifics I heard, the more archetypal these individuals appeared. This didn't make them general or ethereal, but fuller, more substantial. Of course, I had known moments like these before, but never in a stretch of such consistency. I wrote about my travels at least an hour every day. I took pictures. I paid attention. The road brought me understanding.

The road also bought me time. Being on the road was seductive because there I was neither home nor away. I hovered between leaving and arriving, graduating and beginning again, being single and married. Being in between amounted to an invitation to be at once a stranger and an intimate, seeking connections without establishing commitments. If one pit stop or interstate exit didn't respond to me, I moved on. The only person I was accountable to was me. The only decisions I had to make were where to stop and when to get going.

I figured that this in-betweenness liberated me from vague though well-established boundaries of behavior. It made sense that Duke University sophomores wouldn't say amen in a High Holiday service. They were among their own and had to answer for their behavior. In temple especially they felt obliged to blend in, toeing the line between appearing nonchalantly engaged and seeming resolutely bored. From firsthand knowledge I knew this to be the appropriate spiritual life of a late-teenaged Jewish congregant. I'm sure that in my temple, if I *had* a temple, I would behave just the same way. The room would be filled with acquaintances, elementary school girlfriends, and friends of my grandparents, and in this setting "Amen!" would be impolitic, no matter how inspired I felt to testify. On the road, however, I felt free to say amen whenever I pleased.

The pilgrimage felt almost like a vacation.

I didn't consider it then, partly because I had those business cards that said "Tom Levinson, Project Director" on them, but of course, it was a vacation. There was no golf, no hot tubs, no shuffleboard; there had been only a handful of late nights, and few, if any, lazy mornings. Yet a pilgrimage, like a vacation, is an escape from the everyday. I still had routines, still was subject to the ceaseless rhythms of self-care, of tooth brushing and deodorant using. But I had evacuated the dull and the workaday. Instead I made my daily commute to the unknown, not the same old same old. I turned my pilgrimage into a divinity student's Disneyland.

I didn't realize it when I woke up that Monday morning but the next forty-eight hours would be like my very own Space Mountain roller coaster.

A close friend of Liz's named Wesley Hogan was completing her doctoral dissertation in oral history at Duke, and she told me that if I passed through Durham on my journey I should call on her advisor, Larry Goodwyn, a history professor and head of the school's Oral History department.

At two o'clock that Monday, I arrived at Larry's heavy office door feeling a tinge of cockiness. What did I have to tell Larry? That was the question on my mind as I knocked. He waved me in. He looked small behind a standard-issue dark desk cluttered with leaning towers of papers. Piles of books rose behind and on both sides of him. I didn't know this when I walked in, but the core focus of his scholarship was the development of mass-mobilized, democratic social movements. Goodwyn had authored books about the Populist movement in America and Solidarity in Poland. He was a historian who argued that "ordinary" people were not only the foot soldiers but also the leaders of these movements. His texts focused on firsthand accounts and people's personal stories. Goodwyn chose conversation as his way of discerning the truth.

Considering this backdrop now, I shake my head with embarrassment at my first hour with him. After our first stretch of chit-chat, what followed seemed proof of Larry's total self-centeredness. He dominated the conversation. I had arrived on time, courteous, respectful, armed with questions, but fully expecting that *he* would interrogate *me*. I, the pilgrim, and he, the head of Duke's Oral History department, had clearly defined roles. His monologue had to be some kind of practical joke.

But the professor kept talking, with some kind of southern twang bubbling up, about the research he'd done for the first book he'd written. He described the ways that unconnected rural Americans, from their small towns and local churches, had created the Populist movement in the late 1800s, first by organizing into area committees to learn about the federal economic policies that stunted their development as small farmers. Within a few years, they'd grown into regional communities, and within a few more years, a national party. The subject interested me, and I listened with active eyes, but only for so long, because at a certain point, anticipating that he'd pass the conch my way, I assumed I could begin to tell him about my project. I thought that was the drill. It didn't happen, though. So finally, with the clock a few minutes from three, calculating that I neared the end of my allotted hour's worth of time, I heaved all deferential protocol out the window.

"Larry," I said, butting in, "I'm sorry to interrupt but, look, I've got this one question for you." He looked at me expectantly, neither surprised nor offended. "Look, all I want to know, all I came here for really, was to ask you something: How do you get your subjects to feel like they *have* to tell their stories?" As soon as the question left my mouth, I second-guessed it. Was it really the single question I most wanted answered? Maybe just getting a few words in rewarded me with a victory of sorts.

Larry nodded at the question. He said something about my having cut into his story, and I almost said, "Come on man, enough already; just answer my question and I'll get out of your office." I didn't have to take this. I was a pilgrim. Clenching my jaw, I waited for him to proceed.

"Why'd you cut me off?" he asked.

"Honestly, because it didn't seem like you would stop unless I jumped in."

"How did it feel when I was talking so much?"

"Not great."

"Did it feel like you had to break in?" he asked.

"Yeah," I answered, my frustration suddenly tinged with sheepishness, "kinda."

"That you had to break in to tell your story, that asking your question was a necessity, speaking your peace something urgent?"

"Uh huh."

"Well," he said, not exactly concealing a half-smile, "that's one way."

I laughed. His whole ramble had been an exercise for me—one long, meandering prelude to my asking the question, then answering it for myself.

"So you're the big-time oral historian," I said, teasing and nearly blushing, "but you just spent a long time talking, telling your story to me. I have another question then. As the person asking the questions, how much of oneself is one supposed to share?" I exhaled. As soon as this question left my mouth, I knew it was the one I had meant to ask had I only been granted time for one.

What followed was a Ripley's Believe It or Not kind of moment. If a moment could be poured into a mold, baked in a kiln, glazed, and set on a mantle as a centerpiece, I would display Larry's next gesture. He unbuttoned a button at the top of his shirt, as though the heat from a North Carolina September midday was getting to him. Then he unbuttoned the next one down. And another, and still another until he had undone every button but one above his navel. I felt certain he would have headed for his belt next but I interjected, in between my laughter and my incredulity, to tell him I got the point. The scene was the furthest thing from a striptease one could imagine. A teacher simply showed a student how to ask good questions. To elicit the stories I drove from and toward, he showed me, I had to be willing to share my own. The perfect stranger revealed himself, and in the process encouraged the self-revelation of others. It hit me like a thunderbolt: here was how amens could be extended, how my "*Hineni*'s" could become "Here we are."

"That much?" I asked, grinning.

"All you've got," Larry said, suddenly dead serious.

Larry and I sat and talked in his office for nearly three more hours. We got down to my trip, what I made of what I had heard so far. We spoke of democracy, and when I asked him what it meant to be a lowercase-*d* democrat, he said, "A democrat is someone for whom no one is an other." This was precisely what I had been sensing, and as we spoke I started to wonder if my drive led me toward an understanding of American democracy as well as American religion. That the two were connected, I knew, but precisely how, I still struggled to figure out. Larry said he was not a religious man, but I saw him driven by a personal kind of dogma—his faith in people, something documented through his scholarship. He said that as a child his father, a military man, issued only one order repeatedly: "You must not lie." It seemed to me that Larry had turned this commandment into his life's work; his oral histories are a sort of encyclopedically researched form of reprobation for those who try to pass off fictions for history. He exhorted me without raising his voice, and our conversation touched me as political without focusing on politics. Transformation needed to be personal before it could ever become public.

A few minutes before six, Larry suggested we finish the afternoon off with a beer at a local bar. He led me to the history department building's vending machines, where he bought two packs of peanut butter and crackers. He hadn't eaten lunch.

The bar straddled the campus and downtown Durham. The dried tobacco stench of a nearby warehouse wafted through the bar's windows on breezes. There we drank a couple of Bud Lights as the dusty yellow light of the setting sun reflected off of the bottles. The humidity had been rising all afternoon. Hurricane Floyd gathered strength off the coast of Florida as we spoke, and local weathermen expected the storm to hit the Carolinas the next day.

In the booth, Larry undid, once again, a few of the buttons on his shirt. While he scratched his back with a fork, his arm cocked as though he was intending to stretch his triceps, I asked him for advice about my interview with Harvey Lee Green the next day—what he would ask if he were in my place.

When he had attended to the itch, he tore open his vending machine packs of peanut butter and crackers, munched on them, then made one of the wrappers into a funnel to pour the last crumbs into his mouth.

"What's your agenda?" he asked. "What would you like to learn?"

"I want to ask about his faith, and his spiritual life," I said, "the role that the inner life has played in his prison world. The man's only ten days from his execution date. I get the sense I'm about to skate a very fine line with Harvey, you know? I want to be compassionate and lend him my support. But he did murder two people. I've been told he killed them with whatever instruments he could grab during a bungled attempt to rob a hardware store. He admits it. He has devastated two families, pushing them to crave revenge for closure. In my time with him, I want to be forgiving, but not too forgiving. And yet I want to see him not only for what he did, but for what he has become in the aftermath."

Larry focused on the table as though he had scribbled a shopping list on it in pencil and struggled to see it. I noticed his jaw moving, and when he looked up after I had spoken, I could see him scouring his gums and teeth with his tongue for any leftovers of the peanut butter crackers. He began to draw on a white cocktail napkin, soggy around its edges. He sketched thick lines, some an inch long, others half that length, that met at right angles. I couldn't make out what he was drafting, so I swigged from my beer and surveyed the bar, pleased with the way the day had gone.

Larry's head still angled toward the table—maybe as the shopping list was finally coming into view—when I heard him say, "Sorry, I didn't quite hear you." He wanted me to repeat what I had said. I looked down, scanned the napkin, and saw that, though seeming to be dreamily preoccupied, he had used the napkin as a chalkboard. He had spelled out his reply. He'd colored in the hatch marks of ink until the thick lines and right angles formed "HOPE" in block letters. He swiveled the soggy napkin around to give me a better angle of his work. Once more, Larry Goodwyn asked me to repeat my question. "Hineni," I whispered out loud before sipping again from my beer, as Larry brushed crumbs off the table.

[13]

The morning in Durham dawned dim and foggy, as though the sullen sky had, during the night, dropped, breaking its fall only inches from the ground. On the walk from Mark and Steph's door to my car, pinpricks of perspiration settled like dew on my forearms. No rain had fallen, at least not yet. There was no wind either: quiet leaves sat still on roadside branches, the calm before the storm. I drove with all four windows down. I turned the radio on, but the wind swallowed the songs. The blurry sky, heavy with fog and anticipation, seemed to swallow up rubber and metal and asphalt, coughing up something melted and mournful. Interstates intersected, and state highways curled from the straight-edged streaks like the arced trigger of a pistol. The day started dark, Transylvania dark. All that was missing was the moan of a pipe organ. I slowed down and raised the windows in the back seat to hear a weather report. I couldn't miss it: local radio station obsessed about Hurricane Floyd, due sometime that afternoon but at the time pelting the coast of South Carolina. In Savannah and Atlanta, Georgia, mandatory evacuations were making interstates look like funeral processions.

My mind roamed forward toward my destination, the state prison in Raleigh, and backward, too. I recalled the stark white, halogen-lit classroom in the maximum-security prison where I'd volunteered every Thursday night throughout my two years of divinity school. I thought back to how I'd first gotten involved, and how naturally (or maybe not so naturally, but easily enough for me) I had assumed that I'd headed inside to help. The prisoners needed the wisdom of Harvard Divinity School, and I would be generous enough to show up and dole it out weekly, as though the server at an intellectual soup kitchen. I had quickly learned that the prisoners, though lonely and angry, were also wise. They were Christian and Muslim and agnostic, some over fifty and others still in their teens. During bouts with loneliness and addiction, as lovers left them and children forgot them, in their shame at the sorrow they'd caused and their rage at the sorrow they'd endured, their souls churned struggle into insight. As in the plotline of every tragic drama, through their suffering they had tunneled into awareness. In the examples of their stories I heard echoes of the spiritual struggles of the religious exemplars I'd first learned about in high school. Over the course of humbling, often soul-stirring evenings, Thursday night had come to feel to me the way Saturday mornings must feel to a synagogue's devoted attendees. My time in the presence of the incarcerated had become the anchor of my weeks; our banter, the temple auxiliary social league; their monologues, my rabbi's homilies; their prison, my sanctuary. What dawned on me then seems like an obvious plotline now. Still, at the time, the realization struck me like a lightning bolt: maybe it's the places we don't look, the people we don't see, who have the most to tell us.

I flashed forward, back to the start of my trip, when Mark had put me in touch with his summer employer, a public defender who represented Harvey Lee Green. Convicted in 1983 of a double murder, Harvey had experienced a conversion and become a born-again Christian while on death row. His attorney agreed with Mark's suggestion that he would be a good subject for my project. She in turn reasoned that I could be reciprocally useful if, after audiotaping my interview with Harvey, I found some way to broadcast it. Coverage of any kind would generate some much-needed public pressure in Harvey's bid for either a judicial stay of execution or an act of executive clemency. Harvey was, at the time of my visit, nine days from a scheduled execution date.

Nervous, I practiced possible greetings at the steering wheel. "Hi, Harvey, I'm Tom." "Harvey, Tom Levinson, hi." "Tom Levinson. Damn glad to meet you." I immediately felt like a plagiarist, as though my nervousness was hollow because it mimicked those movie scenes in which we watch the protagonist preparing to meet someone important, someone he's been traveling miles and miles to see. Still, I visualized the meeting: maybe he'd be in the room when I got there, maybe he'd walk in to find me. I thought about the cache acquired from going inside, behind clanging steel doors, to find a story. And I wondered whether, in truth, I'd be as anxious for a meeting with the families of the victims. After all, their faith had most likely gone through tremors as substantial as Harvey's. Where were they? I turned the radio off; I drove in a haze. I heard only wind and the greetings I was planning for a dying man.

I drove into the parking lot, pulled the penitentiary's front doors open, and announced my arrival at a window shielding the lobby from the prison's mission control. Captain Hudson, a graying white man of average height and medium build, came out to greet me. He led me through doorways and hallways, steel doors sliding open, thundering shut, until we reached a pale white room, washed in industrial lighting, with a white table bordered by a few wooden chairs, dulled and smoothed with wear in their centers. A desk with the state seal emblazoned on its front was on a slightly raised platform near the room's only door.

The captain sent somebody to bring Harvey into the room. He settled me into a chair at the table in the middle of room. He sat behind the desk with the state seal.

"You just staying until he comes in?" I asked Captain Hudson.

"Nope."

"You gonna be in here while we talk?"

"Uh-huh."

I was readjusting the microphone in its stand for at least the sixth time when Harvey entered the room. I had been told he was thirty-eight, but he looked several years, if not a decade, younger. He wore a standard-issue burgundy-colored uniform. A white undershirt poked out against his dark skin beneath the shirt's wide collar. I noticed the heavy clop of well-worn-in Converse basketball sneakers—the kind the Detroit Pistons of 1989 and 1990 used to wear: high tops with a royal blue star and a sideways "V"—as we met to shake hands. I hadn't planned in my series of possible introductions to begin by praising his footwear. I decided against it as we sat down across the table from each other.

"Harvard, huh?" he said, clearly taken with the only piece of me he knew, information gleaned from his attorney. I tried at once to meet his expectations and downplay this status with a nod.

Harvey was an inch or two shorter than me, broad but not bulky. A thin layer of afro receded near his temples, sloping gradually to the center of his forehead, making his hair look like an artist's sketch of a segment of an umbrella. A wisp of a moustache, so thin it looked penciled in, rested above his upper lip. He looked like any early-middle-aged guy you see on the bus or in the line at Subway. He bore no distinguishing marks that indicated his imminent fate. Most of Harvey's conversations were observed and overheard, so he brushed off the presence of Captain Hudson. I was a little more sensitive to his presence.

"I always believed in God," Harvey told me. "I was taught about God at an early age by my mother in the church. But I didn't profess God 'til round about 1985. Well, I professed God, but I didn't try to live as a Christian. Matter of fact, I didn't know how to live as a Christian. I still have trouble with it today."

I asked Harvey what it meant to live as a Christian.

"To love my fellow man as I love myself." And just how did Harvey do that? As someone condemned but forgiven? Lost and now found? Harvey drew three stages in his evolution as a believer: in the first stage, he merely believed in God; in the second, he declared his personal belief in God's saving grace; and in the third, the biggest struggle of the three, he aspired to live as a Christian. In this setting (as in any setting, I guess), that was asking a lot.

I had a book in front of me, a coil-bound journal my brother and his wife had given me a few years ago for my birthday, ornamented on front and back covers with the New York City subway map. I had taken the book into all of my conversations so far. It was on this book's pages that I legibly rewrote the questions Liz and I had drafted in those nights before the trip began. The questions provided me with a script that also functioned like a crutch. I could refer to them either to get the ball rolling or to keep the ball rolling. While my head scanned the pages of the journal, I watched from the corner of my eye as Harvey brought his hands from his lap to the tabletop. The hands were brown, a bit on the pudgy side, his fingernails clipped cleanly. Not a single question felt like it fit the occasion. I looked up at Harvey. He had been told by his lawyer that I was a student, that I had come to hear his story. He offered a smile, both suspicious and curious, at my silence.

Looking up, meeting his eyes, I felt suddenly bashful. "How's it going?" I asked. This was not among the questions listed in the subway map book.

"Pretty well." He shifted in his seat. "Things are happenin'. I'm hopin' for the best. I put it in God's hands long time ago. After the crime I said, 'Lord, take this from me. Whatever happens, let your will be done.' Although I got a tendency, as every man do, after putting it in the Lord's hands, to keep going back and pick it up again." Did this "take it from me, Lord," this articulation of surrender represent an abdication of responsibility? Or was it more like a recognition that the process of forgiveness begins with the ability to forgive yourself? Perhaps, I thought, this process begins with the desire to be forgiven, and whether forgiveness is granted by God or not, that initial impulse comes from the individual.

Emboldened by Larry Goodwyn's suggestion, I proceeded without a question. "I've spent a few years working in prisons, so I have a sense of it, but I never had a conversation like this."

Harvey chuckled, an encouraging, keep-going kind of chuckle. He seemed to understand that I needed some help. I had not broken quickly out of the gates here, and I wasn't asking what I wanted to learn. He started talking, throwing me a conversational lifeline about, appropriately, the things that are not said. "In our society, we really don't speak of death too much, except in the movies: bang you're dead, and that's it. But death ain't nothin' but a transition. Now, from my point of view, I believe I'm goin' to heaven. I believe in the Lord and I believe in his Holy Word. He don't never lie. Death is something where you don't experience it until you experience it. I'm still hopin' I don't have to experience it. But if I do, I believe the Lord will be right by my side."

"Are you praying every day?"

"I been praying every day since I been in here, day in, day out."

"Is that what you spend most of your time doing?"

"Right now it is. But most times I also work on my college courses. I got sixteen lessons in social interaction. I done finished lessons one through five. I also do my artwork. I just finished up all the artwork I was doing and sent it out. So the only thing I got now is just my Bible study."

"What's your art look like?"

"I do many things. I work mostly with acrylics, but I like working with pastels and watercolors. Also, pencil, pen, and ink. They won't let me have no oils in here. The last one I did for John Hilpert, for down at his retreat center in Cedar Cross, was a forty-inch by thirty-two-inch." John

Hilpert was the pastor of a Raleigh church that had built a relationship with Harvey. Harvey squinted with one eye, staring over my shoulder at the blank wall, re-imagining his canvas. It was a medley of different scenes from the life of Jesus.

"Is your cell decorated with your art?"

"Nah, they won't let me do that. Nothin' on the walls, nothin' on the floor. Most of my artwork, right now, Pullen got." Pullen, I learned, is the downtown Raleigh church where John Hilpert pastored. "It's supposed to be on display right now. Matter of fact, Pullen ain't but a five-minute drive from here."

"I'll have to go check it out," I said. "How do I get there?"

"I couldn't tell you that. I ain't never been there." Harvey belonged to a church he had never seen. While the community he formed on death row helped get him through his days, Harvey had hungered for the fellowship of a community outside the prison walls. He began an active search, asking the prison chaplain if she knew of anyone on the outside willing to begin a written correspondence with him. The chaplain considered the request and forwarded Harvey's name and address to John Hilpert. The pastor and the prisoner started a correspondence by mail, and after a number of months the church invited him to become a member. He said that before he'd joined, he'd alerted the church to his "whole history, the liquor, the drugs, and all that. But I also said I'm a changed person." A year into their letter-writing relationship, Pastor Hilpert suggested that Harvey begin written conversations with members of the church's youth group. The church even picked up the cost of Harvey's college courses on sociology when the state cancelled the program. The people at Pullen Memorial Baptist Church had been good to Harvey, and in return, I learned, Harvey had been good to them.

"Why sociology?" I asked.

"Well, it dawned on me as I was writing to the youth, and I started to see all the drive-bys and hate crimes and high school shootings. Sometimes it's safer being in prison than being out there on those streets. But those youth out there today, some of them just ain't got no one to talk to. Their mom and pop ain't gonna understand. So I figure to myself, I like sociology. I like the concept of it and what it's doin' for people. I want to be a counselor. So I'm taking these courses now. And what I'm learnin' I'm applyin' to the letters now.

"I had some of them write me to say thank you. One girl had told me that one of her friends was about ready to commit suicide. So that night I spent a couple hours writing to that girl's friend. And I mailed the letter to her, to send to her friend. Well, her friend wrote me and told me thank you 'cause she just needed someone to talk to. I *know* that feeling. And I said, 'Aw, thank *you*.' That kind of sadness don't make no sense no how. Their lives are just starting. Shoot. They just need somebody to listen to 'em."

I tried as I listened not to romanticize this whole scenario, the death row inmate counseling the teenagers on the outside, expressing concern and support in ways their parents have not, perhaps cannot. I felt I could say amen to a lot of what Harvey was saying. I had an experiential predisposition toward expecting wisdom from the prisoner. During divinity school, months passed where what I learned in the academic world was trumped by the head-nodding, heart-pounding lessons I received in that harshly lit, white-washed penitentiary classroom, so much like the space in which I now talked to Harvey. My impulse to say amen to Harvey was born on a hundred different Thursday nights in the prison in Bridgewater, Massachusetts. But Harvey didn't know about all that. In fact, he didn't know about *any* of that. The emphatic "uh-*huh*," the effusive "I heard that," and the melancholic "mmm" running through my head as Harvey talked might seem, if I loosened the valve and let them all out, to be a kind of sycophantic applause meter. I started to praise him for these relationships he had built, but when I opened my mouth what came out was, "That's, you know, that's really, um." The words felt lodged somewhere between my heart and my tongue. I wanted to tell Harvey how sorry I was, how humbled I was, how divided I was, seeing him without arranging time with the parents and spouses of his victims. And I could have, but I didn't.

How easily I could forget that Harvey was responsible for two people's deaths. Yet how easy it was for lawmakers and cultural executioners to forget that Harvey constituted more than that crime. Like soap bubbles, the shapes of lament and the outlines of praise floated through my head, rising only to burst without any close examination. My mind wandered. Still more questions blinked in front of me, remaining in my peripheral vision long enough for me to recognize that they were unwanted and not particularly useful. Naturally these were the ones that remained, lodging themselves like deer ticks in my mind, reducing me to a stumbling, page-turning, question-groping fool. With all this in my head, I couldn't express a single damn thing—not my background, not my admiration, not my ambivalence. Finally, with the help of his words, I emerged with the sense that I rose as though from underwater, gasping for air and grabbing for the life raft.

"The pastor told me," he said, referring to John Hilpert, "and most of the whole church told me, 'The life that you got in there, and what you're doin', is helpin' me a whole lot.' My other pen-pal says, 'I know you don't see it all the time, but you help a whole lot of people.'" How many of us could use that same praise, I thought to myself. "I don't know what's going on out there. I'm locked up behind these walls. Only thing I can do is write and offer advice. Most times with men in prison, society already says the man died. But I'm a new man. And I'm trying to be that new man with the people over at Pullen." Harvey folded his hands into one another on the table, eight of his fingers interlocking, while the other two, both index fingers, pointed like a steeple toward the base of his chin. The church is the people, I thought, looking at those hands.

In a bungled robbery attempt at a Bethel, North Carolina, dry cleaners in 1983, Harvey Lee Green killed two people, beating them to death with a blunt object and those hands. He was found guilty in the deaths of the store's seventeen-year-old employee and a thirty-three-year-old customer. The jury sentenced him to death. After acknowledging errors in the initial sentencing process, the state allowed for a new sentencing hearing eight years later. Once again, Harvey was sentenced to die.

Harvey's letter writing did not begin with the pastor and young parishioners at Pullen Baptist. The search for family that stretched from death row to a nearby church was initiated by the loss of family while he was on the inside. He communicated his remorse and his apologies to his mother, whom he wrote to and remained close to over the course of his imprisonment. He did the same with his father. His parents had divorced and his mother had remarried.

"My father and my stepfather died within two years of each other. It was hard to deal with my father's death. I got angry at the prison system for not letting me out for the funeral. But I knew they weren't going to let me out no way, so I just said, 'Lord, take this from me.' And the brothers in the church, from all the denominations, Muslim and all, passed cards around." When he referred to the "brothers in the church," he meant the men on death row. "They told each other, 'Yo, you know Harvey's father died.' And they came to me and told me, 'Yo, man, it's part of life, bro.' 'Everybody goes.' 'Just keep strong.' 'Keep going, homes.' 'God looking out for you.' 'Allah bless you, Bro.'" From Harvey's mouth these remembered consolations emerged rapid-fire, each commiseration beginning where the prior one left off, bleeding into the one that followed. "You know," he said, "they kept me up. Matter of fact, by that time I didn't have no board. I had paint but I didn't have no board. They went and found me some board to keep me busy. We try to do the best we can. Even though we do have our arguments and fistfights and what not, we still got to look out for each other."

Muslims invoked Allah's blessings on the lives of Christians, Christians invited Jesus' grace into the hearts of Muslims, and Harvey spoke as though this was standard operating procedure on the row.

"You don't see that all that much," I said.

"No. Unh-unh. When I got here in '84, I had a couple dollars in my pocket. The brothers on the block got together and asked me, 'Yo bro, whatcha need from the canteen? Either shaving cream and toothpaste or smokin' cigarettes.' I looked at 'em, I said, 'Whatcha mean?' And they said, 'Just whatcha need?' I told 'em what I need. They went and got it. They said we do this every time a brother come in. No matter whether he white or black or Puerto Rican or whatever, help that man out when he first get here. And the only thing you have to do: when that next man come in, help him out.

"Sometimes you see a man that come in and you see a quality in him, and you might pull him off to the side and say, 'Yo, bro, how you doin'? You makin' it all right?' And you say, 'You can do anything you want to in this penitentiary, or any other. But I'm gonna tell you how I made it in here.' You know? Get talkin' to him. And pretty soon, you get to learnin' about that man, he get to learnin' about you. If that man's a troublemaker, you could tell right off. But if this man come in and seem like he want to make a change, pull that man to you, talk to him. Get to know him, get to know his family. 'Cause we all family here. We all facing the same thing. Just that right now, I'm in the seat, and the brothers down there, they're tryin' to keep me lifted up. You know," Harvey said, letting out a small sigh, "sometimes it get a little tiresome. I know they mean well, but when they get to peepin' in there, and I be readin' or something, and they askin' me, 'Yo bro, you doin' all right?' I say, 'Yup.' And they'll be down here in five more minutes, askin' me the same thing." He laughed at their unflagging persistence in checking up.

"So you feel them looking at you a certain way? A different way?"

"To a point, yeah."

"That'd get on my nerves," I said, trying momentarily and failing miserably at imagining how the "What's ups?" and "How you doin's?" of friends would grate on me as I bent under the weight of a calendar's inevitability.

"Yeah," Harvey said, "but I understand where it comin' from. Cause they concerned. You get some strong brothers in here. They lift me up. I lift them up. The one thing we don't talk about is dyin'."

"So, on your row there's a real code of conduct," I said.

"Uh-huh."

"And the code changes in different contexts."

"Right."

"And they've just kicked into a different kind of code with you now." Harvey nodded.

The first guy I volunteered with during my time at the prison in Massachusetts was a fifty-something black man, an Evangelical, who reported to me that the prison's volunteer coordinator had shuddered when told of my biographical sketch. He heard Harvard and white and Jewish—especially the Jewish, with all the representatives of the Nation of Islam in the group—and predicted that I would get eaten alive. My fellow volunteer told me that for my own safety it was in my best interest to avoid the subject of my religion at all costs. So I did, for months shielding myself from a hypothetical though seemingly ever-imminent barrage of propaganda-laced epithets and millennia-old violence funneled and focused onto me. Eventually, though, as I learned more about Judaism, I began to understand what I had ignored in Hebrew school: the central storyline of Judaism is a people's liberation. This story is remembered and recounted daily in prayers and reenacted annually through holidays, all the while fueling our present-day focus toward the stranger, the suffering, and the enslaved in our own community. The rituals, the laws, the folklore, even occasionally the caricatures, all radiate from this central motif. One Thursday night in the prison, late that first fall, perhaps anticipating Larry Goodwyn's advice, I opened up, though I didn't find it necessary or prudent to unbutton my shirt at the time. There were looks of befuddlement and a smattering of snickering. But most of the guys inside just nodded and moved on. It was the memory of that experience that encouraged me now, to share part of my own story with Harvey. The decision was the product of deliberation, not the spark of spontaneity, and months later I'd wonder whether this paved a new route in my pilgrimage.

"I'm a—" I said, uncertain with the directness of my self-admission. "I was born and raised as a Jew." Harvey nodded and, in the background, unmistakably, Captain Hudson's head darted up from his reading material. "It's an interesting time of year for us," I told Harvey, and I sensed Captain Hudson as well. "Saturday night—the Jewish day begins at night, actually—was something called Rosh Hashanah. The holiday basically refers to the Jewish New Year. Then there's a space of ten days called the Days of Awe, which ends with another holiday called Yom Kippur. That's the Day of Atonement."

Harvey nodded.

"We're in this stretch of ten days now, this time of new beginnings, when the tradition teaches that repentance is most important. It's the time when everyone has the opportunity to turn," I said, thinking of the importance Rabbi Arnold Wolf placed on the direction, not the location. "Do you feel—" I started before catching myself. "I shouldn't start with that. So I'm trying to turn. In my own life, in my own way—"

"Uh-huh."

"—in my own experience. With the people I love and the people I don't love, maybe as importantly."

"Yeah," Harvey said.

"Trying to turn," I said and took a breath. Together we were almost freestyling, a death row, Day of Atonement, rapped call and response. "Do you feel like, in your own experience, that the people who have needed to see you turn have seen you turn?"

Harvey nodded. "Yeah," he answered. "My mom's only fifteen years older than I am. Basically, to a point, we grew up together. I didn't think she knew me as well as she did. But my mom has said that over the years of my writing her, she could see through my letters that I had started to change."

"You mentioned the families of the victims. How about them?"

"Well, I ain't really had no contact with them. The closest I ever came was in court." Harvey inhaled. "From where I was sitting in court, before they announced the sentence, I told them I was sorry for the crime, and I hoped they would forgive me." He paused. "I just hope that they will forgive me." He looked at me, not searchingly, not pleadingly, but stoically. He emitted an anxious laugh, something curt and muffled. "What more can I say?"

"I don't know," I said. "Your desire for forgiveness is a beautiful thing. But I know it would be *real* tough to be the ones on the other side. If it were me, I hope I'd be able to forgive, but that's a tough position."

"It is. It is. Very tough." He checked himself, considering, maybe even inhabiting, their mournful anger before he shook his head left and right and left again. With each back and forth, he sighed, offering up a noise that sounded to me at once shaken and sad. "Mm, mm, mm," he hummed, softly.

Oftentimes people on the outside look with deep skepticism at the integrity of death row turnarounds and foxhole conversions. They see someone who committed a crime cowering for the protective embrace of the supernatural. They resent the wrongdoer for the refuge he seeks when the victim has no such opportunity. Prisoners, it's true, are prime suspects in looking for what religion offers, whether consolation, forgiveness, or new possibility. A God who asks for obedience, bartering forgiveness in return, appears too good to be true for those suddenly locked up. That most of these conversions are opportunistic, there can be no doubt. But that given raises a question: does that make it wrong, a perversion of the religious path and the spiritual search? My answer is no. In fact, throughout scripture God is custom-made for the outcast, the despised, and the wrongdoer.

Some of these jailhouse conversions are short-lived, firecrackers of the spirit. But in others, faith finds fertile soil. Harvey Lee Green had lived as a "professing" Christian for more than fourteen years when we met. He helped organize church services on death row, led the liturgy, and joined a church on the outside. His conversion, no doubt motivated by an urgent, self-interested concern for the fate of his soul, had been nourished in a community of fellow believers. A conversion is proven authentic only over a lifetime's aftermath. Some people cheat, steal, and kill, get locked up, fall down on their knees, pray for a second chance, are released, and use that second chance for another shot at the same old life. The conversions that prove lasting, however, depend on a faithful community of support. I believe that Harvey Lee Green had that community. Whether he lived the rest of his life behind bars, or whether one day he was let out, I think he would have remained faithful. Why? Three reasons: one, because there were too many people watching his back to let him fall down and stay down with any ease; two, because he did his time, and in it seemed to have learned about the place of personal accountability in the life of faith; and three, because I remain hopeful despite evidence to the contrary.

Nine days remained before his scheduled date with lethal injection at the hands of the state of North Carolina. "I'm a Christian, and born again, and I know them sins is forgiven by God," he said as Captain Hudson announced that our time was up. "Still, people hold you to your past."

I asked for permission to take photos of Harvey. Permission was granted. I thanked Harvey for his time. A guard whisked him out of the room. Captain Hudson waited with courtesy for me to pack up, then escorted me from the room to the prison's entrance.

When I left, a gusty wind from a heaving sky rattled the chain against the metal flag pole in the parking lot.

Only a handful of direction signals away, Pullen Memorial Baptist Church, the size of a city block, teemed with little children. In the day care center on the ground floor, I asked a woman where I might find the paintings of Harvey Lee Green. She sent me upstairs to the church office. The people in there pointed me down a carpeted corridor toward the sanctuary. On an easel in the back of the church, behind a couple dozen tall wooden benches, in the space in between pews that forms the center aisle leading up to the pulpit, I located one of Harvey's paintings. Outside, the swirling wind hoisted discarded burger wrappers and Raleigh newspaper pages from the garbage can on the corner, sending them helicoptering through the street, into storefronts and onto windshields. Inside, the carpet swallowed the sounds of rubber-soled shoes walking toward me. This was the pastor, John Hilpert, alerted to my visit.

He guided me from the sanctuary into his office, where we talked about my conversation with Harvey, my trip, and his own path, from the borough of Queens to the city of Raleigh. Against a plain white pillow beside a dusty brass bell and the base of a halogen lamp in a corner of Pastor Hilpert's office leaned another of Harvey's paintings. In it, a blond-haired female angel wears a loose-fitting robe. She is depicted midway between profile and back shot. From the back of her neck rise three tiers of wings, like the wide fingers of comic book hands. She stands against a black background blanketed with a couple of hundred stars made from dabs of white paint. She holds in her right hand a horn, its long neck leading to the flared opening. One could call the instrument, without keys, without plungers, a bugle. This angel sounds her horn against the starry nighttime sky: maybe it is the tune of a ghostly, sonorous "Taps," signaling the day's end, reverberating amid the silent, hollow night. Maybe it is the voice of a celestial shofar, announcing the new year's arrival, the time of our repentance. Perhaps it is both.

Leaving Raleigh, the sky was so dense with moisture it should have burst.

The front edge of Hurricane George bounced rain drops off my windshield as though they were pennies. The weather pummeled parts further South, but the next day, outside my sister Lynn's apartment in Bethesda, Maryland, the forecasted hurricane traveling north amounted to a heavy, windy rain for a couple of afternoon hours. By seven o'clock that evening, the sun erupted through the dense gray cloud cover, and puddles in crosswalks gleamed like new snow.

Eight-months-pregnant Lynn, her husband Roderick, and I ate dinner at a Mexican restaurant that night, and after our plates were cleared, we lingered at the table for a couple of hours. I heard about the anticipation of their firstborn, and they asked of news from my trip.

My sister is a high school American history teacher, and Roderick had been a physics teacher in the same school—that's how they'd met—until starting medical school a year earlier. As teachers they'd both spent a lot of time thinking about pedagogy: how students learn best, how they themselves teach, and in turn how they themselves were taught.

Amid this conversation we turned to the subject of religion. Lynn and I agreed that in our family we learned about religion largely from its omission from our lives. We learned not to think too much about it, not to pay much attention to it, not to ascribe any real relevance to it.

You know," my sister said, pulling another tortilla chip from the basket on the table, "I'm amazed that I haven't asked you this before, but what do you think sparked this ambition to learn about religion?" In some respects, it was amazing that my sister hadn't asked me about this before, both because she was invested in and connected to my life and because she was a teacher who thrived on learning about her students and colleagues. But in another way it wasn't all that surprising, because the subject we hadn't discussed was religion. My sister admits to an agnostic outlook, and maybe she deduced that, given my theistic leanings, I might interpret her questions as a rebuke, and what began as dialogue would necessarily devolve into argument. To forestall any potential misunderstanding, I had not offered and she had not asked.

"I'm still not sure," I said, "though I've been running the stuff over in my head. I know I can narrow it down to a bracket of time, but I still can't pinpoint it." I said I knew that the extended moment came sometime between the two barbecued chicken sandwiches I ate during lunch on Yom Kippur of my freshman year, when the seconds I took in the cafeteria felt like an unrepentant raspberry to my fasting comrades, and Passover of my senior year. My girlfriend Laura and my friends Mark and Fathead decided too late to attend the campus seder, and there was no space available. So we appropriated four *haggadot,* the Passover seder scripts, from the Jewish dining hall, then spent an hour hopscotching along the main commercial strip in Princeton searching for matzah and horseradish and hard-boiled eggs and Manischewitz wine and paper plates and plastic cutlery, until we located an empty and surprisingly intimate classroom, where we held our own seder. It was there that, maybe for the first time, I felt like religion was something *I* could do, not solely something that *others* did. Somewhere between those two poles, in the time when I became a religion major, when I first considered divinity school as a viable option, lay an answer.

"Was it Laura?" my sister asked. True, Laura, my girlfriend that senior year and for a little while afterward, was the most convincingly sentimental Jew I had ever met, and her stories of raucous family Bat Mitzvahs and Jewish life in West Los Angeles had, in their own time, made me smile with an unknown recognition.

"Maybe she's part of it," I answered, "but I don't think that gets to it fully."

And there in the booth in the Mexican restaurant, I scrolled through my college life, through classrooms and corridors, through girlfriends and acquaintances, back to my freshman hallway, where among a vibrant and motley cast of characters there lived in a single room overlooking a courtyard filled with bicycle racks and cigarette butts a bustling, scrawny young man named Mikail. Wisps of black hair, scattered like magnetic iron filings, flickered from his perpetually ruddy face. He was, if I remembered accurately, sixteen when he entered college as a freshman. He was born in the Soviet Union and later moved to Brooklyn to live with his grandmother. His heavy accent signaled his Russian upbringing, and his voice still cracked as though he were twelve. Sitting on the decaying sofa in the common room of our fourth floor hallway, shooting the shit with roommates, I watched him scurry from his front door toward the common bathroom. He seemed always on his way to wash, with a thin white towel draped over his shoulder and a bar of white soap floating in milky water in an uncovered dish on his flushed palm. As he was on his way to the bathroom, he and I would chat. I liked him and the way he was bashful and intense and inquisitive.

He was born and bred in the Soviet Union to be a secular scientist. No safe place existed there to express Judaism, even had he wanted to. He came to Princeton to be a physics major. He told me that in Brooklyn as a teenager he attended synagogue services one Friday night with his orthodox grandmother. He looked around that dimly lit, musty sanctuary and noticed—and it couldn't have been hard to notice—that he was the only one under sixty in the room. On another Friday he returned, and found the same thing. The community was wrinkled and white-haired and dying. He might have brushed this recognition off, and in the process blown off the ritual and the tradition, calling it antiquarian and forgotten. But he didn't. Instead, he chose immersion, and observance, and with that choice he assumed the burdens of tradition for the sake of tradition. There on that hallway, amid the empty cans of Old Milwaukee Light and the repetitive, too loud blaring of the Spin Doctors' first album, I met a contemporary leading a life of rigorous, and for him rewarding, obligation.

After our freshman year ended I never saw Mikail again. I wish I could say I looked for him, but I can't. In truth, I felt the inclination to hide from him. From afar I inflated his commitment into a kind of promethean sacrifice of youth, an elemental stand for survival and renewal. Because to have seen him, ruddy-faced, twitchy, committed and called, walking with a lowered head and a raised soap dish, was to witness someone who said, "Hineni" every day of his life. "Here *I* am," he might have said. "Where are *you?*"

PART THREE

[Preponderance of the Small]

[14]

There are three words for sin in the Torah. The least severe, *chete,* essentially means "messing up," an unintentional offense. Another, *avon,* describes a transgression, the deliberate breaking of a law. And the third and presumably most damning form is *pesha,* a rebellion against divine order and authority. Whatever your degree of wrongdoing, Yom Kippur is a holy day dedicated to atonement, to getting straight with yourself, the people in your life, and by extension, God. So in retrospect it is ironic that during my return to New York, in the choice of where to attend Yom Kippur services, I made a choice that gave me something to atone for in the following year.

My grandma Ruth was still a member at the synagogue where I went (or didn't go) as a kid. People often maintain their annual memberships to guarantee tickets to High Holiday services, which are standing room only events that sell out like Springsteen shows at the Meadowlands. Adroitly she managed to locate a ticket for me to join her at services when she heard I'd be back in town after my trip to North Carolina.

"I'm sorry, Gram," I told her. "I have other plans."

Back in Manhattan for a day and a half before flying out west, I walked across Central Park on the morning of Yom Kippur, attended a service by myself at a synagogue on the Upper West Side, and ambled my way back to the East Side after the service concluded. I spotted an empty park bench under a canopy of prodigious trees, sat down, and shut my eyes. A soft breeze turned the hazy day comfortable. The thousands of leaves above me bristled against each other, and the shushing sound they made sounded like the breaking of a small wave. There in the park, I had myself a moment. I forgot that my stomach rumbled from the fast and I overlooked the puniness I was supposed to feel on that most holy of days. I saw how the world is full and beautiful. I marveled at its structure and my place in it. At precisely the same time, my grandma, less than a mile's walk away, heard my grandpa's name announced during the memorial Kaddish and dabbed with a handkerchief at glassy eyes.

Yom Kippur, the bookend to Rosh Hashanah, is a day of abstention from the things that make us human. Jews don't eat, don't drink, don't work, and don't have sex, and this day of negation puts a spotlight on both the fragility of our lives and our capacity to start over. The holiday enshrines what Rabbi Arnold Wolf described in our time together in Chicago: what is of real importance is not the accomplishment but the direction. Ideally, you take a hard look at your life, acknowledge what you've done wrong, ask for forgiveness, and turn in a new, better direction. It's a day for humility. The assembled Jewish community stands together, confesses its sins as individuals and as community, and prays for forgiveness from above and self-awareness from within.

I saw my grandmother later that afternoon, at the customary breaking of the fast, and she asked how services had been.

"They were good," I said.

"Who'd you go with?" she asked, figuring my plans were with friends.

"Nobody," I said. That had been the point. I wanted to sample the liturgy in a space where I was unfamiliar and unencumbered, and where I could grasp the gravity of the day. I wanted to be able to say amen if the spirit moved me.

"Nobody?" She drew a sharp intake of breath, as though she'd been elbowed in the stomach by a straphanger on the Third Avenue bus. "That's terrible. Tommy, you really shoulda come with me."

"I'm—I'm really sorry, Gram." I had not known my grandpa's name would come up, one among the dozens of congregants whose names were announced, a roll call of the synagogue's recently departed. Had I taken to heart that Yom Kippur is a day dedicated to remembrance, had I known that the *Yizkor* prayer is recited during the service to honor the memory of the deceased, I certainly would have accompanied her. But I had not. In a manner befitting my trip I went alone, and so a private vision took the place of a shared observance. Perhaps I honored my grandpa's memory in moments like those I had with Wallace Johnson in Rockford, Illinois. But I performed a disservice to my grandma's life when dumbly, unthinkingly, I sat on my own instead of next to her. It wasn't a Golden Calf kind of sin, not a trespass or a transgression. I apologized again, told my grandma I loved her, promised I'd see her soon. But it was a *chete*, a mistake, and it made me wish I had thought longer about priorities.

The reverse red-eye to Sea-Tac Airport touched down a few minutes after 3 A.M., Pacific standard time. Taking the plane was cheating, I know. But before the trip began I faced a tactical quandary: though this was a road trip, would I rely solely on my car to get me around? When I scrolled across America in my 1997 Rand McNally atlas, I looked at a lower forty-eight that stretched three thousand by two thousand miles, six million square miles all told. Somewhere between driving through and flying over was, I believed, a middle path.

At 3:55 in the morning I arrived at my close childhood friend Danny's apartment. I had to ask a cop how to get there. Apparently the cab driver didn't recognize the address, but he neglected to tell me that. He cruised the streets ignorantly while running the meter, so at twenty to four I spotted the cop, got directions, and walked the last half a mile to Danny's place. I spent $35 for the fare when I should have spent only $29. Six dollars wasn't much, but it was the *principle* that got me. I didn't blow up at the cabbie, but my irritation seeped through his car like incense. Yet I wound up frustrated with myself more than the driver because he had a little shrine to the Hindu god Shiva above the meter (naturally, I couldn't take my eyes off either the bobbing god or the rising fare) and already I had blown another golden opportunity to talk and learn.

My travels, like faith itself, could easily descend into a scorekeeping exercise. There is the ethic in America that more always seems to mean better: getting more means not only that you've done more, but that you've become more. The impulse in me that sought subjects from taxi drivers to shopkeepers to monks represented, I think, my American tourist side. This was the part of me that barked approval when I visited five congregations before lunch and plotted six destinations over two days, the me that could see everything before sitting anywhere. I saw this not as an expression of a personal wellspring of antsiness, but as a natural, inherited tendency to see quality in quantity. This was my megachurch side. Megachurches of twenty and thirty thousand people flourished across America, in large part because they offered incontrovertible proof to their members that God is listening and that their prayers of abundance are being answered. For me, the days of frenetic activity patted me on the back. They could also occasionally trip me up. After all, when everyone's a possible partner for conversation, you can't afford to burn bridges with anyone. This leaves you, on occasion, a forgiving sucker.

I woke up the next morning to an empty apartment, a car key, directions to Danny's office downtown, and a somber sky. Two hours later, from the gleaming lobby of his towering building, I called his office.

"Mr. Rosenberg is in a meeting," a woman's voice said, "but he left a message requesting lunch with Mr. Levinson. Can you return at noon?" It was 10:30.

"Yes, of course," I said, dropping my voice to sound as professional as I could.

The weather was cold and drizzly: Seattle as advertised. I planned to spend the day wandering, learning the lay of the land, but given the conditions, my number one objective turned to finding a little cover to wait out the rain. Sheltered beneath the protective scaffolding of Danny's office building, I scanned the streetscape two blocks in both directions. My gaze focused skyward, so I almost missed, amid all that glass and steel and sheen, the architectural anomaly right across the street. It was a huge church, assembled with rust and beige bricks, and crowned with a domed roof like a monk's bald head. I sprinted across the street and into the darkened sanctuary, spending a few minutes sitting, strolling between pews, and flipping through Methodist hymnals before wandering downstairs in the direction of voices.

In the cavernous dining hall area in the basement, a seniors' coffee klatch was well under way. I remained on its margins for a while, waiting in the shadow of a doorway to the cafeteria-sized room, as the crowd murmured on the other side. Before entering I couldn't shed the anxious sense that they would see me and assume I'd arrived to sell them Bible-themed flatware.

I walked over the squeaky floor in damp sneakers. I introduced myself, telling the folks about the mission of my trip.

"Care to sit for a cup of coffee?" a woman asked. Though not a coffee drinker, I knew not to turn down expressions of hospitality. I thanked her for the offer, filled up half the Styrofoam cup, then dumped in two plastic teaspoons full of sugar and stirred until my stirring became superfluous. I wanted something to do with my hands. The crowd around the table was cordial but reticent. I stayed patient. On the group's periphery, a woman painted with watercolors. Beside her, another woman sculpted peeled potatoes into swans. Maybe they were turnips; I couldn't decide. Initially, the painter seemed the least interested in my presence. She sprinkled indifference with a sporadic glower in my direction. But when the subject of conversation turned to religion, and one of the women around the table asked me, "So, are you a Methodist?" I answered, "Actually, no, I'm Jewish." The painter, suspicious above her watercolors, jerked her head up.

"My daughter lives in Borough Park, Brooklyn," she said. Huh? I knew Borough Park as one of New York's most concentrated Orthodox Jewish areas. This woman sat in a Methodist Church's basement. Was she teasing me? "She's married to a Hasidic man. They have three kids. I was just there for two months." She didn't have any overt reason to string me along, so I nodded.

The woman with the watercolors was husky. She wore a satiny, floral-patterned blouse under a black and white checkered jacket, framed on each side by shoulder pad inserts. She used a white plastic clip, the kind designed to keep potato chips crunchy once the bag has been opened, to prop up a mop of sawdust-colored hair. Her face was smooth and puffy, almost as if a porcelain vase had been inflated with a bicycle pump.

"Are you Jewish, too?" I asked.

"No," she said, "I practice the wisdom Confucius himself used." She set her brush down and yanked from a bulky purse a mustard-colored, hard-cover book. "The *Eye Ching*," she said. She held the book aloft with an outstretched arm and announced its presence as though she'd pulled Excalibur from the stone. Ladies and gentlemen, I thought at that precise moment, we have a winner. In an effort not to be rude to the others, I excused myself, then swung my chair around to the watercolorer's side of the table. Within a few minutes the other seniors dispersed to the opposite end of the room for a singing class, and Dolores Ledbetter remained behind to talk.

Dolores said she was sixty years old, and she described the *I Ching* as a book of wisdom that acted as an intermediary between her questions and "the Almighty God's" answers. I had picked up copies in used book-stores and flipped through them, but never had any clue how the *I Ching*, also known as the "Book of Changes," worked until meeting Dolores.

The *I Ching* (pronounced "ee-*jing*") is a product of China in the second millennium B.C.E. It is a sacred scripture, but not the kind one reads like a continuous, intelligible narrative. The product of centuries of oral traditions and folklore, it performs like an oracle. An *I Ching* user flips three coins a series of six times, and the sequence of those tosses corresponds to a fortune recorded in the book. The user looks up the fortune and finds in it the answer to her question. Just about any question can be asked of the book, though focused questions, I learned, work best. So the *I Ching* won't tell you what to eat for dinner, but apparently it will respond knowingly if you aren't sure if you want Chinese tonight.

I interpreted meeting Dolores on my first morning on the West Coast as a serendipitous jackpot. From what I knew of the *I Ching* and Hasidic Judaism, the two occupied different poles of the spiritual spectrum. I understood the *I Ching* as a staple of New Age bookstores, a tool for solitary individuals looking not just to divine order out of chaos, but also to have fate make decisions for them. Hasidic Judaism, on the other hand, I knew to be an Old World, insular, community-centered tradition that followed strict guidelines and set tightly controlled parameters of inclusion and ex-clusion. Yet for all its New Age fanfare, the *I Ching* is probably older than Judaism itself. Both of the traditions stress obedience to the wisdom and insight of a higher power. Still, finding these two traditions swirled together in one person made me think I heard the faint sound of an avalanche of quarters piling at the base of a slot machine.

The clock in the cafeteria read 11:55. I knew I had to leave Dolores to meet Danny for lunch. I asked her if she was available to talk in the early afternoon.

"That's not going to be a problem," she said. She suggested we meet in another wing of the church. "Walk in through a side entrance. You're looking for the Mary Magdalene Chapel. That's where I'll be."

Danny worked at a venture capital firm for Internet and new economy start-ups during a boom time of unprecedented proportions. In his office I was a dot-com voyeur, and I briefly considered the idea of making my-self a Web site, putting together a PowerPoint presentation, and asking for some modest sum in the high five figures. I gazed out the window at the skyline. Money flowed from these buildings like sweat from pores. Everything seemed a can't-miss prospect.

"How's the trip, Odysseus?" Danny asked over a lunch of Japanese noodles.

"It's good," I said. "It's really good. It's almost like I'm doing my own Celestine Prophecy. I find the people I need to meet, hear them, and in-evitably bounce from them into someone else I feel like I have been sup-posed to meet. It's like clues keep popping up in front of me, you know?" I reported the stroke of dumb luck I'd enjoyed that morning, ducking into the church next door and finding Dolores Ledbetter, the *I Ching*-citing mother of a Brooklyn Hasid.

"That's ridiculous," he said, and I nodded my head. I know the phrase well, use it often, understand it as a combination of congratulations and envy, a sort of lowercase awe. I don't know if I sought my best friend's admiration, but in the way he sketched lines with his chopsticks in the traces of oil on his empty plate, I could almost make out the hypothetical cartography of his own route. We parted, agreeing we'd meet back at his place later in the evening.

"I can't wait to hear more about this woman," he said as we slapped hands.

"Can't wait to tell you more."

He returned to his office and the Internet, and I returned to the church and the *I Ching*.

Dolores was right where she said she'd be, near the entrance of the church office. A dozen or so women lounged in plastic chairs, watching afternoon television in a room next door. I asked Dolores if there was a quiet place to sit. She hummed to herself for a moment, then pointed to a corner away from the TV. We pulled two of the plastic chairs together. I had to ask one of the women seated at a desk for an extension cord for the recording equipment.

We talked a little about her time in the Hasidic neighborhood of Borough Park with her daughter Jasmine, Jasmine's husband, and their three children, and about her stay in the Manhattan apartment of her son, a surgeon in training. A few months ago, weary of playing the guest in her children's homes, she'd left. She'd wanted to come, she said, where the air was clean. She'd boarded a Greyhound bus in July and spent four days and three nights on her way out to Seattle from New York. I didn't know if Dolores's children knew where she was, or even if they knew how to reach her.

Dolores had consulted with the *I Ching* about her move. She had consulted the *I Ching* for most decisions ever since she'd picked it up in a used bookstore a couple of years earlier. She was onto her second copy. She'd worn out the pages of her first.

We had been talking for a while when I thought of a question from my notebook that I had yet to ask any of my subjects. I wanted to give Dolores a question with which she'd have room to roam. "What is faith?" I asked.

Dolores's eyes compressed into a thin, horizontal stripe of mascara. She looked at me as though I was a precociously and admirably naughty fifth grader. She nodded her head and the hair clip jiggled up and down. "Faith is knowing that things are going to work out right if you're doing the right thing. Understand, the *I Ching* deals with order. That's because *life* is about order. The *I Ching* tells us about life. And in life, one has to have faith." And then the thought came to her: "I could ask the *I Ching* about it. 'How does the *I Ching* feel about my faith?' Oooh," she said, and it sounded almost like a purr.

"Is that an appropriate question?" I asked.

"Sure. Any kind of question. You want me to ask that? What does the *I Ching* have to say about my faith? You'll hear the truth," she said, delivering the line like a prizefighter predicting a knockout in the third round. Her faith in the *I Ching* was unflinching.

She rose from her chair and moved to her bags, bundled onto a cart and held together by a bungee cord. "This is my homeless cart," she said, and I chuckled, because she said it as though bragging. "No, it is. It's taken tremendous pressure off my shoulder. We had Bingo last week. I won three games. I never won anything before. But I got points for each game, and Scarlet, who organizes Bingo, said, 'Dolores, you have enough points for that cart there.' I didn't want to look homeless totally, so I said, 'Oh, no. No thanks.' And then my old shoulder thought differently of it. I said, 'Well, maybe we'll try it.' I already look homeless anyway."

I had no idea Dolores was homeless until she told me. I gathered we spoke in a shelter of some kind, given the church locale and the glazed faces of women milling around in slippers. But I thought that Dolores just hung out here once in a while. The coffee klatch, a periodic event for the church's older congregants, attracted Dolores, who was able to wile away a few mornings a week there. She told me that immediately after she confessed her homelessness. I cocked my head a little bit to the right, so that instead of looking at her I was peering. "I'm sorry," I said. "I really, really, really don't mean to offend you in any way."

"It's not a problem," she said and kept right on talking. I guessed that Dolores was newly homeless. From the sound of it, she had chosen to become so. Dolores was eccentric, no doubt, but she also seemed smart and coherent. I would learn that she followed the rules of *I Ching* readings meticulously. Though in her personal world she may have been coming undone, she seemed both sane and fully conscious of the consequences of the choices she made—though what motivated her to make these choices, other than the encouragement of the *I Ching*, I had trouble figuring out.

She had sunk her arms into her bag nearly up to her shoulders when I heard, "Ah hah!" After fumbling through all of her earthly belongings, she pulled an Altoids mints container from the bag. She opened the small tin only to scratch her head at what she saw. "They're not in here," she said. Dolores kept her special *I Ching* coins in the Altoids box. "I guess I didn't put them back in here. I must have put them in a different place."

I patted down my own pockets, afraid that sometime during our conversation I might have accidentally taken sacred paraphernalia. "Did I put them in here?" I muttered out loud, fingering an airplane boarding pass, a receipt from the White Hen Pantry in Boston, and lint. "I don't think I did. But I might have some change."

"Any three coins," she said. "It doesn't matter." Having scrounged around my bag, I assumed I had solved the problem when I extended my hand to give her three coins: a penny, a nickel, and a quarter.

She looked at them. "No," she said, nodding her head from side to side, "it has to be of the same weight. It can be three dimes, three nickels, three pennies, three quarters." This was official *I Ching* divination policy. The three coins used had to be the same kind of coin. Disconsolate at the unknown whereabouts of her coins, she perked up with a discovery. "Here's one penny."

"I got another," I said, holding up the one I had already located. "If we can scrape up one more"—what a sight, both of us digging, each head buried in a hobo's bag of belongings.

"Yes!" I shouted, turning a few heads in the shelter. I raised my right hand at the women who looked at us, part greeting, part apology, as we reappeared from our bags. The women smiled respectfully. The scene was comic. How was I to contain myself, though? Dolores held up her hand like she'd recovered a fumble. She found a third penny. Never have I been so excited about a penny.

She pulled a pencil and piece of paper off of a nearby desk. "Writing the question out helps you focus a bit." In her hands she held the paper, the pencil, the *I Ching*, the Altoids tin, and all three pennies. She looked burdened.

"Can I hold something?" I asked.

"No," she said, waving away my concern. "What does the *I Ching* have to say about my faith?" She transcribed her words, asking the question with a mechanical deliberateness.

Then she went through the routine. Each round of three coin tosses produces a sequence that can be rendered as a line, either solid or broken, depending on the result. When the six sets of tosses are completed, the user has six lines. The lines, stacked one on top of the other, form what is called a hexagram. With the hexagram, the user consults the *I Ching* for the corresponding reading. The readings are a series of interpretations: one level really is like a fortune cookie, except it would be the most archaic, unintelligible fortune you've ever received. Another level offers a more coherent response to the question. Devotees stress that the *I Ching* chronicles the inner life and the outer world. They say it does not simply foretell the future with its answers; it also describes the present.

Dolores whispered each toss's result under her breath. Only when all the coins had been flattened, only when each result had been recorded with a scribble, could we then effectively consult the book for our answer. She finished her tosses, turned the *I Ching* right side up, and thumbed through the book's dry pages. They scented the three feet of space between us with the mustiness of a used bookstore. Dolores shook her head. "See, you can't fool the *I Ching*. Here's what it says: it says, 'Everything has its proper measure. Even modesty in behavior can be carried too far. The confidence of the man in the superior place must not be abused, nor the merits of the man in the inferior place be concealed.'" She was reading the different interpretations that her tosses had pointed her toward. Okay, I thought. Is that it?

She clutched the book close to her, as though reading on a crowded subway car. I wanted to see what the reading said for myself. I also felt curious to see what a page of the text looked like. So I got up from my chair to walk behind hers. I checked the page from over her shoulder. The heading for that section read PREPONDERANCE OF THE SMALL in small capital letters.

Dolores read aloud: "It says, 'Success, but perseverance furthers it. Small things may be done; great things shouldn't even be tried.'"

I gulped. The instant I'd read "Preponderance of the Small" above the reading, I'd known, in a gut instinct way, that Dolores had stumbled onto, or the *I Ching* had delivered, a stunning answer to the question we'd asked.

"Preponderance of the small" hovered in the air, like the ad text strung behind a prop plane at the beach, as I considered my pilgrimage thus far. A fortuitous turn off a Dayton off-ramp had led me to Hayder Almosawi and Roxanne Masni; newspaper notices of events in different cities had led me to Brother Gus, the Dalai Lama, and Elvis Miranda. You want preponderance of the small? Dolores and I had just scoured our possessions for one measly penny, the laughingstock of currency, to begin an extemporaneous series of random coin tosses in order to answer a question on a wet weekday afternoon in a Seattle shelter. This was neither earthmoving nor world-changing. Yet our small exchange weighed heavy, like a ritual. Suddenly the white noise of the television, the clang of ringing phones, and the soft shuffle of slippers across carpet faded, and Dolores and I sat at attention for the *I Ching*.

Yes, I thought, *yes*. In truth they are big things, these small things. And they're not simply big because they add up in the cosmic balance sheet to a big thing. No, then and there what struck me was that the small things *are* the big things. "Preponderance of the small" represents the areas where we have choices to make that determine who we are and how we participate in the world around us. Faith is less about theological grandness than about the ordinariness of the day-to-day. This is what the Hadith of Islam teaches, what pizza meant to Kisna Duaipayana Das's parents, and what the grittiness of the holiness chapter, Leviticus 19, that Arnold Wolf had cited, preaches. It was these things, the tangible expressions of fidelity to God or covenant or community that told me about faith. Dolores Ledbetter assured me that "Confucius himself used" the *I Ching*. I didn't have any clue whether Confucius had actually used the *I Ching* (though I later learned that indeed he had) or if Dolores had assembled some sort of creative anachronism. I did not care. What was true did not have to be factual. What was real did not have to be proven.

I sat back down. Dolores continued the reading. "'It is not well to strive upward. It is good to remain below.'"

Dolores explained with an interpretation from the text. "It says below is Earth, and you need to do earthly stuff. You don't need to be flying around in the heavens, mentally thinking you're above it all. 'You got to rely on your earthly principles'—Bob Dylan," she said, chuckling at her own allusion.

While she stroked the book's grainy cover, I chewed on her reading for a minute. I held my tongue for a moment, a little disbelieving, because these words seemed so obviously to address her life right now. I didn't expect the *I Ching* to be so direct, pinpointing Dolores' predicament so acutely. In all honesty, I had assumed that I would hear, "A chance of love awaits you," or "One in the hand is worth two in the bush"—both true, of course, but both bubblegum prophecies. Of course Dolores knew firsthand how good it was to remain below; she was living underground.

"Do you see your being homeless as a way of being more earthly than you've been?" I asked. "Is that a greater challenge for your faith?"

Her eyes followed an almost perceptible arc, from the book up to my face. "See," she said, "to my way of thinking, what I'm doing, to have left Massachusetts and New York and come here, has saved my life. I could hardly walk, so we never went anywhere. I had other problems: sitting too long, standing. I couldn't breathe, and I weighed about twenty pounds more than I do right now. I was isolated with my daughter, because I didn't have any friends. In my own little way of thinking, this is not negative. This is positive. I've forced myself down these Seattle hills, and I've got the cart now. I've saved my life."

What had led her to feel like escape was an antidote to her problems? Why as a homeless person was she able to walk whereas as a woman housed by family she had felt immobilized? I didn't sense it at the time, because I was too engrossed in her analysis of the reading, but in describing her own path to a migrant's life, had Dolores hinted at the deeper reasons behind my own choices?

"See," Dolores said, "to me, *being* here is very positive. I'm saving my life." She gazed down at the *I Ching* on her lap, patting it with one hand, then raised it, holding the book the way a trial attorney lifts a piece of evidence. "Small things." She pointed to a spot on the page. "It says right here, 'A bird should not try to surpass itself and fly into the sun. It should descend to the earth, where its nest is.'"

"I found it today," I said a few hours later in the kitchen of Danny and his girlfriend Carly's apartment. My friend Kim from college was there, too. While not bragging, my words could well have sounded as if I had led a successful excavation. "I found the phrase. It was revealed to me by the *I Ching*." Like an honest divinity student, I took care with my citations, lest through some act of spiritual hubris I failed to acknowledge the source of my finding and faced karmic punishment afterward for my oversight. "This woman Dolores handed it to me. I asked her, 'What is faith?' and she started this." I recounted her divination technique and our finding. I took a slug from my glass of red wine, allowing the words to waft through the kitchen.

"Wow," Kim said. "That *is* amazing." In her fourth and final year of medical school, Kim had the kind of flexibility in her schedule rivaled only by the jobless. Month-long rotations give medical students the chance to sample a number of hospitals where they might want to work, so she was working for a few months in Seattle before heading south and east to do research at the Center for Disease Control in Atlanta.

"Wait, what?" Danny stammered, stepping back from the tomato sauce he was tending on the stovetop. In Kim's tone he recognized that something had happened. While preparing the meal he had listened the way one pays attention to *Entertainment Tonight* with one's back to the screen. But now he turned around and asked me to repeat the phrase. "Preponderance of the small," I said. "It was a pronouncement from above." I told my friends that it seemed like I had been traveling toward this phrase. An *I Ching* reading felt like one of my preordained destinations. "When I got up and walked around her and saw the words over her shoulder, the hair on the back of my neck rose. It was like, *bam,* the *I Ching* had spoken."

"That is *ridiculous,*" Danny said.

"Totally ridiculous," I said.

A few hours later, Danny and I drove Kim back to where she was staying. Kim asked what my plan was for Seattle.

"I'm going to see what I can find on the Internet," I told her. Maybe it was Danny's influence, maybe regional propaganda, but a search on the Web for "Seattle and Religion" seemed like a culturally appropriate next step.

Driving back home, I told Danny that Kim and I had gone out in the past.

"Oh, dude, you totally want to go back," he said, darting his hand to the blinker in preparation for a hasty U-turn.

"Nah, man. I got my girl."

"Come *on,* T." His words were an effort to wring desire from what he heard as the party line.

"Not even." Danny shook his head in mock indignation. He drove, up hills and down hills, and I dozed the twenty minutes back to his driveway.

[15]

I called Liz early the next morning. She was studying at home before classes. Life sounded grim in Chicago. Her workload was mounting, her free time was evaporating, her anxiousness—about school, the cadaver in her anatomy lab, us—was spiraling. She missed me, she said, wanted me there in her second floor studio apartment. She asked something along the lines of did I miss her, and did I want to be there, too? I answered, naturally, yes, and left it at that. I hoped the answer would soothe her, but my terseness irritated instead. She didn't believe me when I said it. I had called to check in, and she heard me checking out. I let out the mother of all sighs when we hung up. I was ready to talk to Seattle.

Yahoo suggested a few leads. I scribbled the address of the local Zen temple on my notebook and, again borrowing Danny's car, drove east through the gray city.

Two hours later, stuck as the first car in the middle of a three-lane street at an interminably long red light, lamenting the outcome of my failed expedition to hang out with some members of the Seattle Zen community, I remembered with a wistfulness too saccharine for the passing of only one day about how easy, how clear, how self-evident the life of faith had seemed to me with Dolores's help twenty-four hours earlier. I had driven over to the house that doubled, I thought, as the Zen Temple. I had knocked on the front door. No answer. I had wandered to the rear, knocking there. Again, no answer. Clearly, I was spoiled. The Zen people ought to have been expecting my knock. I had considered trying the doorknob, but figured a well-intentioned breaking and entering wasn't the best way to start a conversation. Finally, I had the answer to one of the lesser known Zen riddles: What sound does a hand knocking make that didn't dial first to make sure somebody is around? Apparently, no sound. I couldn't help but think what a might-have-been day this had been. There I was, all set to listen, and no one was around to talk.

I had walked back to the curbside and the car. I'd figured that the Zen community, another Eastern tradition, presented a topical follow-up to Dolores. I had been foiled.

The red light endured so long, I thought it must be broken. I couldn't tell: had I missed a cycle of green already? Had I, daydreaming about the *I Ching*, neglected the blaring of horns from behind me? I had planned to go straight. But with an increasing fidgetiness, I checked the passenger-side mirror and noticed that no car had filled in the right lane. It was early in the afternoon and Danny's house was twenty-five minutes away. Then I felt the force behind the fidget: my bladder. The light was still red when

I turned my signal arrow and spun the wheel right. Initially I thought the right turn was an expression of exasperation. I was only looking for a bathroom.

Not long after I took the right, a couple of blocks after the turn, I spotted a blue neon sign that read, "Caffeine Saves." Next to it was a neon cross. This might do fine, I reasoned, so I pulled over and parked.

The place was a coffee bar, kind of. The storefront had all the requisite coffee shop qualities—a choice of blends, a domed window that showed pastries like they were museum pieces, a condiment table and its containers of milk and cream and honey that rose in cylinders and squares like the model skyline of an imagined metropolis. Pierced and tattooed twenty-somethings sipped from chipped white mugs at small round tables, and frayed upholstered cushions lined the seats against the wall. Above the booths, however, adorning the walls, were at least a dozen paintings of Jesus. The images had the visual quality of Eastern Orthodox icons, in which Jesus' face hangs long and narrow. Next to these pictures, above the booths, portraits of clowns with red honking noses acted as the alpha to the Jesus pictures' omega. I saw a collection of T-shirts for sale behind the cash register. On your pick of white or black cotton, in several different sizes, was an ironed-on portrait of Jesus hanging from the cross. Floating above the image were the words *Coffee Messiah*. I stepped outside for a second to double-check the sign outside the place. I nearly pinched myself. Sure enough, of all the turns I could have made, of all the establishments I could have entered to relieve myself, I'd walked into a place called Coffee Messiah, a kitschy hipster's café with a sacred side.

Trying to camouflage my giddiness at this discovery with a surface of blasé cool befitting the clientele, I coolly asked the woman behind the counter if I could talk to the owner or the interior designer of the establishment.

"Tim isn't around," she said, "but he'll be back later. I can tell him you stopped in. Or you could call him if you wanna set something up."

She gave me the number of a man named Tim who had conceived of and created the Coffee Messiah coffee bar. I thanked her. I was in the car another ten minutes before remembering that, maybe because of my focus on coolness, I had forgotten to ask to use the bathroom. I pulled over again, walked into a restaurant, used the facilities, and left relieved and without a revelation of any kind.

The next day I returned to Coffee Messiah.

Tim Turner, thirty-three, wore a gray cardigan sweater, Birkenstocks with wool socks underneath, and a bandana tied and knotted around his neck. His black hair, flecked with gray streaks like the first few drops of rain on a windshield, touched his shoulders. He was tall enough that at the table where we sat he needed to move his legs from under the table to cross them. He looked like the young dean of a New Age college on staff picture day.

"Because I can't do Coffee Messiah's style justice," I said, "can you describe what you were going for when you put it together?"

"Coffee Messiah is decorated in sort of a high-Gothic style, with lots of icons, and it has a coin-operated discotheque bathroom." I nearly spit out my mouthful of the free mug of tea Tim had given me. "It's a discotheque in hell. The walls are painted in different peoples' interpretations of hell. Mostly medieval liturgical pamphlet prints. Pictures of devils and Satan, and the different hells for the seven deadly sins; a lot of Hieronymus Bosch prints; a lot of dripping blood and skeletons. It's a discotheque, and with a quarter it plays 'Disco Inferno' and an evil devil laughs at you."

"What's that devil laughing at?"

"He's just laughing that you're in hell. And that you paid him a quarter. The original concept was going to be a heaven bathroom and a hell bathroom, but we got hell finished and ran out of money. So what I really wanted was a heaven bathroom where you would see the face of God. I never figured out what the face of God was going to be, but I knew you had to pay to see it, and that it was going to cost a quarter."

I replayed my serendipitous coincidence of discovering his place. "And when I came in and looked around, the burning question I had was: parody or piety?"

"Skating the thin line between the two," Tim answered, his deep voice unexpectedly serious. He spoke with a kind of colloquial gravity, like a Valley Boy theologian. "I never wanted to offend anybody, but I did want them to think about and question the meaning of these images. There's nothing overtly sacrilegious here. There aren't crucifixes hung upside down. People give me a lot of pieces that I can't use. Like this ridiculous space alien nailed to a cross. But I find it offensive, because *that* is parody. I'm more offended by its mindlessness than by taking the crucifix out of context. I believe in that for artistic purposes; but pieces like these are just lacking in artistic merit.

"I don't show disdain for the objects in the way I display them." Tim pivoted his body and gazed up at the wall to his left, where a few of the paintings were displayed. "Some people take umbrage that I have my own little santería-esque version of an altar to Andy Warhol. In it there's a can of Campbell's soup and a couple Andy Warhol prints in the same altar space with Jesus and a Pee Wee Herman doll." I missed this nook on my first look around. Sure enough, Jesus, Warhol, and Pee Wee—all together. They looked comically scrunched, as though forced to sleep three to a train berth made for two. "For me, what that is about is a comparison of these different images and icons. I think it's interesting for a devout Christian to come in here and look at that and ask, 'What does this mean, that he has Jesus next to Pee Wee Herman?' You know, does Jesus suffer by comparison?" I couldn't imagine a devout Christian walking in here, unless goaded by some fire-breathing pastor who wanted the believers to glimpse what their adversaries looked like. Nonetheless, Tim had designed the space, if one took his words at face value, as a benign challenge to the pious of the Christian world. "For me, Andy Warhol is there because Andy Warhol was a master at following his bliss and making money. And that's what I'm trying to do here. I'm trying to find some truth about my life and exploit it for profit, basically."

This sounded perfectly logical and appropriate coming out of Tim's mouth. What I had in front of me was a self-evidently savvy, sardonic entrepreneur fusing his own path with the culture's, his quest for truth with the American worship of the dollar. This was smart marketing, not automatically a crass commercialization of the spiritual life. Coffee Messiah was a concept, but also a store. Andy Warhol was an artist and, at the same time, a salesman. This didn't diminish the purity of their paths. But, I wondered, would I feel the same if Tammy Faye Bakker said those same words?

"Let me back up," Tim said. "I first started to understand the powers of icons when I was a student doing a children's theater tour in Moscow in 1990. We got to go to this cathedral in the middle of Moscow on a Sunday night. Aside from us few dorky American students, the only people there were five or six peasant women. As they stared at the icons they started this guttural chant they all knew. It turned into a really Gothic-sounding hymn. Their connection seemed to be all about the icons and the space. There wasn't a priest there telling them what to do. They were having a divine experience in the presence of a painting. That's what made me start to explore what images mean. Why was that possible? Why were they able to have what seemed to be an incredible, transforming experience in front of this flat object? On that trip, I bought a couple icons.

"My plan to open a coffee shop was years in the making, but the concept for Coffee Messiah came suddenly. I really had not planned on doing this. I was originally leaning toward a dorky French bistro approach, but I kept thinking, ugh, that's so boring. There are so many of those in Seattle. So one night I went to bed and woke up with Coffee Messiah in my head. I already had a large collection of icons that I hadn't really planned on putting on display, but it just seemed to make sense. And the longer I've owned it, it's made more and more sense."

"Was that an entrepreneurial epiphany?" I asked.

"No. The epiphanous part came later. I started it not knowing that I was going to be able to talk to people about spirituality. When I started it I was very shy about my spiritual beliefs and my spiritual path, and I didn't talk to people about it at all. For some reason I had never considered that if you open a shop called Coffee Messiah and you display religious icons in the way you want to, people are going to come to you and ask about your spiritual beliefs. And at the time, if I had thought about it, I would have said, 'No, I don't want to talk to total strangers about my spiritual beliefs.'

"It's ironic that I've grown into the shop and have come to a space where I'm more than willing to talk about it. In fact, I sometimes do performances about it. This started two and a half years ago, and it's only in the last year that I've been really vocal, or really comfortable, about what I believe personally. I was always willing to talk a little about the shop, the icons, and their history, but what ended up happening was that more and more people kept coming here wanting to know, 'What's *your* deal? What's motivating *you*?'

"One of the reasons I opened up the shop was to have a performance space. I'd been experimenting with different forms of performance art. All of a sudden I found my performance art starting to slip into a religious vein. I would get up in front of fifty people and stand up on a soapbox for twenty minutes, basically, telling them what I thought. I didn't plan it; it was a very organic experience that just evolved out of my performing. Suddenly I found myself in the role of a postmodern preacher at two in the morning at our late-night cabaret."

I smiled. "I find that holding a beer in my hand at two in the morning is when I do *my* best preaching." Tim laughed, maybe not knowing how sincere I was. "If you're preaching at two in the morning," I asked, "what's the congregation looking for?"

"It depends on what event I'm preaching at. Our regular cabaret is sort of a mixed crowd of drag queens and drunks and poets and spoken word people, and some of my friends." Tim cobbled together a community of the religiously unaffiliated and the spiritually uninhibited. The people attracted to Coffee Messiah, and to its monthly cabarets, was a rowdy, motley array of the inebriated, the outlandish, and the explicitly unorthodox. "They're all looking for something different. For the most part they're just looking for a little entertainment while they're still drunk before they go home and go to bed. Many times, the last thing they want is me trying to bring them to a divine state of grace. But, on the other hand, preaching is quite an amazing experience. Preaching is not drama; it's what *you* think, it's what *I* think. Performance-wise, it's the ultimate limb to go out on and say, 'Here's my belief,' or 'Here's part of my belief,' or 'Here's something that I think can help you understand the world better.'

"It's stunning when people really receive it and appreciate it. To have drunks and drag queens and spoken word people sitting in awe and total silence for ten minutes after you're done. And you know you've moved them because nobody is moving. Nobody's applauding, just silence. That's happened a couple times. And I looked around the room and I thought, 'What a strange congregation.'"

Tim and I both shook our heads at the thought. "We also do another venue on first Saturdays," he said, "a trance show that we call Jungle Jam. We clear everything out. I have Turkish tapestries that cover the floor. And everybody sits around on pillows or on a bench. We have a deejay spinning low grooves—trance grooves—and about four or five musicians playing— a couple guitar players, a sitar player, and a couple of bass players. Then we give everybody in the audience percussion instruments, bamboo or shakers or rattles. Usually bamboo sticks are the best. And we just jam out. Everybody's invited to do spoken word. In fact, we're doing one this Saturday that's going to be a wedding." I cursed to myself. I'd be gone, down south in the Bay Area by then.

"For real?" I asked.

"For real. It should be really cool."

"Who's getting married?"

"A guy named Masa who hangs out here."

"Who's marrying him?"

"One of the Sisters of Perpetual Indulgence, who's also a registered minister with the Church of Life. The sisters are drag queens gotten up as Catholic nuns. They are much more sacrilegious than I am, for the most part. One of them is a registered minister. So he's going to come and perform the ceremony for Masa and his girlfriend, Robin. It's going to be a trance surrealist wedding. The first one in here. I'm very excited. I've wanted to have weddings in here for a long time. We have mock weddings on Valentine's Day, and we've said we'd like to have real weddings, but nobody has taken us up on the offer until now."

"That's fantastic." I was a little stunned. At that point the wheels had really started turning in my head. Cataloguing all the activities that go on in this coffee bar after the coffee bar closed amounted to a major undertaking. I loved that Tim described Masa's wedding as Coffee Messiah's first trance surrealist wedding, as if it wouldn't also be the planet's first.

Each of these separate elements of Coffee Messiah seemed to add up to something larger, something incongruously orderly. I needed to ask Tim if he saw what I was seeing. "You know," I said, "there are a few elements that I need to catch my breath on. One, dozens of icons; two, times here when it's late night and there's the feeling that you're preaching to a congregation; three, the wedding; four, altars." I made a list by touching the tip of each finger on my right hand with my thumb. "I mean, I could bring up other stuff, but what I'm getting is that this is a different kind of church."

Tim started nodding well before I reached the end of my point. "A while ago I realized that, in many ways, this space is becoming a postmodern church. I did not plan that. I didn't think of myself as a preacher or this coffee shop as a church when I opened it, but that's almost what it's turning into. I think the spiritual evolution that's been developing in the past ten years is really, really amazing. My little corner of the world is really just a small, minor bump in the road in terms of how many people it's affecting." Listening to Tim, I considered the way that a preponderance of the small, including Tim's minor bump of a postmodern congregation, amassed in such an evolution.

What did Tim mean when he suggested that Coffee Messiah was becoming a "postmodern church"? This question hinged on two others: What did *postmodern* mean when used as a description? And how did a functional, quasi church grow out of a smirking café?

First, postmodernism, as a way of thinking about and understanding the world, challenges the claim that any one story is *the* story, that any one belief is the *only* belief, and that any one faith is the *true* faith. True stories change from person to person, according to the postmodern perspective, which denies the possibility of universal unanimity in values, morals, doctrines, and dogmas. Each of us, it stresses, sees through our own lenses, tinted by our own lives.

What would seem to sit on the opposite end of the religious pole from postmodernism is fundamentalism (an umbrella term related to but more general than Protestant Fundamentalism). Fundamentalism aspires to an idealized version of a mythic past of cultural purity, and grounds its search in timeless standards and moral absolutes. While postmodernism maintains that there are no universal truths, and that the truths of one culture are as arbitrary and artificial as those of any other, fundamentalism believes there is but one single truth, that its adherents know it and are protected by it, and that everyone who believes otherwise is doomed here, now, and ever after. Both fundamentalism and postmodernism in their own way reject the worldview of modernity. Modernity sees potential progress everywhere and affirms all peoples' and cultures' access to truth. No one path is exclusively right: any number of paths pave an equally accessible route through the thicket of the world to the clearing of wisdom, faith, and holiness. This is the bedrock conviction of religious pluralism and the liberal religious perspective.

While Coffee Messiah has postmodern particularities, Tim's place stands more in the modern than in the postmodern tradition. Because ultimately Tim Turner believes that his trance jams and cabarets and individual spiritual search has led him, and others, to a form of his, and their, own truth. The world isn't empty and devoid of meaning; it just demands an infusion of our own meaning to make sense. While Jeff Paul at Liberty University represented the certainty of a fundamentalist perspective, Maureen Scowby, the Cafeteria Catholic, and the Coffee Messiah community could be seen as models of a modern consciousness.

Coffee Messiah transformed into a "church" because of its evolving function, not its original intent. At the cabaret where Tim preached, at the trance surrealist wedding where a Sister of Perpetual Indulgence presided, Coffee Messiah made tentative, tiptoeing steps from irony to earnestness. A self-conscious café turned into a sacred space because *why* people hung there replaced *what* hung there as the storefront's main focus.

Tim continued: "One of the lessons I've learned is that you have to be willing to talk about this stuff; to be willing to say, 'Yeah, I'm on a spiritual path, and I'm not a geek.' You have to be willing to be out there and say that spiritual matters are worthy of study, and that there's another way to look at the world besides through yuppie eyes. We live in this environment that teaches us that what's important is a new Lexus, and a nice tract home, and buying our clothes at the right stores, and looking a certain way. I've been encouraged to see more and more people who are willing to say, 'That's not important to me. But what is important is finding a state of grace.' Ultimately I think that's what most spiritual pursuit is about."

Tim's faith journey hinged on balancing his search and his coolness, and assuring others that the one did not compromise the other. I nodded my head in agreement, but I felt like, in my experience, it wasn't a challenge to stay cool while searching. The wanderer, I think, whether scripturally sketched in a figure like Jacob or popularly drafted in a book like Paolo Coelho's *The Alchemist,* is a portrait of archetypal coolness. Though I might have tried to dismiss the claim, my own trip, truthfully, attempted to tap into that source. So Tim and I shared that sensibility.

The challenge lay in remaining cool when you've actually found something, presuming that the search was not an end in itself. While part of me agreed with the notion that "the only finding is in the looking," another part of me clung to the conviction that looking could in fact lead to a finding. And what then? What if the finding rendered you a geek? What if what you found sparked an impulse or stoked a desire to do something really dorky, like join a church or embrace a doctrine?

Tim and I are similar, because to us, as to many in our generation, icon-oclasty seems to be the chosen path. If a path has actually been shared, if our essential uniqueness has somehow been subverted, then the com-monness of that journey demands a level of irony, which affirms that while we may have joined up, we were never sucked in. If a path is common, then it is not only shared but ordinary. And it is ordinariness, I thought, that ter-rifies us. Tim recoiled at the idea of creating a French bistro-type coffee shop, in the same way, before the beginning of my trip, I had feared that I followed in the footsteps of another pilgrim. We didn't want to follow. While I imagined Tim and I would agree that competitiveness had no place in our spiritual searches, we both were motivated by the desire to be the first. And yet we didn't want to be pioneers in a way that led oth-ers to mimic our routes. No, it might signal our failure as trailblazers if others found their answers in our stories. Tim and I subscribed to an in-dividualistic doctrine. We preached the postmodern gospel of the partic-ular, and the modern, liberal road to truth.

I tilted my head: had I been driving to stave off ordinariness? Why was this something I stiff-armed if the perspectives I drove to explore hinged on such ordinariness? If the ordinary was where others located meaning, why couldn't I? Was taking a pilgrimage a unique life decision? In the grand scheme, no, not exactly: millions of people travel to Mecca and Jerusalem and Varanasi in India and the Virgin de Guadalupe in Mexico City every year. But certainly it was among my peers. In the same way that divinity school illustrated a desire to break from the pack, so too did this trip. But wasn't it possible then that my pilgrimage existed only as a means of stamping me further with uniqueness, loading me up with more barroom and cocktail party, though clearly not resume-padding, ammunition? Damn, I thought: if the underlying foundation, the prime motivating fac-tor of my pilgrimage was to make me feel special, to prop up my ego like some New Age cosmetic treatment, I would be so deeply demoralized. If this was my reason, then wasn't it possible that other paths and pilgrim-ages necessarily suffered the same syllogistic fate? Were our soul search-ings and spiritual stirrings powered by self-involvement? Tim and I were both pilgrims, both searching, both creating community as though a col-lage. But at the end of the day, or in Tim's case, by the end of the cabaret, we both remained solitary. Both of us hoped to find community the next day, but we were unable to rely on it.

Considering Tim Turner's unanticipated calling, I reasoned that Coffee Messiah was thriving as a loosely affiliated congregation because its spiri-tuality was subtly, self-consciously ironic as much as it was iconoclastic. People went for coffee, or to people watch, or to write in their journals, or for a trance jam, and left feeling connected to the place and one another.

But if Coffee Messiah advertised its legitimate spiritual component, I reasoned it would lose its cache as a place to find underground religion. Tim Turner agreed with what the *I Ching* had told me and Dolores Ledbetter. In the life of faith, "it is good to remain below."

Tim and I spoke for a while longer, though soon the time arrived for me to hit the road. Of course I understood, particularly in light of my initial biological impulses that led me from red light to blue sign, that no trip to Coffee Messiah was complete without a visit to the bathroom. I searched my pockets but couldn't come up with a quarter. Tim plucked one from the open cash register so I could experience a minute in my very own inferno. Underneath a strobe light, shuddering a little at the grim laugh of a caffeinated devil and the detailing of the burgundy-tinted frescoes on the walls, I stood, shaking my head, uncertain whether I should laugh, pee, or boogie.

[16]

Danny drove me to the Seattle bus station to say good-bye. A piece of me wished I could lug him and the rest of his city onto the overhead rack on the bus. There, detours and rain shelters precipitated everyday encounters with revelation. When my friend pulled away from the station, I felt like I had just waved "so long" to my parents at the end of a summer camp visiting day. I was energized and sentimental.

It shouldn't come as a surprise that in Seattle, the home base of Starbucks' conquest of the American streetscape, a sanctuary would link caffeine with deliverance in its title. Even in meeting Dolores Ledbetter, coffee had been a prelude to prophecy. Questions bombarded me: Could this be dismissed as coincidence? Or was it fate? What did coffee have to do with it? Why didn't I like coffee? Was this some sort of conspiratorial collusion by the coffee industry to sway me? Would Juan Valdez appear on my bus down to San Francisco?

Seattle's bus depot was a one-room waiting area with a handful of vending machines. Compared with the Port Authority in Manhattan or Boston's South Station, the place was a broom closet. The duffle and army bag I carried, the former filled with clothing, the latter with notebooks, recording equipment, camera, and toothbrush, sagged, looking as if they shared my nostalgic mood.

My fellow passengers and I boarded in the mid-afternoon. I assumed I would collect testimonies from seatmates like tickets. Once the sun set, however, the highway blanketed the bus with quiet. I slept fitfully through that Monday night. The Greyhound paused hourly for driver and passenger cigarette breaks. Seven or eight times, from sundown to sunup, the sound of the bus's brakes punctured its hum. What followed was a parade of insomniacs, rattling up the aisle, down the steps, and into the night air along Interstate 5 to inhale the smoke from their butts hungrily, before climbing the steps, wobbling down the aisle, and tumbling back into their seats to await the next break. Nearly all of the passengers filed off the bus for those breaks, and I figured that Greyhound must post special deals on the insides of cigarette packs.

Dolores Ledbetter had taken a Greyhound bus for four days and three nights to reach Seattle from Boston the previous summer. From my seat in the middle of the bus, I peered over my shoulder, after the 4 A.M. stop, to survey my fellow travelers. One kid had pulled his wool hat down to his nose. An older Mexican man stirred in his seat, clawing after a comfortable position. A young woman in her mid-twenties reapplied her lipstick. Who, I wondered, might the Dolores be on this bus? Though they were strangers, I sensed that if we had a few moments to talk on the bus on the highway south of Eureka, they wouldn't be. They were, I knew, all Doloreses. Every stranger had become a source for me. Did the person across the aisle know how I felt? To look at the foreign and understand that it is only the familiar in gestation? At 4 A.M. I propped my pullover behind my head as a pillow and stared out the plastic window toward the asphalt underneath us, and toward the forest, cloaked with night, that bracketed the bus. But all I could see was my own face.

The bus pulled into San Francisco late in the morning, nineteen hours after we pushed off from Seattle. I wandered around San Francisco but found no Doloreses. It was not for lack of effort, but there were days, and the Tuesday at the tail end of September was one of them, when nobody looked in my direction. Numbed by their inattention by the mid-afternoon, I stopped searching, stopped gazing, stopped approaching.

It was dinnertime before I emerged from temporary social hibernation to meet up with my good friend from college, Laura Wolf. We had gone out and broken up several times in the previous four years. Laura worked at an Internet start-up, making little money but sitting on her stock options. It was Laura whom my sister had asked me about during our Mexican dinner in Bethesda, Maryland, the day after I spoke with Harvey Lee Green.

Seattle and San Francisco marked the first in a succession of cities where I would visit women friends from college and after: the relationships ranged in past intensity from platonic to serious. In my planning, in the phone calls and catching up and requests for short-term housing, I never struggled with the notion that staying with any of them signified a conflict of interest, an unadvised traipse into temptation. I was with Liz. Though they hadn't met Liz, or she them, they knew I was attached. And Liz knew I was seeing these friends. Yet I don't know why I kept staying with women Liz didn't really know and consequently couldn't quite trust. In retrospect, this was an incredibly foolish, naive decision: not because I expected or intended or even wanted anything illicit to go down, but because my girlfriend and I were presently navigating through somewhat rocky waters, and instead of looking for a calm spot to drop anchor with her, I chronicled the gusts of breeze and the lure of the sea with relish and little regard for her mounting seasickness.

Laura and I walked twenty minutes to reach dinner. On the way there, at the corner of Bush and Pierce in the Western Division neighborhood, she found cause to tease me.

"Look, Tom—a church! Go on, boy. Get it!" She taunted me in her best dog-owner's voice.

Dutifully I walked across the street, panting as I went. Sure enough: there on the corner was a white building, freckled with divots of chipped-away paint. Above its entrance, a sign read, "First Apostolic Faith Church." Emblazoned across the sign was its thesis statement: "Jesus Saves." Jesus did it decaffeinated here. I scrolled down the congregation's weekly schedule of events. "Beautiful." I couldn't contain myself. "It's a Pentecostal Church. They've got a prayer service and Bible study tomorrow at noon."

We had already put back a little bit of red wine, giving Laura cause to cackle at the extraordinary, coincidental ease of the process. "That's incredible," she started, only to pause herself mid-breath. "Wait a minute. That's not incredible. Look who I'm with. Of course there's something tomorrow at noon. So you'll sleep in, roll out, and hit the twelve o'clock service," she said, crafting a mock itinerary of leisure like Julie, the Love Boat's cruise director. "Perfect."

The search for a subject was over, Laura assumed, and she was right, in part. She was right that the gods of scheduling had conspired in my favor. And she was right that stumbling into this church was not solely coincidence. But she was wrong that the search was over. The blessing of a discovery like this still demanded follow through. I still had to open a door the next day come noon, take a seat in some pew, smile, blink back anxiousness, sing if others sang, amen when others amened, act like I belonged when I knew how glaringly obvious it would seem, to me even more than my hosts, that I didn't.

Fully expecting to barge in on a crowd of regulars, I showed up at one minute after twelve. It was premeditated punctuality, but with the subtlest hint, the most minuscule dash, of casualness. I pushed open a wooden door and entered a small anteroom decorated with yellow and sky blue church flyers along one wall and an old school soda machine with options like Tab and Fanta against another, before I entered the small, cozy sanctuary. The space was flooded with natural light and lined with well-worn wooden pews.

I didn't know whether I had read the sign wrong the prior evening. A trim black man, seemingly in his mid to late fifties, tidied up the sanctuary as if it were his child's bedroom. He was humming when I tiptoed in. He smiled at me, shook my hand and, still humming, guided me to sit. I chose a fourth-row pew, in a couple of seats from the aisle—close enough to the pulpit to see the preacher, far enough away to avoid an invitation to join him. Playing the stranger who, though foreign, wasn't threatening demanded some strategic thinking. I folded my hands, crossed my legs, unfolded my hands, uncrossed my legs. I figured he would take a seat soon. We would sit together as other congregants walked in, taking reserved seats in familiar pews, all of us waiting for the pastor.

Before I'd entered, I had been afraid that I might disrupt the service. In truth, my arrival marked its beginning.

As it turned out, this man was the pastor. We were alone together, and as the clock on the wall behind the altar inched past 12:05, he had already rolled out his prayers. There was no official beginning to the service—no "Good afternoon," no "Let us pray," no whistle—just a sudden immersion into one man's inner life, spoken out loud. My peripheral vision caught a blurry glimpse of a portrait of a seated woman next to the clock. 12:08 came and went, and so did 12:09. The last time I remember looking at the clock it read 12:13, and no one else had joined us—still and only the pastor and I.

I suspected that the setting was a particularly cruel practical joke. Laura must have set it up somehow and walked me past the church, goading me to check it out because she knew the fix was on. Friends had hired this man to play a preacher. His thick, yellow, v-neck sweater was a particularly surprising, hence believable, costume choice for this slender, older black pastor. He'd go on and I'd pick at my cuticles and the conspirators would be cackling as they watched on closed circuit or behind a two-way mirror. I half-expected Ed McMahon to break the tension.

The pastor wasn't fooling, though. He started calling out to Jesus, and his words found their rhythm. He called out the names of congregants, the names of congregants' cousins, friends of congregants' cousins, local police officials, and statewide elected politicians, and asked for blessings to rain down on them all.

I stared down at the space in between my Chuck Taylors. Something poked at me from inside. Stop poking me, I told it. It persisted. There was no course in divinity school called "Prayer." I hadn't had much practice—at least not like this, where you were expected to be heard. I had taken part in silent prayer, had found myself to be a capable head bower, believed I had contributed an emphatic "mm-huh" and a heartfelt "Amen" with the best of them. As far as spoken prayer and spontaneous worship went, though, I counted myself a novice. But there I was, being told by that still, small voice that I had to catch an ounce or two of the Holy Ghost there and then. The pastor, closed eyes and all, knew there were only two of us in the sanctuary, and yet I figured he must have wondered why he heard only his own voice.

I felt commanded to join in, because it seemed so clear that I was refraining. As the preacher called out for the Holy Ghost to join us (pending the Holy Ghost's arrival, I calculated that the congregation would grow by 50 percent to three), I leaned over, looking as though bathroom-bound with a bad stomach cramp, and began murmuring amen as if it were an assignment. I didn't know what else to say.

Before I'd arrived, I had figured I would be one of many, join a chorus, melt into a pew. I'd been wrong. What comedy, what squirmish, awkward, mesmerizing comedy it must have been to those I still suspected were watching.

I'll tell you one thing about fervent prayer and a bowed head, though: time flies a lot faster than you think it will. A woman joined our duet about twenty minutes into the service. Her voice rang with a comfort that implied she might have grown up in this church. Slowly, satisfyingly, her prayers flowered from a greeting, "Hello, Jesus" to a moan, "Ohh, Jesus," rose to an apex, "Yes, Jesus!" and then calmed to a graciousness, "Thank you, Jesus." It almost could have been X-rated prayer. Some time after she began speaking in tongues, a language of Pentecostal prayer that sounds like intoxicated gibberish, I heard the church's door open. Down the aisle came the heavy thud of footsteps, past my closed eyes and lowered head, up to a pew near the altar. Baritone-voiced, the man started repeating "Oh God, oh God, oh God" like the sound had been dubbed and mechanically looped. The voices, though unchoreographed, started to move in time like a kick line.

After a few more minutes, I realized I was listening to unorchestrated jazz for Jesus, Pentecostal a cappella, in which the pastor sang and the woman wailed and the front row thumped like a standing bass. Stunned that these three people could turn out this music, I wanted to find my own instrument to play. Yet while I wanted to join, at the same time I preferred not to be acknowledged; my aim was to participate as if I had always been a part, rather than as the newest walk-on addition. Maybe, I considered, they were so focused on Jesus that they wouldn't notice me. Then again, maybe when I raised the volume of my own prayers, they would all stop and stare, as if I were one of the white fraternity brothers in *Animal House* when they open the door to the all-black club. The needle would skip, the record would scratch, and I, apologizing earnestly and repeatedly, would backpedal my way out of the church. But after a couple more minutes of quiet deliberation, I let go. I began to mutter my prayers like a drumbeat— a deep-down drumbeat—whispering amen as a kind of salute to their full-throated pleas, sighing "hallelujah" at the thought of where I was a little after noon on a mid-autumn Wednesday.

I wouldn't say I dove in. No, not by any means. A dive would have consisted of giving myself to Jesus, then and there. Trust me, I did not dive. But I waded, and the water felt warm enough. And somehow, since everybody else was already swimming, remaining on the shore felt far more awkward than getting wet.

When the music dissolved, as the quiet of a San Francisco midday returned, I lifted my head and opened my eyes. Yeah, I thought, I might be just a *little* out of place.

Like a lot of white people—and yes, this is a generalization, but one I'll stand by—I know that I am apt to indulge every so often in delusions of pioneering grandeur. The thought crossed my mind that I may be the first white person to pray here. It was, admittedly, an odd fantasy of boundary-crossing—presumptuous on the one hand, sappy on the other.

"Forget about that nonsense," I told myself. "Just be here now." A pause in my thinking: "But what if I am the first? Could that be possible?" I gave a discreet glance at the other attendees. "It'd be sort of cool if I were." I jumped in almost immediately. "Shut up already!" I feared my internal monologue might spill into the church aisles at any moment.

The pastor rescued me from excessive self-inquiry when the Bible study began. "We're going to be talking about sanctification this afternoon," the pastor said, and the three of us smiled. That was okay by us. Sanctification, he claimed, is a setting apart. "When I'm through, there isn't going to be any doubt in our minds that the Word sanctifies." I jotted that down: "The Word sanctifies." Transitively speaking, the Word must set apart, then. In a Pentecostal context, the Word denotes Jesus, the Holy Spirit, and the inerrancy of the Bible. But I was taking my own reading into the "Word." Anytime the pastor said "Word," I understood it to mean words, conversation, contact. If this pastor felt emboldened to interpret, so did I.

"What's gonna reform the world?" he asked. "The Word. What's gonna renew the world? The Word." The Word, he said, fuels our soul, ignites our testimony, and cements together our lives as believers. This time I said amen audibly, making certain they could hear me. The pastor made his points, and my shoulders and head bobbed up and down as if still hearing the rhythm of their prayers. By 1:30, the sanctification of the Word sounded like something other than a setting apart. It seemed as though the pastor offered praise for conversation. Maybe he amened small things, too.

I waited around after the service to talk to him. He introduced himself as Pastor Johnny Lay. He requested I call him Johnny. I walked with him past the pulpit and through the choir benches, to look up at the woman's portrait—the one next to the clock, which at that point read 2:20—which had been too far away for me to make out during the service. She appeared matronly, the painting old-fashioned, almost like an heirloom that had survived one of the congregant's migrations from the South out West. She could have been Harriet Tubman for all I knew.

"Who is that?" I asked.

"That's Mother Booker," Johnny said. "She is 102 years old. She started this church. Started it in her living room. She was the pastor here until eight years ago. That's when I took over."

I double-checked my math, following a quick calculation. "She was the pastor until she was ninety-four?"

"Uh-huh. Still comes to church, too." He was bragging now. Wow. Pentecostalism, the most explosive, charismatic, and successful religious movement of the twentieth century, and the brand of faith practiced by the congregation at First Apostolic, was still several years away from its conception at the time of Mother Booker's birth. It'd be cool to track *her* down, I thought, wherever she was.

I asked Johnny if he might be willing to sit down and talk. He gave me directions to his house across the Bay in Alameda and told me to visit him the following morning. "Meet my wife, too," he said with a smile.

Johnny stood on his lawn, green with some patches of brown, when I pulled up in my brother Nick's car next day. "Make it okay?" he asked.

"Just fine. Excellent directions, Pastor."

He ushered me up the gray porch steps, through the screen door, and into the large wooden house, which was across the street from an elementary school and playground.

Ellen Lay rose from the living room sofa to greet me. Several Snoopies danced on her well-worn white shirt. The images looked a little like a learn-to-dance diagram: Snoopy with both paws raised, Snoopy with ears perked high, Snoopy with legs scribbled and scrawled in—Charles Schulz's way of showing the beagle in an excited tither. We chitchatted for a few minutes. I told Ellen that I was a New Yorker and was staying with my brother, his wife Julie, and their baby boy Nate at their place in San Francisco.

I was having trouble focusing. Though I consider myself a pretty open-minded guy, I am still occasionally blindsided by my own preconceptions and misconceptions, clichés I cling to and caricatures that function like default mechanisms when I grow weary of being attentive, which is often. When I first started speaking with Dolores Ledbetter, she was painting with watercolors at a coffee klatch in a downtown Seattle church. When she asked me if I was surprised to hear that she was homeless, I stuttered, "No, no, of course I'm not," as a reply. The obvious answer, naturally, and the only honest answer I could have offered, was "Yes. Yes, Dolores, I am a little surprised that you sleep on mats in shelters and wear clothes donated by urban relief organizations, that the *I Ching* guided you across the continent to a homeless lifestyle you see as a recuperative calling." When I met Pastor Lay, heard him lead a prayer session, and listened to his congregation sing, I assumed that I possessed enough information to fill in the spaces of other parts of his life. In the moment immediately after he introduced me to the woman sitting on the couch in his living room, I still felt inclined to ask him when I would meet his wife.

The day before, when I had slid into the empty row of seats at the First Apostolic Faith Church, I had imagined, momentarily, that mine might be the first white backside to touch that pew. Now I knew otherwise. Johnny Lay, a black Pentecostal preacher, had been married to Ellen Lay, a white agnostic, for nearly thirty-five years and counting.

There was no room for feeling out of place there.

Perhaps I shouldn't have been so surprised. Although Pentecostalism is perhaps best known today for its ecstatic praying and meteoric growth, when it surfaced in the early 1900s, first in Topeka, Kansas, and later in Los Angeles, its headlining evangelist was a half-blind, itinerant black preacher named William J. Seymour, who proclaimed the transforming power of a colorless, classless God. Seymour led a revival at a run-down warehouse on Azusa Street in Los Angeles in 1906, and the event attracted thousands of people—white, black, Mexican, Native American, poor, working class, and wealthy—who discovered there a faith based more on personal experience than on impersonal doctrine. Pentecostalism began preaching a "baptism of the Spirit," in which a believer felt the Holy Spirit, the manifestation of the Christian God, in the contemporary world. The Holy Spirit made the believer dance and sing and shout and shriek and sometimes even bark. But most significant for the Pentecostal movement, the experience made the believer speak in tongues. This "glossolalia" was a gift of the Holy Spirit, and it called to mind the experience of the early followers of Jesus in the Book of Acts. While gathered in Jerusalem to celebrate *Shavuoth*, a Jewish harvest festival that commemorates the giving of the Law on Mt. Sinai, those gathered experienced the Holy Spirit. Their proof was their speaking in tongues. (Pentecost itself refers to the Greek word for fifty, alluding to the fact that Shavuoth falls fifty days after Passover.) In their *glossolalia*, these believers witnessed a new revelation that they felt superceded the one at Sinai. The Los Angeles press loved the hubbub, and the coverage that local newspapers provided brought more people down to the revival, and spread word of the revival throughout the country. Missionaries soon started to spread the faith worldwide.

Pentecostalism's message signaled a radical injection into the American religious landscape. Black and white can and must be together in God's Church, the early Pentecostals of this century preached. Women and men, too. On the second floor of the Lays' cluttered house, near the bathroom, a beautiful, grainy, black and white photograph of the attendees at a 1914 Pentecostal conference—black faces, white faces, young and old—was framed on the wall. It seemed to be an early portrait of the Pentecostal vision.

"What does that picture tell you about Pentecostalism in its early days?" I asked Johnny.

"That God is a God of unity, not division. Man has brought division in the races, in denominations. Sundays are the most segregated period of the week. But God is not that way."

Seymour's efforts at building a multiracial religious community moved swiftly forward until 1914, when the Assemblies of God—designed to be a segregated white Pentecostal church—came into being. In the intervening eighty-five years, Pentecostalism had spawned a number of different church bodies, from the Church of God in Christ to the Apostolic World Christian fellowship to the Assemblies of God to the Church of God.

Whatever the name of the particular church community, the Pentecostal faith emphasized personal, unmediated experience of the Divine. Other than that, religious practices varied from church to church. No central religious authority existed in Pentecostalism, so individual pastors enjoyed an essentially unopposed effort to create whatever kind of church they wanted. Unlike Roman Catholicism or the mainline Protestant traditions such as Episcopalianism and Presbyterianism, Pentecostals weren't bound by doctrine, tradition, or centuries-old liturgies.

Because I studied Pentecostalism for a semester in divinity school, and because the course remained relatively fresh in my mind, I was curious to hear how Johnny would describe his tradition. "Maybe I wouldn't come from the angle of being a Pentecostal," he said, "but from the angle of becoming a child of God." As he spoke, I flashed back to the way Jeff Paul at Liberty University saw himself not as a Baptist but as a Christian, and how Roxanne Masni said she followed only the Koran as the source of her belief and practice, not the dictates of any ethnic culture. Many of the most ostensibly religious people I had spoken to did not drape themselves with specific names or particular titles. I figured that members of any orthodoxy would be the first to affirm these labels. Instead, they rejected them. How I described them, how the popular culture might pigeonhole them, was not how they pictured themselves. Their self-identification fell under a larger umbrella of belief and practice—although they were quick to assert that if one stood outside the protective force field of the broadly understood faith, one was in deep trouble.

Johnny Lay made this point, too. "Jesus came to Earth to pay the penalty for sin. By accepting Jesus on belief, believing something you can't see, you're rewarded." For someone to "accept Jesus" essentially means that the person believes that Jesus died for him or her on the cross, and that in this faith the believer can have new life here in this world, and eternal life in the world to come. "But at the conclusion of your life's journey," Johnny continued, "you're going to have to give an account of the decisions you made or failed to make, with devastating consequences for the wrong choices. We believe that those who are judged to be wrong will not go to heaven, but end up in hell."

Maybe out of courtesy, maybe out of fear, I had refrained from asking Johnny the one question that had careened around my mind since I'd been introduced to Ellen: Was he worried about his wife? As a guest in his home, I didn't want to put him on the spot unnecessarily, but this was a crucial question, one they must have grappled with and, consequently, one I suspected was out there for discussion. Because if accepting Jesus were *essential* to one's salvation, then what did he think was going to happen to Ellen? "For you it took a belief in God," I said, pointing out as gingerly as I could, as though bringing my lips down to a mug of hot tea, "and yet your wife—she doesn't seem to have that."

Johnny paused for a moment. He gave a gentle tug at the collar of his short-sleeved Hawaiian shirt, then stumbled through the beginnings of a response. "Well, no. She has it, but she doesn't"—he flipped through his mental dictionary of faith for an adequate word—"pursue it. We do a lot of entertaining. Sixty or seventy people could be right here. Or at the church." His voice suddenly received an infusion of volume. "Who does

the cooking? She does. She'll make three turkeys, a ham. We have barbe-
cue grills out here, and we'll line 'em up, and we'll cook eight or nine slabs
of ribs. We'll cook twenty chickens.

"When I'm not here, who counsels the one in trouble? She'll do it, right
over the phone. 'You do this, you do that. He's not here but he'll be back.
You can reach him on his cell phone.' No, she doesn't go to church daily
every time we go over there. But," he stopped for a moment, then nodded
with increasing certainty, "I have observed that she gets closer and closer,
Tom." By closer and closer, I figured Johnny meant to his way of believing.

I had heard Ellen and the sound of plates loosened from cupboards and
the refrigerator door opening and closing in the kitchen. She stepped into
the living room, where we were sitting, to tell us lunch was ready. My invitation was implied, my acceptance assumed. A pilgrim gets so many unsolicited perks.

The Lays, appropriately enough, featured at least five different brands
of chips on their table. There were Doritos, Kmart-brand Doritos, potato
chips, Fritos, and Jeff Gordon Fritos in the shape of Indy 500 race cars.
Wheat bread, a big bowl of tuna fish, and all the condiments a boy could
wish for sat in the center of the table. I was never a huge fan of tuna fish
sandwiches growing up, but as a stranger I had been learning to bend toward my disinclinations, putting my arm around notions and noshings
that I might typically have shied away from.

"Well, thanks so much for lunch," I said, preparing my plate.

"You're welcome," Ellen said. With the back of her hand she pushed
her straight gray hair off her forehead.

Johnny, who served in the Marine Corps for nearly twenty years, met
Ellen while in Turkey, where he was stationed for part of his service. When
they met they went out together to clubs, listened to jazz, and fell in love
before coming home to the United States. I figured their return would have
crushed their relationship, but no: they had two grown children and one
grandchild.

I sat between Johnny and Ellen at the small table in their yellow kitchen.
Johnny softly announced that he would say grace. He dipped his head.
Mine dropped, too. I couldn't tell if Ellen's did or didn't. "Father, we thank
you for this fellowship. We thank you for Tom being in our midst. Lord,
we thank you for the food. I ask you to bless it and sanctify it. In Jesus'
name, Amen."

"Amen," I said. Yesterday he'd prayed for the San Francisco White
Pages. Today he prayed with me in mind. And it's a strange thing to admit,
particularly seeing that I hadn't grown up in a community or among people who prayed, but being mentioned in a blessing, being a presence that
a pious person thanks God for before we sit and eat together, is a novel

and moving experience. I smiled at the memory of Wallace Johnson's blessing at the Appleby's in Wheaton, Illinois.

"In an interracial marriage I wouldn't have suspected that religion would've been the hurdle," Ellen said as we dug into the food. When she spoke, the deep vertical wrinkles on her face seemed to shift shape, creasing horizontally from the corners of her mouth to the back of her cheeks. "Especially since neither one of us was active in any way when we first met. I grew up in a small town in Vermont that had a Catholic church and a Congregational church. We went to the Congregational church, sang in the choir, attended Sunday school, did all that. Johnny grew up in St. Louis. His mom was religious, but he wasn't when he was younger. Along in my teens I recognized a disconnect between what was going on in the church and what was going on in the village. And from then on," she said, looking for a diplomatic way of phrasing this point, "organized religion has not been easy for me."

"Do you remember a particular moment where Johnny came back and said, 'You know, I'm thinking about this religion thing?'" I asked.

"The summer after our son Fred was born, he went to a lot of different churches. We were stationed in Virginia then, and he was obviously seeking something. I didn't completely understand it or pay a lot of attention to it. And then he went home to St. Louis. When he came back, I remember he came in the bedroom and flung himself down on the bed. He was so happy. He'd been baptized.

"And then the first time I ever went to his church, it was totally different from what I had experienced growing up. In a Congregational church, in those years, you were quiet. To go to a church where people were shouting was quite an experience. But it's not a church that ever attracted me. I used to go occasionally, because of the kids."

"Did they take to it?" I asked.

"Well," she chuckled, "they had no choice. When they were little, he dragged them." But their children weren't active now. Ellen said that when their son Fred turned sixteen and Johnny didn't force him to church anymore, that was the happiest day of Fred's life up until that point. Johnny expressed hope that they still might return to the fold, because he himself was thirty-two when he was first baptized. But he admitted it didn't seem likely.

I looked at Ellen. She adjusted the wide, plastic rims of her glasses up to the bridge of her nose. "Johnny says that while your faith isn't explicit, your contributions to the life and faith of the church are enormous."

"Because he's always volunteering 'em." Ellen giggled. She jerked her hand to her mouth to keep the food from falling out. "The church is having a dinner," she said, imitating one of his requests, "could you roast a turkey?" She tried to catch her laughter but couldn't. "I think it probably would have been harder for us if I had been a little bit more worldly than I am. But I'm a small town girl with a country background."

Ellen described the first ten or fifteen years of Johnny's life of faith as a real challenge to their family. Religion put a major strain on their relationship. In Ellen's clear-eyed interpretation of that period, I caught a reflection of Liz and me, and the way my religious walk led me away from her. He belonged to a church that made unusually extensive demands on his time, and sometimes he brought the kids to church and they stayed with him until one in the morning on school nights. Surveying the rigidness Ellen described, Johnny shrugged his shoulders. "A lot of the things with the children that we did early on," he said, "I found out that I was going overboard. And I apologized to my children and my wife for carrying them through that period of time."

"Yeah," Ellen said. "But then we got out of there and got to Mother Booker." The two of them grinned together. It was Mother Booker whose portrait hung next to the clock at the First Apostolic Faith Church. "She was just like a lovely grandmother to the children. Completely different."

Over lunch Ellen had painted over the spiritual portrait Johnny had made earlier that morning. Johnny had airbrushed Ellen to the point that she had seemed a tireless aide to the church's mission. But in spite of their different interpretations of her faith, I found myself getting a little misty-eyed over the tuna fish. That Johnny Lay, a speaking-in-tongues preacher with what must be a nearly, if not entirely, all black congregation was married to Ellen, a white woman who spent her adult life disregarding all of organized religion, including her husband's own church, struck me as hilarious and beautiful. There I was, struggling to keep up with my girlfriend in Chicago over the phone. Now *this* couple had had some things to work through.

"So I guess you never envisioned when you were growing up that you'd end up being the wife of a black Pentecostal preacher?" I felt I had to ask.

Ellen laughed. "It was the last thing in the world. The church that I grew up in was so different than the one that he's a part of. You went on Sundays and you went to choir rehearsals. Everybody knew the minister and the family. The minister's wife gave piano lessons to the kids. But there weren't all these rules and regulations, that if you didn't believe this you were forever damned to lakes of fire. Organized religion is just more than I can comprehend. I don't remember any of that in the teaching that we had. But it's probably just as well, the way it's worked out. I'm sort of areligious. If I had more intense or rigid belief, I think we would have had some real problems. All the sisters in the church, they say, 'Mrs. Lay, you should get saved, you've got to come to church.' And I think, 'Now, if I've been with Johnny for thirty-four years and I haven't been motivated to do it, then their words are really falling on some really deaf ears.'" Even Johnny joined in this joke.

Before I said goodbye to the Lays, I asked Johnny if his mentor and the founder of First Apostolic, Mother Booker, was in good enough shape to share a little of her time with me. Johnny mulled over the possibility before concluding yes. We arranged to meet at his church a couple of days later.

[17]

Johnny Lay was already waiting in his flatbed truck in front of his church at the corner of Bush and Pierce when I arrived. Maybe because we were going to visit his pastor and mentor, Johnny had on a blazer and a cool-looking, beret-type hat. He looked, in a way, semiformal. Within fifteen minutes and a dozen hills, we reached the home of Mother Booker's grandson. He owned a hardware store down the block and had come home to open the door for us. Johnny and I took seats in the downstairs living room on upholstered chairs.

"She'll be down in a minute," Johnny promised.

A couple of minutes passed. I fidgeted, rubbing my cuticles with the tip of my thumb on the edge of my seat, in anticipation of Mother Booker's arrival. I felt as though I were backstage, a celebrity hound, some advance scout for Willard Scott. Then I heard the soft creak of wooden stairs. Mother Booker poked her head in the doorway. She was small—maybe five feet tall in high heels—mahogany, and ancient, but she could still shuffle her own way into the living room. Johnny greeted her with a two-handed shake and a squeeze.

"Praise the Lord, Mother Booker," he said.

"Praaaaise the Lawd," she squealed, stretching the phrase like silly putty.

I approached her anxiously and extended my hand. "How're you doing, Mother Booker?"

She gazed up at Johnny, who stood at least a foot taller than her, with a puzzled look that suggested that the ambassador from Israel had made a diplomatic gaffe. Mother Booker, consciously or not, stonewalled me. I fumbled out loud for a minute, searching for other appropriate greetings. After a moment of bumbling, the certain success of mimicry dawned on me. "Praise the Lord, Mother Booker."

Her pupils, specks of coal encased in ivory, shone with recognition. "Praaaaise the Lawd," she answered giddily. Her reply was almost Pavlovian. How many times had she said this in her life? I would need a calculator with exponents to do the math.

Johnny and I eased her into the seat between us. We were careful not to disrupt her snack. Her mouth, stocked with the crumbs of biscuits she clutched in a napkin against her lap, looked parched. Achingly, she rested a mug of tea into her lap with her right hand. I knew I was in the right place when I caught a glimpse of the print on her mug. Here, in my presence, was this 102-year-old woman who had started a Pentecostal church in her own living room. The pastor of that church for nearly sixty years, she cradled a cup that extended the red carpet for me. The mug read, "Selma's Bat Mitzvah, November 1998." Praise the Lord, indeed.

Mother Booker began suddenly, without a question having been asked. She made reference to a man named Elder Walker who led a revival years earlier in San Francisco. "Did you know him?" she asked Johnny.

"No, I only know him through you telling me about him. Tell us about that revival."

"Well, I could show you a picture. But my pictures, they're all burned and destroyed." A house fire in May of 1997, Johnny told me while Mother Booker sat in sad-eyed recollection, had consumed many of her own photographs and the church's archives. This fire ultimately brought her here to live with her grandson and his family. The way she said "burned and destroyed" sounded like she had not forgiven the blaze.

"You know he's dead?" she said. "Dead" from her mouth sounded like day-id. She squinted. I thought she must be trying to visualize this particular man in the compression of the years. "I wasn't saved then."

"When was she saved?" I asked Johnny to clarify.

"1921. She got the Holy Ghost in '21 in Yuma, Arizona."

"Been so long ago, I hardly remember. But you cain't argue when you get the Holy Ghost," Mother Booker said. I didn't think she even knew I was present in the room. She looked only at Johnny, who asked her the questions. Lulled by her slow patter and Johnny's questions, I never expected her to turn so suddenly and dramatically toward me. But in a moment she had swiveled her head to look in my direction. "*You* baptized in his name?" From a voyeur I became a participant. At point-blank range she asked if I was a believer in what she had spent her life professing. Even Johnny hadn't yet asked me this question. Maybe I had intentionally not told him. Whether he assumed the answer or I avoided the question was of little importance in that moment. What I wished I could say was how much respect and admiration I had for Jesus. "Rosetta," I'd say, sidling close, a whisper among friends, "he's one of my three or four all-time favorite Jews. And no, while I'm not saved, I've gotta tell you, I am a very, very big fan."

"No," I said, "I'm not."

"Nooo?" I startled her with my reply. "You can come to church, get baptized, and we'll tarry with you, till you get the Holy Ghost." Then she began to speak of her children. She ran down the list: of her five, four had died. I couldn't decipher if she imagined the birth order she traced or if she had it right.

When I'd sat in the pews of First Apostolic Faith Church, I'd assumed that the pastor perceived my otherness the same way I had, on the basis of race. But what hit me was that perhaps an Evangelical tells people apart first and foremost by their salvation, as though they had a gift of spiritual X-ray vision. For them, there was no greater chasm between one person and another than "saved" and "unsaved": not gender, not race, not sexuality, not class. Salvation was the one difference between me and Jeff Paul, but it was the big one. During our conversation at Liberty University, I'd felt that the difference was of minimal importance; he'd maintained that it was of ultimate significance.

Mother Booker pawed at the veins that rose from the backs of her hands like an aerial photograph of a river's delta. "I can't tell the story just as perfect as it is," Mother Booker said. I felt a sudden shiver at her words. This admission offered my first inkling that despite her disorientation, she still recognized the length of her life's arc. In other words, she didn't think she was only forty-five, or that we were speaking in 1966. In her shrunken frame and her bony shoulders, I saw how she had bowed under the weight of her years, had surrendered—while seemingly a function of neurological necessity—the need to remember chronology. This phrase in particular, "I can't tell the story just as perfect as it is," a beautiful potential introduction to the autobiography she would never write, italicized itself in the same way a teacher might twist her enunciation to inform you that what she had just said would most definitely be on the test.

Rosetta Booker hadn't even meet Johnny Lay until the middle of the 1970s, after Johnny had served his twenty years in the Marines, a full forty years into Mother Booker's ministry. I was thinking about that chronology as Johnny tried unsuccessfully to nudge Mother Booker into the space where the events of her life were laid out neatly and clearly. "Did God tell you to start a church in your house in 1936?" he asked.

"When I got the Holy Ghost," she mumbled, "where was we living at that time?"

"Yuma," Johnny and I said in unison. I was getting the hang of it.

Before we arrived at Mother Booker's, Johnny had driven me past 1709 Baker Street, the house where Mother Booker heard the call to start her own church. I was wondering about what moves someone to start a church, or for that matter, a coffee shop? Was the idea necessarily well defined, or

could it be more inchoate? Is the seed always a need, a niche that needs to
be filled? Or as with my pilgrimage, does it begin with a whim? Johnny said
that Albert and Rosetta Holton and their children had attended a church
in Oakland in the first half of the 1930s, and the Sunday drives across the
bay had become too burdensome for her and her growing family. Necessity
being the mother of epiphany—to revise a phrase—she heard the voice and
converted her living room into a sanctuary. Need then prompted the whim
that became the church.

"There was no church in San Francisco?" I asked Johnny.

"Not Apostolic. That's why that's called First Apostolic." Part of the
potency of the then-adolescent Pentecostal worship tradition derived from
the lack of hierarchical church structures. If somebody got the call—man
or woman, white or black—and found the space to hold prayer meetings,
then that person became a preacher in the very act of convening a community for worship.

Mother Booker turned toward me again. "Where you from?"

I removed my wallet from the front pocket of my pants, opened it up,
and pulled a "God Is" card from the crease where the cash goes. I held it
up to Johnny, asked for approval, and when I received the go-ahead, I
handed the card to her.

"God Is," she read slowly from the card. "That's true. An Oral History
. . . of Faith . . . in America. . . . God Is."

In the Copy Cop that anxious morning in July, I had assumed that the
"God Is" of the title was part of a prologue, the opening phrase of a sentence that people would finish in vastly different ways. Mother Booker
transformed "God Is" from an introductory subject to a complete sentence. In my planning, and in the five minutes I had spent sketching the
look of the business card, I had failed to consider that possibility.

I suddenly suspected that Mother Booker and I spoke some private language, and she might be willing to share it with me if only I asked. "So
you started a church. That's what Pastor Lay's telling me. That you started
a church."

"You all give me some shoes, some clothing." She thanked Johnny for
something out of the blue.

"See," Johnny said in a whisper, "when the church burned, when her
house burned, the Church bought her a new wardrobe."

"Talk out," Mother Booker said with a surprisingly booming voice. "You
can talk out." I fought back a giggle.

Johnny dutifully repeated what he told me. "At the fire at your house, we
lost a lot of records." He was almost shouting now. "A lot of your clothes
and a lot of your pictures. May 18, 1997."

"Oh yes. Oh yeah." She might have wished she hadn't requested volume. She looked up at the ceiling, then down again at my card. "God . . . Is," she started to read again from my card. "an Oral History . . . of Faith . . . in America."

"Yes," Johnny said. "This is the gentleman here."

"I think he'll find something, too," she said.

Johnny kept talking, diverting Mother Booker's biographical snippets my way, though once again my attention refocused on her. In that moment, minuscule and fleeting as it was, I hoped, maybe even trusted, that Mother Booker knew, without my having told her, what I sought. "You think I'll find something?" I asked, anticipating a phrase, expecting a moment, one single moment, a gesture, a wink, less even, a twitch that would reveal that she understood why I traveled. I was poised to ask her what would I find, what might I uncover. Did she know? And if so, how did she know? Had I arrived hoping to find an oracle, a prophetess, a still breathing *I Ching*?

"If you're walking with the Lord, I believe the Lord will make a way for you," Mother Booker said. "He says, 'Come out from among them.' That's what *I'm* trying to do." There was something in Mother Booker's voice, a note of assurance, the wrinkled oblivion that nearly camouflaged the century-old knowledge, that again hinted that she intended something other, or at least in addition to, what Johnny transmitted back to me. Was this wishful thinking, or some unspoken understanding? I didn't know. But when she raised her hand, with its long brown fingers like a tree's roots, my gut signaled to me that her words were mine and that the Lord would make a way for me, too. I can't explain that. I simply felt it.

I asked Johnny whether she spoke often of her life while still in the pulpit.

"All the time. Hammered it home." He suggested that he couldn't not know about her life, given the extent to which she talked about how the Lord had called to her, how she had converted her home into the first Apostolic church in San Francisco, about her time in the Mexican church in Yuma, and all the orbiting minutia that constituted the years since 1897.

Pastor Lay narrated Mother Booker's life to her, for me, from the time she was Rosie and Rosetta to the years she was known as Sister Booker, and from the years when she was Mrs. Albert Holton until her husband died, up through and including the moment someone first called her Mother Booker and the title stuck.

I carried a release form around with me, so that after an interview I could secure my conversational partner's permission in transmitting their story. When I placed the release in front of Mother Booker, she asked me, "Which name do you wish me to use?" We listened to her deliberate for

half a minute—Mrs. Booker, Mrs. Albert Holton—wobbling through the
merits of one name to another, before Johnny stepped in to help.

"Just sign it Rosetta Booker, Mother Booker. That's right. That's you."
So she did.

A person hopes for a long life, prays for it even, only to watch her children die, as Mother Booker had, one by one. Someone who lives this long
endures in such a way that she can't recall precisely which of these children are dead and which are not. So she must ask for clarification. One
lives so long that one outlives one's own memory, living so fully that the
years overflow and drip down the side of the mouth like crumbs. Mother
Booker had lived fully enough, though, shared her life enough that as her
memory scuttled away, someone stood poised to retrieve the life for her
when she lost track of it. Somebody has continued to minister to you,
Mother Booker, because you ministered to him. He absorbed your history
as a tributary of his own, considering himself privileged and duty bound
to narrate your life back to you.

When Johnny and I had spoken at his home, he had acknowledged that
he did not know who would carry on Mother Booker's legacy. "I'm doing
it to this point, but none of her family, no grandchildren, no sons, no great-
grands, have carried on her legacy. And you know, Tom, I wonder who
will take on my legacy. My children aren't in the church. They're not following." He conceded these points with a deep regret in his voice, sounding resigned to the breakdown in baton passing.

When I praised the Lord to Mother Booker when we parted, and after I
thanked Johnny for his generosity and his time, I felt something wash over
me—urgency tinged with nostalgia—that made me feel larger, almost physically heavier—something inspiring and melancholy all at once. I wanted
to recount to Pastor Johnny Lay the parable of the stranger.

There is a stranger who arrives in your empty church one Wednesday
afternoon. He is timid, his prayers muzzled by his insecurities. He does not
look up, he prays with his head down, while the other congregants—the
two of them—sigh and soar. He remains after the service to hear the Bible
study, and after the lesson ends, he asks for a moment. Is he a journalist
or a student? A Pentecostal or an undecided? You have not seen him before. The moment he requests turns into an hour. Because you are hospitable, you are willing to meet him the following morning to talk more.
A few days later, the stranger sits recording the perambulations of your
mentor. Somewhere between his anonymity and his immersion in your life,
he changes shape. Under cover of ignorance—or was it just innocence—
the stranger becomes a torchbearer. You watch the stranger fade in the
rear-view mirror, still not sure how he found you, or what you left him.

When I was bracketed by Mother Booker and Pastor Lay during our ninety minutes together, and when I left them—Johnny in his pickup truck, Mother Booker anxiously staring out the window at sidewalk-colored clouds—I experienced a shudder of recognition, suddenly aware that I had become a leg in their relay. Admittedly I was not much, if only because I had been in their midst for days, not years. Regardless, I had learned enough to want to proclaim that I, a seemingly small thing, had arrived.

Of course, Dolores Ledbetter had shown me, right from the source, that small things are big things. That I was Jewish, that I had not accepted Jesus as my personal savior, that I was a stranger, these were, in the end, inconsequential attributes. Johnny and Ellen and Mother Booker had taken me into their homes and their lives, and we had spoken. They had received me hospitably. And so I carried them with me. Religion, I was beginning to realize, hinges on this transmission from one generation to another, from teacher to student, parent to child, and sometimes, stranger to stranger. What we receive from our families, how we break from, ignore, and rebind those inheritances: this is the backdrop against which all of our searches take place.

There came a time when, having lived so long, your pupil, your congregant and successor, came to remind you who you are and who you were. He introduced this young man who traveled from the East, who watched you fade in and out. The young man heard the pupil speak of legacies lost, genealogies disintegrating. The young man even watched the mentor wander while sitting still. But by the time he said good-bye he understood that the slivers of history he'd heard, the lessons of the life he'd learned, had become a part of him. The pastor's privilege, like his duty, was his as well. And if he failed to transmit them, small and sacred as they were, then he would somehow be culpable, alongside that house fire, of turning a life, a church, and a mission into ash.

———————— o ————————

At my brother's place in San Francisco, I logged on to the Internet on the computer in his guest room. More than ten days had passed since my conversation with Harvey Lee Green, and I suspected that a search of the on-line version of the Raleigh, North Carolina, daily newspaper would inform me of Harvey's current circumstances. Whether the governor had issued a stay of the execution or the state had killed Harvey by lethal injection, the outcome had already been decided. For a few days I had deliberated, bouncing between the impulse to find out and the longing to hover in the space between willful ignorance and knowledge. The night before I departed San Francisco to drive south, I ended my equivocation and searched for Harvey's fate.

The pleas for clemency had been denied. The wishes of the victims' families had been granted. The judgment of a North Carolina jury had been carried out. Harvey Lee Green had been executed on schedule.

My brother and his wife were upstairs, preparing their son for bed. In the guest room off their garage, with Nate's laughter barely audible, I logged off the Internet and recalled the thickness of the afternoon when we spoke. Before I left him, before I stepped out into the heavy air that preceded Hurricane Floyd's arrival, I took a few photographs of Harvey. After I snapped six or seven pictures with my manual camera, Captain Hudson, the prison officer who sat in the room, motioned that the time had come to go. I asked for a moment to take one more photo. Captain Hudson waved his hand, granting permission. Harvey stayed seated in his chair. For half a minute I kneeled, then crouched, then shifted back to a kneel, while I clicked the aperture back and forth, letting in more light, then less, in the dimly lit room. I wanted to get a great, last picture. I watched the air leave Harvey's nostrils and his shoulders rise with a gesture of slight exasperation. And then, as I focused more, I realized that as long as I continued to focus, nothing would happen to him. So I intentionally turned the lens blurry, and then refocused. Harvey sat, the prison staff stood, and I fumbled to ensure myself and Harvey more time. In that long moment, I almost pretended that there was no crime and no sentence, no two victims, and no dead man walking.

I walked upstairs to say good night. I woke up early to pick up the rental car I would drive down south. In Harvey Lee Green, I now had another story I felt bound to pass on.

[18]

Along the Pacific Coast south of the Bay Area, Highway 1 offers a blur of cars that whiz in both directions. Driving south and looking for an address on the east side of the road demands hyperattentiveness and a left turn. And a left turn on Route 1 is a tall task. With patience punctuated by a moment of bravado, I made the left and pulled onto a gravel driveway fronted by a metal mailbox. I shifted from drive to park in front of a California ranch house. My rental car was the only car in the driveway. Behind the house was a field of browning grass. I knocked on the door.

"Usilinanda?" I asked a dour-looking, middle-aged monk.

"Upstairs," he answered, opening the front door wide enough for me to enter. As I entered the Burmese Buddhist Monastery of Half Moon Bay, California, the stairs swallowed the sound of my steps, and led to an airy, second floor space. I noticed several gilded, larger-than-human Buddhas lining the room's walls. One sat cross-legged on a pedestal at the back of the room. Another lounged at the base of a narrow stage, its arm propped behind its head as though the reclining Buddha sat poolside.

Usilinanda was seated on the second story's carpeted floor. He smiled when I walked into the room, though he did not move. He had a youthful quality for an elderly man. He'd draped a burgundy robe over himself, tucked it under his legs, and slung it over his shoulder. Unlike the wardrobe worn by Brother Gus, which covered him from chin to toes, the monastic uniform of Usilinanda revealed his skin and the body's shape. The robe left one thin, brown shoulder bare. There I was, in my nearly ubiquitous Chuck Taylors, khakis, and short-sleeved, collared shirt greeting a seventy-year-old religious leader whose garment left the slightly sagging skin of his chest and the charcoal-shadowed crease of his armpit exposed. Etiquette questions I hadn't thought through rushed over me. What do you do when meeting a Buddhist monk you've never met? Shake hands? Bow? High-five?

I chose none of the above. Standing, I towered above him, so I sat. My position framed him between two of the statuesque Buddhas. "Were you born and raised to be a monk?" I asked after I'd crawled across the floor to set up my recording equipment.

"Not born and raised," he answered, his voice soft, his accent clearly indicating that English was not his first language. "It was my own decision. It was during the Japanese occupation, during the World War II, when many Burmese people joined the resistance movement and fought against the Japanese. I was sixteen: too young at the time to join, too young to go out and earn a living, and too old to be home and doing nothing. So I decided to get a taste of the religious life. My decision then was for only one month. That one month stretched into now more than fifty years."

"You liked what you found?"

"Oh yes."

Before he became a monk, Usilinanda did what all Burmese boys do: as a seven-year-old, he spent three days as a sort of monk-in-training. The monastic life is deeply revered in Burma, and little boys wear robes, have their hair shaved off, and spend a few days and nights at a sleep-away monastery. The idea is both to inculcate respect for the institution and pique the interest of potential future monks. My friend Colin Evans grew up in Allentown, Pennsylvania, but he did this, too. The son of an Irish father and a Burmese mother, Colin visited Burma with his parents as a young boy and lived for three days as an initiate. Today, he's a night-life-adoring entrepreneur. Actually, it was at a party Colin invited me to that I had met Liz, so I considered him something of a rabbit's foot. Colin suggested that while out west I should call his aunt, Kin Kin Min, a devoted member of the Buddhist laity and a student of this monk named Usilinanda. It was Aunt Kin Kin who arranged my conversation with Usilinanda. Colin wouldn't lead me wrong.

The monk told me that after his three-day cycle ended, and as he grew older, the sight of older friends choosing the monk's life stirred him with a sort of religious envy. So at the age of sixteen he decided to try it.

"At first," he said, "my father didn't believe me when I told him I wanted to become a monk. To my teacher, he says, 'Bande,'—bande means teacher—'my son says he wants to be a novice for one month, but I don't know.' But as soon as I changed to the robes, I think I changed also. I became a very serious person. And so in a few moments I was changed from a frolicking kid to a serious adult."

"Was being a serious person something that you assumed monks were?"

"Oh yes," he said. "They were always serious when I saw them."

"Do you have a different opinion of monks now, now that you are one? I mean, are monks always serious?"

"Always serious," he said, the hint of a smile passing over his gray lips. "As a monk, the main thing is to be dignified." But just as he said this, a strange thing started to happen: Usilinanda couldn't keep a straight face. "We should always be serious," he said, and what had been a smile turned into a gut-busting, breath-losing laughter attack. For a moment I thought I might have to rise, step behind him, and offer a few good chiropractic whacks on the back. Just what was so funny? Was he reminiscing about the straight-laced, no-nonsense monks of his youth? Or perhaps, recalling the glum monk who'd answered the door, those of his present? "I am different," he said, squeezing words out past his breathlessness. "Talk to other monks: they may not be as smiling as I am."

He struggled to gather himself. "Once I visited a meditation center belonging to another religion, and I was talking to a man there. The man who accompanied me asked the other man whether he had seen a Buddhist monk in the building, and this other man said, 'No.' My companion said, 'You are talking to a Buddhist monk.' The other man said, 'Is he a Buddhist monk? I did not think Buddhist monks smile.'"

The thought sounded familiar. I think I, and maybe other people, sense that the people who take religion most seriously lack the sense-of-humor gene, the intensity of their religious commitments somehow precluding their ability to look lightly on anything. The world is at stake in every moment, souls are being won or lost, the true faith is being corrupted, and it is their task to halt the deterioration. I imagined they believe that they take their cues from God. In my reading of the Torah, I could not recall a moment in which God smiled or laughed. Perhaps the commentaries of the rabbis expound on that. Perhaps there is a reason. But certainly, humorless zealots model their behavior from somewhere.

Buddhism, however, didn't strike me this way. Buddhism revolves not around a god or a doctrine or a dogma, but around a person and a story. A young prince renounces his royalty, chooses to live as an ascetic, and achieves a level of clarity about the world, the suffering he feels and sees, and the path to the cessation of that suffering. Carved into many of the faces of ancient, hulking statues of the Buddha from Thailand to Tibet were smiles.

Though in a number of countries the Buddha has been transformed into a larger-than-life, supernatural being, the tradition's earliest teachings consistently show him to be a humble man with a self-subversive side. Enlightenment was not his to experience alone; others could find it, too. He had no interest, it seems, in being deified or glorified. Rather, he is said to have instructed his disciples to analyze not only the content of his teachings but the teacher himself. Thanks to his example, Buddhism stresses practice over belief. If there is a Buddhist motto, it is, "Come and see for yourself." I believe it may well have been Buddhism that, several millennia ago, gave birth to our beloved American notion that the spiritual path is a self-guided tour.

Yet Usilinanda conceded that the agency and independence of the individual practitioner eluded many in his native country. "In Burma, there is so much respect for the monks. Sometimes people come to this monastery with questions, but mostly they come and listen. People think that if they ask questions, it might be disrespectful to the monk or something like that."

"Has that changed here in the United States?" I asked.

"Oh yes. It's very different here. Here we have to leave room for questions and answers whenever we give a talk. People here are trained to ask questions and they are not reluctant to ask. They don't think that asking questions is disrespectful to the speaker. They're more open, like the audiences in the Buddha's time. And of course the Buddha taught by asking questions." Clearly, Usilinanda would feel at home at the Islamic Center of Greater Toledo, where ceaseless inquiry was the party line of the faithful I'd met. "I like people asking questions. Because then I know that they are interested in my talk. There is interaction. If they do not understand something, I can supplement. If there were mistakes in my talk, I can correct. Sometimes there are tough questions," he said, emitting a little giggle. "But yes, it's very different here."

Buddhists first started arriving in the United States during the California Gold Rush of the mid-nineteenth century. Hundreds of thousands of Chinese Buddhists immigrated to California and the western territories before the U.S. government incorporated them as states. They worked as farm laborers and on the track-laying teams of the Transcontinental Railroad. The immigrants established the first American temple in San Francisco in 1853. By the turn of the century, the entire Pacific coast was dotted with hundreds of Buddhist shrines. As more Buddhists immigrated, especially in the same tide of immigrants that brought an influx of Muslims and Hindus to the country in the 1960s, Buddhism seeped into the American religious vernacular. Although the Buddhism practiced by immigrant communities retained elements of their home cultures, Americans, in particular college-educated white Americans, developed their own Western form of the Eastern tradition. At the Seattle Zen Center, for example, where I knocked and nobody heard, I fully expected to see a meditation circle filled with middle-aged white people. To a demographic disenchanted with organized religion, mistrustful of authority, and inclined to seek spiritual independence, Buddhism offered a made-to-order blend of spiritual self-initiative and nontheistic spirituality. Practical, see-for-yourself religious paths, Buddhism and American spiritual experimentation were in some respects made for one another.

And yet, despite the growth of Buddhism here, an acceptance of the Four Noble Truths appeared anathema to American culture.

"Our American culture," I said, "is really permeated with desire, and craving, and suffering. In fact, it seems that our culture doesn't see desire as a negative thing, but quite the opposite."

"Ahh yes," he said. Usilinanda looked glum for the first time. "People need to be realistic. Those who follow this desire and sensual pleasures are deceiving themselves. They don't want to accept that there is suffering. When this suffering is caused by craving, they don't want to give up the craving. We must understand the First Noble Truth of suffering: What is suffering? According to the teachings of the Buddha, suffering is not just painfulness. It is more than that. Every experience in the world is suffering, because every experience has a beginning and an end. You enjoy sensual pleasures, but there is the beginning of these pleasures and then there is an end. Anything that has a beginning and an end is impermanent. This is what the Buddha meant by the Pali word *dukkha*." *Dukkha* signified the suffering caused by impermanence. Pali is an ancient Indian language.

"Whatever is impermanent *is* suffering, according to the criteria given by the Buddha. We are constantly bombarded by the arising and disappearing of our desires and our cravings and ourselves. Whatever you look at, wherever you go with your mind: *here* arising and disappearing, *there* arising and disappearing.

"But we want things to be permanent. You buy a car and you want that car to be always new, but you know that from the moment you buy it, it becomes older and older. And you yourself are also becoming older and older, no matter how much you say you want to become young. You may undergo plastic surgery, but even when you are on the operating table, you are getting older and older, second by second. That we must realize.

"But that should not depress us or make us give up hope. We must do whatever we can for our happiness. But happiness does not mean just enjoyment of sensual pleasures. Happiness you get through spiritual practices. Happiness you get through helping other people. Happiness you get through improving the conditions of life for others as well as for you. But nowadays," he said, beginning for the first time to sound like a wizened seventy-year-old, "people are driven to just that one thing: enjoyment. Enjoyment. Enjoyment of sensual pleasures."

The mat squeaked as I readjusted my sitting position. "I think many Americans would say they're willing to accept self-deception," I said. "And so a response to your teachings might be, We understand that the world is suffering. We understand the world is impermanent. We don't want to pay attention to that; in fact, that's *why* we work so fastidiously at own our self-deception."

Usilinanda was laughing again. This logic looked silly to him. "You *have* to pay attention to it. You cannot escape. You may not want to think about it, but you have to experience it. It is inevitable. Life is not just a bed of roses. Suppose I want to own a car: I have desire for the car, and if I don't get it, I will be sad. And after I get it, I have to look after it. I will have to see to it that it does not get bumped, or stolen away. See, there are two kinds of *dukkha* regarding things: before you get it you have to make the effort to get it; that is one kind of suffering. And after you get it you have to protect it; that is another kind. But if you don't want to buy a car at all, then you don't have to worry about the car." We both laughed.

"No doubt about that," I said. "But you still have to worry about getting around places. If you have a bicycle, you have to worry about the bicycle. If you take a bus, you have to worry about the schedule."

"Yes, this is true."

"So, unless you resolve to spend your life within walking distance, there will be things you still have to worry about."

The monk shook his head, smiling matter-of-factly. "Not as much as when you have a car."

Okay, so clearly Usilinanda had an anticar bias. Mine was the only one in the monks' driveway. Pining for a car, then buying (or leasing or renting) it, driving, parking, repairing, protecting: these aspects of a driver's life that to most Americans signaled convenience and mobility represented freedom's underside to the Burmese monk. Car advertisements stress that we drive to feel free, and in a profound way I invested heavily in the mythology of the American road, tracking the landscape of the Beat poets and the lure of the cross-country adventure with the attentiveness of financial analysts to the figures that might make them rich. Usilinanda, on the other hand, saw the car as one more shackle, one more source of suffering, one additional totem of impermanence. The car culture fed my personal, and our collective, imaginations, stoking our desires to see what life is like elsewhere, to believe the grass is greener, the air cleaner, the highway clearer, elsewhere.

Yet even before I met Usilinanda, I had been planning to abandon the car when I reached Los Angeles, an act that, in a world of small things, approached the treason of outing oneself as a Communist during the McCarthy hearings. No car in LA? Impossible. Without the keys, minus a car, I would be bound to go only when I could find a ride. Yet being bound did not feel binding. I agreed with Usilinanda. A car demanded responsibility and was a prime source of *dukkha,* while a bus stop, for example, invited an opportunity for surrender. Of course the bus offers thirty-one flavors of suffering too. You go when the bus comes. You sit only if there are seats. You don't use the quickest route. You are subject to odors not your own. Nevertheless, being a passenger seemed at once a white flag and a declaration of independence. Part of me agreed with the monk, but I felt certain that I couldn't pull off a road trip without a car, unless I wanted to follow in Dolores Ledbetter's Greyhound footprints.

This emphasis on mobility, I thought, must have an impact on the Burmese Buddhists that Usilinanda teaches and tends to. "America," I said, "has a tradition that encourages, or at least tempts, immigrants to turn away from their home cultures and native languages and become American. When you move among different Burmese communities, do you worry about the children who are not being taught how to preserve your tradition?"

"Ahh." The monk paused. "I worry a lot about that. I'm always telling them to keep this tradition alive and to hand down this tradition as much as they can. I tell them not to worry about pure Burmese culture. After two generations, their children will lose this anyway. They will be Americans and they will not much care about Burmese culture. But a lot of Burmese culture is based upon Buddhist teachings. So when you hand down the Buddhist culture to your offspring, you are handing down the Burmese culture also. So I tell them, '*Please* hand down the religious inheritance to them.' Although they have become Americans, they can still keep that tradition with them."

Painted portraits lined the stairway at the Half Moon Bay monastery. Each was a conventional, framed oil painting of a bald monk in a burgundy robe, staring from the picture, stoic, almost severe. In one of them I saw Usilinanda. He had a stare on like he was a boxer at a prefight weigh-in. Usilinanda saw Americanness as a threat to the handing-down of Burmese Buddhist religious inheritance. In Lowell, Massachusetts, Sokha Diep shared the monk's anxiety for her own Cambodian Buddhist practice and identity. To be American and remain culturally Buddhist were not mutually exclusive, but the specter of the indigenous religious tradition's evaporation on American soil haunted both the monk and Sokha.

I rose from the mat and thanked Usilinanda for his time. While driving south down Route 1, I shook my head, impressed and bewildered at the monk's steadfast refusal to smile for a picture. I had tried all my tricks: the keeping-up-the-banter-while-I-focused routine, the asking-politely-then-pleading bit, and yet his lips did not budge upward even once. He laughed half the time we were together, giggling, guffawing, almost gripping the carpet for a crutch as he described the seriousness of the monastic life. I couldn't decipher which face was the more authentic—the smiling monk or the serious monk, the self as defined by experience and personality and perspective, or the self as defined by title and tradition and expectation. If the latter were the party line, then why would he have shown his playful side to me, a first-time visitor, a novice just passing through? But if his purpose was to expose me to the joy of his calling, then why not smile for the camera, permitting those who would see his picture a glimpse at what I had seen? If the Buddha could smile for posterity, despite what he knew of the First Noble Truth and the suffering of the world, why couldn't the monk?

I met Usilinanda a day after visiting Mother Booker. Not surprisingly, his words resonated amid those of Johnny Lay. Both had mounting concerns, as aging religious leaders, about the perils of ensuring a lasting religious bequest. "Keep this tradition alive," Usilinanda tells the young Burmese he teaches and who visit the monastery. "Hand it down. This is your inheritance." In former cultures, other places, and onetime homes, the words are commands, inevitabilities. In America, they sound like pleas.

[19]

After a day in Salinas, California, I drove south to Los Angeles, where I dropped off my rental car and spent the weekend with Chris Greene, another childhood friend who had relocated out West. He lived in Santa Monica, a block away from the Pacific Ocean. He commuted to his job in radio sales along LA's choked highways, and learned to surf on the weekends. I figured he was about as geographically removed from Manhattan as possible without living out at sea. I arrived at his apartment just as the sun dipped beneath the distant waterline.

"It's Friday night," I told Chris after we had spent twenty minutes catching up.

I pulled tapered white candles, a bottle of red wine, and a loaf of French bread from my bag and self-consciously started to turn his round table into a makeshift Shabbat center. Because I had never done this in front of Chris, the self-conscious part of me figured I would be subject to a hazing for toting my road-show ritual into his place. But graciously Chris, dragging slowly on a cigarette plucked from the pack on his coffee table, observed thoughtfully, as if taking in a surprisingly compelling show on the Discovery Channel. I asked if he had a light. Holding his Bic lighter up to the candles' wicks, I smiled, grateful and surprised at how routinely the process had gone. Instead of ducking under cat calls of "Rabbi" and the teasingly murmured asides of "Freak," I shared with Chris the hallowing of the evening. I invited Chris into the ritual, as though I were the host, and he responded by playing the unexpectedly gracious guest.

We broke off chunks of bread and alternated between the wine and the bottles of beer we had opened when we arrived at his place. Chris was raised Jewish much the way I was, attending Hebrew School until he was thirteen, having a Bar Mitzvah, then treating the tradition like the nerdy cousin who had to be invited to the party, and neglecting him as soon as the event ended. The prayers I recited were standard one-liners, opening with the ubiquitous *Baruch Atah Adonai*—Blessed are You, O God—and closing with gratitude for the day of rest, the wine we drink, the bread we eat, and the hallowing of our time together. I toyed with a creative addition, blessing the cigarettes we were now both smoking and the beers we were both drinking. This was a most unorthodox observance. And yet, there we were.

"Everything is holy," I said, and in that moment I believed it to be true.

I asked him about the week that had passed, then told him about my time with Mother Booker. Her life soaked the space like a light rain.

While in Los Angeles I heard Dolores Huerta speak at a meeting. Huerta is a legendary union organizer and the co-founder, along with the late César Chávez, of the United Farm Workers. She could barely see over the podium, but her words made the audience rise from their seats to cheer her. Perhaps this was her discreet way of ensuring they could see her, too. Almost seventy when we met, Huerta stood just five feet, one inch tall in her flat, slipper-like black shoes. One could surmise that she had spent a lifetime walking and marching: her plain black skirt extended just below her knees, and she had calves like a sprinter. She was a whirling dervish of energy, chatter, and observation who paid attention to about seven things all at once. Befitting someone who had spent much of her life with her fist clenched in protest, she had a firm handshake.

Huerta was the first almost-celebrity I encountered on my trip. She was one of those untiring, unflappable, largely unwritten-about figures who leaves you with the indelible impression that you didn't learn much or enough in American History classes. I'd be lying if I claimed I knew of her or her work before I heard her speak, but clearly she stood as a figure of legendary importance in the movements for labor, farm worker, and Mexican American rights. She changed from anonymous to iconic for me within twenty minutes.

My brief conversation with Huerta fit snugly under the thematic umbrella of my previous week. I suppose this was in large part a function of the questions I asked—how she became involved in the labor movement, whether her kids were active in the same struggles she had been involved in—but Huerta seemed acutely aware of the role of transmission in her political and religious identity. Born in small-town, Catholic New Mexico in 1930, Huerta moved as a little girl with her siblings and her just-divorced mother to Stockton, California. Her mother remarried and worked as the proprietor of a local restaurant and hotel. Japanese, Chinese, Jewish, Filipino, and Mexican families came through those restaurant and hotel doors. This babble of immigrants worked in the fields and on the farms, lay track for railroad companies, and eked out meager livings as merchants. Huerta's mother allowed migrant farmworkers to stay in her hotel for free. Huerta's father, meanwhile, still in New Mexico, worked as a coal miner, became active in labor unions, eventually earned a college degree, and in 1938 won a seat in the New Mexico state legislature. Huerta's own activism was forged watching both of her parents' struggles and commitments to the poor and politically underrepresented.

Her Catholicism, as well as Chávez's, became a central, stabilizing feature for their farmworker rights movement. Because many of the workers were Catholics as well, the two leaders melded religious expression with material aims. In one famous episode that prefaced others, they consciously turned a political march into a penitential walk, transforming rally into confessional. They encouraged priests to say Mass for the workers in the fields. Religious devotion opened up political opportunities. Whether it constituted practical opportunism or authentic atonement is difficult to discern, perhaps because the practices seem to have been so distinctly both.

"Has faith changed over the years for you, or is it something that has remained a constant?" I asked her.

"I think it's gotten deeper. In the '60s and the '70s, during those years of the civil rights and peace movement, it was almost like anything was possible. You just felt like you could change the world. But then the work gets really hard, and it doesn't seem like you're making any progress. But to me faith is knowing that, despite that, something will happen. Everything around you says this can't possibly happen, and yet it does. I think you need faith to be in the labor movement, because the obstacles are just so enormous. The farm workers went up against the president of the United States, Richard Nixon, and the Governor of California, Ronald Reagan. Today we face the biggest agricultural companies in the world. But somehow you know you're going to survive. And you know that it's going to take time. And *that* takes faith."

In the midst of her own work with the union, Huerta gave birth to and raised eleven children.

"They grew up with the movement," she said. "They were on picket lines when they were babies. They went to jail with me."

"They went to jail when they were kids?" I asked.

"Oh yeah." She shrugged. "Some parents would say, 'My kids don't want to go picket.' And I'd always say, 'Well, why are you asking? Just take 'em.' My kids never had a choice. I said, 'Hey, we're gonna go picket.' I'd take them out of school and we'd go to a march. Perfect attendance was not in our family."

Dolores Huerta led her family in the same kind of migrant existence that her union's members lived. With her children in tow, she drove from city to city, leading grape boycotts; she visited the squalor of migrant labor camps where her members lived; she nursed her babies in between meetings. Huerta acknowledged the pangs of guilt she felt for the lifestyle she had imposed on her children, along with the poverty and peripatetic path she had chosen. But it was clear that in this matter she believed she had no choice. There was *La Causa*, "the Cause," at once her life and her calling. Her organizing work for the union paralleled the single-minded devotion of an itinerant, circuit-riding preacher, whose evangelical mission demands that everything else take a back seat. The United Farm Workers union was her flock, and a megaphone on a picket line was her pulpit.

History is rife with the messed-up offspring of world leaders and revolutionaries. Huerta's kids sounded as though they had matured well enough: among them were a doctor and a lawyer and a poet and a nurse and a teacher. But her children were initiated at birth into a community where a commitment to *La Causa* was more important than homework, prom dresses, and personal ambition. Huerta, and Chávez, too, promised family members and union members alike that from their sacrifice they would secure their dignity. That was the trade-off. And it was nonnegotiable. In her upbringing, Huerta received the rigors of Catholic life. In her adulthood, she transferred that rigor from orthodoxy to orthopraxy, from faith in right doctrine to faith in right practice. The movement took faith, and eventually every act of persisting in the work became an expression of faith.

I thanked Huerta. Then, on my way to catch a bus for the long ride from downtown LA to Santa Monica, my cell phone rang. My mom was on the other end. She asked what was happening, and for twenty minutes I talked about the last week, about Mother Booker and Usilinanda and Dolores Huerta. I had so much to tell her that I didn't gauge the tone in her voice that said she had something to tell me. When I finally took a breath, she told me that my brother-in-law Roderick's only brother Robin had died in a car accident two nights earlier in Topeka, Kansas, where he lived.

"How's Roderick?" Okay, she said. "How's Lynn?" My mom said my sister was all right, too. I hadn't known Robin well, had spent only about half a dozen family occasions in his presence. But good Lord, to have something like this happen, especially given the circumstances of Lynn and Roderick expecting their first child within weeks, was stomach turning. The memorial service was to be held the following Sunday in Washington, D.C. When I told Liz the bad news later that night from Chris's apartment, I was wavering about the importance of my presence there. She said I needed to go. That's all it took. When I got off the phone with her, I called to buy tickets.

I didn't know it at the time, but just a few blocks away from where Dolores Huerta and I had spoken, a painted mural honoring Latina women blanketed a wall under the First Street Bridge. A four-foot-high portrait of Dolores Huerta was a prominent part of the mural, entitled "*La Ofrenda*." In Spanish, an *ofrenda* is a ceremonial offering of thanksgiving. It celebrates the life and, in the case of the departed, honors the memory.

How do you create an *ofrenda* for someone you hardly knew? I wondered on the long, soothing bus ride back to Chris's place.

[20]

On that bus ride, I experienced the recurrence of a vision I'd had with some frequency over my past two weeks out West. In it I drove through the desert toward a distant glow, and I wandered, something pulling me with an almost magnetic tug. It was a wedding chapel on the Las Vegas Strip that I felt pulled to. Not for myself, mind you, but because I believed I was meant to find a minister at one of the wedding chapels, to learn how he developed this calling. The vision propelled me to rent another car that Monday morning, this time just for twenty-four hours, and drive east through the desert to Las Vegas.

Las Vegas's landscape derives nearly all of its seductiveness from nightfall. When you enter in the evening, either by car or plane, darkness unfurls for miles and hours until the glow of the city emerges, suddenly, as though a gopher poking its head from the ground. When I arrived in the early afternoon of an early October weekday, the Strip looked like an overeager postcard rack in the offices of the Travel Network. I exited the interstate and drove slowly down Las Vegas Boulevard, past the Eiffel Tower, the Manhattan skyline, and a pyramid, all of which looked pasty and unflattering. There I was, cruising for wedding chapels.

Las Vegas was the fastest growing city in America when I visited, and it owed most of this growth to the lure of Sin City. Hundreds of thousands of people lived on the periphery of the Strip and its service and gaming industry, working as hotel maids and casino cashiers, as well as Roman gladiators and wedding chapel clergy. There were about sixty wedding chapels in Las Vegas, and it seemed to me, at least from the movies, that they, too, existed on the fringe of Sin City, offering a weird fusion of the titillating and traditional. I thought of questions for my still-unknown subject, who I assumed ran a shop with a name like Vows of Vegas or Wedding Wonderland. Had he been trained as a traditional minister and found this work more stimulating? More lucrative? Or was he a faux-minister, a gaudy version of the real thing, and in this way, a mirror of the Las Vegas landscape itself?

I saw my first wedding chapel, parked nearby, walked in, and requested a moment with the minister. Did I want to set up an appointment for a ceremony? I was asked. No, I said, not really. Then why did I want to see the pastor? I told the woman behind the desk in the waiting room who I was, what I was doing, and why I had arrived. She shook her head no. He's very busy, she said. I wouldn't take much time, I told her. Can I call him? No, that's not possible. I can't even get his number to see if there's a time when he might be available? I asked. No, that won't be possible.

The scene made me think I was a struggling screenwriter trying to wriggle my way into Steven Spielberg's office. All I wanted was a minute with the minister. But he was in a lifelong meeting.

I got back in the car and resumed my cruise. Across Las Vegas Boulevard from the Stratosphere Hotel and Casino, a towering Seattle Space Needle-like concoction of neon and glass, I spotted a cement sign, peaked with a slanting, shingled, upside-down V. The sign rose up alongside palm trees and a façade for the bare-bones Yucca Motel. This was the Little Chapel of the Flowers. The chapel offered, "Your Wedding Live on the Internet FREE" on its marquee. A stretch limousine with the Little Chapel's logo and phone number photographically rendered on the side idled next to the entrance. I stepped into an air-conditioned office, where four people worked at desks without cubicles.

I started talking, concluding by the end of my pitch, "So I'm looking for either someone who presides over the services or, I don't know, maybe one of you, if you'd be willing to share some time with me." Based on my experience at the previous chapel, I had begun to hedge on finding a minister.

As it turned out, a middle-aged Mormon named Yvonne Mickelson sat at one of those desks. A wedding reservationist and a devoted believer, she thought my project sounded like a good opportunity to share her faith. So we arranged to meet at her lunch hour the next day, back at the chapel.

I walked out of the office, almost greedily rubbing my hands at this bounty. Did it get much better than a Mormon at a wedding chapel? Come on.

My experience with Mormonism up until then had been confined to three points of contact: infrequent exchanges with well-scrubbed, post-teen white guys in short-sleeved white button-downs, their front pockets pinned with name tags, on New York and Boston public transportation; in occasional TV viewing of the high-flying offense of the Brigham Young University (BYU) football team; and in the idea of polygamy. I had had close encounters with none of these, though the series of talented quarterbacks BYU produced for the National Football League—Jim McMahon and Steve Young, to name a couple—did a whole lot more for Mormonism's marketing in my opinion than the lean missionaries who walked in twos like they'd just left the ark's health club. It's true, Mormon missionaries had always stirred a competitive, sarcastic streak within me, the kind that brownnosing classmates produced, too. It was an irrational response that typically culminated with my wanting to challenge them to an arm-wrestling match or spelling bee, some nonperilous, adolescent test of power.

And yet, snicker all I wanted, Mormonism had come to be absolutely central to an understanding of American religion. It represented, in 1999, the fastest-growing faith in the world, multiplying by 500 percent between

1980 and 1999. Yet Mormonism remained, for all its growth and despite its domestic coming of age, an almost foreign faith to the larger American culture. Later, its insularity switched for an extended moment to openness at the time of the 2002 Winter Olympics in Salt Lake City. Even after, however, the tradition felt strange and foreign. Hence my juvenile inclination to contest it, I suppose.

Conceived in the 1820s in the western part of New York State (what was then known as the Burned Over District because of the way revivals had lit spiritual fires across the region), Mormonism symbolized something both indigenously American and exotically other. Over the first quarter of the nineteenth century, as America expanded to the west and to the south, territorial acquisition and commercial expansion were accompanied by a new religious fervor. This was the Second Great Awakening, which swept through the young country, carrying camp meetings, emotional revivals, and a host of enthusiastic, evangelical circuit riders to new towns on the frontier. At the same time, a collective sense of mission flowered in the new nation, a sense that America was planting a kingdom of heaven here on Earth.

But this was before denominational consolidation, and so many preachers bounced around the frontier, testifying with different visions and doctrines, that it must have been confusing to be a religious consumer at the time. Certainly it was for the Smith family of Palmyra, New York. As circuit riders came and went, some of the Smiths joined this church, others joined that one, while still others remained unaffiliated. The story goes that in 1820, then-fourteen-year-old Joseph Smith received a personal visit from two figures he *knew* to be God the Father and Jesus. They told the boy not to join any existing church. Over time, the boy learned that the creation of a new church, on the model of the biblical Israelites' community, would restore the religious clarity and the patriarchal authority of the Bible to his own muddled, frazzled time. That new church, born amid the fervor of America's millennial aspirations, was to be a signal that the Kingdom of God was nigh. Young Joseph Smith believed himself to be the man to declare its arrival.

Like Mormonism, the evangelical impulse of the Second Great Awakening spread west, saturating the American landscape. Indeed, I saw it in the hamburger I ate that evening in Las Vegas. Quotes from the Bible lined the wrappers of the In-N-Out Burger fast food chain's products: there was something from the Gospels on the inside of the burger wrapper, and something from the Epistles on the side of the pouch of fries. Every moment represented an opportunity to preach the gospel, spread the Word, and save souls. I looked for a separate recycling bin, something special for the disposal of religiously themed refuse—a kind of conversion center, if you like. Actually, Orthodox Jews do have a special ritual for the dumping of products with God's name written in or on them. But In-N-Out Burger hadn't gotten to this point of religious obsessive-compulsiveness yet. They had one type of trash there, good for sacred and profane waste alike.

Liz and I spoke for a couple of hours that night from my room at the Motel 6 along the interstate. It was a good night for us, and we longed to be with one another. We would be soon, when I got to Chicago in a couple of days.

Perhaps strangely impelled by my In-N-Out burger, I drove the next morning to the Las Vegas Chabad, the community center and sanctuary for Sin City's Orthodox Jewish community. Chabad is an organization with offices and *shuls,* or worship spaces, around the country and the world. It considers its mission to be to bring all Jews back into the fold of observant Judaism. I chatted up the receptionist, who reported that phone call requests for blessings amid the background din of slot machines reached her daily.

Then I met the rabbi, an outgoing guy with a sense of purpose and humor about leading a religious community in Las Vegas. He talked with me in the reception area for a few minutes before asking me to come pray with him. I followed reluctantly. When Orthodox Jews ask you to pray, they don't just want you to sit there silently or mumble the occasional amen, as I had at Johnny Lay's church. Perhaps that was a function of a split between being an outsider and an insider: the former could get away with being an observer, while the latter needed to participate, even if he felt as disoriented as the outsider. In my case, this rabbi wanted me to say the prayer, even though I didn't know what the words meant. And he felt compelled to outfit me in religious uniform. So the rabbi wrapped my arm in the worn, brown leather straps and crowned me with the leather headgear of *tefillin.* I thought I must have looked like a Jewish miner, with my liturgical pith helmet. Frankly, I felt ridiculous, at both my own discomfort and the rabbi's insistence. The rabbi led me through a Hebrew prayer of thanksgiving, syllable by syllable. Even though it was just he and I in that cluttered library with the Torah scroll, I had the distinct impression I was performing for some audience of observant Jews at their own improv club. Again, as at the First Apostolic Faith Church two weeks earlier in San Francisco, I almost detected, in the space between the syllables, the sound of laughter.

My time at the Las Vegas Chabad marked the first time I had ever prayed in this formal, regimented way. I left the Chabad Center embarrassed at what a pushover I'd been, but ten minutes later, singing along to Van Halen on Las Vegas's classic rock station, I felt strangely exhilarated. After all, why should I feel emboldened to be curious and open among all other faith bodies but my own?

Much as liberal Judaism is taboo to kids who grow up cloistered in today's Orthodox shtetls, Orthodox Judaism was the same way to me as a kid. In my youth, nobody and nothing, including the Mormons, was more alien than the Jewish Orthodox, because let's face it: at least the Church of Jesus Christ of Latter Day Saints had the good sense to advertise during after-school cartoons. Consequently, all I knew of the Orthodox was what I imagined and what I gleaned from the critical talk of secular grown-ups. Sometimes, though, the only way you enter a house reputed to be haunted is by getting dragged in. Then you realize it's not so scary after all. So, driving to meet Yvonne, while one part of me registered a sense of violation, another detected a measure of gratitude.

As a wedding reservationist for the previous two years, Yvonne Mickelson helped many customers for whom a Las Vegas wedding was not the result of a lost wager or a trough of liquor. There were people, I was flabbergasted to learn, who actually planned their Vegas nuptials. We sat and talked in the Heritage Chapel, a reasonably appointed little space with a few rows of pews and a gazebo-type picket fence structure near the altar that wasn't as cheesy as it might have been.

"Some people get married here because Mom wants it this way and mother-in-law wants it that way, and Aunt Mary wants it that way, and they want it their own way," Yvonne, a forty-eight-year old mother of five, told me. "So they find their way to Las Vegas. At our chapel, we try to make it very traditional: the walk down the aisle, the bride's bouquet, everything. And we try to do it as quickly as we can," Yvonne added without any hint of irony.

"That's an interesting combo."

"We give 'em more time than most wedding chapels do. Thirty minutes here on property. That gives them time to talk with their minister, do their ceremony, and have their photos." Yvonne said that there was a chapel down the street that bragged that it could marry and move out a couple in six minutes.

"That sounds like a drive-thru wedding."

She nodded her head. "There's a real drive-thru up the street. People come through the little driveway, pull up to the window, the minister marries them, and they drive off. They never get out of their car."

"Do they get fries with that?"

"I don't know."

"Would you encourage Mormons to get married here?"

"No," she said. "As part of our faith we believe that families can be together forever. We have to be sealed to one another: the husband, the wife, and the children. That can only be done in temple. My husband and I were married in a temple, so automatically our children have been sealed to us."

I was confused. I didn't know what this phrase, "sealed to us," meant.

"'Sealed to you' means that if we live our lives following God's commandments, then when we die and go to heaven, our families will be together. I'll still be married to my husband, because I've been sealed to him for eternity. If our children follow the commandments, then we can all be together in heaven as a family unit." I hadn't heard of this before—the Mormons' celestial family reunion. A couple was sealed to one another in a temple as part of their wedding. The sealing ritual was sacred and serious: church leaders interviewed not only the couple who sought to be sealed, but also potential witnesses who wanted to be present at the ceremony. Yvonne added that cousins and grandparents, even the family dog, could be sealed, too. "We recognize that we're all one family. So if Grandma and Grandpa weren't sealed together in a temple while they were alive, we can do the work for them vicariously." After they die, in other words.

This seemed to be a radical reformulation of the Christian notion of the afterlife, because this wasn't each person accountable for his or her own salvation, but something considerably different. Mormons pushed for conversion in this life, but if it didn't work out for some reason, sealing could be done posthumously. In the Mormon religious platform, eternity spent with immediate family and distant relatives constituted a reason to believe. I love my family a great deal, but I thought we'd run out of movies to watch pretty soon into our afterlives together—unless heaven was a place where new releases were available, in which case maybe it was doable. The sealing doctrine promised that no one was left eternally out in the cold, although the flipside of sealing was that people who made the deliberate choice to leave the faith were subject to spiritual Monday morning quarterbacking by those whose pious self-interest diverged from theirs. I thought then about Tim Turner, the proprietor of Coffee Messiah. Tim grew up a Mormon but had renounced his membership years earlier. Did somebody tinkering with his soul after he died fill him with dread, or could he just brush it off as a fiction of the faithful?

Mormonism is, in part, a quintessentially American faith because of its optimism and its sense of chosenness, and both of these features stand out in the sealing doctrine. All believers have direct access not only to God, but also to other people's souls. Everyone fits into the Mormon spiritual cosmos, even those from other faiths. Baptism in the Church of Jesus Christ of Latter Day Saints represented a choice, but the whole world had been saved, whether they acknowledged it or not, by Jesus' sacrifice. This seemed outlandish, and yet simultaneously I saw the appeal to it. If you think you've got the truth, and you want everybody to join the party, then you construct a theology and a worldview that allows everyone to be invited, even if they never picked up their mail.

Even so, inactive Mormons were a source of anxiety for otherwise devoted family members. Yvonne mentioned that a couple of her kids didn't go to church anymore and had strayed from the faith. "Is your primary objective to get them active so you can be together for eternity?" I asked. She nodded. "So it's less about now and it's more about eternity?" I asked, needing some clarification.

"Exactly. I question why my children, my two boys in particular, have to go through what they're going through. One of them had a very serious drug problem for a while. Why did he have to go through that? Why can't they be active in the Church? I know the Lord lets us make our own decisions, but I also know that in his case a lot of it was peer pressure."

"Was he with Mormon friends?" I asked.

"No. That doesn't mean they're bad kids. I like these kids. I didn't like the things they were doing. And unfortunately that's the way he went."

As Mormonism expanded away from Utah, where 90 percent of the citizens were in the Church, the community clearly struggled to retain the insularity at its core. The more Mormons connected with different faiths and cultures, the more the world collided into Mormonism. Yet despite the Church's insularity, Mormons were perhaps, per capita, the most well-traveled, multilingual religious community on the planet, given the missions that late-teenaged Mormons took around the world.

Yvonne inhaled. The memory riled her up a little. "Becoming a parent has made me see how our heavenly Father feels. Because he loves us like I love my children. When my child makes a decision that I know is wrong and will ultimately hurt him, I feel the same way that our heavenly Father feels when he sees us making decisions that will ultimately hurt us."

I realized listening to Yvonne that nowhere on the American landscape, not even among Christian Fundamentalists, are believers more certain that God is created in their own image than are Mormons, who view God as an idealized version of themselves. I nodded at my recollection of the way Joseph Smith's vision of God the Father and Jesus coming to visit him is portrayed in Mormon iconography. The two divine figures look like Ken dolls, buffed and shined fans of the Osmonds, back from the future.

Despite her struggles with her children, Yvonne found a way to see how her predicament was paralleled in God's own troubles. The Mormon can understand how God feels. The Mormon can relate to God. This is a Christian understanding of the Divine, in which God can be accessed through the human experience of Jesus. But it is something other than that, too. The Mormon's familiarity with God approaches a domestic kind of closeness. As much as Mormons were foreign to me, this familiarity with God was, too. Moses had known this kind of familiarity, but in the history of Judaism as I knew it, no one else came close. In Mormonism, everybody was that close.

The model for the Mormon intimacy with the Divine comes from the experiences of Mormonism's founder, Joseph Smith. In 1823 at the age of seventeen, three years after his first divine vision, Smith was visited by an angel he called Moroni, who told him about a collection of ancient gold plates buried in a nearby hillside. It took Smith a few years more to discern the exact location of the plates, which were inscribed with something like an Egyptian hieroglyphic that Smith, an unschooled frontier kid, ignorant of all ancient languages, somehow found he was able to translate. But Smith seemed to corner the market on the miraculous. His translations revealed the plates to be a fully formed scripture. He claimed he had located the Book of Mormon, God's third and final dispensation after both Old and New Testament. The Book of Mormon was meant not to supplant but to complement the Bible. The people of western New York learned from the Book of Mormon that they were living amid the end times prophesied in the book of Revelation. Most of his neighbors branded Smith's discovery a bunch of hocus-pocus mumbo jumbo, a fly-by-night cult of the Second Great Awakening era. But a number of them found Smith, his miracles, and his visions convincing.

"A lot of people say the Book of Mormon is the Mormon Bible," Yvonne said. "That's not true. We believe in the Bible. But when you go to court and you have one witness, it's okay; when you have two witnesses, the testimony is stronger. That's what the Book of Mormon is: it's a second witness for Christ. We believe that when Christ was crucified, he said, 'I have other sheep not of this flock. I go to see them.' He came to the American continent and visited the people here." Yvonne maintained, if I understood her correctly, that Mormons believe the resurrected Christ traveled to America. "We believe the Native Americans are a remnant of the people who came here at the time Babylon destroyed Jerusalem."

"Why do you think that?" I asked.

"Because that's what it says in the Book of Mormon." Okay, so that was a dumb question to ask a believer. I might see it as pulse-pounding but preposterous fantasy literature, something from the mind of a poor man's Tolkien, but Yvonne believed the Book of Mormon told her story, and she understood the doctrine derived from it as inerrant. This rift distinguished faith from skepticism.

What I admired in Yvonne's relaying of the Book of Mormon's narrative was Smith's ingenuity as a storyteller. Random characters from the Torah—I mean seriously little blips who dissolved from the storyline nearly as soon as they appeared—became the seeds for Smith's Mormon Bible's new narrative. The Book of Mormon begins with Lehi, the son of a Jerusalem prophet, Nephi, telling his own story: his father has warned the people of Jerusalem to change their ways; they haven't heeded his advice; the prophet's family, with Jerusalem in rubble, sails west in an ark of their own making. Smith's "found" scripture begins with just enough recognizable elements from the Hebrew scriptures—the prophetic errand of Jonah, the dire warnings of Jeremiah, the post-catastrophe sea voyage—to strike Smith's audience as consistent with biblical reality. From there the story line could stretch and pull in different directions while staying bound to that central familiarity. Smith had much of the Bible memorized, and he understood his task to be the resurrection of the biblical past. Part of how he did that was explaining how the biblical past found its way across the Mediterranean, and then the Atlantic, and then settled here in North America.

The Mormons transformed the American landscape into a road map of revelation. They were run out of Palmyra, a forced exit that began the Mormons' move westward in the early 1830s. They set up villages in Ohio, then Illinois, and then Missouri, before conflict with the locals in each place drove them further west. From Smith's discovery of a new scripture in a New York hillside, to his vision that the biblical Eden could be found somewhere in Missouri—perhaps one more reason that state's motto is "Show Me"—to the recreation of the Exodus in the trek from Illinois to what would become Utah, Mormons not only professed faith that America was the new Zion; they also dedicated their lives to proving it. The Mormons didn't suffer from any self-esteem trouble. They felt no need for a self-help pick-me-up, and didn't doubt that the task of establishing the Kingdom of God here on Earth was too big an initiative. They were Americans to the core, people dedicated to the proposition that they had been called to do great things.

But this Americanness produced another, subtler feature that reflected and was inspired by the egalitarian ethos of the new faith and the new nation. Seeking to substantiate the claim that they were God's new chosen people, Mormons set out to prove that they were the descendants of God's original chosen people. They did this the same way the Bible did it: through the use of genealogy. "Prominent church leaders can trace their genealogy all the way back to Adam," Yvonne said. "People say, 'It can't be done,' but it can. I try, but I'm not real strong at genealogy. I'm missing a few generations." To meet the demands of genealogical exploration, the Mormon Church created one of the most authoritative resources on the world's population. Buried inside a mountain outside Salt Lake City, an enormous weather-protected and climate-controlled cave holds the most comprehensive records of the human race in existence. Retired missionaries travel throughout the world combing the archives of churches, mosques, city halls, and local governments in an effort to keep track of just about everyone. The records they find are sent to the archive and stored on compact disk.

Just as the Torah uses genealogy to link Adam with Abraham, and just as the Gospels use it to connect Jesus with King David and Abraham and Adam, so too is genealogy used in the Book of Mormon and subsequent Mormon scriptures to document the Mormons' ties to biblical predecessors. Here, though, there is a twist, because it is not the Messiah alone whose genealogy matters. It is Mormons everywhere, all of whom see themselves as the latest stage in a lineage that started with Adam. The Mormons have turned genealogical arcana into a shared, sacred story. For a people who left behind their lives in the East and Midwest to build a new community, Mormonism offered a tantalizing consolation to their isolation: the truth, Mormons grew convinced, was that they weren't isolated at all. Yes, they lived apart, and yes, the building of their new Zion demanded their communal solitude. But they saw themselves not as an invention but as a fulfillment.

Their genealogical research isn't only for Mormon use. The Mormon obsessiveness with bloodlines is responsible for what I know of my own ancestry, too. On a visit to my grandparents' apartment while still in college, my grandma Ruth showed me a copy of U.S. immigration records from 1886. There, on a chart of the arrivals to Ellis Island, were the names of her grandparents, then young adults. Their port of embarkation had been Hamburg, Germany. They'd traveled, we concluded, overland from Russia or Poland or the Ukraine. Frankly, that side of the family wasn't quite sure of its history. On the other side, my dad's side, there were records that we hailed from the bustling Black Sea port of Odessa.

America has represented entirely different things to Jews and Mormons: while Jews have sought an escape from history, Mormons have been busy burrowing their way through it, toiling to reach its beginning. For Jewish immigrants, America was a new start. For the Mormons, America has provided a chance to complete an ancient process. However perplexed the Mormon tradition left me, I felt at the same time equally indebted. In their rush to prove their place they have deposited a series of bookmarks for those of us still uncertain of our own, those of us still striving to order the past like a collection of unnumbered pages.

Mormonism appears to demand a uniformity of outlook among its adherents. Believing that they possess the truth, the Mormons appear to look at other faiths with a condescending mixture of piety and pity. I didn't get this emotionally from talking to Yvonne, but their doctrines and scriptures and worldview necessarily make those outside the fold the objects of Mormon concern. Salvation is found one particular way. This means that dissidents within the Mormon community, would-be reformers, people floating on the faith's fringes, seem destined for one of two choices: to shape up and join the community of believers, or ship out and live as outsiders until others try to seal them after their deaths.

Tim Turner had once found himself at this crossroads. When he quit the Mormon Church a decade earlier, he went so far as to have his name officially removed from its rolls. Tim grew up in a small town called Montesano, Washington, and was one of the only Mormons in his school. During our conversation at Coffee Messiah, he described himself as having been "the perfect kid: quiet in Sunday school, respectful to my elders." But as he grew older, he "started to feel unworthy. Honestly," he said, "one of the first things that did it for me was masturbation. I was a big fan, and the church was very antimasturbation. I just felt like a failure. I had a relationship, I thought, with the Divine. I had some kind of understanding as a fourteen-year-old of a divine presence. But I *really* started to feel unworthy. To be successful as a Mormon, you can't masturbate. And you can't like boys. And I was beginning to realize that I liked both. So I knew something was wrong with me.

"People put on all this pressure when you're young and in the Mormon Church and male to go on a mission. To go serve God for two years. It's like everybody's going, and if you're not, then something's wrong with you. I just knew that I could not do that. Luckily I got to escape to this Mormon school in Idaho. It was the lesser of two evils. Well, they had a dress code there. And part of the dress code was that you had to wear socks. This was 1984, and at the height of fashion I was running around in little leather boat shoes without socks on. And I got sent to the dean's office for not wearing socks. Okay. I said I'd wear socks. And then I forgot. I got sent to the dean a second time. So a conflict ensued with this dean about why I needed to wear socks. 'Explain it to me. I don't understand why God cares whether or not I wear socks.' The dean looked at me and said, 'You're not being humble.' And I said, 'I don't think I'm not being humble. I just want you to explain why God wants me to wear socks.' And he's like, 'God wants you to prove you're humble by following our dress code.'" Tim bit the corner of his mouth. Though he might have relished this part of the story, he did not. It still seemed to pain him. "That was so hollow. That just didn't make sense that a divine being cared whether or not I wore socks." When his alienation from the Church reached its rupturing culmination, it was a policy on sock wearing that drove him out. Tim left the Mormon Church and his home, and came out as a gay man. When he left, he found himself alone.

"I left most spiritual tradition for years, and then started to look for it again. I studied Santeria, Buddhism, Taoism, Zen." Tim's personal spirituality was a collage of these traditions—no, better put, a blended latte of these paths. The orthodoxy required by the Mormon Church had such a profound impact on Tim's spiritual journey that he had reversed field, making himself his own guide. He used what he called shamanic drumming CDs; their repetitive, thumping beats helped him engage in a "real simple shamanic journeying technique in a trance state to explore, to find teachers, to ask questions. I've found so many different connections," he said, "that, unlike the Mormons I'm no longer obsessed with finding the one that's right."

Tim's search reflected both a deep spiritual hunger and a gnawing spiritual loneliness. Coffee Messiah brought a number of other individuals on personal paths into a shared space. Maybe on especially inspiring nights their time together left them with a feeling of community. Still, Tim sought his spiritual guides in a trance, in between beats, not in the light of day.

Tim seemed to have traveled about as far from the Mormonism of Joseph Smith as he could. But he admitted that once he started sifting through the world's religions for material that gave him space to be himself, he remembered the bond with God that he had felt as a kid in the Mormon Church. "Some of the connection came back without all the dogma. And I started to realize that I wasn't just confused about my sexuality and my religion. I did have a connection." Tim found it ironic that he felt a connection now similar to what he had felt then, but as I drove west toward Los Angeles, after saying goodbye to Yvonne, as I recalled the blinking blue neon of Coffee Messiah, like a glimmer of Technicolor Las Vegas in moody Seattle, I thought the irony was that Tim had unwittingly grown closer to Joseph Smith the person, while moving further from Joseph Smith's religion. After all, when had Smith and Tim experienced their first crisis of faith? At the age of fourteen. How had each responded? By staking out new territory. By creating a community built in his own image. By moving west. By challenging the sexual mores of the larger society. As has happened so often, the founder of a faith is precisely the kind of renegade that the faith, once calcified, needs to excise. Joseph Smith couldn't exist in Mormonism today. He'd get thrown out. That's not to say that Coffee Messiah represented the cornerstone of a new faith. Not at all. But Tim Turner had created a spiritual community in his funky coffee shop. Whether a new religion developed from trance jams and postmodern preaching would take decades, if not centuries, to discover.

Nevertheless, amid the similarities between Tim Turner and Joseph Smith were chasms of difference. In fact, Tim's shop symbolized his most stinging rebuke to the Church of his youth, because the neon sign in Coffee Messiah's window blinked "Caffeine Saves," and because Mormons, after all, are forbidden to ingest caffeine.

[21]

I intended my time in Chicago as a respite from my journey and from Liz's grueling school schedule. It offered an opportunity to see firsthand how life was treating her. On phone calls exchanged three to five times a week in the month and a half since I'd last left her, life in Chicago had come to seem predictably erratic. On some evenings, she reported that molecular biology came easily, how she spent fifteen minutes chatting with her dad's old barber, and why her studio apartment felt as comfy as a pair of favorite gloves. On others I heard that sawing through a cadaver's torso disgusted her, how the sight of a terminally ill mother of an elementary school classmate aggrieved her, and why the new construction going up around the campus annoyed her.

I could detect all this up and down in our initial embrace. When I stepped from the van that drove me from Midway Airport to the University of Chicago's campus on a chilly Tuesday afternoon in mid-October, I spotted a solitary, small figure a long block away. I couldn't tell if the figure moved away from me or toward me until I took another twenty or so steps. I walked north and could just make out the shape of familiar hips and shoulder-length blond hair. I recognized the figure to be Liz, but I was loaded down with two backpacks and felt physically incapable of running. As she came closer, I walked as bouncily as I could. From Liz I detected little bounce. There was no hop, no skip, and definitely no jump.

The smile from twenty-five feet away was white with teeth but heavy, as if her joy had dropped an octave. Then came the comprehensive embrace—the closeness of the mouths, the caressing of the cheek, the stroking of the hair—which, warm though it was, did not match past levels of gushing enthusiasm. I don't know if I could have put all that into words then, but in the light of our conversation that first night before dinner, the impression grew clear.

I had been thinking of Eduardo's deep-dish pizza, stuffed with mozzarella and spinach, since we had eaten it six weeks earlier, so we ordered one and the woman on the other end of the line said, "Forty minutes."

We reclined on Liz's used blue couch, and it was then that I first detected the almost tactile change in her voice. It was time, I heard, now was really the time, to look long and truthfully at us, at one another, and most concertedly at ourselves, to figure out if we were right for one another or—and when she offered this possibility, tears tumbled down her cheeks—whether we might be somehow "fundamentally incompatible."

How? In what way? It felt as though she had launched a fist into my chest while I wasn't looking.

In our ambitions, she began. In the different ways we go after getting where we want to be. In the ways we had learned to be accountable to one another.

Where we're going? I thought. Shoot, we just get there; that's all there is to it.

Could you say a little more? I asked, uncertain if I had suddenly downshifted into interview mode. I adjusted my position on the couch. We now sat in opposite corners.

She sounded angry, almost resentful, about my trip. Did I have a sense of where I'd be a year from now? She asked. How about five years? I sat stone-faced and breathless, like an impassive, secretive oracle. When she prodded me for answers, she sounded as though she demanded certainty about what I would do a decade from that moment, when I didn't know and didn't much concern myself with where I'd be the following day. With regard to my future, I had great trust that something would arrive. My pilgrimage had seemed to validate the merit of the unchoreographed, and to undercut the value of the planned. Just as I had found Tim Turner and Coffee Messiah, I would find a path to walk down. But when I said as much to Liz, my convictions made her cry.

She wiped her flushed face and with wet hands, rearranged the tautness of her ponytail. She needed all of me, she said. She felt she had portions of me, pieces that she loved, that listened and liked to listen, but those pieces in sum didn't form the complete package.

Do you think I have the whole of you? I asked. She nodded, now weeping. I looked over at the thinness of her front door. A young couple lived right across the hall. Could they hear us? Our voices? Her sniffling? You don't think you have the whole of me? I asked, uncertain. Again she nodded.

It just might be, she sobbed, that we miss each other in the passing. That was worth grieving over, she assured me, but that just might be how it was. The way she said this, I felt like the passing had already happened.

By then the pizza was surely ready. Good Lord, I thought I had arrived to strengthen her and enjoy my own recharging, but I had walked instead into a buzz saw. I staggered my way through half of the four-block walk to pick up the pizza when the possibility arrived that my pilgrimage might not be about my search after all but about the path to us, Liz and me. Our path. When I first started in with Larry Goodwyn, the history professor in Durham, I asked about the yin-yang tension between listening and speaking, each an essential offering, obviously, in the process of an interview. He answered with an illustration. He began to unbutton his shirt. His point had been well taken, and I had made a concerted, if only occasionally successful effort ever since to turn interviews into conversations.

What Liz was asking, for the future of us, was the history of me. She hadn't even needed to take off her shirt to show me this. This was my choice to make if we were to be partners.

What dawned on me as I carried the pizza back those four blocks, transferring the bottom from one hand to the other when the cardboard got too hot, was that the mission of my pilgrimage had been to hear the stories of the unconnected, offering pieces, intimate pieces, of my own story in order to feel as if, when we parted, we left one another parts of ourselves. In the pursuit of forming a more perfect union, the equitable bartering of autobiographies was of world-creating importance. This was what Liz was asking of me—no more, no less. To ensure our own domestic tranquility, we had to share the way Larry had suggested, hear the way I had been trying to, and speak as if the lives we would create together depended on the details of our days, on the preponderance of the small. Because to have faith in us, ultimately they would.

As we lay in bed the night before I left again, to fly south to New Orleans, Liz told me that every morning she walked to medical school along the block that she had walked to elementary school fifteen years before. She was building this new life, she whispered, in such an old place. Her second day with a cadaver began when she bumped into her fourth grade teacher on the street. Each day she felt like she was completing herself. "Does that make any sense?" She lifted her head from my chest, up toward my chin.

"It's the quintessential American story," I said. "It's like," and I mentioned Johnny Lay, who at First Apostolic had returned to the faith of his childhood, and Yvonne Mickelson, whose genealogical search had led her back to a biblical beginning. "All of our journeys are returns. You know, there's no place like home."

Liz nodded and tucked her head into the nook between my jaw and left shoulder. Her body felt warm against my side. Her hand surfaced from beneath the covers to scratch her nose in that cute, rapid-fire way, and to rub her eyes. Allergies? I wondered to myself. When she lay her hand on my stomach, I thought I felt once again the moisture from her eyes. I said something wrong, I thought, but what? Liz settled into sleep. I stared at the street lamp through a slat in the blinds. We had once galloped through our time together; now we had to tiptoe. The worst part was, I fell asleep feeling like I didn't even know how to start walking again.

[22]

On the plane ride from Chicago to New Orleans I sat next to an aggressively funny salesman, a Louisiana native in his mid-twenties, recovering from a recently broken engagement. This was not the karma I needed after my shaky few days with Liz. My seatmate was off-handed and defiant about his loss, as if narrating the story on Jerry Springer; yet as with most of that program's guests, if one were to catch them on stage but off camera, he had a glazed, distant look in his eyes. "I'm glad it's over. I mean really, that thing was over before it even began." He paused to take a sip from his Bud Light. "Bet it's nice doing what you're doing. Just driving around." He heard the sentiment in his own voice and swallowed it down with another sip. "You're looking at one old twenty-four." He raised the plastic cup, a gesture of triumph that poorly veiled an admission of defeat.

Before landing he told me what my first destination had to be upon arrival. "The Quarter. No doubt. You're not gonna have any trouble finding people to talk to in the Quarter."

That night, Meredith Wells, a friend from college and a New Orleans native, picked me up at the airport. We dropped my stuff at her apartment and went into the Quarter to have dinner and hear some music. Meredith is friendly with the family that runs the Preservation Hall Jazz Band concert hall, a small, plain room where visitors pay five bucks to hear half-hour sets of old school, Dixieland jazz. A line snaked outside when we arrived, but Meredith hugged the bouncer hello, kissed the owner, and introduced me as her friend from New York. "Come on in," they urged us, and I shrugged not exactly apologetically as we moved past the people forking over the price of admission. Everyone plops right down on the floor there, so I sat at the rubber-soled feet of the trombonist, basking in the music, the warm night air, and the chance to resume my exploration after a brief but bracing return to my alternate reality in Chicago.

The following afternoon I chatted with Dorothy Wells, Meredith's mom. An Alabama native and former college English professor who embraced Episcopalianism as an adult, Dorothy had married her husband, Meredith's father, when he did not know he was Jewish. She described the eventual disclosure of his background as having had the curtain-opening dramatic oomph of "the Madeline Albright thing."

"Meredith's father's family never discussed religion. In fact, it's as though they didn't have a past. It was a total blank. The Wellses were Wallensteins before they immigrated from White Russia and settled in Manhattan. They brought construction skills, built skyscrapers, made a lot of money, intermarried, and then Lester, Meredith's grandfather, changed his name from Lester Wallenstein to Lester Wells. Meredith should be Meredith Wallenstein, not Meredith Wells." Dorothy chuckled at the thought, and presumably also at its twin: that she, a Southern girl raised next to an Alabama prison, where her father worked on staff, should be Dorothy Wallenstein, not Dorothy Wells. "I had been married many, many years before I found any of this out."

I opened my mouth tentatively. "If it's too personal we can just move right on, but if it's not, then I'm curious as to how your husband heard about his roots."

She didn't mind at all and swatted my concern away with a swipe of her hand. "Some of it has slowly been revealed. He certainly knew that his grandmother was Jewish, but it just was never talked about. They didn't have that let's-go-over-the-past-and-remember-it thing. Going through family papers, we found birth certificates. And then I happened upon this incredible series of letters that had been sent from Meredith's great-grandfather, who had been a lawyer in Berlin for forty years, to his brother in America. The letters were written from Berlin in June, and then in July, and then in September, 1939. It was like reading a novel or something.

"In one of them, Per, another one of Meredith's great grandfathers who died before she was born, got this letter from Berlin saying, 'I need what they call an affidavit. I know we haven't written over the years, but it would be very helpful to me if I could have an affidavit.' Very genteel. Then the next letter is, 'I wish I could send you some mementos but I can't. I had to move out of my house two years ago, and I'm not allowed to practice law anymore. I have no means. Mother has been taken to a home for the aged. I really need that affidavit.' Then the third letter is written by his daughter, who had married an American, on the boat over to New York. It expresses the hope that the affidavit can get there. That was September of '39." Dorothy paused, allowing the weight of the date and the finality of that third letter to fill the quiet space like a tipped hourglass. "The Holocaust certainly had something to do with their reticence to be known as Jews, with their desire to make it in this society and not wanting to acknowledge any of their past."

Who could find any fault with Lester Wallenstein's decision? I mean, back then, when simply being Jewish, whether you practiced or identified with or shunned the religion, meant you were marked for death, who wouldn't jump at the chance to be more American than Jew?

But this thought brought to mind a conversation I'd had that morning, down in the French Quarter, with a street trumpeter named Hack Bartholomew, who played for dollar bills and change outside a café beside the Mississippi River. He wore saggy blue jeans; beat-up, untied high-tops; and a white T-shirt decorated with an image of the Ten Commandments in tablet form on its front. He told me he belonged to a church with 25,000 members. A born-again Christian grateful to Jesus for saving him from his sinful ways when he performed as a jazz musician in New York; a devoted member of an enormous, thriving church; and a man who wore explicitly religious clothing, Hack struck me as a representative religious person in America. But he asserted that he was not religious. And Christianity, he said, was "not a religion." Religion was closed-minded, the province of the avaricious and the powerful, a space for empty doctrine and hypocritical piety. True Christianity, he said, was a personal, unmediated relationship with God through his son Jesus Christ.

In Hack's religious life there had been a turnaround, a dramatic and life-changing transformation. When he professed his faith in Jesus, he acknowledged that his life had cleaved in two. All born-again Christians, even those physically born into the community, experience their own personal B.C.'s and A.D.'s, the period of their lives before they were saved in his name, and the period after. Their former lives dissolve. The slate of their past sins is washed away.

This escape from one's past, I realized, was a hallmark not solely of Evangelical Christianity, but also of American history. A genetic relationship developed between the spiritual movement and the national culture. Instead of stressing the possibilities of upward mobility and western expansion, born-again faith turns the individual rags-to-riches story inward, away from the world and into the individual, away from history and toward the eternal. The born-again sensibility touches every American. When

Hayder Almosawi and his brothers arrived in Dayton from Iraq; when Sokha Diep reached Lowell, Massachusetts, from Cambodia; and when George Pejovic and his surviving family members came to Wheaton, Illinois, from Sarajevo, they were quite literally escaping from their pasts. To the born-again person, the soul is a battlefield, no less divided than the countries these immigrants have emerged from over the past twenty years.

When Dorothy said that her husband's family lacked "that let's-go-over-the-past-and-remember-it thing," her phrase struck me as a funny way of referring to memory, and curiously it made me think of both Hack Bartholomew and my grandfather. I wondered if this was the bargain the Wallensteins, along with millions of others, had made with their new culture and its promise. By coming to America, succeeding, acculturating, and changing their name, Dorothy's in-laws had undergone a different, though no less transformative, kind of born-again experience. It made sense that the Wallensteins made their money in construction. Like the Evangelical convert, these American immigrants wiped their history-filled slate clean and built a new one. They could no more speak openly of the Holocaust than they could of their Russian ancestors. Somewhere along the way they forfeited that memory. Thus Wallenstein became Wells, and the new life they found in America demanded a silent sacrifice of the life they had left behind.

Was the letter I wrote to my grandfather on his deathbed an invitation to divulge pieces of the past that, on that ruffled hospital bed, beside those Caribbean nurses, fluttered through his mind and out of his mouth like a moth that finds a hole in the window screen? Did he have something to tell me, something he had bundled and secured in his own cold storage decades earlier, something of deep value and deep loss, his own religious "Rosebud," a spiritual bequest? Perhaps. But as much as that unrealized possibility blanketed me with loss, there was something else, another possibility, that struck me as even sadder: that he in fact had nothing tucked away. That he, and those who preceded him, had left their history behind them. What, I wondered, were Jews without their memories? Jews still, but the born-again kind, saved by America, not Jesus.

[23]

I called Hollis Watkins from New Orleans. A professor of mine had suggested that Hollis was someone to get in touch with in Mississippi, because Hollis "knew everybody." When I reached him, Mr. Watkins said I could pay a visit to his office anytime the following workday from 11 to 3. I'd find him two blocks from the Mississippi state capitol and across the street from the Sun and Sand Motel in downtown Jackson, about a three-hour drive from New Orleans. I realized that after a few days of trolley rides and walking, I would need another rental car. While walking down the street, I received a call on my cell phone. Michael Brown, a colleague and friend of mine in Boston, a middle-aged man who had spent his adult life as a community organizer, was calling. I said I'd be on my way to Jackson the next day to meet someone named Hollis Watkins. "Do you know him?" I asked.

"Hollis Watkins!" He actually yelled the name into the phone. Either Hollis had been a mentor, or Hollis owed him money. "Hollis Watkins. Yeah, sure, he's famous. Wow." Hollis had been a prominent activist, I learned—a high-profile organizer in the Mississippi voter registration campaigns of the early sixties. "You oughta do a little background so you know something going in."

"I will." I was perched on the steps of a branch library when Michael called, about to head inside.

"Wow," he said once more. "Hollis Watkins."

I said good-bye to Michael and stepped inside the library. I asked the librarian if she'd run an Internet search for Hollis Watkins.

"Who?" She asked.

"Hollis Watkins. He's famous."

Twenty minutes passed. She found nothing on Hollis Watkins. I asked for possible alternatives, and she suggested a visit to the Amistad Research Center at Tulane University, a mile or so away. "If anybody's gonna have it, Amistad will," she said.

The day was gorgeous, bright sunshine, in the mid sixties. I walked up St. Charles Avenue, away from the downtown part of the city and the Seventh-Day Adventist Church I had penciled in for my afternoon. The day's itinerary had changed, and I now considered myself on a Hollis Watkins fact-finding mission, an informational search for a man who ranged from celebrity to anonymous, depending on whom you consulted. On the way to the Amistad Center I passed by a casually well-dressed black couple. They might have been extras in a Dockers ad. We exchanged smiles. Then the man called to me. I turned. He extended his hand and asked if I knew anything about Jesus Christ.

"A little," I said.

"Would you care to know more?" He reached for the stack of leaflets in his hand.

"I would love to but I'm kind of doing something right now. Can I be in touch?"

"Of course, of course. Come by our church Wednesday night," he said, "or just call us. Our number's on the pamphlet." I waved goodbye to my new Jehovah's Witness contacts, a couple in all likelihood I would never see again, with the familiarity of first cousins I'd see at Thanksgiving.

A young black man in a Technicolor African print shirt, his eyebrow pierced, sat behind the information desk at the Amistad Research Center.

I started, "I'm looking for a little info about a man named Hollis Watkins, who's affiliated with—and I think runs, as a matter of fact—an organization up in Jackson called Southern Echo." My professor had filled me in on Hollis's work. Southern Echo is a nonprofit organization that trains citizens to be community leaders on political, educational, and environmental issues. The young library staffer swiveled toward the monitor. As if synchronized with his move, a voice called down from above the exposed railing of the room's second story.

"I know Hollis Watkins. He and I used to work together for a long time." My words now took on an alchemical potency, ushering in the acquaintances of strangers from stage left. I looked toward the voice and saw a man, approximately sixty-five, easing down the stairs. He wore a navy blue Howard University sweatshirt and a pair of black corduroys.

"Thanks," I said to the staff behind the desk. "Looks like I've come to the source."

"Come over with me," the man said, waving me in his direction with a wag of the forefinger. "I can help you with your search." I introduced myself to Clarence Hudson, the Amistad Center's archivist. Librarians offer to help people with their searches dozens of times a day. Through rivers of information they are gondoliers. The Amistad Center had created its own oral history of the civil rights movement, and somewhere amid that mass of audio recordings, Clarence told me, was an interview of Hollis. He shuffled to the stacks and within a minute located the recording.

After he asked one of the student staff members to confirm the adequacy of the sound, Clarence turned toward me. "So what's Hollis up to?"

I didn't have much to report: he was organizing, working with an organization called Southern Echo.

"He still doin' that?" Clarence asked, startled and admiring. I opened my hands to show him they were empty. I believed I knew one thing, and that's that I knew less than Clarence. "Hollis and I were working on a project trying to buy art for the Tougaloo Museum. That's north o' Jackson. But I haven't heard from him or contacted him in quite a while. Hollis was involved in everything down there. Knows everybody. You know he's in the Nation of Islam?" Clarence asked.

"Huh?"

"Yeah, he doesn't make a big deal about it, keeps it quiet, but yeah, he's in the Nation." Clarence said he hadn't even known Hollis had become a Muslim until one day, while stopped at a red light in Jackson, Clarence glanced up at two men selling *The Final Call,* the Nation of Islam's newspaper, in the intersection. When they approached his window, Clarence looked out to tell them, "No thanks." And then, "Hollis," he remembered his response, "that *you?*" Clarence didn't know why Hollis had joined, or why he had remained, but he looked forward to speaking to him soon, and told me to extend a hello to his long-lost friend.

I took the earmuff-sized headphones, and though I had to strain to discern the scratchy voices of Hollis and his interviewer, I could make them out. When the questioner inquired about one of the civil rights era's early civil disobedience episodes, Hollis responded with details. He said that the community assembled on the steps of the McComb, Mississippi, courthouse. One by one, those gathered stepped to center stage and offered a prayer. As each person knelt to pray, each was handcuffed by the local police. The goal, Hollis said, was to show that folks could be arrested for doing nothing other than praying, and that the ones doing the arresting were supposedly God-fearing people themselves, Baptist and Methodist churchgoers. They were the ones who unleashed fierce dogs on little children, he said, the ones who set fire hoses on women. Hollis's recounting of his role sounded neither sentimentally folksy nor grandly self-promoting. His voice was a little bit raspy, and as he relayed his information, the anger of those memories remained potent, lending his voice a simmering quality, as though it was controlled by a low but steady pilot light.

I arrived at Southern Echo's offices a little after noon the next day.

"You're late," Hollis said, greeting me at the entrance of a large, open, industrially lit room that had the worn though still-tended-to feel of a high school teachers' cafeteria. His eyes crinkled as if he smiled, though his mouth said he was serious. Hollis was slight, though not frail; he had the look of a seasoned boxing trainer, sinewy and no-nonsense, perhaps once a contender in the featherweight division himself. He wore a windbreaker, open down the front, and under it a thin white oxford shirt, buttoned all the way to the base of his throat. Even inside on a temperate day, he kept his black wool hat on and folded it up and over itself to leave his forehead and a few wisps of white hair at his temples exposed. He was not solicited by students and journalists and interview seekers so often that he required a press secretary, but Hollis clearly possessed a skeptical side and did not like his time wasted. In an effort to establish my credentials, and in a solicitous effort at absolution for my tardiness, I told Hollis that my professor, Marshall Ganz, and Clarence Hudson at the Amistad Center sent their greetings. I admitted my meeting with Clarence to have been an episode of incidental good fortune. Hollis's face brightened.

Clarence had handed me a thumbnail sketch of Hollis's current religious perspective, but I wanted to hear it from the source. "Are you part of a religious community now?" I asked.

"I'm both Christian and Islamic." Hmm, both, not just one: this was interesting. How could you be both? Didn't you have to choose?

"How are you able to make that kind of fusion work?" I asked.

"I grew up as a very religious person, African Methodist with—" he paused to find a way to phrase his former religious composite, "Holiness leanings into the Baptist Church."

"Whoa," I stopped him there, "you're talking to someone who's Jewish, so work that out for me."

"See, I grew up in the rural areas. So our African Methodist church met once a month. On those other three Sundays I was going either to the Holiness Church or the Baptist Church, and sometimes I'd double up, because I'd go to the Baptist in the day and the Holiness that night. My grandfather was a Holiness minister. My father was an AME deacon." The Holiness Church was a part of the Pentecostal movement. Former slaves who had become free men formed the AME, or African Methodist Episcopal, Church in 1816. A Northern-based movement, the denomination's creation reflected the religious autonomy of free blacks in the mid-Atlantic states where it blossomed. "I got to the point where I was a junior deacon in the church. I sang in the choir, the whole bit.

"I accepted Islam in 1970. But I continued my relationship with my former church. Accepting Islam deepened my understanding of religion: one, because of the style of teaching, the way questions were encouraged and invited; and two, because of how we were taught that there's only one God, and how God sends different prophets to different people. See, that takes me back to where you are," Hollis added, chuckling, "'cause I have a little Jewish in me."

"Really?" I blurted. "Who? Where from?"

"My great grandfather. From southwest Mississippi."

"See, I knew you looked familiar." Hollis giggled, and the former suspiciousness of his expression faded. "What did Islam sound like when you first heard it?" I asked.

"I first heard about Islam as a part of SNCC in the early sixties." SNCC, the Student Nonviolent Coordinating Committee, was an organization formed in 1960 in the wake of the first wave of sit-ins at segregated drugstore counters throughout the South. With students as its leaders, SNCC (pronounced "snick") organized around challenging the institutional racism of the South, while in turn pushing more established civil rights institutions to greater grassroots activism. Members were black and white, from the South and the North. "Islam sounded foreign, because it was almost 180 degrees different than what I'd been taught as a submissive Christian, which was to submit and accept and wait on God to come and change your condition. Instead, Islam's teaching said, it's all right to pray, but you got to get up and try to do something, too.

"One day it finally clicked: what I was learning about Islam, like taking action to fix what's wrong in the world, was the same as the things we were doing in SNCC. I had always had a belief in standing up for what is right, but I just couldn't see the connection between my political life and my religious life, because I had politics and religion in altogether different corners."

I was confused. That someone as invested in the political struggle of the civil rights movement, which I had learned about in classrooms as an explicitly religious undertaking, segregated religion and politics surprised me. What was civil disobedience if not a political act of religious significance, an active turning of the other cheek to real, current oppressors? But for Hollis, even though he and his fellow protesters prayed and as a result were arrested, and sang spirituals on protest marches, perhaps religion had remained an interior, or church-centered, pursuit.

"What prompted you to visit a mosque for the first time?"

"Very close friends of mine had gone. They had accepted the faith, and they thought I would, too, if I allowed myself to listen to a whole lecture, where I could get some kind of start-to-finish cohesive points about it. So I went, and that's what I did."

"That day?" I asked. Hollis nodded. "What was the lecture about?"

Hollis thought for a moment, allowing the content that sparked his conversion to mount like kindling in a fireplace. "It was about not depending on or waiting for other people to do what you can do for yourself. It also had to do with defending oneself, how it's natural for a person, or an animal, when attacked or aggressed upon, to defend themselves. The speaker said Islam did not encourage aggression, but that if somebody attacked you, you didn't have to turn the other cheek. Defend yourself. It made sense to me. I said, I think I can dig this."

The Nation of Islam was born in Detroit in 1930, its founder a door-to-door salesman named Wallace Fard. Fard's theology hinged first and foremost on a categorical rejection of the American status quo. He preached that the white race was the devil incarnate, Christianity was the religion of the oppressor, and black people had neither hope nor need to assimilate. His message found its market in the living rooms of family homes and tenement apartments, amid the backdrop of bleak economic times and rampant racial prejudice. Detroit's black community learned from Fard that their African ancestors were Muslims. Fard had arrived, a divine presence come to Earth, to help the black population retrieve its ancient faith. His pool of converts, nearly all Christians, heard Fard indict Christianity using the Bible as his proof text: while Christianity taught slaves to love and serve their masters, and to pray for those who hated them, Islam, as Hollis heard that first day in the temple, offered a different response. It wasn't that Islam advocated violence, but it permitted self-defense. In Fard's message, the Bible was a springboard to the Koran, and Christianity was the dark bottom of a slave ship that led to the bright light of liberation through Islam.

Fard passed on the torch of leadership to Elijah Muhammad, the son of a Southern Baptist preacher, in 1934, and Muhammad presided over an era of expansion for the fledgling community. The Nation of Islam opened temples and schools in the cities of the industrial Midwest and the Northeast, created black owned and operated businesses, and began recruiting new members on city streets and, perhaps most famously, inside prison walls. Malcolm Little, a petty thief and junkie, himself a son of a Baptist preacher, was serving seven years in a Massachusetts prison when he first learned of the Nation of Islam. Inside that prison, Little converted to Islam, joined the Nation, and changed his last name to X. An explosively charismatic teacher and preacher, Malcolm X brought thousands into the movement, helped open additional temples in the South and Northeast, and became a magnet for both widespread attention and massive indignation in his fiery rhetoric about race in the United States. More than any single figure among American Muslims, Malcolm X testified to the braided relationship between religion and politics. Antipathy and enemies sprouted up among the white establishment, and within the Nation of Islam itself. When he was murdered in 1965, it was alleged that members of the Nation committed the crime.

Five years later, with cities burning, with movements that preached radical violence supplanting those using nonviolent civil disobedience as the common tongue of protest, Hollis Watkins joined the Faith.

By the early 1990s, when I was graduating from high school, right before Spike Lee's Malcolm X bio-pic hit the theaters, the *Autobiography of Malcolm X* seemed to have become required reading among the white, privileged, predominantly Jewish community I grew up in on Manhattan's Upper East Side. In fact, in my freshman face-book at Princeton, the one with the headshots and addresses of all incoming students (which soon succeeded *The Autobiography of Malcolm X* as the most dog-eared volume on my bookshelf), there was a wonderful example of this trend. The grandson of a Jewish New York real estate tycoon grinned for the camera while wearing a black hat with a white X embroidered into the front. The choice of headgear was hilarious and embarrassing, because I knew that I too was implicated in the silly hollowness of that image. The X hat was a type of urban shorthand, a visual synonym for being "down." During this X craze, we gobbled up Malcolm X items like they were Cabbage Patch Kids.

Embracing a figure like Malcolm X had a deeper significance, too, for these gestures of ours were snapshots of a larger, unstated rebellion, wherein our sterile and brittle tradition was supplanted by a fiery and relevant spirit. The faith of Malcolm X was not doctrinaire—or for that matter, dull—but political and potent and personal. This certainly was appealing.

Even so, reviewing now the way I saw Judaism and Malcolm X in 1992, the difference, if I'm being honest, is plainer: Malcolm X was cool, Judaism was not. There's a moment early in *Jesus Christ Superstar*—one effort of Hollis Watkins's generation to make religion cool—during one of the musical numbers, where Caiaphas, the high priest, belts out, "One thing I'll say for him: Jesus is cool." While traveling to visit Hollis, these memories had flooded back, and I'd wondered if a piece that threaded together the lives of religious leaders martyred at an early age was this: their followers thought them cool. I couldn't decide if this was funny or scary, but I did recognize this to be a peculiarly perilous piece of American martyrdom. Once the revolutionary critique and infectious passion of the life were snuffed out, what remained was an image, a poster, a slogan. The life could be whitewashed, dry cleaned, shrink-wrapped, and tossed in the air like a jump ball. Whoever came down with it staked a claim to the myth and accompanying fame.

Yet here was Hollis Watkins, "famous," in the words of my friend from Boston, though that fame was a form of stealth celebrity, a fame that endures, perhaps because on the cultural radar screen it is a consciously concealed blip. Hollis grew up in southwest Mississippi, the twelfth child of sharecroppers. As a twenty-year-old, he was one of the first two people arrested in McComb, Mississippi, for staging a sit-in at the local Woolworth's. His was the first student-led direct action in Mississippi, and it landed him thirty-six days in the county jail. As SNCC built its strength in the rural South, Hollis became project director of the first voter registration drive in his native state, and served as field secretary for SNCC from 1961 through 1965. He didn't tell me about any of it the day we spoke, though. I learned about his work later. In the process I developed the sense that in the movies and documentaries and photographs and film stills and anecdotes and historical notes about the civil rights movement in Mississippi, Hollis Watkins stood always just off stage left, amid the crowd, planning tomorrow's event, envisioning the next possibility. Locked down, beaten up, threatened with lynching, a witness to visions enacted and sometimes turned to ash, Hollis perhaps deserved to be famous most of all, because he had survived this.

"When I was talking to Clarence yesterday," I said, "there was a moment when we were talking when he did *this*." I tried to demonstrate for Hollis the way Clarence's eyebrows had arched with disbelief at hearing that Hollis still dedicated his life in and to the same community, "He said, 'There's so few of us still doing that.' So I guess what I'd like to know is, what keeps you doing this when other people haven't?"

Hollis nodded. "Number one, I made a commitment to do it. You know, when I made it I was very naïve and I had no idea the depths of what I would be getting into." Hollis paused; a just-barely-perceptible smile cracked on his mouth, as though he were recalling a private joke about past mischief. "But regardless, I made that commitment. And I'm still trying to fulfill it. I see that there's still a tremendous need for what I'm doing to be done. And I have not lost any love for my people; matter of fact, the love for my people has grown. I don't want to attempt to pass off to somebody else to do when I can do part of it myself. And it's a religious foundation that gives me the courage to go on, like it did back then. When you understand that you have both a right and an obligation to do what you're attempting to do, to struggle for dignity and justice, then you know you've got to keep going. Even though you are being met with billy sticks, clubs, dogs, and water hoses, you understand that ultimately evil and injustice are wrong, they won't prevail, and your major fear should be your fear of God rather than fear of man.

"The other thing that keeps me going is young people. That's part of the mistake a lot of us have made. You see, we look around and say young people are our future. That's true. But they're more than our future. Young people are part of our present. I look at a lot of the young people and I see myself looking at me thirty years ago. And with all I could do then, with the limited things that I had at my disposal, I think about Hollis Watkins—" he waited a beat, "here—" again he paused, "now, with all of the technology and all of the educational material and everything that's available to him. That's part of the problem a lot of us older folks have today. We don't bring young people into the process as equals because we're afraid they would take us into areas that we have not thought of, and are not prepared to go into. But that's where part of the true freedom comes from."

"Their freedom or your freedom?"

"Both. Most of us don't realize it as our freedom, but as their freedom comes about, more of it comes about for me as well."

I was rocking back and forth in my plastic chair, moved by Hollis's words. "And then," I said, riffing off of what Hollis had just said, thinking about the transmission of wisdom, "it seems the older generation won't feel left behind because they've been involved in the process of finding a new synthesis for the new time."

"Absolutely. And that's the beauty of intergenerational interaction. The culture that we are brought up in teaches us that the young folks should be over here and the old folks over here, which results in people not seeing themselves as a part of a group, or part of a family, but seeing themselves as individuals." This is the American mythic ideal of the rugged individualist, the lone ranger, the solitary frontiersman who by dint of grit, smarts, and occasional good fortune, makes his life and his fortune on his own. "They are their own individual selves, isolated and separated.

"But the question that was not asked is: How do you define self?" Hollis said. "When you don't ask that question, then you instantly begin to think about the isolated, stand-alone individual, which is a false perception, because people do not exist in isolation. If you're connected to me, then when you say that you've got to be true to self, then that means that you got to be true to me, too. Even the way the original question is framed is limiting. How can you ask which is the single most important?"

Hollis was on a roll. "I posed that same kind of question to people about our activities in the civil rights movement. I asked the question, Who played the most important role? Was it the people who housed and fed us young people? Or was it we young people who beat the pavement and got people to come out to all of the various meetings? Or was it the national leaders who came in and spoke to the people that we young folks had gotten to come out? Who played the most important role? Now if you're honest with yourself, you'd say it's an improper question. Because there were three major roles that had to be played. They were all interrelated, and one was just as important as the others. If the leaders had not come in and spoke to the people in the way that they did, then the people may not have become interested and motivated. If the young folks had not beat the pavement and gotten people to come out to the meetings, then these leaders who came out to speak wouldn't have had nobody to speak to. And if it hadn't been for these community people who fed the young people and provided them with a place to stay, they wouldn't have been able to beat the pavement to get the people to come out. So forget about what's the most important." I gestured to say something, then instead simply kept nodding my head. Hollis let out a soft chuckle. "There's a role for everybody to play to be part of that process. Let me hush so you can ask me something." He laughed again.

"No, no," I said. "Amen. Amen." Many of us knew a handful of figures, the ones memorialized and secularly canonized, who appeared, like embroidered Xs on baseball caps, on Happy Meals during Black History Month, and in Hollywood reenactments of the time. But the task of progress, of movement, required years, and all those years were filled up with days, and all those days were filled up with people, hundreds and thousands of them, cobbling together with seemingly anonymous actions a platform of possibility. And *that*, to paraphrase Dolores Huerta, required faith.

"Let me ask you this," I continued. "Has your conception of what religion is changed since you made the choice to become a Muslim?"

"In a way it's changed, and in a way it hasn't. After coming into Islam, I had a better understanding of a lot of the whys of religion. In the church, when we would ask various questions, they would tell us, 'You don't question the word of God.' Now I understand that part of that was coming from the leaders themselves not knowing. If you're running things and you don't know the answers, you don't want anybody to be asking you questions.

"But I was real inquisitive. That was such a tremendous relief for me coming into Islam, when at the end of a teaching they'd ask, 'Have you got any questions?' I could say, 'Yeah, I got some questions. A whole bunch of them, and I've been fixing to get a chance to drop them out.' And they'd say, 'If you got questions, then questions need to be answered. And you need to be honest with each other: if questions can't be answered then tell the person to give 'em some time and you'll try to find the answer.'"

In Hollis's words I heard echoes of Kisna Duaipayana Das and his conviction that the questions he asked as a Hare Krishna helped him better understand the Catholicism of his youth; and of the Muslims of Toledo; and of Usilinanda, the Burmese Buddhist monk in Half Moon Bay; and even of Dolores Ledbetter, whose questions led her to answers supplied directly by the *I Ching*. For each of them, the act of asking questions, and in a large sense, the process of maintaining a conversation—between students and teachers, between communities and tradition, and between people and scriptures—was a vital element of the American religious walk.

Hollis Watkins made a straightforward but radical point, a Martin Buber-type point. We live in relationship to one another, each of us a someone connected to others. And yet we claim, and oftentimes cling to the notion, that we are self-contained, solo units. I know I did. The uniqueness of my pilgrimage seemed to depend on it.

Drained from a day that began in New Orleans and was winding down in Jackson, I felt enticed by the $25-a-night neon sign advertising the

Knights Inn on the Mississippi interstate. I pulled off the highway and into the parking lot, and walked through the doors of the motel office. An Indian man walked from a back room, where a TV flickered, to the front desk.

"Do you have any rooms available for the night?" I asked.

"Many rooms," the man answered.

It was almost eight o'clock and I was nearly asleep on my feet. I leaned against the desk and saw, beyond the man and his computer monitor, a foot-high sculpture of a Hindu deity, with a caption at the statue's base inscribed in Hindi. At the opposite end of the counter sat what seemed to be an incongruously added icon: a six-inch-high tourist-trap totem of the robed, risen Christ set against a backdrop of seashells, illuminated in the spotlight of a raisin-sized light bulb.

The Indian proprietor's name was Bruce, and I complimented him on his religious art. "Thanks," he smiled. "The Jesus statue I got in Biloxi." Did the little knickknack represent a way to appease the Christian majority he lived among? Or was he maybe a Christian himself?

"Are you a Hindu or a Christian?" I asked.

"I pray to Jesus, Krishna, whoever. I pray to everybody. The key is belief." He leaned over to the corkboard on the wall where room keys hung on hooks. "All religions are one. When you believe, God is everywhere. We take God with us everywhere when we believe." He handed me my room key.

"Even to the beach, I guess."

"Sure," he shrugged, "anywhere. All religions have the same goal, you see. There are many ways to get from Jackson to Biloxi. You can take the interstate or the local roads." Yeah, I liked that. Many ways to get from Jackson to Biloxi.

On the faded bedspread that covered the bouncy mattress in Bruce's Knights Inn, I called Liz. In the aftermath of my conversation with Hollis, the memory of one of Liz and my earliest evenings together flashed back in my mind. Amid our recent rocky patches, I hoped that the telling of the recollection would soothe, for a few minutes, the mounting tension we felt. "D'you remember—" I began, and I recalled the unseasonably balmy night in late January, nine months earlier, and how on her quiet street, where months later I would call twice for a tow truck, we strolled arm in arm. Mist rose from the melting snow, and streetlights shone with halos of glare. Her neighborhood had felt like a movie set, abandoned in the after-midnight evening, and we seemed to be the only people in Boston. We were already in love, had been from the night we met at that Beacon Hill Christmas party. Sometime on that walk I told her I had written a couple of columns for the newspaper of Temple Number Seven, the Nation of Islam's mosque in Harlem and the community Malcolm X once led. When I visited the Temple while researching a paper during my last year of divinity school, the people there welcomed me with courtesy and hospitality. We spoke for a couple of hours that afternoon, about what Islam meant to them, and about the huge areas of overlap that Judaism and Islam shared, from sacred characters in scriptures to *halal* and kosher kitchens. Our two communities could learn from the particular perspectives they shared, from the similar emphases they placed on communal self-sufficiency, to what they had learned about their status as others, as subhuman, as a despised race, and how to make sense of that predicament. Instead, they chose to fail miserably at mutual recognition.

That day, after I thanked them and retraced my way through cubbyhole cubicles in their storefront office to the slate gray of a New York winter day, one of them, as I pushed open the door to head back to the street and the subway back south, called out to me, "Are you a writer?" and from the open doorway I replied with an enthusiastic nod of the head. Was I interested in writing for their paper, *The Thinker,* he wondered, because they were looking for a voice from the Jewish community? In my recounting this to Liz on that winter night, she sighed and smiled and—do you remember this? I asked her as I told the story—caressed the back of my neck with cold fingers.

Of course she remembered. "It wasn't so long ago," she said. But it was.

[24]

I took a circuitous route from Jackson back to New Orleans, driving west through southern Mississippi to Natchez, then weaving down local Louisiana roads until I reached Baton Rouge. I stayed with an acquaintance of a friend from Boston, and together we attended Friday night services at one of Baton Rouge's Reform synagogues. The rabbi preached a sermon about Abraham. The book of Genesis says that Abraham heard a voice that commanded him to "go," to pack up his belongings, gather his family and his accompanying entourage of servants and livestock, and leave his home. The Hebrew for "go" is "*lech lecha,*" also accurately rendered in the more colloquial "get going." Citing Abraham as a model, the rabbi said that the religious walk is a solitary one. There is a voice, a command, and a decision to obey or disregard. I knew what he was saying, but I also found myself softly shaking my head no from the pew. I had heard a voice, heeded a whim and followed it, yet my religious walk, my own *lech lecha,* didn't feel lonely; on the contrary, it felt crowded. The voices of the people I had spoken with waited in my head as though the members of a jury pool: some lounged, distracted; others paced, jittery, anxious to be called. Each voice seemed immediately accessible.

Just before the service ended, the rabbi called on the congregation to recite in unison the Kaddish, the mourner's prayer. He asked the forty or so of us to offer up the names of the recently departed. Uttering a name serves to resuscitate the recently departed in the life of the community. Though they are dead, by mentioning them we speak them back into life. The rabbi's head scanned the room like a searchlight, and when he caught my unfamiliar eyes I raised my hand and said the name of my brother-in-law Roderick's brother: "Robin Kreisberg." I was a stranger in that synagogue, so the name was a mystery to all the regulars there, though in truth it was something of a mystery to me, too. The last I had seen of Robin was at my sister's wedding sixteen months earlier. We had shared seats at the head table, congratulated and passed butter to each other, but we didn't have much of a relationship. He was the general manager of a rock station on the FM dial in Wichita, Kansas. He was Roderick's older brother by six years. He was sharp-witted but reserved, divorced, balding. He had died a little more than a week earlier, killed when his car was hit at an intersection by a truck.

Other people called out other names, and from the congregation came murmurs of sympathy and groans of recognition. But there were no "I'm sorry's" after I offered Robin's name, and no sympathetic crinkling of the eye from the rabbi. He surveyed the crowd like this every week. Death was, for him, a part of the job. Yet despite the congregation's indifference, I nevertheless experienced a kind of consolation. The sound of his name, for that one moment, wafted above the pews before nestling into the rafters. I had planted his name as though it were a seed, and together our anonymity to this temple was transformed in the act. His name—once a life, now a memory—in being spoken, became an offering, and my own form of introduction. I thought Larry Goodwyn would be nodding.

To make it back for Robin's funeral, I had scheduled a flight from New Orleans to Washington, D.C., at 7 A.M. that Sunday. With the sun setting behind me on Saturday, I drove back to New Orleans and stayed the night with a former boyfriend of Liz's who had become a friend of mine, too. We had a good time together, but he was a harbinger of misfortune to come. That night in New Orleans, we grabbed a few beers and shot some pool with a couple of his friends. One of them, a strapping former college linebacker named Josh Blum, and I got to talking.

"You headed west at all?" he yelled over the pool table.

"Yeah. I'm just heading east for a funeral, and then I'm flying back out to Texas."

"You makin' it to Colorado?"

"I'd like to."

"Well if you do, you should give my grandma a call."

My ears perked up. "Where does she live?"

"In a town called Alamosa. It's in the southern part of the state."

"How far from New Mexico?" I asked, because I was planning to fly from Dallas to Albuquerque and then rent a car to meet the Southwest.

"Not all that far," he said.

"Wouldn't that be weird?"

"Are you kidding? She'd love to have you. She loves guests. I could call her and let her know you'll be coming."

On the night before I left Louisiana I made arrangements to spend an evening the following week in the prairie town of Alamosa, Colorado, with eighty-four-year-old Ruth Blum. The country seemed bound together by fewer than six degrees of separation.

○

Don and Dusty Kreisberg called the event for their son Robin a memorial service, not a funeral. I didn't know the difference. The weather had turned cold—more than crisp but less than icy—on the East Coast, and people arrived at the church in overcoats. My sister's husband Roderick and his parents stood inside the door to greet people. What do you say to someone whose son has died? "Sorry," obviously, but is there a place for hopefulness? Does one express grief but also the promise that one will return to one's former self? Is that appropriate? Is it possible? I entered with my parents and my grandma, and when I saw Roderick's dad I shook his hand and cupped the burlappy tweed under his left elbow.

"I'm sorry, Don," I said. "I'm really so sorry."

Don shook his head. "Tommy," he said, "you went to divinity school. Maybe you can explain this."

The most I could do was smile and keep the procession of grief-givers moving steadily. My sister, then thirty-eight weeks pregnant, sat in the front row, her left arm resting across her husband's back. They stayed in that position through much of the service.

At the reception after the service, my grandma went nuts on the hors d'oeuvres, grabbing three and four broccoli florets at a time, cradling too many diced chunks of cheese in a paper napkin. To see her like that, with flecks of crackers sitting like scabs on her top lip, made me realize that the last funeral she attended was my grandpa's six months earlier. It almost seemed that in her uncharacteristic behavior she was the only one who captured the mourners' collective befuddlement. The rest of us talked about our daily worlds; I told clusters of threes about the Bible-thumping trumpeter Hack Bartholomew. My grandma, on the other hand, couldn't stop praising the creaminess of the dip. She was appropriately out of sorts.

In their car, I drove my parents and my grandma back to New York. How odd it was to drive up the familiar I-95, with its Maryland Crab House rest stops and signs for Philadelphia, Trenton, and Newark, on a chilly Sunday night with sleeping passengers, as if they were my children and had school tomorrow. The East Coast suddenly felt foreign, roles had been inverted, and I savored the quiet while they slept.

PART FOUR

[Death and Texas]

[25]

By noon the next day I was eating beef noodle soup in a half-full restaurant in Martinsville, Texas. An early-morning taxi, a flight to Dallas–Fort Worth, a rental car pickup, and a car ride down I-20, then a handful of state roads had brought me to a table equipped for four, draped with a plastic tablecloth and set with paper placemats. Two men across the room lay their cowboy hats on empty chairs. I took a mint on my way out and, as I pushed open the door to head back to the dusty parking lot, I noticed that a flyer had been posted in the restaurant's entryway advertising Thursday night religious services. This in itself wasn't so unusual; the unusual part about Thursday night services in Martinsville, Texas, was that they took place in a livestock auction barn known to locals and cowpokes passing through as the Cowboy Church. I received directions to the barn from the woman behind the cash register and drove over to see if the cowboy pastor was available. I pictured him strutting to the altar, tobacco packed tightly in his lower lip, bearing crosses of rawhide, each sermon a high noon for the soul. Disappointingly, I saw no pastor in the corral. Maybe it was the stale stench of cow dung, maybe it was the imagined echo of "going once, going twice, sold to the man in chaps," but I found it difficult to see the auction barn, a quiet, dark warehouse, as a sanctuary.

Yet not long after, on the way out of town, I marveled at how permeable the wall between sacred and profane is in this country. On Wednesday afternoons at 1 P.M., cattle sales take place; on Thursday nights at 7 P.M., thirty hours later, the market became a congregation, the barn, a church. Maybe it was a Texan allusion to the manger scene, the smell of farm animals serving as a veil to the holiness of the scene within. My timing to hit the Cowboy Church hadn't worked out, but just knowing it existed made me swell with satisfaction. It sparked a mental slide show, back to the Orthodox Jewish synagogue in a Las Vegas strip mall, back to Harvey Lee Green leading his co-congregants through the death row Protestant liturgy, and back to Tim Turner and Coffee Messiah. In unexpected places, amid incongruously outfitted communities, faith peeked out from under secular covers. The lines we draw that separate sanctuary from street corner, sacred from profane, us from them, are real, but at the same time more perforated, more easily crossed than we believe.

———————— ○ ————————

The people of San Antonio wore heavy parkas as the people in Washington had a few days earlier. Summer was gone, but somehow it seemed like years, not months, since I had spoken with Darnell Lyman, a sixteen-year-old San Antonio native, in Boston back at the end of July. He had been a camper in the sailing program for kids that Liz had run the previous summer; a Boston relative had hosted him and his younger stepbrother. Near the beginning of my trip, I stepped onto Community Boating's dock on the Charles River to meet him. Liz thought he'd be a good subject, and given my antsy anticipation, I jumped at the chance to listen to what he had to say. It had been my conversation with Darnell that had turned San Antonio from a possible pit stop to a must-see destination.

When I first saw him, he had on a yellow life vest over a white tank top and jean shorts that sagged a few inches below his knees. He held court with three or four girls, grabbing the sides of his shorts and yanking them above his hips to prevent excessive sagging. Darnell's cornrows—braids woven thick like rope—revealed lines of brown scalp so geometrically arrayed that, seeing his head from a bird's-eye view, I might have felt like I was glancing at an arid city grid from a blimp. His legs, narrow and light brown like empty paper towel rolls, looked like they belonged on a little boy, though his shoulders rippled with a young man's muscles. He wore a gold hoop in his left ear. Maybe, *maybe*, he had some peach fuzz above his lip.

"I guess I've been raised Catholic," Darnell told me that day. "I've grown up going to a Catholic Church. When my mom and stepdad first got married, I was seven, and I started going to his Pentecostal church for a while. But after a while I told them that I liked going to Grandma's church better. So they just gave me a choice.

"What did you like about the Catholic Church that made you want to keep going there?" I asked.

"I think it was about relationships. My grandmother goes there, and from when I was one to six I was living with her. So my grandmother's kind of like a mother to me. Even when she's out of town or sick or some-thing like that, I still go. A lot of my friends don't believe I still go. They're like, 'Darnell, you go to church?' I'm all, 'Yeah, every Sunday.' And they're like, 'Whatever.'"

I liked the thought of that moment—Darnell responding, not even apologetically, to a friend's bewilderment at his persisting church atten-dance. In high schools where the cool kids drape themselves in "What would Jesus do?" gear, the pressure obviously inverted onto the disbeliever (or better said, the believer in something else). For Darnell—whose smile gleamed and whose gold hoop sparkled, who talked with the knowledge that he had the gift of gab, and walked with a perceptible swagger—this conversation with his friends was a declaration he could have withheld or offered tentatively. One could see how, in varying environments, declaring oneself a person of faith, a believer in God, could be either a ticket for ad-mission or a velvet rope slung across the door, barring entry.

I asked Darnell what he liked about church. "You know, I feel bad when I don't go, and I feel good when I do go. Like, say something happened before I go and I'm still feeling down; church takes a weight off my shoul-ders. A lot of people from the church would say that's Jesus, or that's God, working his ways." Darnell dipped his right shoulder, and with this ges-ture his head tilted right, too. He was thinking, though he looked for a moment like he had frozen during a dance move. "I don't really know if that's it or not. I just know I like that feeling. I like having a place to go so I can talk to someone if I need to." This was why Darnell could admit with satisfaction, albeit to occasional ribbing, that he still went to church. Actually, in his next breath he told me about his stepdad's church, where the services lasted five hours and where his stepbrother bugged him in-cessantly for pieces of gum. Darnell didn't care much for those services. To their credit, I believe, his mom and stepfather handed him the keys to his own spiritual life. And so Darnell decided to switch back. Not out of compulsion, or devotion, or obedience, or obligation, though each or all of these might have been mingled into his number one reason for attend-ing: Darnell went to church with his grandma because he liked it.

"My grandma's church is on an Air Force base, so everybody knows everybody there. It may not be that everybody knows everybody, but every-body knows somebody that knows somebody. And everybody knows me cause my grandma's been going to that church for so long."

"How long?"

"Since 1963. They have this plaque of the people who've been there the longest and done the most for the church. My grandma's the first one on the list, and then there's ten years before the next person. Usually the priests are in for six months at the most, and then they're gone, going to Saudi Arabia or Turkey or different places like that. So people know my grandma more than they know the priests. Everybody knows that if you want something done, ask Jean. She'll talk to the priest, or try to get it done herself."

"Jean's your grandma?"

"Yeah. People ask me where's my grandma, but it's a big church, you know? I don't have an alarm on her." Darnell shrugged and smiled, more like the parent of a precocious child than the grandson of an active woman. "I can't just push a button and she'll come. I tell them, 'Just stand still. She'll come around eventually.' She's pretty unstoppable when it comes to church. She's been there so long, a lot of people call it Jean's house. I see people at the postal exchange, where you buy your groceries and stuff, and they'll be like, 'Let's go to Jean's house and see if she's there.' I think they're going to her *house* or something, but no. They're going across the street to see if she's in the chapel."

The more Darnell told me about his grandma Jean, the more I wanted to meet her. Our conversation would be the first of several subsequent occasions that triggered the search for a relative of someone I'd spoken to. Just as Darnell's words led me to his grandmother, Dolores Ledbetter's reflections about family piqued my interest in a possible visit to her Hasidic daughter in Brooklyn. So too, when I learned of Harvey Lee Green's death in the online newspaper, did I read that his mother was a minister. I planned to try and reach Mary Gooding, Harvey's mom, at some point.

"Seems like it might be a tall task to be Jean's grandson in Jean's house," I said to Darnell.

"I used to think that a couple years ago. See, 'cause I used to have my hair braided a different way. My aunt did this thing called micro-minis: they're little tiny braids, like string braids. I knew my grandma didn't like them in the first place. But I had 'em, and I didn't want to take them down cause it took me like two days to get them in. I'd spent the night over there, and she must have thought I was going to church with my parents. But I got up early so I could go to church with her.

"She was like, 'You're going to church?' I go, 'Yeah.' 'With me?' 'Yeah?' 'Like that?' 'Yeah.' 'But they're gonna laugh at me.' It was kind of funny, 'cause we got there and she was all like, 'Okay, walk in first.'

"But everybody there has known me since I was little, so they know me for what I am, especially all the older people. They're like"—Darnell changed his voice to parody a doddering old lady—"'I used to change your diapers'"—and then again, to the tone of a barrel-chested, know-it-all man—"'and I remember when you used to stick your whole hand in your mouth.' I get reminded of that every Sunday."

Three months later, on a San Antonio Saturday evening, I arrived at Jean's home (as opposed to Jean's "house"). I had introduced myself by phone a week before, told her about the project, my time with Darnell, and my desire since my conversation with him to come and speak with her. She said Darnell had told her about our conversation. She'd be happy to talk.

Darnell's grandma lived in a squat but comfortable one-family house on a cul-de-sac, an exit and a few turns from the interstate. A couple of twenty-year-old cars sat parked at the curb in front of neighbors' houses when I pulled up. From the rest of the street, too, I got the feeling that this corner might have looked the same way in 1981.

Jean had the kind of bearing that made me think of a disciplinarian teacher tickled—in a private moment, perhaps during a covert cigarette break outside the faculty cafeteria—at the recollection of her favorite target. A member of the Air Force for more than thirty years, she presented a generous, matriarchal side that dispensed wisdom and offered hospitality but didn't take kindly to fools and cynics. Her voice, polished and contained, sounded as though she used 10 percent of her vocal cords' capacity.

Jean, sixty-nine when we spoke, had lived and worked and worshiped in San Antonio for more than thirty years. In 1958 she joined the church that would come to be called "Jean's House."

"When I was talking to Darnell," I said, recounting our conversation back in July, "he said that a lot of what he believed came directly from you. He was right up front about that. He said your influence, not only on him but on the larger community, was pretty big."

"Uh huh."

"The way Darnell spoke about you made me know I had to get down to San Antonio and speak to you myself. He said the church is called Jean's House." Her eyebrows rose above the red plastic of her eyeglass frames. "Had you heard that before?" The curiosity implied by her response made me think, maybe not.

"The kids must say that. I'm there a lot, but I'm not there all the time. I think most people in that church look at me as someone who's sincere—and sometimes I say, 'Boy, don't I have them fooled.'" Jean laughed. "I also think sometimes they think I'm very naïve, that I think that everything is okay."

As though seized by the smell of something burning in the oven, Jean surged to a posture of readiness. Yet it was a difficult task, because her sofa looked as though it were stuffed with quicksand. "My mom and dad always allowed me to say whatever was on my mind, as long as I did it respectfully. But see, there were people in the Baptist church where I grew up—" Conjuring the memory, Jean slid back into the sofa. "When I was a girl, I went to church one day with no stockings on, and I got chewed out. 'You don't have on stockings,' they said. And I said, 'Why do I need on stockings?' 'Because you're coming into God's house.' And I said, 'You know something? God created a universe. He can handle me not wearing stockings.'" *Whoa*. Jean's anecdote of teenage subversion, coming just about four weeks after Tim Turner recounted his crime of wearing boat shoes without socks, was, in my friend Danny's word, ridiculous. What was it about bare calves and naked ankles? "In a sense," Jean said, offering a tidy summation of her faith journey, "I guess I've been a rebel. But the thing is: I believe in a sensible God."

Clearly, the rebel gene had passed from grandmother to grandson: what were Darnell's braids if not a reenactment of Jean's own iconoclastic, stockingless religious impulse. Jean's words struck a chord in me, and not solely because of their preposterous likeness to Tim Turner's. Both Jean and Tim had smart mouths as kids, and they used common sense to call into question matters of strict obedience in their stifling religious settings. Both of them had had faith as children. Jean told me that as a three-year-old she stood on a stump near her church, flapping her mouth and waving her hands, testifying about her faith, to the delight of congregants, one of whom, an old woman, foretold the day that Jean would be a missionary. Tim thought of himself as a perfect little fourteen-year old Mormon kid who had a connection with God. Jean and Tim's rebellions, in other words, were grounded in a yearning to comprehend, not merely a propensity for protest. In each of the moments they cited, they asked the treacherously simple, devastatingly threatening, "Why?" They both believed in a reasonable God, and viewed with suspicion a divine being with an unnecessarily anal retentive side with regard to footwear and legwear.

At some point on the religious walk, after early years of imitation and subsequent years of initiation, the time arrives for innovation. Maybe it comes within the tradition in which one was raised, and perhaps it manifests itself in a rupture with that tradition. But through every one of our religious walks runs a tension, a fault line on which the subterranean plates of obedience and inquiry strike each other with massive effect on the spiritual Richter scale. Religious traditions greet these moments the way parents react to nose pierces: some, expecting the behavior, understand that rebellion is a part of maturation. They consequently line the borders of the tradition with the kind of netting that breaks the falls of acrobats. Others, vilifying the behavior, rail against the rebellion and lock the storm windows from the inside in an effort to ensure that nothing and no one else gets in or out.

But when you walk into a tradition already wearing a metaphorical nose ring, like I had, with the pack of cigarettes wrapped tightly in the sleeve of your white T-shirt, a Hebrew school incarnation of Marlon Brando in *The Wild Ones,* your rebellion precedes your education. My entry into and exit from Judaism went this way, and the process made for a specious, toothless rebellion. In my case, maybe the only way to rebel authentically, perhaps predictably, was in my reentry.

I admired the deftness of Jean's own rebellion, and wondered how and when she had come across Catholicism as a Baptist growing up in Mississippi.

"I used to play coronet," she said. "When I was a little girl Artie Shaw used to come on with his clarinet at eight o'clock in the evening on WWWL in New Orleans. My mother would let me stay up, and I'd play my coronet while he played his clarinet. This one night, I was in my room—I had to be about eight years old—I heard someone speaking what sounded like gibberish. I was flipping the stations when I heard it, and I honestly did not know what it was. But I remember thinking, that is of God. They were speaking a language I did not understand. They were repeating the same words over and over and over again. And I thought, that's what I want to be." In a deep whisper, Jean offered a recital of the Hail Mary she remembered hearing that evening.

"When I got to college, one day I heard this same talkin', and I said, 'I've heard this before.' The girl that was my roommate said, 'Yeah, that's the Catholics. They're doing their Mass.' Well, I thought the Catholics were pagans. Oops." Jean pointed up to the wall of photographs. She requested I zoom in on one particular picture. "When this child, the one with the baby, was born, she did not breathe." Jean was pointing up to one of her daughters. "The doctors were working on her, and the nurse said to me, 'Mrs. Apollon, do you want me to call the priest?' I said, 'Why would I want you to call the priest? I'm not Catholic.' And she said, 'Mrs. Apollon, you were saying the Hail Mary. And you were saying it over and over again.'" Jean stopped to take a sip from her glass of juice. Her hair, blown straight, was parted on the right, and a wide strand dipped across her forehead, away from the rest of the obedient hair that sat still across her ears. "I promised to God that if he would let my baby live, there would be nothing that would stop me from becoming Catholic.

"Had I been raised Catholic, I probably would have become a contemplative, a nun, because they see God and recognize that we don't understand it all. They know that God is within us, and yet we have our own selves. And once we know all that we think there is to know, then we learn that we don't know anything. I am 69 years old, and if I lived to be 169, I still would not have reached all there is to reach in just knowing God. The kids I teach, they wear these bracelets that say, 'What would Jesus do?' This man, although divine, he was so *fully* human. You know why?"

Jean looked to me. I said nothing; I took her question as rhetorical. "Because he knew who he was. And maybe that's what it is: if you know who you are, it makes a difference in how you think, and what you do, and how you say it. Because if you've read the New Testament, when they were going to stone the lady for adultery Jesus said 'Go and sin no more.' When he was healing the blind, he said, 'Your faith has healed you.' To me he was always getting the individual to take part in what was happening to herself."

When Jean described Jesus, her voice reached an emotional crescendo when she said, "He knew who he was." *That* was what made him fully human. More than his compassion, more than his sacrifice, more than his ambition, it was self-knowledge that defined the core of Jean's Jesus. He knew who he was, knew where he came from, knew what he was called to. Yes, I thought. This was the great example he, and other religious teachers and visionaries, set. The array of bumper stickers and T-shirts and headbands that ask, "What would Jesus do?" "What would Buddha do?" or the exceptional "How would Jesus drive?" all missed the point, all asked a good but unessential question. Asking "What would Jesus do?" inspired a moment's thoughtfulness and a lifetime's imitation. But gaining insight into how he came to know who he was, aye, there's the rub. That was teaching a man to fish, not giving him a grouper.

In the moment when Jean walked over her dark carpeted floor from kitchen alcove to living room sofa, I suddenly saw with clarity that knowing who you are depends on a sufficient knowledge of where you come from.

With Jean I rewound back to my conversation with Darnell and how he thought his grandma had converted to Catholicism because the Baptists were so strict. The truth of the story was less pragmatic and more cinematic. One can picture the scene: second-generation radio, straight-back chair, cute black girl, nappy hair pulled taut into pigtails, small nail-bitten hands cradling a silver horn, hearing a sound so foreign it jolts her with a paradoxically familiar recognition. Jean's first encounter with Catholicism hit her not on the rational level, but on the emotional level. What she did not understand just felt right.

When Darnell attended church with his grandma Jean, it was not solely the religion he chose, but the approach to the religion as well. Both he and his grandma made their religious choices at an emotional level. But beyond that was another, key similarity. Back in July, talking about his grandma's change of faith, Darnell offered this hypothesis for how it had taken place: "I think when she got of age, like eighteen or whatever, when she moved out of the house, then it was her choice. She gave my mom that same choice. And you know, my mom already gave me that choice. When you turn eighteen, you're your own person. So pick your own religion." That Darnell was not yet eighteen when his mom gave him the choice was of little importance. That there was a choice, that's what stood out. Both Darnell and Jean had chosen their faiths from several options—perhaps not a smorgasbord of options, but a menu, at least.

In Darnell's words, choosing your religion made for a rite of passage in which one's soul became one's own responsibility at a particular, set time. What you did with it was up to you. The First Amendment ensures citizens the freedom to practice their own religion, and Americans have crafted for themselves the complementary rights to choose what to worship, and with whom to worship. Through great awakenings, revivals, immigration explosions, the flicker and formation of new faiths, and the legal protection of an individual's religious freedom, America has fashioned a religious climate that is democratic, antihierarchical, and universally accessible. The freedom that began as a safeguard protecting people from a state-sponsored church developed, among many communities, into a coming-of-age ritual. Individuals could remain in the faith of their families, or choose from among door numbers 2, 3, or 4. (And if they wanted, they had access to doors 2, 3, *and* 4.) In such a culture one found Muslims who remained Christian, Hindus who prayed to Jesus statues, and postmodern preachers born into Mormonism who looked to Japanese, Caribbean, and Native American faith traditions for a spiritual outfit that suited him.

Now, for others, this right to choose lay dormant. Because for them, having the choice meant not that there was a choice among equivalent options, each one potentially appropriate and sufficient for the chooser, but that one's choice was a test on which there was but one acceptable response. For Jeff Paul at Liberty University and for the New Orleans street trumpeter Hack Bartholomew, every individual had a choice, but only one was the right one.

Earlier, during my drive through Texas, I'd met a twenty-two-year-old woman named Jessica Campbell. Our conversation touched on this exact topic. A senior at Texas A&M University in College Station, Jessica had grown up in Fort Stockton, part of the ranch country of west Texas. Raised around horses and a student of agricultural development, she stood at least five feet and nine inches tall, and the weathered cowboy boots she wore that poked out from tapered jeans added a couple of additional inches to her height. Jessica had been brought up by her mom and grandparents in the Church of Christ, a conservative, evangelical denomination found mainly in the South and Midwest.

"Do you still go to church?" I asked her.

"No. I haven't been going since I came to college. I'm confused about religion, because in Church of Christ, if you're not one of them the way they think, then you're not going to heaven. But I don't think that's right. My mom and my grandparents view things differently than I do. Baptism is such a big thing in the Church of Christ. We're taught that you don't go to heaven if you're not baptized, no matter how much you believe. A lot of other people get baptized when they're little kids, but we don't get baptized until we're ready to give ourselves to Christ—until you believe and you're ready to repent and you do it yourself. My mom always left it up to us." Jessica paused. "I oughta get baptized because of what I believe in, but I don't want to do it here, 'cause it doesn't seem like it'll mean as much in such a big church. I'd like to do it around the people I grew up around. But then again, I'm embarrassed because I'm twenty-two years old and I haven't been baptized. I think one reason why I never did it is 'cause I was so worried about my mom and my grandparents saying, 'We don't think you're ready to do it,' no matter how ready I think I am." She paused, absorbing the prospect of her salvation as a tug o' war between necessity and uncertainty.

This decision—or better said, this indecision—on whether and when to be baptized pinpointed a quandary of faith for Jessica Campbell. Like a pair of blindfolded messengers unsuccessfully reaching for one another, Jessica and her family could not connect. "I don't wanna 'cause they don't think I'm ready," she would say, and "We wish you were ready and you'd just do it," they'd reply as each side imagined the expectations of the other and envisioned the haunting implications of the delay.

Accepting salvation in the Church of Christ takes the form of a self-initiated rite of passage. In fact, that Jessica's say-so determined her preparedness for baptism and salvation reflected a most democratic strain in the conservative Christian ethos. That she resisted making this choice indicated not so much that she wasn't sure if she wanted to be saved but that she wasn't sure what kind of believer she wanted to be.

Jessica wavered about being baptized at least in part because the choice seemed like no choice at all. For her there existed two possibilities, with everlasting import: salvation and damnation. She did not perceive the life of faith the way a Cafeteria Catholic or Mess Hall Muslim might. She did not explore faith as if in a mall for the soul, where she could dabble, enter, try on, head upstairs, peek around downstairs, then rest. She did not think herself able to browse different congregations. She could not pick and choose, dared not mix and match. For Jessica, because there was no choice, there seemed to be no good answer. And so the fear associated with the decision overwhelmed the prospective comfort that accompanied the choice once it was made. Sometimes choice feels like a jail cell.

In July I had asked Darnell, "What's it mean to you to be a religious person?"

He had said, "I guess I'm not considered the exact religious person, because when it comes down to it, let's say there's a guy standing across the street with a gun and he's gonna shoot me. I'm not going to sit there and pray to God. I'm gonna either duck or run, or go and get somebody else's gun. I think the last thing I would do is sit there and pray to God. Maybe because of that I'm not a religious person. But to me, that is me being as religious as I can be.

"I know a couple of people who don't believe in religion at all. They say they're not devil worshipers or atheists or anything like that. They say they're just regular people, which I guess is okay. They figure that afterward we're just going to be in dirt somewhere. I mean, we are, but I guess we need something to hold on to that's not there. Everybody believes in something that they can't see. They're holding on to something. Maybe not with both hands, though."

"How many hands are you holding on with?" I asked him.

"I'd say one and a half. I don't want to hold on with both hands. Because maybe I believe in myself more than I believe in anybody else."

When juxtaposed against Darnell's and Jean's religious decision making, where there was real agency and power in the choice, Jessica's choice, trailing her like a shadow, seemed sadly hollow. In Jessica's words, "I can't win for losing," one could hear, "It's no use." I couldn't fault her. Take an example: If you knew an election was rigged, that one candidate was a real person and one was, I don't know, let's say, a corpse, you would probably stay home on election day. After all, what's the point? You already know the result. You've got no say. You've got nothing to do with it. (Presumably this, or an analogous feeling of impotency, is what keeps droves of Americans from the polls every November.)

Now, perhaps if someone came to Jessica, allayed her anxieties, told her she was ready, told her she was welcome, shared with her that what waited on the other side of her dread was peace, that the candidate would make a great leader—perhaps if faith was sold to her that way, she'd recognize that at least her one option was a sure thing.

Jessica's predicament shone a spotlight on my own, because all my conversations with Liz had made me feel a similar kind of paralysis. I was out on the road, meeting people, seeing friends, piecing together and finding myself in a story larger than my own, and what I heard from Liz was, *that ain't gonna work*. I need you, she said. I need to know you're with me. I need a sense of a longer commitment than just your next destination, she said, a knowledge that you're walking with me. She spent three hours a day with a hacksaw in her hands and goggles on her head. She scribbled notes on index cards, pierced body parts with small pins, flagged arteries, and labeled muscles. She was exploring, inspecting, surveying the body of a middle-aged, white male corpse. I supposed that when one spent that much time in anatomy, one couldn't stop oneself when class ended. She was dissecting me, sketching an anatomy of us, and while I felt whole and expanding, she seemed intent on exposing that the whole had parts and the parts had holes. That inclination fed her impatience. The more I told her, with an air of naïve and knowing nonchalance, that I couldn't tell her where I'd be in five years, that I didn't know and that, in truth, didn't want to know, the more hounded I felt for details, for certainties, for something, anything, she could count on from me. And I, because I was a pilgrim, because I believed that planning with her would somehow compromise me, my journey, this story, I interpreted her need as her problem. I didn't quite realize it at the time, when I was in Texas and she was in Chicago, when I was on the road and she was in anatomy lab, but both of us felt like Jessica Campbell, paralyzed by choices we didn't want to make. There I was, listening to my soul and bad-mouthing my heart.

I drove to Austin and stayed in the guest bedroom of my friends Greg and Margaret Connor. The bed they provided was exquisite, lined with soft flannel sheets and cottony, breathable blankets, and topped with a beautiful quilt, a wedding present from a loving relative. Why did other peoples' spare beds feel more comfortable, more practically luxurious than any bed I had ever called my own? Seriously, this was like the bed everybody gets in heaven.

Before sleep, we ate dinner at their local Chinese restaurant.

"So what are your plans for tomorrow?" asked Greg, who was in his first year of residency in some incredibly impressive, awe-inducing surgical specialty at the University of Texas Medical Center.

"I think I'll try to find some pagans early in the morning around Austin, and then drive the three or four hours to Waco to locate a Branch Davidian." My friends nearly spit up their Moo Shu Chicken. I didn't bother trying to keep a straight face, even though I was completely and totally serious. "I did a little search for 'Pagans comma Austin,' then 'Pagans comma Dallas,' all in quotes, on Google a few days ago," I told them. "See, I wanted to meet up with pagans either today or tomorrow, because our Halloween is for the pagan community a spiritual observance known as Samhain." Pronounced "*sow*-in," Samhain is a contemporary celebration of a holiday that has archaic Celtic roots in Northern Europe, Ireland, and England. The ancient holiday commemorates the Celtic new year and the end of the annual harvest. Like the Mexican Dias de los Muertos (Days of the Dead), Samhain, also known as Ancestor Night, marked the time of year when the dead returned to visit the living. "I got a couple of phone numbers of some leads here in Austin, and scored something of a jackpot in Dallas." I'd happened upon the Web site of Betwixt and Between, a Dallas community center "celebrating spiritual exploration" and a gathering place for the city's pagans. "And with regard to the Branch Davidians, I figure everybody in Waco can point me in the right direction. Their compound's probably like a theme park by now."

My friends nodded and offered encouraging smiles. I believed they were in part dazzled and in part perplexed. My response to Greg's question was playful, bordering perhaps on flip, but only to let them know I shared the humor of the scenario. With respect to my plans for the following day, I wasn't kidding—that really was my agenda; but an itinerary of this kind, set in pencil for the first Monday in November, seemed to all three of us implicitly decadent. Obviously not decadent in the Robin Leach, *Lifestyles of the Rich and Famous* way, but in the I-get-to-do-exactly-what-I-want-to-do, go-anywhere-I-want-to-go, with-no-set-objectives-except-those-I-create kind. I had no boss, no supervisor, no officemates, no office. On the road I thought of this as work, these nine or ten hours a day of driving and looking, finding and hearing, so I never understood the sadness I caught in Liz's voice when I'd recount for her my ready-made schedules. I felt sorry that she was struggling as much as she was, staring down as much academic asphalt as she was. But we were just doing different kinds of work: hers rigid, mine fluid; her path set for the next four to eight years, mine for the next two to three weeks. Such imminent uncertainty didn't concern me the way it did her. She didn't ask me every day about my plans after Thanksgiving; in truth, in most of our daily conversations she permitted me the privilege of floating on this pilgrim's soap bubble I had blown. I don't think I understood how much restraint this took for her, this refraining from asking what the future held for us once I was done with this chapter. For her, such questions were stabilizing, grounding; for me, they appeared as needles, pinpricks, whose unstated intent was to bring me back to Earth. We talked, but much remained unsaid. We could have used a translator and two sets of those headphones they use at UN General Assembly gatherings, so a bilingual fluent in "Anxious, Future-Focused Young Woman" and "Naïve, Present-Minded Young Man" could facilitate intelligible communication.

At dinner, Margaret, no doubt inspired by the next day's interview prospects, asked me if I had interviewed anybody who was *really* strange.

"That's an interesting question. I guess I hadn't even considered it." I thought for half a minute. I'm the one hurtling through central Texas in a rental car to meet the people you live next to: that was the first thing that came to mind. Maybe *I* qualified. "Nobody really," I said, shrugging, and I immediately felt disappointed for having no answer. Surely there had been some unusual characters. I scrolled down a list of possible suspects: I had met a death row prisoner and a homeless devotee of the *I Ching* and a Hare Krishna devotee and the proprietor of a coffee shop that doubled as a postmodern church. But honestly, *strange* doesn't really cross my mind when I think of them. The recognition made me shake my head in amazement. At the core, all were struggling with how to hope, how to remember, how to act, how to be. In fact, we were closer together than most of us knew, maybe than most of us wanted to know. And no time would I see that more clearly, more surprisingly, than the following afternoon.

[26]

Mid-morning on the first Monday in November, gnawing my way through a fingernail, I had a destination but no directions on how to get there. Driving north up I-35 from Austin, I headed for Waco and the remnants of an American cult. More specifically, I was driving toward the Mount Carmel Compound, the one-time home and last stand of the Branch Davidians, a self-cloistered breakaway sect of the Seventh-Day Adventist Church led by David Koresh that once hid in, and from, the glare of the national spotlight.

After I woke up in that almost unbearably cozy bed in Austin, I quickly came to the conclusion that my day's focus had to be on the Branch Davidians. Pagans I could find elsewhere. Branch Davidians and Waco constituted a one-shot deal.

Once on the road, my practical navigational hurdles made a threadbare camouflage for my private fears. The Branch Davidians had not exactly rolled out the red carpet for visitors in the past. The last visitors to Mount Carmel were greeted with a barricade. Of course, those guests arrived in armored tanks, not a compact car. I approached with a nervous expectancy, because as much as I wanted to meet and speak with a Branch Davidian, I wasn't certain they'd have any interest in meeting with me. And of course there was one additional concern: that there weren't any left with whom to speak.

Waco long felt to me like an essential stop on this road trip, because there a small-scale American apocalypse played out before a national audience. To approach an understanding of religion in America, one had to come face-to-face with the self-identified fringe of religion in America, and the venomous responses it inspired. A community of devoted believers led by a charismatic figure regarded by followers as a prophet, the Branch Davidians were demonized by the press and later decimated by the government in the late winter and early spring of 1993. During a climactic showdown with government agents on April 19 of that year, following fifty-one days of an FBI siege, the Mount Carmel Compound burned to the ground. Eighty-six people, many of them children, died in the inferno.

Nearing Waco, I started to remember scenes from that spring, a few from the television, but one in particular from the dining room of my grandparents' apartment during our Passover seder. I was in the second semester of my freshman year, and midway through a class on the relationship between the Jewish tradition and the Christian Gospels. My family conducted its annual sprint through the Haggadah, the Passover script that recounts the Exodus story's arc from slavery to freedom, produced by the Maxwell House coffee company. We were partly through the gefilte fish course when I said something like, "It's kind of amazing that biblical stories like the Exodus are still so relevant today." This realization had come as something of a shock to me, because at the time I still seemed certain that Judaism was yesterday morning's news.

My uncle passed the horseradish, the symbol of the bitterness of the Hebrews' suffering during slavery, in its silver serving boat to my grandpa.

"Look at the Branch Davidians," I said. "David Koresh is portrayed by the media and the government in a lot of the same ways as Jesus was by the authorities of his day."

"More matzah," one of my little cousins requested. Matzah, the bread of affliction, a cracker in the cardboard genus, commemorated the slaves' hasty flight into the wilderness, when they couldn't wait long enough for bread to rise.

In truth, though a neophyte in the subject matter, I saw clearly that to flip between scripture and the editorial page was to be startled by the similarities. Each community, Jesus and his followers and the Branch Davidians, bore the mark of heretics, a fringe group of misguided zealots and unstable fools. Each community maintained that one in its midst was a prophet, a precursor to the return of the kingdom of David, of heaven on Earth. And each railed at the mainstream, defiantly proclaiming the imminence of judgment on the status quo and the ascendance of their peripheral teaching as the universal truth.

"Wasn't it possible," I wondered, "that Jesus was the Koresh of his day?"

My grandma pushed her chair back and, with the assistance of the housekeeper, started to clear the gefilte fish plates and ladle the matzah ball soup. The question floated in the air, a few tentative thoughts emerged as replies, and the head-scratching implications of the analogy remained like a leftover.

Only minutes from Waco, I nodded at the recollection. This Texas terrain wasn't all that different from the Judean hills. It was a bare enough landscape that little things poking up from the ground loomed ominously on the horizon. Soon I couldn't help but smile at the fact that, minutes from Waco on that autumn Monday morning, my most pressing concern was how the Branch Davidians would greet me, if any remained to receive me.

A billboard on the interstate welcomed me to Waco: "The gateway to Texas history." I stopped at the Visitor's Center and asked for the quickest route to the Branch Davidians. The two women behind the brochures on the counter didn't know how to get there, and didn't seem to care much that they didn't know. Waco, it turned out, was not the blinking yellow town I had imagined, but in fact amounted to a decent-sized city. It had Baylor University, the home offices of Dr Pepper, and a little roadside shack called Krispy Fried Chicken, where I ate lunch before again asking around for directions.

Before I drove into Waco, I assumed that everybody would have an intimate acquaintance with the Branch Davidians and their compound. Waco had gained so much notoriety through the Branch Davidians that I expected to see peddlers on street corners selling buttons and mesh hats and T-shirts with iron-on self-deprecating, self-marketing slogans like "Waco happens." I anticipated that Waco residents would know both how to get to Mount Carmel and how to avoid it.

Much to my surprise, not one of the four or five Waco residents I asked for directions had ever taken a ride out to Mount Carmel—not to kick around rubble, not to pay their respects, not even to see what all the fuss was about. Looking at it in retrospect, this became less strange. I was born and bred in New York, but in my time there I had never visited the Statue of Liberty or seen the view from the restaurant atop the World Trade Center. This is one of the differences between tourists and natives. Passers-through hunger for the particular destination, rise in the morning to visit, then recap once they've returned; residents move in orbits that self-consciously bypass the magnetism of their own tourist traps.

Twenty miles outside the city, the landscape looked like sandpaper. Lumbering cows nibbled grass. I pulled over to verify my navigation with a rail-thin woman who staffed a roadside gas pump. She directed me down a curvy stretch of road. Within a few minutes I had arrived.

Three metal mailboxes, positioned like sentries, sat beneath a white sign welcoming the visitor to Mount Carmel. There was no skull and crossbones, no "Abandon hope all ye who enter," no checkpoint. On the property in the distance, the wooden skeleton frame of a two-story building rose, bookended by telephone poles, bare like winter trees.

Not far from the sign was a one-room building with a gray front porch. I poked my head in. Along the walls of the yellow-lit room I noticed picture frames, standing easels, posters, and glass exhibit cases. Incongruous elements from the siege rested side by side. Spent ammunition, bent and rusted, was displayed beside a mud-caked, parched bag of Huggies. Framed family photographs of the community members who had died in the siege hung in rows. In one photo, a smiling woman huddled with her white dog. In another, honeymooners in formal wear preened for the camera. In still others, families of four and five and six crowded next to each other to fit into the frame. I saw white and black faces, as well as Latinos and Asians. It was a diversity I had not anticipated. Of the 130 people living here in 1993, 45 were black. Community members came from England, Canada, and Australia, as well as from the United States. Next to these photos were others: aerial shots of rising flames and ground-level glimpses of the water from fire hoses spraying onto smoldering rubble, while postmortem inspectors in tall boots surveyed the damage. Noticeably absent was any sort of "cult" team portrait, with the flock assembled and kneeling, their well-scrubbed, brainwashed children seated in front, like some high school German club's yearbook shot. The photographs appeared to be standard Sears portraits and everyday candid shots. The people seemed "happy"; they looked "normal." This room, the Mount Carmel Visitor's Center, doubled as a museum. It displayed recovered *memento mori* as though they were a collection of millennia-old artifacts.

An old woman smiled when I introduced myself, revealing yellowing teeth and a sagging jaw. Her name was Edna Doyle, and she invited me to stay for a while. Thin wisps of silver hair billowed like steam around her ears. When she shook my hand, I felt how her long, wrinkled fingers bulged with knuckles.

Edna stood behind a front counter topped with a cash register and Branch Davidian versions of impulse purchases: a stack of audiotapes of one of David Koresh's last sermons, a rack filled with copies of Koresh's manifesto "Revelation of the Seven Seals" (the coded information Koresh professed to have deciphered from the Book of Revelation, reputed to tell believers what will happen upon Christ's return to Earth), and a collection of academic and not-so-academic accounts of what really went down here, from February through April 1993. Edna leaned on a corner of the counter, one elbow supporting the weight of her torso, and I thought she could be the graying bartender at a retirement home lounge.

Once we started talking, it seemed as though I had turned the knob on a faucet. "I used to not talk nearly as much," Edna said, her native Australian accent still strong even after twenty-three years at the Mount Carmel Compound. "But you learn how to talk because of something that happens to you. If this hadn't happened, I probably wouldn't be flapping my mouth now." A Branch Davidian since 1956, she moved to Mount Carmel from Melbourne, Australia, in 1976. While Waco was a Mecca for Branch Davidians worldwide, the community drew membership from around the English-speaking world. Edna had arrived at Mount Carmel five years before a handyman named Vernon Howell came to live at the compound. In 1990, following a power struggle with the former leader in which Howell wrested control of the compound, he changed his name to David Koresh. He chose David because he considered himself in the line of King David, and Koresh because it was Hebrew for the name Cyrus, and like the biblical, Babylonian king Cyrus, who returned the exiled Hebrews to Jerusalem, Koresh saw himself as the man to gather the scattered remnants of the chosen people in one place.

Koresh was an ambitious man with a big job. But this job had not been Koresh's alone. Each leader of the Branch Davidian sect, since its founding in 1942, believed himself or herself to be a messenger sent from God. Apparently this inflated sense of self was listed along with "strong communication skills" on the job announcement for the position. Founder Victor Houteff was certain he had been sent by God to purify Christians in anticipation of Christ's second coming. Florence Houteff, Victor's wife, prophesied after his death that the kingdom of David would be definitively established in Waco on April 22, 1959. She left the community in 1962, demoralized by the inaccuracy of her pronouncement.

How had all of these scriptural delusions of grandeur come to be? Was there something in Waco's water? How had a seemingly sane woman like Edna Doyle been led across the globe to live here? How, after each prediction failed to come to fruition, did successive prophecies replace them? Did the would-be prophets really believe that theirs was the authentic vision? That God had called *them*? That world history would pivot right there, in their community, just outside the Waco city limits?

A Christian theological term, *typology,* offers the beginning of an answer. Typology is a way of reading the Bible that views the Old Testament as a prefiguration of Jesus. Typology says that all of Israel's history leads up to Jesus like a cosmic funnel. What happens in the Hebrew Bible—the making of the covenant, the giving of the law, the history of the chosen people—serves essentially as a narrative foreshadowing of the life and times of Jesus, who announces a new covenant, proposes a drastic revision of the law, and introduces a radical expansion of the chosen people.

Typology has proved to be a very useful narrative device for peoples as well as for prophets. America has a whole host of examples of religious communities that make use of typology, like the Mormons on their westward trek and the earliest Pentecostals in their *glossolalia;* but Pilgrims and slaves present the country's two most prominent historical examples. Introduced to the Bible in captivity, the American slaves were force-fed a biblical reading that sought to reinforce their submissiveness. But the Bible's interpretive flexibility permitted the slaves to see themselves as the contemporary incarnation of the Hebrew slaves. The pyramids they labored to build were the cotton fields; their pharaoh was the plantation owner. Part of how they came to terms with their suffering, and located hope for an inevitable liberation, was to use the Exodus as a guidebook. They employed an informal typology, through which they heard the Exodus story as a script of their own redemption.

The Pilgrims embarked from England, searching for religious freedom. Sailing to the "new world," their leaders described their journey in terms explicitly evoking the Exodus narrative. They, too, though in a vastly different circumstance than the slaves, understood themselves as a contemporary incarnation of the Hebrews wandering through the wilderness. As the New Israel, they used the old Israel to set the stage for their ascendancy as "a light unto the nations" and "a city on a hill."

These are familiar stories in American history classes. Less familiar is connecting these models of interpretation to more eccentric, marginal communities of faith. One of the enduring refrains in both the Hebrew Bible and the New Testament is the expectation of eventual redemption. Many, maybe most of us, see this as a long-distance proposition. Our lives, our children's lives, and our children's children's lives form the cobblestones on that path. Implicit in that slow walk is a recognition that collective redemption is basically unavailable here and now. It lies forever in the future. On the other hand, the foundation of evangelical Christianity is the conviction that while collective redemption might be a long row to hoe, the personal kind is ever and immediately available.

The Branch Davidians blended typology with the evangelical impulse to produce a potent, threatening concoction of scripturally grounded self-aggrandizement. They weren't misquoting the Bible. They were reading the same one that all Christians read (not withstanding the distinctions in translations), but coming to a dramatically different conclusion. They were the long-awaited New Israel, David Koresh was their prophesied king, and humble Mount Carmel would soon be exalted.

America itself has found in typology proof for its central place on the historical stage. Typology taught the new nation that it was not only an inheritor of biblical prediction, but an incarnation of it. Those who see themselves this way, whether entire cultures or faith communities on the fringes of the mainstream, believe their experiences to be predictive for the rest of the world. They set the standard, and the world will eventually get the picture.

The Branch Davidians, then, were not a species distinct from the American religious sensibility. They were just a strain of it on steroids.

Very early on in our conversation I recognized that Edna Doyle did not fit the caricature of the "typical" cultist. She wore an un-tucked-in white button-down blouse underneath a black cardigan sweater. Her plaid skirt—colored in light blues and pinks and greens, its pattern that of a country club golfer's pants—made her look more like a grade school teacher than a domestic terrorist. Her whole demeanor, from attire to wrinkles to hospitality, conspired to craft an aura of ordinariness that belied the exoticism she and her community had acquired in the public eye. The allegations that stuck to the Branch Davidians—the firearms violations, the sexual impropriety, the doomsday mentality, some of which turned out to be accurate—gave me the distinct impression that upon arriving I would find Holy Rolling, pill-popping, bloodshot-eyed, prophesying Hell's Angels. But that was not Edna Doyle. She looked and talked like somebody's grandma.

At the start of our conversation I learned about the faith of the Branch Davidians. The community had cobbled itself together from the Seventh-Day Adventists and local area seekers, some magnetized by Koresh's claims of apocalyptic possibility, others by the community's emphasis on family, communal discipline, and belonging. Like other Seventh-Day Adventists, Branch Davidians stress the imminent return of Jesus Christ and worship on Saturday, not Sunday. Like Fundamentalists, they revere the Bible as inerrant. But like a "cult," and as with the New Testament's accounts of Jesus himself, they went the extra distance and said that the ancient faith and prophecies had come to fruition in our times, in their community. This constituted their essentially radical, albeit age-old claim.

There was no disproving or debating Edna about her faith. "I used to think I must be mad," Edna told me. "But if God showed you something, and you saw it and other people didn't, it's not *your* fault." Edna believed that the community, under Koresh's leadership, *had* seen something. Even as we spoke, more than six years after the FBI's siege and the deaths of nearly two-thirds of her "people," Edna believed they were "the true church come to light again, as it was in Christ's time." Like the members of that former true church, they suffered and died for their faith. What occurred at Waco, then, seemed to her, and to other survivors and sympathizers, only corroborating evidence of Koresh's prophetic accuracy. Edna believed. No amount of post-siege deprogramming or media-driven psychobabble would change her heart. In fact, that people doubted the veracity of the community's apocalyptic predictions even after those predictions had come to pass seemed like one additional piece of evidence in their corner.

As Edna spoke, I scribbled her words in furious chicken scratch onto the pages of a spiral notebook. I kept waiting for the perfect moment to pull out my recording equipment: a break in her words, an appropriate segue, a chance to identify myself not just as a student and a visitor but as a writer as well. But it never came. Something about pulling out the microphone there, in that disproportionately recorded and photographed place, felt intrusive, as though I were just another in a long line of point-and-shoot camera wielders touring the scene of the crime. And I meant to be more than that. I see now that in the process I became less than myself. I wasn't up front with Edna, in large part because I felt she wouldn't trust me once I identified myself as someone interested in recording her thoughts. There remained something about my own exploration that I couldn't trust—a tendency to hedge around openness and self-disclosure—and an additional sense that I was intruding somehow. At Mount Carmel, it seemed safer to be concealed by my own camouflage.

A few visitors at a time, though not more than seven or eight total over the three hours I spent talking to Edna, trickled in, circled the room, and thanked Edna before leaving. Somebody bought a copy of the Seven Scrolls, what Koresh was writing at the time of the siege, and slipped a couple dollars, in addition to the cost of the manuscript, into the donations canister on the counter. As the sky darkened with clouds and dusk, Edna's testimony moved from ideology to autobiography. She walked from behind the counter to the wall of photographs, creaking over the wood-planked floor. She pointed up to one, tracing a gnarled index finger along the outside of the frame. She pivoted away from the wall and walked back across the small room to resume her stoic lean against the glass countertop. I stepped away from the counter and several feet closer to the photograph, to get a better look at this image of her granddaughter, taken when she was sixteen, before she burned to death. Edna shook her head, more stunned than dispirited. "Truth is stranger than fiction," she said. "If someone wrote our true story in a book, people wouldn't believe it, even though it's true."

The world she described as home developed like a photographic negative of the standard story told. Here at Mount Carmel, the Feds were murderers and the cultists were righteous heralds of the approaching kingdom. Edna Doyle had lost her granddaughter and nearly one hundred other members of her extended family. Her son survived, crawling from the burning building while aflame. Despite the casualness of her posture against the counter, I heard in her voice a tone at once menacing and matronly, a product of what she had witnessed and of the role she played here. All of the small children she used to care for died alongside her granddaughter. She survived, I learned, only because she was away from the compound on the day of the siege. "I used to wish I could have been here," she said, her eyes narrowed, "and burned with the rest of 'em."

Cult status adheres to a religious community when its message is either sufficiently bizarre, like the Heaven's Gate members who committed mass suicide in the belief that they would live immortally on a comet passing Earth, or when it claims contemporaneity with the scriptures. Any group that declares itself outside the mainstream, that answers to a different—what they hold to be higher—authority, necessarily becomes a threat to the center. Across the spectrum of disparate religious traditions, the prophets and progenitors, canonized in scripture and story, are a reviled and iconoclastic lot. Moses and Muhammad seem to have been as abhorrent and threatening to the authorities of their time as Koresh was to his. This is not to say that Koresh heard the voice of the Divine with the clarity of Muhammad, or communicated the will of God with the conviction of Moses. Only that he saw himself, and was perceived by others, in an analogous way.

As long as our sources remain at a distance, I thought, either temporal or geographical, their grueling struggles remain safe to serve as models. But when an individual or group arrives in our zip code or rush hour subway car, to proclaim its umbilical connection with the Lord and the prophets of old, we call the authorities, who whisk them from our midst, restoring the muted moral tones of our prophetless times. By airbrushing the canonized in our past, and by condemning the apocalyptic in our midst, we rob ourselves of the space in the middle of these two poles.

We are prone, as human beings, to desire our icons calcified like marble statues, with our judgments—maybe good, maybe evil—set in bold lettering at their stone feet. In the moments before I left, when I watched Edna Doyle slip rubber waders over threadbare black slippers to protect her feet from the muddy ground, I glimpsed that even the survivor of an anticipated apocalypse doesn't want to walk around with toes wet from mud. The very banality of such details underscores the humanness of our villains, both those made of flesh and blood, and those made from smoke and mirrors. In truth, the villainous terrorist can be seen as fully and terrifyingly human, for precisely the same reason that Jean Apollon in San Antonio celebrated Jesus: because the terrorist knows just who he is. That's a haunting recognition. We might despise someone whose self-knowledge leads to such carnage, but the fact remains, who *we* say he is does not change who *he* says he is. This, too, is faith. And simply because *we* believe in something else does not make his faith something less.

Edna and I thanked each other for the three hours we spent in each other's company. "When I talk to you," she said, "it becomes real. My memories are the one thing they couldn't burn." In some respects, as the widow to an entire sect, Edna lives cursed with the burden of memory. She has charged herself with the mission of transmitting a believable, durable version of this family's obituary.

Edna poked her head out the doorway to speak to a woman walking her dogs around the property. When she did, I plucked a few bucks from my wallet and furtively crammed them into the donations box. The thing was: I felt compassion for Edna Doyle's loss. She and her fellow Branch Davidians believed a certain way and kept to themselves for the most part, and it got many of them incinerated. I looked out at the wooden frame of the new house rising behind me, and I shuddered with a queasy kind of wonder that belief could outlast Armageddon. It had for the Jews who survived the two destructions of the Temple in Jerusalem and the crematoria at Auschwitz. When she turned back into the room, she told me not to leave without the tape of David's last sermon and a copy of the Revelation of the Seven Seals.

"How much do I owe you for these?" I asked.

"Don't bother."

When I pulled out of the Mount Carmel Compound into gray dusk, having waved good-bye to Edna, I thought I heard her say, "Come back soon."

In the end, it's not easy to point to the true story of what happened there. The official findings of government inquiries stated that the Branch Davidians were apocalyptic, hence suicidal. Rather than surrender to the authorities, whose accusations of illegal weapons stockpiling and sexual abuse were well-grounded, they chose to set fire to their home and their church, killing themselves and their children in the process. But if you hear it from the Davidians' side, particularly in the gripping documentary *Waco: Rules of Engagement*, they were law-abiding neighbors, the accusations of improprieties were unfounded, and throughout the siege they sought negotiations, not confrontation. The FBI claims the Davidians started the conflict; the Davidians point the finger right back at the FBI.

On the looping two lane roads back to stoplights and highways, I recalled that Passover seder in the spring of 1993. This time I mentally rearranged the seating chart at my grandparents' white-clothed table. Separating my giggling, feuding younger cousins was Edna Doyle, who praised the brisket and warned us not to treat Passover only as a story.

The Haggadah tells us as much: "In every generation," we recite annually, "one must see oneself as though having personally come forth from Egypt." Edna would surprise my family by sharing how she, in addition to being a member of a cult, was a grandmother driven by loss, a survivor racked with guilt. "Like to see pictures of my Egypt?" she might have asked. "Care to hear stories about my wilderness?"

Three months into the pilgrimage, I found myself redecorating the spiritual topography of my past. Voices from the front page, once anonymous faces, crept into my memories. My table needed to be reset.

If Edna told us how our remembrance of our ancestors' suffering sustained her in her own struggle, would my family nod or cringe? If she said how closely the Hebrews' cries to the Lord paralleled the Davidians', would we ask for details or clear the table? Maybe when we are called to remember that we were once slaves we are closer to the "wackos from Waco" than either we or they believe. Somewhere on the trunks of our family trees, all of us are the descendants of a cult.

[27]

The next morning I arrived at Fort Worth's Wedgwood Baptist Church, a modern two-story building with a smooth, red brick exterior; a silver roof; a jet black parking lot that looks like it just had a shoeshine; and an aqua and pink playground with miniature plastic slides and four-foot ladders. When I drove up and stepped out of my gray Ford Taurus rental car, no kids were playing. A pair of spindly, just-planted trees grew from circular plots of soil and wood chips in front of the entrance. I peeked behind corners of the building, trying doors, finding them locked, then continuing to look for an open one. A woman approached the building with her hand gripped tightly around her little girl's shoulder, and for a long moment I saw myself as I thought they saw me, as a stranger approaching them, and felt for the first time on the trip not nervous but accused. No, it wasn't accused, it was suspect. I was an unfamiliar man, and this community didn't need any more of those.

Six weeks earlier, a deranged man had walked into this church and sprayed the sanctuary with gunfire. He killed seven people—choir members, seminarians, and high school students—before killing himself. I visited Wedgwood Baptist a month and a half after the night that changed the church's life.

In much the same way I had tracked down Edna Doyle, I located Mike Holton. The headlines of the recent past had thrust his home into the national glare, and it was the church's loss that attracted my attention. Mike's extension was the one the church secretary directed me to when I asked for the youth minister. That wasn't his job, but because the youth minister, in the wake of the deaths of seven young people, was understandably deluged, my call was rerouted to Holton's desk.

Holton gave the appearance of a man for whom three sizable square meals were the bare minimum. He shook hands with force, and his body was wide enough that when I hugged him upon saying goodbye four hours later, my hands had to have been six inches, maybe more, from touching each other on his back. His skin tanned, his hair mostly silver, his neck thick, and his button-down collar snug, he still had the pug nose and thin eyes of a little kid. If Spanky from *The Little Rascals* had grown up to work at a Baptist church, he might have become Mike Holton.

We sat in his office, in chairs opposite one another, separated by a few feet. Two decades earlier, before he had spent nearly thirteen years in the Carson City, Nevada, Fire Department, where he eventually wound up as assistant fire chief, Mike believed he was called to be a preacher. "It took me two weeks in seminary, talking to guys that God had called to preach, to realize that I don't like being in front of people. I forget my own name in front of a group." He assumed in the aftermath of those two weeks that he had misheard God's call. He returned to work in a fire company, but by the time he turned forty, he was once again uncertain—unsure if he was called, but certain of his confusion. It was a vocational metaphor that ultimately convinced him of his place: that of a firefighter of the soul, someone who could teach Christian fire prevention and put out the fires in peoples' lives. He returned to seminary, moving his family to Texas, and enrolled in a Christian Education program.

"I believe the Lord wanted me in Texas," Mike told me. In 1991, Mike came onto the staff of Wedgwood Baptist as the minister of education. The following year he became church administrator. "Now I tell people I'm the Minister of Toilets and Air Conditioners."

When I dialed the number of Wedgwood Baptist a week earlier, I asked myself if my visit constituted spiritual rubbernecking. In some respects the answer was, of course. But that answer came so easily that I assumed another question was more relevant to ask. The deeper question for Mike, and Edna Doyle, too, was not What do you believe? but How do you keep on believing? After the flood, after the world you have known is washed away, what role does faith play?

"It's real easy," he said, "especially in the work I do, taking care of the nuts and bolts—the plumbing, the electrical, the heating and air conditioning—to get religious. To just go through the motions. I have to keep reminding myself that the reason we have air-conditioned buildings, comfortable facilities, rest rooms, all that, is to facilitate people coming together, to worship the Lord, to come to know him."

"When you use the word *religious*," I said, "it takes on a negative feel. Where I come from, in New York and the Northeast, when we think about Baptists, we think we're thinking of 'religious' people. But you wouldn't think of yourself as religious."

Mike leaned forward and slowly shook his prodigiously large head from side to side. "I'm no theologian, Tom," he said. "I think it's easy to be religious. But I think there are a lot of religious people who are going to hell, because they're depending on their religiosity. They're going through the motions, they're living traditions, they're doing things the way they've been done for a long time, and they're depending on that to save them. When in fact the only thing that's going to save them is a personal relationship with Jesus Christ. In right relationship with him, our relationships with our families, wives, children, brothers, sisters, all of 'em, are going to be better than if we just try to do what's right. I'm closer to many in our church family than I am to many of my own blood kin, because of our relationship with the Lord. And that is not religious; that's Christian.

"After this shooting that happened, churches from literally all over have responded to us. Take the Church of Christ up the street. Now it's a different denomination. They practice their organization and their polity differently than we do. But they know the same Christ that we do. That's not religion. That's relationship."

The administrator of a Baptist church in Fort Worth, Texas, claimed not to be religious. By this point in my journey, such a statement ceased to be a startling thing to hear. The Baptists and the Pentecostals, the pious church attenders, the devoted Bible readers, and the Evangelicals all appeared to be the very models of modern religious Americans. But each asserted that he or she is not religious. Of course the choosers in our midst—Tim Turner, Maureen Scowby, Darnell Lyman, Kisna Duaipayana Das—didn't see themselves as religious either.

Despite widespread belief about America's religiousness, I now believed that Americans prefer not to portray themselves as religious. The apparently orthodox and the self-evidently searching, despite their many differences, share one sentiment in particular. They profess a spiritual belief, often possessing a personal relationship with their savior, but make certain that I know these points of view are explicitly not religious. They have said, "I'm no theologian," and "I'm not much for religion," and "what I believe is not religion." This is not a matter of semantics, either. Their opposition to the word is too strong to signal simply preference. Religion is formalized, institutional, and centered on tradition. "Relationship," or what others called "spirituality," is personal, particular, rooted in direct experience. At the core of religion is precedent; of relationship and spirituality, experience. Tradition is often seen as a kind of Old World relic, and an elevation of inheritance over experience, history over autobiography, predecessors over self. Americans, then, are believers who predicate their singular faiths on personal experience. As a consequence, the dominant religious impulses on the American landscape—from Pentecostalism and the born-again reliance on emotion and a personal relationship with Jesus Christ, to the self-help ethos illustrated, for example, in the rise of yoga as spiritual practice and physical fitness while removed from its Hindu roots—point to what I had come to see firsthand as the American ambivalence to history.

This ambivalence connects the experience of the "not religious" with the experience of the immigrant. Often hounded by contemporary violence or haunted by the specter of historical travails, immigrants arrive in America looking for a fresh start. This is, of course, the New World. The seduction of starting over has always butted metaphoric heads with the need to remember what had been left behind. When Mike Holton stressed relationship above religion, his point was, in fact, quintessentially American. The Christian's relationship with Jesus gives the believer new life. Jesus turns the soul's odometer back to 000.

When in the New Testament Jesus asks his disciples, "Who do people say that I am?" (Mark 8:27), the question is posed as a demographic query for his own time. But that question survives and endures, because each age absorbs, revises, and retransmits its own multiple answers to his question. Who does America say Jesus is? Messiah and Savior, yes; but also, I was finding, a friend, a best friend, a gentleman, and an intimate—an internal spiritual reality even more than an external historical one. He is painted the way many describe their relationships with their spouses. No longer the Prince of Peace, not really a revolutionary, he has become, especially for the millions of Evangelical Christians, a romantic lead, someone to love and be loved by. This Jesus is no accident: he is the intimate savior, the whisperer of sweet nothings, and the God who will make everything okay. This Jesus encourages starting over. He is the author of the incessant newness that America has made for itself.

"I'll tell you a story," Mike said. "And I'll probably cry telling it, because when my heart gets full, it runs out my eyes. Sunday, my wife and I went to Kim's folks' house for lunch. They showed us a videotape." Kim Jones was one of the victims of the shooting rampage earlier in the fall. "Kim had been doing some traveling for the summer, and she came to Saudi Arabia to visit with her parents, who worked there, before coming back here. She went to speak to some kids, and for some reason, though they don't usually do it, they videotaped it." Mike stifled back a sob. "You had to know Kim: twenty-three, vivacious, excited about life, exciting to be around. Just a beautiful young gal. She said, 'I've been living out of my backpack all summer. I've been spending a week with this family, two weeks with this family, maybe another with this family.' She said, 'It was so good to come home and be able to unpack my backpack and sleep in my own bed.' She said, 'Kids, I want you to understand something. We're backpackers here on this Earth. Our home is in heaven. And one day,' she said, 'this body's gonna die, and I'm going to get back home to heaven and unpack my backpack. I'm gonna get home and sleep in my bed that the Father's been preparing for me.'" Mike sniffled. "It just breaks your heart, how prophetic. We talk about heaven, but when you come to know Christ, heaven begins. You know? I heard one man say, 'When I move into heaven, it's going to be like an automatic transmission. I'm not even gonna feel it shift.'"

Despite the consolation he received, Mike admitted that he had struggled with the Lord in the days and swiftly passing weeks after the killings in his sanctuary. Why had God taken young people? Why not him? He had raised his family, had found his calling and done some good work. "Lord, why take a twenty-three-year-old girl who was just beginning, and leave this old guy?" Mike balled up his fist and rapped it against his chest as he said "this old guy." From the look of his eyes, I guessed that Mike's heart was full. "He could have taken me. I mean, he shot at me twice, and one of them missed me by this far," Mike said, holding his thumb and forefinger two or three inches apart. "Lord, if you'd taken me and left Kim, who knows what she would have accomplished in her lifetime? But her folks were telling us Sunday that they're going to distribute this tape to youth groups all over, as far and wide as they can. Kim will possibly have a greater impact through this tape than she ever would have had in her life."

At the funeral of one of the fourteen-year-olds killed in the attack, Wedgwood Baptist's senior pastor, Reverend Al Meredith, asked how many of the assembled had ever "been to the funeral of a martyr before?" While he delivered the sad, honest truth that martyrdom would not ease the pain and suffering at Wedgwood, he offered this assurance: "History teaches . . . that the death of a martyr is never wasted."

To many contemporary ears, affixing this notion of martyrdom to the deaths of those who did not choose such a designation appears a little creepy, almost opportunistic. I assumed martyrdom to be, at least historically, a choice. At Wedgwood Baptist there had been no chance to make a choice. A deranged man with guns and explosive devices (which mercifully never detonated) had opened fire, and before they had the chance to duck, more than a dozen people, most of whom were under twenty-five, were hit. For some, thinking of these innocent victims as martyrs made the gruesome act something else. When the event was translated as an act somehow sanctioned by God, the particulars were leeched of their realness. It was as if the pews stained with blood were hosed down, the pictures of the crime scene hygienically altered. The event was grisly and terrifying, the lives lost tragic and illogical. Kim Jones sounded like a terrific person. Her dying so young was miserable. Why make it more than it was, and in the process cast the killer in a role larger than was his due?

In reality, though, martyrdom is a title more frequently stamped on a victim by survivors. Whether the dead choose their fate or fall headlong into it, martyrdom is a designation made with the aid of perspective.

"So you were here that day?" I asked.

Mike nodded and blew his nose. "I was in the office, working on the computer, which had a virus. And the band was in there, warming up, re-verberatin' the walls. I'm old enough to where that kind of thing doesn't turn me on." I laughed and Mike smiled. The service was an after-school event for area youth at which Christian rock bands often performed.

"That's when I heard the first shot. From my arson investigation back-ground, and having qualified on the police pistol range, I know a gunshot when I hear it. Then two, three, four, five right afterwards. That's when he was shootin' and killin' the people in the hallway. But in my mind I said no, this is *church*. I figured Jay, our youth minister, was doing some kind of skit. Out loud, just to myself, I said, I'll bet he's using a starter pis-tol in this skit. And I thought, I'm gonna shoot 'im. You know? Because he's supposed to let me know about those kinds of things so I don't get too upset. There've been times when he set off smoke bombs and set the fire alarm off. Then, of course, I'm runnin' around trying to figure out where the fire is, and it's just a skit where he's using smoke bombs.

"So I went running down this hallway. And here's this stranger I didn't know and the hall is full of gunsmoke. And I'm thinkin', What in the world is goin' on? He sees me in the doorway and he crouches and, bang bang!" Mike's voice rose. His simulation of the gunshots punctured the pall hang-ing over the story. "I've seen a lot of gunshots coming from behind me, but that's the only two I ever saw from the business end. And I thought, this is not a skit. Well, by that time, I'd called 911, and they'd gotten calls from all over the place. There was a lady in the church, crouching down behind a pew, calling on her cell phone.

"The day after the shooting," Mike continued, "we met because we had to make some decisions about how we were gonna respond to this thing. The overarching consensus of our staff was that tragedies happen—in

Columbine, in Paducah, Kentucky—you know, everywhere. This isn't something that's just happened at Wedgwood Baptist Church. What we need to do here is to show people that tragedies happen, but that in the midst of tragedy there's hope. And his name is Jesus Christ." Mike's eyes were glassed over. I reached into my pocket and handed him a piece of Kleenex. I did it so reflexively that instinctively I patted down my pocket again, to be sure I hadn't given him something I'd already used. After his recounting of that night, I needed a tissue, too. No, it had been fresh.

The church had received seventeen thousand e-mails of condolence. In one, a Baptist woman writing from Saudi Arabia, where evangelism is prohibited by the government, reported that the memorial service for the kids had been televised by CNN throughout the desert kingdom. Mike said, "She wrote something like, 'What I've been trying to do here for twenty years is now being allowed by the government.'" Mike took a deep breath, then exhaled through his nose. He looked for a moment like a man pretending to be a bull for his grandkids. "I mean, praise the Lord. He used what we saw as a tragedy to spread the Good News.

"The next two or three weeks are just kind of a blur. But during that time the pastor gave a sermon about, Where was God in all that? He said, 'God was right where he was when his own son was killed, on a cross, two thousand years ago. Still loves us, still has a plan for us, still is in control.'"

Faced with a seemingly unanswerable why, the pastor, and by extension the community, chose to consecrate the deaths through martyrdom. This was a model elevated by Christianity but also shared by most other religious traditions. In Islam, for example, the word for "martyr," *shahid,* is also used to describe one who witnesses for the faith. The language and tradition of Islam position martyrs as models, spiritual exemplars who achieve both personal spiritual elevation and posthumous public commemoration.

In the story of Christianity, God is located in the tragic: it is God, embodied in the person of Jesus, who hangs on the cross. The pain, the suffering, the agony of the crucifixion is a central piece of the larger redemption story in Christianity. If Christians sought to be Christ-like and died what appeared to be meaningless deaths, what more suitable way to validate those lives than to brand them martyrs? By decreeing martyrdom, Reverend Meredith found a way to offer a graceful logic to the inexplicable and to endow the utterly random with a higher order.

Martyrs die public deaths, and from those deaths they gain a sacred kind of celebrity. The funeral services for those who died in the Wedgwood sanctuary were attended by thousands, including then Texas governor George W. Bush. Reverend Meredith spread the story of his homegrown martyrs far and wide, on local newscasts and *Larry King Live.*

Though different in kind, this televised testimony is not all that different in form from the eerily triumphant reporting of suicide bombers on stations like the Arabic-language al-Jazeera. The hortatory broadcasts acclaiming the suicidal act and its homicidal impact change the criminally premeditated into something culturally celebrated. Suicide is forbidden in Islam: it is a sign of desperation and hopelessness. But when seen through the lens of martyrdom, suicide becomes spiritual self-sacrifice and an expression of political defiance. These Islamic martyrs, like Kim Jones, like all martyrs, die with many hailing them as champions of the faith.

Despite these similarities, there is, of course, something fundamentally different among the pathways to martyrdom. Kim Jones was a victim. The human bombs, as Imam Farooq in Toledo stressed, are murderers. How their fates are reworked is part of the transformative power of faith. But it's strangely ironic, given Mike Holton's distaste for "religion": this transformative wringing of meaning from meaninglessness is something I understood to be a central task of religion.

Mike and I spoke a little longer. By that time, lunchtime, I figured I needed to let him go. So I thanked him, we hugged, my hands not meeting behind his back, and I headed for the men's room down the hall. Though quiet and darkened during my visit, the hallway remained a work site, because of the necessary repair of the walls from the damage caused by the bullets. A minute later I heard the whistle and heavy footsteps of someone approaching the door. I smiled at Mike Holton from a partitioned urinal. In the small space, in that awkward meeting after we had already hugged and said goodbye, I felt the tug of banter and an obligation to wash my hands with water *and* soap.

"So, what're you doing for lunch?" Mike asked.

Flattered, I said, "Nothing."

"You like Mexican food?" I nodded yes. "Why don't you come with me?"

The minister of toilets and air conditioners parked his sky blue pickup truck outside the restaurant, and the waitress brought us two glasses of water, menus, and a basket of tortilla chips. When with an elder and at a restaurant where chips or bread is served before the ordered food arrives, I don't reach into the basket until they do. It's a habit born of my desire to locate in small gestures appropriate expressions of deference. Mike waited, so I did, too.

"Are you married?" Mike asked. "Do you have kids, Tom?"

"No and no. I do have a serious girlfriend studying to be a doctor up in Chicago." I told him about Liz.

"She sounds terrific," he said in a genuine, avuncular tone. "What's she doing up there and you doing down here?"

A good question. I wasn't about to mire Mike Holton in my few days
with Liz in Chicago and their aftermath, so I chose to sum up. "Well, you
know, I'm just trying to finish up this project." I caught the waitress out
of the corner of my eye pushing open the kitchen doors with our enchi-
lada platters.

While Mike Holton reached for his napkin and lay it in his lap, as the
plates breathed steam in our faces, I grabbed a chip, dunked it in the
tomato salsa, and lifted it to my mouth. The bite had actually crossed
the plane of my mouth when I heard Mike say, with head bent toward
the table, "Tom, I'd like to say grace." Oh, *shit*. If I crunched, I laid waste
to the sensible, sensitive etiquette I had shown thus far. If I bit down, would
Grace be compromised? Would the enchiladas not be blessable? I had only
one chance at escape: with my top teeth I scraped the salsa off the chip
and onto my tongue, and I eased the chip—slowly, slowly, no quick moves
and nobody gets hurt—down to the side of the plate. Whether Mike saw
I'll never know. But he didn't ask for a do-over. My faux pas hadn't compelled him to start again.

[28]

I drove through a broad, combustible political and religious divide on my
way from Fort Worth to Dallas, from a Baptist church to a Wiccan gathering place. The Betwixt and Between Community Center, the pagan holiday
Samhain, and in a larger sense, pagan and Wiccan spiritual observance, had
become political fodder in Texas over the previous six months.

In June 1999, Fort Hood, a Texas Army base, gave official sanction to
pagan religious observance and provided space for its three hundred "neopagan" enlisted men and women to worship. (Paganism and neopaganism
are imprecise umbrella terms used to describe the religions of Wiccans,
witches, Druids, and Earth worshipers, among many other idiosyncratic
belief systems. These terms are not necessarily synonymous, as I would
come to understand.)

Since the late 1970s, the U.S. Army has recognized Wicca under the cat-
egory of "natural religion," featuring an evenhanded description of core
beliefs and ritual observances in its military chaplains' handbook. But Fort
Hood's explicit recognition set off a firestorm of indignation from a host
of conservative Christian clergy. A coalition of thirteen groups went so
far as to call on all Christians not to enlist or reenlist in the U.S. military
until Wicca had been banned from military posts. They couched this fight
in the language of good and evil. The Army's soul was at stake.

In addition, the pagan community's ritual celebrations on October 31 struck many conservative Christians as, well, pagan. To them, *pagan* signaled primitive, pre-Christian, and polytheistic. Conservative Christians, on the eve of the twenty-first century, looked at the ritual of Samhain and the celebration of Halloween and, conflating them, believed them to be two sides of the same satanic coin. This, however, was a historically inaccurate understanding because, as I learned, Samhain, a tradition older than Christianity, has no genealogical link to Satanism, a belief system that depends on the existence of Christianity for its conviction.

In a funky neighborhood bordering Dallas's Fair Park, a collection of Art Deco buildings that plays host to the annual Texas state fair, I found Betwixt and Between along a strip of restored, converted warehouses. One warehouse was now the office of an Internet start-up, another was the setting for a coffee shop, while still others had become loft apartments. Dallas's Wiccan community had planted itself in a yuppie, bohemian enclave.

A tall, rose-colored front door opened into a cavernous interior, dimly lit, scattered with small tables, chairs, sofas, and two bars. The space had been a restaurant and night club before the Wiccans moved in. I asked for the owner or director, and a woman named Maeven Eller came out to meet me.

Wicca is an explicitly modern creation, a collage of beliefs and observances that derive from both ancient Celtic myths and modern Western imaginations. Believers think of themselves as recovering the religious practice of the indigenous people of Europe. When I asked for her own description, Maeven Eller said, "Without trying to sound all light and fluffy, we *are* tree huggers. We don't worship nature, but we revere it, and we honor it with the turning seasons. We give thanks that every day the sun comes up, that we've lived another day." *Wiccan* is a term that replaced *witch* to describe these believers; *pagan,* and subsequently *neopagan,* became other titles used by the community and its adherents.

"How did this place get started?" I asked her once we had sat down on plush velvet couches at a circular cocktail table.

"It's sort of a magical thing," she said, perhaps not unexpectedly. Maeven Eller was thirty-eight, a mom, and the creator of Betwixt and Between. She had straight auburn hair, parted down the middle, a porcelain-white face with flushed cheeks, and an upturned nose. She had the stout roundness of one of those archaic, 25,000-year-old fertility goddess icons found in the caves of Lascaux, France. She wore a necklace of a pentagram—a five-pronged star inscribed in a circle—over a black shirt emblazoned with a white symbol of the Oak King Faire. I didn't know what that was, though I assumed it was a medieval fair or festival that had passed through town recently, given the crispness of the ironed-on logo. Maeven had practiced

Wicca as a "solitary" for twenty years. This meant that she essentially practiced her own faith, whether in meditation, chanting, or prayer with candles or herbs, on her own. A Wiccan can choose whether to worship as a solitary or as part of a community.

"I remember the moment," she said. "It was November 1, 1996, the day after Samhain. I had gone back to the place where we had had the circle in the woods." The circle is a Wiccan ritual gathering. Maeven and friends had held their circle in the woods, but an outdoor location is not mandatory. "There had been seven of us walking in front, leading 120 people carrying tiki torches. We were singing the goddess chant: 'She's been waiting, she's been waiting, waiting so long for her children to remember, to return. We are the old people, we are the new people, we are the same people, stronger than before.'"

Then in the middle of a divorce settlement, Maeven had planned to spend a month or two in Ireland and England when the split was finalized. "That was my greatest hope in life," she told me. "But we have something we call a 'flash on a flame,' where you get a moment of inspiration. All my life I had said, 'I'm just training for the day that it happens.' And everyone would go, 'What's *it*?' And I'd say, 'I don't know, but I'm supposed to do something big. When it happens, I'm just gonna know.' I was standing there, in the woods, and as I turned and looked across the circle, I realized people only got together every six weeks. And I heard a voice, as though someone was speaking to me: I was supposed to open a community center. The idea literally possessed me, and there wasn't anything else I could do."

With her idea and her passion, Maeven did what any savvy spiritual entrepreneur does: she took to the streets, initiating conversations, conducting informal polls to find out what other area Wiccans thought of the idea. "I found out that people could go to open circles and rituals and classes and those kinds of things, but there was no place to gather between festivals. And it was very important that we had an urban sanctuary, a place we could turn to in a moment of need and crisis. It would set up all kinds of new situations we had not enjoyed as a people or as a culture. I took the money from my divorce settlement that I was going to use for my trip to Europe, and I opened up a community center." Maeven brushed her hand through her long hair. I only half-expected a parrot to fly out from under it.

A reliable estimate of the number of Wiccans in the United States, offered by the Web site religioustolerance.org, puts the total somewhere near 750,000. This would make Wicca the fifth largest religious community in the United States, behind Christianity, Islam, Judaism, and Hinduism. Before arriving, I had sensed that Wicca is more a smattering of 750,000 solitaries than a circle of 750,000 adherents. Yet the fact that individual Wiccans like Maeven had molded their own community centers, and that Wiccans in the military had demanded the right to worship as a community on base, implied that Wiccans around the country were beginning to conceive of themselves as a well-defined group.

I suspected that part of the rationale behind being a solitary was a tacit concession that outing oneself as a Wiccan remained a risky thing to do. Maeven told me about an event just months earlier, in Killeen, Texas, west of Fort Hood, in which a local Fundamentalist pastor had called his congregants together for a "March Against Wickedness." The event targeted the military base's Wiccans and a store in nearby Copperas Cove called the New Age Connection, co-owned by a Wiccan high priestess. Forty marchers turned up at the shop on Labor Day, 1999, the same day I met with Sokha Diep two thousand miles away in Lowell, Massachusetts. The marchers arrived with signs reading "Turn or Burn" and "Napalm the Witches." But like the climactic scene in a stirring after-school special about religious tolerance, more than 150 Wiccans and friends stood in front of the store, holding signs that said, "Love Thy Neighbor." Both sides chanted, and the showdown ended peacefully.

Wiccans who identify themselves to the wider culture understand this move as a spiritual coming-out, perhaps no less risky than the sexuality kind. By doing so, they put themselves at personal risk. Of course, the fewer people there are who came out of this "broom closet," the less reliable information and the less constructive contact between the broader culture and the Wiccan community there will be. And the damaging cycle of misinformation about Wicca will run on.

The notion that articulating a belief in God, or in the case of Wicca, a goddess, might be considered a coming out made me think of a conversation I'd had with a forty-something woman named Sunny Schwartz while in San Francisco three weeks earlier. Sunny, a tall, garrulous, husky brunette, Chicago native, and friend of mine, worked in the San Francisco prison system.

"I always believed in God," Sunny said during our conversation in her living room. She had sustained her Chicago accent, so "God" from her mouth came out "Gahd." "My friends are very activist people, and most all of them are atheists. And one day, it was back in the '70s, I'll never forget it, they were talking about all these God-believing people, and blah blah blah blah blah. And I said, 'You know folks, I believe in God.' They were like, '*What*? We've known you, we've talked about everything under the sun, but we had no idea you believed in God.'"

I asked her, "Was that like a coming out in its own way?"

"It was totally a coming out. I mean, here we *did* talk about everything under the sun, from sexuality to politics to our activism, but we never talked about the classic question, 'Do you believe in God?' I remember my friend Ruth said, 'You know, I never had a friend who believed in God. You're my first.'"

At the time, Sunny's personal declaration blinked with a neon sort of familiarity. When I was in divinity school, my childhood friend Noah used to send bogus updates to our high school's alumni office for use in its magazine, which was printed and mailed semiannually to the school's several thousand alumni. A couple of the updates were in fact printed in the Class of '92 section. In each update, Noah concocted a fiction that played wildly with my religious education. He wrote in one that I lived somewhere in the mountains of Jordan, in another that I spent my days roaming the pastures of New Zealand as a shepherd.

These claims were not unlike the plans I had offered at my divinity school graduation, when the acting dean read aloud the statements of future plans for each of the hundred-something graduates. Around me were ministers-to-be, future high school religion teachers, budding specialists in the feminist hermeneutics of a sixth-century desert community, and documentarians of ashrams for HIV-infected prostitutes in India. These were serious people with definite futures. I, on the other hand, was slated to conduct an oral history of religion in America. That's how I summed up my project for the dean's announcement. In addition, I had written that I planned to begin a highly profitable tele-rabbi program. The commencement audience, composed of classmates and their families, professors and alumni, basically exploded with laughter after hearing my plans. I blushed and looked down at my feet, both humbled by and adoring of the extended moment of laughter at my good line delivered by a straight man at an unexpected time. The latter prediction was a tease, but a classmate I hadn't known too well approached me afterward and asked what channel I'd be on. "No, I was just playing," I confessed, and she seemed genuinely disappointed. I left the ceremony that day feeling, to be frank, like a bit of a clown. In June 1999, I had been sitting on the idea for my pilgrimage for almost a year, rubbing at the writer's callus on the middle finger of my right hand, imagining the people I would meet and the conversations I would have—in short, considering the path as if it would soon be a pilgrimage. And in its initial public offering, I had served it up as the preface to a punch line. In the echo of their laughter, with the when of the whim growing imminent, I got nervous.

For both me and my friends, humor disguised an uneasy curiosity. My own self-parody, and their fruitful attempts at sketching a caricature of my unconventional exploration, drew a veil over my religious coming out. Yet faith was about stepping up, being visible, "coming out from among them," as Mother Booker had said. In my moments of coming out, the people I told, whether my friend Chris Greene during our ad hoc Shabbat or Harvey Lee Green during our conversation in his Raleigh prison, appeared grateful. They pulled closer rather than pushed farther away. They sought more information from me, and shared more of themselves in the aftermath of my sharing. What repeatedly struck me in these expressions might be a shared element of many kinds of coming-out: every time I said I believed, I believed more. Just as cynicism and mistrust are contagious, so too is possibility.

Betwixt and Between gives the pagans of the Dallas–Fort Worth area a launching pad for their coming-outs, and a landing pad for the aftermath of their leaps into public identification. Before Betwixt and Between opened its doors, a Wiccan in Dallas or a spiritual seeker like me had no explicit, physical place to go to learn. Betwixt and Between offers classes on Wicca and Celtic studies, provides meeting space, organizes concerts, hosts parties, and convenes spiritual gatherings. This is not just a community center; it is also a congregation. Betwixt and Between resembles Tim Turner's Coffee Messiah: one doesn't have to call the storefront a congregation for it to behave like one. Yet Maeven has a more conventional religious ambition than Tim. She has a license to serve as a minister, and Betwixt and Between is a nonprofit religious organization seeking church status. Maeven, then, wants her community to be considered mainstream enough that it isn't a threat to the social order and distinct enough that it can create and maintain its own identity.

One tool Maeven used to establish a pagan community is the Internet. "The persecution we suffered before won't happen again," Maeven assured me, "because we are so connected through the Web." Being wired enables small communities in disparate places to link into one large, self-identified culture. "We can, within an hour, make almost every pagan community in this country and Europe aware of what's going on. And we are a letter-writing bunch of people. Not only that, but we vote, and we're going to keep voting." Religion and politics are inseparable for a religious organizer like Maeven. An active role in the political process functions as the public means for Wiccans to carve a foothold in the culture. Through politics, Wiccans like Maeven have outed themselves. Interestingly, this is the same path that the Fundamentalist Christians traveled on their way to cultural clout. This is how Pagans have told the world who they are, and *that* they are. In chat rooms, through Web sites, by creating virtual circles, and by connecting geographically remote solitaries, the Internet has allowed the Wiccan community to be at once underground and above board. But a brick-and-mortar sanctuary like Betwixt and Between was the next step in that evolution.

Maeven's solitary voice had nudged her, whispering "community" loud enough that she could no longer ignore the message. She had turned her whim from fantasy into reality. What a weird twist from Baptist minister of education Mike Holton that morning. The people who seemed most obviously religious renounced the term. And those who seemed most explicitly spiritual were in fact creating the religious in their midst.

"There was no room for me in Christianity," Maeven said when I asked how she had become a pagan. "I will never forget when I was a kid in Batesville, Indiana, driving down the road with the minister and his wife. We had just eaten lunch at some fast-food place, and we still had all the wrappers in the car. As we were going down the road, the minister rolled down the window and threw the bag out on the road. I asked him why he'd done it. He explained it away with, 'Someone'll clean it up.' But I was horrified.

"Then it was frustrating to be a girl in the church: I could run the youth group, I could put on the Christmas pageants, but I was never allowed to speak before the church because I was a woman. They told me the root of all sin was women's fault, and the best thing I could ever be was a wife to a good man." In Wicca, Maeven discovered a spiritual path that allowed women to take leadership positions, to be in charge of their own spiritual progress, and to create the kind of community she wanted to find.

Another thread that neopagans have woven through their solitary practices and perspectives is a common heritage of oppression. Though Maeven may be the first witch in her family tree in several thousand years, she has embraced the pagan history of persecution, of forcible conversion and being burned at the stake. I'm not sure it was a conscious act, but the neopagan community has torn a page out of Judaism's playbook. The tradition's survival is predicated on remembering the suffering of predecessors and highlighting the culture's fragility in such a way that the contemporary adherent feels as though she has endured those tribulations herself. "It's always been okay to hate us," Maeven told me, and it didn't sound all that dissimilar to "Remember you were a slave in Egypt."

"You would never see someone on television commercials making fun and being discriminatory toward your tradition," she said, referring to Judaism. "Because the coalition would go after them. But we're fair game.

We're sport. They come after us with a vengeance because we're evil in their eyes. Well, how did we get to be evil? Who decided? What makes that right? If they just took a little time to get to know us, they would see how incredibly spiritual we are. We recycle. We use biodegradable things. We use soap that doesn't hurt the environment. For goddess' sake, we don't put our cigarette butts on the ground." For goddess' sake, I said to myself: too, too good.

Winners claim the right to write history. But losers, if they survive, can write their own. "How did we get to be evil?" Maeven asked, though the words could have come from Branch Davidian Edna Doyle's mouth just as easily. Who writes the rules? Why them? Why not us? The Branch Davidians were a cult because that's what we, the American media-consuming public, heard several times a day during the first half of 1993. Witches, or rather, Salem residents who were branded witches, were considered to deserve their immolation in the New England colonies; getting rid of them purified the community. But sides change. Shapes shift. Stories are retold. Who gets editing privileges? Whoever makes it their business to tell one version of the story. This, too, is a cardinal expression of the postmodern ethos and its multicultural manifestations. A single, authoritative history is replaced by many histories told from many perspectives, each history a reflection and an interpretation of reality.

Maeven has turned vision into creation. In the process of outing herself, she has given hundreds of other Wiccans and witches and neopagans in Dallas and the surrounding areas permission to do the same. "I really would like to enlighten the world that we're just the indigenous people of Europe," Maeven said. "We've just had two thousand years of bad press, and I'd like to work on that." To make herself into what she was not yet, Maeven had done what I did more than three months earlier: she had pulled out her wallet. With money from a divorce settlement, she had effectively named herself a regional public relations director for the Wiccan faith, and declared that she was as much "indigenous European" as Indiana girl.

"Most of us are on the path of ourselves," Maeven said. "I'm on the path of Maeven. Everything I learn lends itself to the path of Maeven. Whatever works for me and enhances my idea of spirituality, that's what I do. But we're all Wiccans."

I thanked Maeven, wished her and Betwixt and Between best wishes for a secure and prosperous future, then spent forty-five minutes or so wandering around the adjacent Dallas fairgrounds. On the hard floor beneath a concrete half-shell canopy, I surveyed the vast, quiet, hollow space. On other days, summer days, barkers shouted, I was sure, and ice cream melted and Ferris wheels spun. And from inside humid, stuffy tents, the kind with canvas flaps, came the zealous holler of preachers as people rose from their seats, waving their right hands in the air like a Texas state flag in a soft breeze. My mind wandered into those make-believe tents, then back up the interstate toward Fort Worth and Mike Holton's office. When we had spoken, I hadn't known if he knew I wasn't a Baptist, or that I wasn't even a Christian. So I told him, "I'm Jewish," and Mike held his head still.

"Tom," he said, shrugging those hulking shoulders, "I'm not a theologian."

I shook my head. "You are as much as I am."

"But let me ask you about a gift, Tom." Mike reached into his denim shirt's front pocket. "I'm going to give you a pen." It was a nice pen, somewhere between a Bic and a fountain pen in quality. "Now, you don't know me real well, but you figure, well, 'he's associate pastor at a church, he must be pretty reputable. If he says he's gonna give me a pen, he's gonna give me a pen.' Whose pen is it?"

"In your hand?" I asked, pointing down at the pen in his palm, plush and creased like a slept-on sofa.

"Yeah."

"Well, I think it's your pen right now."

"When does it become your pen? If I'm offering it to you as a gift?" Ooh, what had my dad said was the law's perspective on possession? I couldn't remember.

"When I accept the gift," I said with a gulp.

"Mm huh," Mike hummed. "Now, you might say, 'Well, I don't deserve this gift. Let me do something for you, Mike.' No, no, no, no. Then it's gonna be wages. It's gonna be something you try to earn. You can't do enough to earn this pen. See, I just want to give it to you. You really have two choices: you can either accept it or you can reject it. That's all you can do with a gift."

I knew where he was going, had known since he pulled the pen from his pocket and started speaking about gifts.

"God has offered his son Jesus Christ as a gift to mankind, to pay the price for our sin, so that spiritually, we can have fellowship with him. 'For God so loved the world, that he gave his only begotten son, that whosoever believeth in him would not perish, but have everlasting life.'" Mike handed me the pen. Holding my breath, biting my lip, I took it from him and gripped it with quivering fingers I tried futilely to calm.

Mike continued: "He's taught me over the years that I can't know enough, I can't find out enough, I can't analyze or learn enough. All I can do is recommend him to others. He says in the Book of Revelation, 'Behold,

I stand at the door and knock. And if any man hears my voice and opens the door, I'll sup with him and he with me.' Today Christ is standing at the door of your heart, Tom, knocking," Mike rapped his knuckles against the top of his desk, "and he's saying, 'I want to be a part of your life.'"

I exhaled. "Oh, but he is a part of my life," I said, my tone sounding as though I protested when I agreed. "Absolutely. See, when I read the New Testament and when I look at Jesus I say, 'This is a man I want to be like.' This was a man who many considered, and then many denounced, as a rabbi. This was a man who understood himself to be within the Jewish tradition, but trying to learn from it, trying to grapple with it, trying in his way to revitalize it. He wanted to be with other people. I believe I have taken those lessons into my heart. And if you want to say that I'm—" my mouth stopped, my forearm clenched as again my fingers tightened around the pen.

"You know," I continued, "I think about it. Certainly I consider myself Jewish. But if being saved is about taking Jesus into your heart, trying to know him, trying to have him influence your life, do I also then consider myself saved in some respects? Absolutely."

"Good." Mike nodded. "And there's no conflict between the two."

"I couldn't agree with you more," I said. "And what I'm realizing is that you can be both—"

"That's right—"

"And it doesn't make you less of the other—"

"Amen."

I wasn't talking about being a Jew for Jesus. I was talking about being a Jew *with* Jesus. What was the difference? It seemed perfectly clear to me, I thought, and I hoped Mike understood it the same way. He might not have. At that point I didn't care. A Jew for Jesus appropriated Jewish symbols and customs and rituals to act Jewish, though in his core beliefs, in his understanding of Jesus as the Messiah, as the Risen Christ, he believed as a Christian. A Jew with Jesus was a totally different ballgame, because this approach found meaning solely in Jesus' Jewishness, discarding the millennia of claims and costumes and customs attached to Jesus that had made him the Christ and not merely a man.

The Christian religion, from its fledgling early days to its decree as the Roman imperial faith, through the authoring of creeds and the convening of councils, over centuries of evangelism and missions and crusades, not only appropriated Judaism, transforming the Hebrew scriptures into the Old Testament, but also filtered the Judaism from Jesus so that he became the first Christian and no longer a Jew at all. But Jesus was a Jew, lived and died as one. So for Jews to yield our communal right to claim him as our own, because we'd been ostracized and marginalized and tortured in his name for many centuries, was to forfeit one of the hallmarks and landmarks of Jewish thought and life, and a benchmark of the postmodern perspective as well: the right to reinterpretation.

If Judaism had a hall of fame—and thank you God that it does not (imagine the arguments on where we would put it, Jerusalem or New York?)—surely the carpenter from Nazareth would be enshrined. After all, here was one of the all-time great Jews, and we as a community no longer consulted him, no longer thought of him as a resource, as a teacher, as a guide. We as a people no longer considered him one of us, and that, to me, was a tragic loss.

So yes, I thought while in the Dallas fairgrounds, consider me saved, Mike Holton and Wedgwood Baptist. Consider me saved, Johnny Lay and Mother Booker. Consider me saved, Jeff Paul and Jerry Falwell. Except I'm going to make that mean something else, something new, something my own—not to diminish the way you know it, but to expand the way I do. In the process of reshaping and retrofitting Jesus to make him both applicable and appropriate for my life, wasn't I engaging in a most American form of interpretation?

I stood up, hopped down from the stage I had been sitting on and back onto the sidewalk. I walked back in the direction of Betwixt and Between, where my car was parked. I felt good. The Wiccan notion of being a solitary in a circle, following your own ripple amid the current of a larger community, suddenly felt especially well-tailored to my pilgrimage. Create your own path in the context of a wider, evolving story line, that's what Maeven meant when she said, "I follow the path of Maeven." All of the Wiccans at Betwixt and Between were bound together by the fact that each of them had searched out her or his own truth. "That's one thing that's important in a lot of the pagan religions," Maeven had said. "*You* find what *you* believe." Of course, this could make for spiritual anarchy, but the pagan community of Dallas seemed to be making strides toward establishing perimeters, securing a flexible kind of order for their faith as a community. Somehow, in their individual rebellions, they were finding each other. If the witches could do it, so could I.

Maybe, I thought to myself as I opened the car door, turned the ignition key, and pulled out of my spot—maybe I'm not just saved. Maybe I'm pagan, too. I could be, as Johnny Lay had suggested to me back in his home in Alameda, California, a "disciple of many people."

I didn't put the pieces together until I had left Maeven and drove into November and the three-month marker of the pilgrimage. I didn't connect the afternoon spent with Edna Doyle with the tragic loss at Mike

Holton's church, my brother-in-law's family's grief with the Wiccan pre-occupation with the spirit world at this time of the year. But each and all of them are connected. We had moved past Halloween and All Saints' Day. November 1 and 2 also marked Los Dias de los Muertos, the Mexican holiday in which the living celebrate the homecoming of the dead. Over the centuries, as the Aztecs and other Meso-American religious traditions had commemorated the holiday. Los Dias de los Muertos depicted death as neither a taboo subject nor a tragedy, but as a familiar, honored guest. This was the time of year, so it was said, when the space between living and dead was thinnest, most gossamer. For these communities, death was a comma, not a period.

Maybe it *was* the time of year, and maybe it was a divine elbow in my side, but the deeper into Texas I drove, the more commonplace encounters with death became. I was beginning to think that on an American pilgrimage there were two things one could not avoid: death and Texas.

I had dinner that night in Dallas with a group of friends, and I talked with a woman who asked me if I'd ever visited a huge congregation, like Riverside Church in New York. I told her I had, but never for a service. She said she had considered it, too, without ever following through.

"I think I'd be embarrassed," she said. "Like I wasn't supposed to be there and they knew it." She was afraid of being singled out as a tourist, or a voyeur, or a spectator. She worried that in attending she would turn sacred time into visiting hour, sanctity into spectacle.

I told her no. "I totally understand that feeling, but I don't think that's how it works. Those are our own fears, not their responses." We feel uncomfortable in those religious settings because (1) we assume everybody knows more than we do, (2) we believe everybody knows we're outsiders, and (3) somehow we consider ourselves unworthy of sitting in that setting. So many of us feel like imposters, even in our own faith traditions. As a consequence, we tend to think that crossing faith boundaries, expressing curiosity or interest or uncertainty, is especially off limits, that we have to have ourselves and our traditions figured out before we encounter others. But maybe we need others to begin to grasp our own.

"My experience has shown me that they'd welcome you," I told her. "They'd welcome the chance to show off, to share their world and speak their minds about it. They wouldn't even eye you like the potential convert you are. They'd just like that you made the effort to come out."

One could look and one could touch: the traditions wouldn't break, and they wouldn't infect. It is in the searching that we gain a better sense of where we stand. It is in the encounters with the other that we receive a clearer picture of who we are.

[29]

Every detour has its own logic.

I took an early flight from Dallas to Albuquerque that next morning, and a couple of hours later the wrong turn I took on the way to visit Chimayo, New Mexico's famous healing church, proved to be a serendipitous mistake. In the process of making a three-point turn on a dusty back road to retrace my steps and get back on the highway, a Camaro, its color faded like old blue jeans, screamed out of a driveway, its screech sudden and jolting. The car's front bumper headed straight for the side of the gray Corolla I had rented from the Albuquerque Airport's Budget Rent-a-Car not two hours earlier. But at the last minute the driver must have jerked the wheel the way one does when a race car video game is ending badly, and one final, furious spinning of the wheel is your last chance to get a full quarter's worth. Somehow, his car missed mine, and he gunned the engine as a farewell, leaving a plume of yellow dust rising and hanging in the crisp, late-morning air.

Cursing to myself, wondering how high the Camaro's driver had been, I pressed gingerly on the gas pedal when I looked up, back in the direction I had come from, and through the settling yellow film I spotted the gleam of a gold-plated dome rising above a row of trees. I kid you not. It was low enough that I hadn't seen it while driving past the first time. Slowly (what at most was a five-mile-an-hour pace) I drove toward the dome.

Just about a year earlier I had gotten into a conversation with a woman who sat next to me in a class. She was an undergrad at Harvard who had been raised in New Mexico. She looked like hundreds of other twenty-year-old women do at Harvard: shoulder-length brown hair, white skin, blue jeans, and a backpack on both shoulders. She gave no external cues, through dress, behavior, or language, that she was a Sikh, but she had been one since birth. While preparing to hit the road I wrote myself a dozen notes to contact her, so I could visit the congregation where she had grown up. The notes nagged and nagged, but never were they so persuasive as to convince me to contact her. I had chalked it up as "Oh well, I guess that stop isn't meant to be," when in truth it was straight-up laziness.

But laziness and bad navigation had, through contagion, acquired the silver lining of providence; only because of the wrong turn and near crash did I wind up visiting Española, New Mexico's Sikh *gurdwara,* the congregation's sanctuary and my classmate's spiritual home base. *Ridiculous,* my friend Danny would have no doubt said.

Virkaur Khalsa, "an Anglo," in her own words, wore a white turban around her head, revealing only the slightest hint of hairline at the top of her forehead. It was Virkaur (veer-CAR) I met as soon as I parked my car and walked in, and she who told me to come back a little bit later in the afternoon if I wanted to talk.

"That's great," I said. "But before I go, one question: could you maybe help me out with directions to Chimayo?"

The *Santuario,* or healing church of Chimayo, was a Catholic shrine where miracles were reputed to have blessed the infirm, the lame, and the crippled. Apparently the dirt there had holy, medicinal properties. A jumbled pile of abandoned crutches, canes, and braces were testaments to the miracles performed in the church. The stack of metal and wood looked to me like ready-made iconography, as though French poet and painter Marcel Duchamp, the parish priest, and a football team's injured reserve list conspired to create a shrine with what they carried.

Dusk had already inked the sky violet in Española when I returned to the Sikh *gurdwara.* I knew I didn't have much time before I'd need to hit the road again if I was going to make it at a reasonable hour for my visit with Ruth Blum, the grandmother of the guy I had met playing pool in New Orleans. She lived a three-hour drive away in Alamosa, Colorado. Most of the people wandering through the *gurdwara* were Anglos like Virkaur. Walking down the long hallway from the front door to see her, I passed a tall man, his head wrapped in a turban. I said hello. He returned with "How's it going?" What was he doing saying, "How's it going?" Shouldn't he offer me some traditional greeting? I wondered as I passed him. Over my shoulder I heard him call out to somebody leaving for the night, "See you mañana." What was that about? The whole scene felt a little incongruous. I expected to see many people who looked like Baba Singh, the Sikh I'd met at the Indian restaurant in Des Moines, Iowa. Here in northern New Mexico, the Sikhs' white faces and turbaned heads made me think I had wandered into a forty-something, New Age potluck, where each month the members wore the garb of a different faith community to convey their multicultural leanings.

Sikhism had come a long way since its inception in Punjab, Baba Singh's home in western India, at the turn of the sixteenth century. Its founder, a man named Guru Nanak, fused *Bhakti,* an emotional type of worship rooted in Hindu spirituality, with components of *Sufism,* the mystical thought and practice of Islam, to create an independent amalgam. Following a mystical experience and a series of pilgrimages through India and what today are Pakistan, Sri Lanka, Afghanistan, Saudi Arabia, and

Iraq, Guru Nanak preached a radical inclusiveness in which Muslims and Hindus, high and low castes, men and women were to live in community with one another. He rejected asceticism and elevated a dispassionate worldliness—"To be in the world but be not worldly," in Nanak's teaching—as the essence of a Sikh's way of life. Guru-ship was the foundation of Nanak's vision: believers had teachers, who helped guide them to *moksha,* what in Hinduism (and Buddhism) means "liberation." There was no messiah, no *avatara* (living incarnations of the Divine), just the guru, a human spiritual guide. After Nanak's death, another guru succeeded him. This means of succession continued until the tenth guru, Guru Gobind Singh, ruled that no longer would the guru be a single living person. Instead, the Sikh scriptures, the *Sri Guru Granth Sahib*—a compilation of the teachings and poetry of the first four gurus, interspersed with wisdom excerpted from other spiritual traditions—became the permanent spiritual guru. And the *Khalsa,* the baptized Sikh initiates, would live as a communal guru, holding each other responsible for the teaching and transmission of the written wisdom.

To generate a sense of communal identity, a guru who followed Nanak required all Sikh men to take the name *Singh,* which means "lion," and all Sikh women to take the name *Kaur,* translated as "princess." *Khalsa* is a Persian word for "the Pure." It is another name taken by many in the Sikh community who have undergone a Sikh's baptism. *Vir,* Virkaur told me, means "brave." So Virkaur Khalsa is a descriptive name that means "Princess Brave in Spirit." "We take spiritual names to aspire to something that's more lofty," she said.

Virkaur, in her early forties, grew up in a family of seventeen children. Two of her other siblings are now Sikhs. She stated her own reasons for becoming Sikh like this: "Even before I was a Sikh I just knew I was going to become one. I had a jam for my seventeenth birthday. A friend of mine came who knew someone who'd been a Sikh. He said Sikhs are vegetarians, they don't cut their hair, and they do yoga. I was into all those things, so I decided then and there to become a Sikh." She also had liked the way Sikhs sing and dance a lot.

I might have branded Virkaur's conversion and subsequent faith journey as irretrievably flaky, an emblem of New Age whimsy, had I not heard more. I learned that she had been a Sikh for over twenty years and had raised her kids as Sikhs. Many Sikh parents send their children to Amritsar, an Indian city and the Sikh spiritual center, for learning in their teenage years. Virkaur had sent hers. She had changed her name, changed her dress, changed her community; she had formed her family around Sikh values, trained them in Sikh customs. What in its inception sounded as though it had been a hippie's whim had solidified, over time, into religious conviction. For her, the congregation in Española provided a *sat sangat,* a company of the holy. This "group consciousness," as she understood it, solidified with the rules and stories handed down through the *Sri Guru Granth Sahib,* the Sikh scriptures.

I asked Virkaur if she had ever worried that people saw her Sikh lifestyle as a product of some New Age phase she was passing through.

"I used to think people thought of me as New Agey," she said. "Then I asked my friends, and they said no. I was relieved that they didn't think I was flaky like that."

I asked her what made New Age practitioners flaky.

"Well, I'm not dolphin channeling in some hot tub in San Diego. I hated crystals even before I became a Sikh. I was never into them. The New Age wants the good things in different traditions but they don't want the tradition. Me, I like tradition."

Virkaur appeared as the flipside of Mike Holton. Mike, a Baptist, a church administrator, a faithful Christian, decried religiosity. Virkaur, a Sikh who had come to her faith not for salvation but because the tradition fit into her lifestyle, looked at first glance like a poster girl for the spiritual lifestyle. Yet to use Mike's definition, she was religious: she was "living traditions, doing things the way they've been done for a long time." But I didn't think Virkaur would have any trouble with those descriptions. She found meaning in a tradition, as had the other Anglo Sikhs in the *gurdwara. Gurdwara* means "gateway to the guru"; tradition, in the form of the teachings of the gurus, had been Virkaur's gateway to a fulfilling religious community. Like Hollis Watkins's immersion in Islam, Jean Apollon's entry into Catholicism, and Maeven Eller's choice to live as a Wiccan, Virkaur had handpicked the tradition she wanted to adopt for herself. The collective memory that accompanied the tradition had not handcuffed or handicapped these converts. For them, tradition was neither hollow nor isolating; in truth, tradition gave them access to the memory they chose.

From Española I set out for Alamosa, Colorado. I had told Ruth Blum I would arrive at her door by eight o'clock. I was still sixty miles away from Alamosa at eight, however. The road was dark, rest stops were few and far between, and my cell phone had no signal, so I decided to drive faster and not waste time searching for a phone booth at one of the sporadic exits between northern New Mexico and southern Colorado.

When Ruth answered her doorbell at five minutes to nine, she asked me where I had been, why hadn't I called. With her greeting I knew I had arrived in the land of Jewish grandmothers. Ruth was small and wrinkled, in her mid-eighties, and still independent. She had moved to Alamosa when

her son and his family moved there more than twenty years earlier, when
her husband was still alive. They had since moved away, but she had chosen to stay. She felt comfortable there, had made friends, had built a life.

She had already prepared for me a dinner of Cornish game hen, broccoli, and rice. It had been ready an hour earlier, at eight, when I had said
I'd arrive. She'd eaten already. Her hand shook as she shaved a sliver of
butter from a stick and dropped it on the broccoli, now cold. The butter
pat did not melt. I ate around it during the meal, and it still floated like a
raft amid the detritus of bones and skin and lonesome grains of rice on
the plate at meal's end.

That meal, prepared lovingly by unsteady hands for a friend of her
grandson's, and her home, thickly carpeted and abundantly decorated
with family photographs and perhaps too much furniture for the space,
induced in me a deep-down homesickness and a curious kind of amnesia.
How they both boiled up to the surface at the same time, pangs of memory and pockets of memorylessness, I didn't know. I went to sleep in a
narrow bed with cold sheets and a wool blanket, in a room typically reserved for her grandchildren. I had woken up that morning before six in
Dallas, flown to Albuquerque, driven an hour and a half to Española, visited a Sikh *gurdwara,* then driven another two hundred miles to Alamosa, Colorado, where a Jewish grandma's dinner and guest room greeted
me like a homecoming. But it was weird. If there was any Circe on my
odyssey, any single person and island that encouraged somnambulance
and forgetfulness and peaceful isolation, it was Ruth Blum's home. Three
months and nine thousand miles, twenty-five states and a hundred testimonies covered me like a sarcophagus of wet sand: my temporary immo-
bility felt like a balm. I could have stayed in that place, collapsed under
the burden of that pile of time and words and miles, indefinitely. My cell
phone seemed hopelessly out of range, but this inability to reach and be
reached by those who knew me, by parents and friends, by Liz and her
questions, by Liz and my choices, by Liz and our future, felt then like a
toy one knows one must return. Waking up in that brown room, as though
having been drugged by a familiar nostalgia not my own, was the first and
only time on my journey when I did not know where I was, or how I had
gotten there. I went to take a shower, saw the geriatric safety bar installed
in the bathtub, and only then knew for sure where I had spent the night.
Ruth Blum made me feel so close to home, but that night and morning in
Alamosa, I had never felt further away.

Ruth's closest friends in town were a couple of nuns. They suggested I
drive to San Luis, about forty-five miles away, where a series of sculptures
depicting the stations of the cross, Jesus' path to crucifixion at Golgotha,

had been erected on a craggy hillside above Sangre de Cristo, the town's Catholic church.

Local expressions of do-it-yourself iconography dotted the landscape in southern Colorado. Before I left that morning, before I hugged Ruth Blum and pulled away from Alamosa and forgetfulness, I visited a Catholic Church a few blocks from her home. There, a ten-foot-high, hand-knit tapestry of the Virgin of Guadalupe hung beside the altar. It had taken a group of local women six years from start to finish to complete it. In San Luis, the oldest town in Colorado, an itinerant *santero,* a sculptor of the sacred, cast fourteen bronze figures of Jesus before, during, and after the crucifixion. On a gravelly path bordered with small rocks, the visitor to the San Luis Via Dolorosa (Way of the Cross) walks from station to station, taking in each scene. My walk began with a sculpted reenactment of Pilate's sentencing, moved toward the agonizing crucifixion, and was punctuated with an exultant Christ, pirouetting in the air as he rose from the cross. The sculptures were magnificent, crystallizing moments of weariness and pain and horror against the dramatic setting of scrub brush and distant hillsides.

There were fourteen stations of the cross in San Luis, fourteen descriptions of the scene depicted, fourteen listings of the donors who had helped support their creation, fourteen pleas from the local church that we pray for those donors. But there were only thirteen sculptures. Number thirteen, in which the crucified corpse of Jesus is laid in the tomb, was missing. On the path from crucifixion to resurrection there was no entombment, no two days of crushed hopes, no weekend's worth of wondering how one would ever hope again. Father Pat Valdez of the Sangre de Cristo Church said that the scene had stayed like that, majestic and incomplete, for four years. He admitted that he didn't know when the Via Dolorosa would be completed. As for the artist's delay, Father Pat couldn't say why the guy hadn't completed the job.

A tiny, mostly Catholic town, San Luis has one Catholic Church, Sangre de Cristo. The building has a clay-colored, stucco façade and is peaked by a shingled steeple. A white clapboard, shuttered window on the second floor stands out against the light adobe brown of the surface. Father Pat introduced me to Juan Olivas, who serves as a lay tour guide for the church and the town.

Juan is a stocky, older man who favors one leg. He has a raspy voice and the accent of a native Spanish speaker.

Juan and I sat down in a waiting room just off the church's entrance.

"Do you want my story or the story of San Luis?" Juan, seventy-four, asked me.

"A little bit of both."

Juan had lived in San Luis as a young boy. He made it only through the fourth grade before he had to start working. He spent thirty-eight years as a track repairman for the Union Pacific Railroad in Wyoming. He married in 1949, but his wife died of cancer in 1960. He married again a year later, this time to a woman from San Luis. "I raised two families: my first wife and my girl, and my second wife and three boys." He also worked as a Spanish-speaking deejay for a station in Rollins, Wyoming, before there were any Spanish-formatted stations in the region. Following his retirement, he returned to San Luis in 1984.

"Is it strange being where you grew up?" I asked. "You must have a lot of memories and flashbacks."

"Oh yes," Juan said. I could barely see his eyes through the rose-tinted eyeglasses that framed his dark eyebrows and reddish, bulbous nose. I noticed the tip of a pen cap and the top of a spiral notebook in the front pocket of his blue plaid shirt.

"Sometimes Father Pat asks me about an event and I say, 'Yeah, it happened in June 1935, or it happened in July 1938.' I've always kept things in my head. I don't figure I know that much, but when people ask about a past event, I just seem to know when it happened."

"So it's like, 'Ask Juan?'"

"Yah." He chuckled. Juan had the easy demeanor of the elderly man who now drives the ice cream truck around the neighborhood on hot summer afternoons. "My uncle and my aunt, they live in a nearby town. He's seven years older than me. People will ask him, 'Do you remember so-and-so?' And he says, 'No, but I'll give you my nephew's phone number. He'll know.'" Juan laughed, a sudden exhalation that sounded as though he was choking on something. "He doesn't even know when his mom died, but I do. He remembers it was wintertime. 'She died on February 25, 1935,' I said to him. Not too long ago, we were talking about the church that burned down in Chama, a town right next door. It was Christmas Eve, 1933. They raised their own money to rebuild the church by forming a baseball team that played other towns and by having people pay at the gate. The church was finished five years later. The cement steps are still the same." In the light streaming through the window, I saw the Knights of Columbus insignia on the navy blue hat he wore. The tragedies that had befallen San Luis half a century ago sat in Juan's mind, accessible and jumbled, like a bowl of mixed nuts at a party.

"Is someone here writing down everything you remember?" I asked.

Juan shook his head and laughed. "Oh, no. One of my boys just gave me a book. He said, 'Write some of your memories of the past.' 'I don't know where to start,' I said. He told me to start with my parents. 'Well, my father, he used to shear sheep,' I said. I didn't figure that would be interesting, but Richard, my boy, said, 'No, put it down. It will be very interesting.' So I wrote it down."

I agreed with Juan's son. "It sounds like you have an amazing memory, and an amazing mind for dates," I said, complimenting Juan.

He shrugged. Juan was recognized by his pastor and by his family as the first and last word on San Luis history. Cultures used to have people like Juan, I thought, who understood both the arc of their community's development and the daily details that colored in the arc's segments. He provided an intriguing counterpoint to Maeven Eller, the founder of Betwixt and Between, and to Edna Doyle, the Branch Davidian survivor. Maeven's and Edna's personal lives were dedicated to, and consecrated through, a retelling of their communities' religious histories. Both understood that the voices of their opposition, those telling a different version of their stories, were vociferous. So both consequently saw their task as sacred and urgent: if they didn't tell their stories, their stories risked disappearance, or worse, a drastically altered, negative retelling.

Juan didn't have this concern. His religious history was bound up with his hometown's history. For him, a church offered a stage set for his memory, the backdrop of his past: cement steps survive a fire, a wintry funeral for a great aunt. His faith was not at stake the way Edna and Maeven perceived theirs to be. But *something* was at stake, or else Juan wouldn't have found a niche as town timeline. At the outset of our conversation, Juan had asked me whether I wanted his story or San Luis's. The two were actually one and the same. Here I'd come across a guy who *was* his town's story. Telling San Luis's history, Juan talked about his own life, in much the same way that in talking about pre-Christian Europe and Wicca, Maeven Eller had rooted her own life in a larger storyline. Maeven understood herself in a story, Juan in a place.

I left Juan while the sun was slinking below shadowy mountains. I could see him as I pulled off, from my rear-view mirror, shuffling slowly away. As I drove away from the Sangre de Cristo Church and Juan, something he had said popped into my mind. It was the assumption that his knowledge, precisely because it was his, wasn't worth much. "I figured I know it," he said, "so everybody knows it." Those were his words, and they sparked a question as I headed south from San Luis. How much of our history is lost because we assume it is history people already know? Juan Olivas was an oral historian, literally. He was the chronicler of a town's history, the keeper of his town's collective memory. Somehow, even though he understood that he was relied on for this task, he didn't quite get that without him the knowledge would dissolve.

I appreciated Juan's son's effort. He recognized what his father overlooked, that what Juan knew was precious, an heirloom for the Olivas family and the town of San Luis. I thought that the ethos that helped Juan's son nudge his father into remembering on paper was the same one that encouraged me to start driving. It was an autobiographical impulse, a tributary on America's mightiest river, Old Man Tell All.

No culture's history has ever, ever been more copiously and bountifully chronicled than America's. So complete a coverage is fueled by an underlying manic drive. It's as though we possess the unspoken self-knowledge that those who succeed us will, as we have, choose to forget us and recreate themselves. We know that the best defense against that is a good offense, so we embark on our own cataloguing and bronzing campaigns. We keep journals (especially Mormons, who are urged at an early age to record the evolution of their faith in a diary), make photo albums, applaud for the Eagles reunion tours, and admire public square memorials for the Spanish-American War. In the process, Walt Whitman's call to "sing a song of myself" eventually comes to express the gnawing need of the Breakfast Club theme song: "Don't you forget about me" becomes an anthem, tinged with both rebellion and desperation.

America's ahistorical impulse is linked intimately with its general opposition to religiousness. If you turn your back on your history, you have to be willing to embrace a new religious tradition. So newness becomes the culture's gospel. Woven through our American fascination and love affair with the new, with rebirth, with the reset button, is the tension we feel, below the surface, between religion and spirituality. Many of us choose spirit over religion in order to "stay true to ourselves." We hunger to tell our stories, neglecting the fact that we never really knew them in the first place. Juan Olivas, on the other hand, knew his story but was inclined to think it didn't matter much. Most of the people I had met, with few exceptions, hadn't paused on this question. That their lives mattered was an article of faith. But Juan's humble, shoulder-shrugging assumption that his story was common, his knowledge nothing special, lingered with me.

It's the small stories from otherwise anonymous characters that determine the fate of the world's religious traditions. Take Hagar, for example. In Judaism, the character of Hagar is a meaningful bit performer. She is Sarah's servant who gives birth to Ishmael after Sarah, believing herself barren, persuades Abraham to sleep with Hagar. (Note: I'm not saying Abraham needed that much persuading.) Years later, after Abraham and Sarah have finally conceived and Isaac has been born, Sarah forces Abraham to throw Ishmael and Hagar out of their camp and into the desert. Ishmael shrieks, Hagar weeps, their deaths appear imminent. In the crisis, Hagar hears God tell her that Ishmael, like Isaac, will be the father of a multitude of nations. Flash forward, where the descendants of Ishmael appear periodically throughout the Hebrew Bible, always as adversaries of the descendants of Isaac. They are, of course, cousins.

The earliest Muslims, seeking a story line of their own, plucked Hagar from the Torah's cutting room floor. In the midst of their meteoric rise to power in the seventh and eighth centuries, Muhammad's followers envisioned themselves as the children of Ishmael. Hagar's exile became theirs, her promised redemption their predestined triumph. The Mormons have done this, too, using little-known figures from the Old Testament as central figures in their earliest history. This is typology at work. No religion is created out of whole cloth. Every tradition is indebted to another before it, even if in its adaptation it renounces the tradition that preceded it.

History is made in much the same way that religions are born. The individual makes the assertion that he or she is more than an extra, more than a stunt double; that he or she is central to the storyline of this world. Before my trip began, I worried that if someone had written a book similar to the one I envisioned, I could not begin mine. Like Juan, I figured others would have already learned what I sought, so what use was my going out and trying to find it after they'd found it already? In recognizing my indebtedness, I feared I would lose all grip on inventiveness. But each of our histories is somebody's child, a genetic fusion of debt and invention.

It was no accident that Juan's son, the one who asked his father to preserve his memories, had trained to be a priest. My day in southern Colorado confirmed for me that religion is the vessel that funnels history from one generation to the next. The Catholic faith, steeped in ritual reminders of past events and ongoing traditions, persists—as does every religion—only because it convinces followers that its history is theirs. Intriguingly, the Catholic community I ran across in the Southwest was committed to the preservation of other peoples' history, too. It was Catholic priests who helped create a mural depicting Sikh history for the Española *gurdwara*.

[30]

No express route had been paved from San Luis, Colorado, to Window Rock, Arizona, my next morning's destination, a projected six-hour drive away. The best I could do was what I had already done: retrace my tire tread back south through New Mexico until I hit I-40 outside of Albuquerque. Then I would head west.

When I reached the outside of Albuquerque, I took a right onto the interstate and joined the flow of the heavy rumble and looming headlights of big trucks on long rides. Soon, the deep blue dusk became soil-dark night. Roadside towns and their electric glow were an hour's drive apart. I tapped the digital tuner with a relentless fidgetiness until, at a point east of Grants, New Mexico, there wasn't anything at all. I succumbed to the scan button to do my FM searching for me. The radio dial looped mutely from the bottom of the dial to the top: a rapid-fire flip book of inaudible playlists, none close enough to be heard. I turned the radio off. The shape of mesas and buttes a few hundred yards from the highway had been swallowed by the evening. In the absence of sights, in the absence of songs, there was the straightness of road, the changing of lanes, the passing of trucks. The highway droned, endless and uncomplicated. The rental car hurtled deeper into the night. Escape took no effort here.

But memory, I would learn the next morning, did.

After a short sleep at a run-down motel off the interstate, I followed I-40 until it crossed a state highway called, no joke, Route 666. It's the highway that leads toward Window Rock, Arizona, capital of the Navajo Nation, and I figured some federal cartographer had made an editorial comment about either the terrain or the people who occupied it. The largest indigenous tribe in the United States, the Navajo live on 25,000 square miles of land, a reservation the size of New England. Window Rock is close to the Four Corners, a traditionally sacred spot for the Navajo that today marks the point where Utah, Colorado, New Mexico, and Arizona meet.

I had read that Navajo medicine men describe this land as the meeting place between Mother Earth and Father Sky. My drive that Friday morning revealed a setting far more prosaic. Driving slowly down the central road that cuts through the reservation, I passed Airstream trailers, their aluminum shells reflecting the morning's haze like shiny quarters on a sheet of sandpaper, and prepubescent Navajo boys in oversized Phoenix Suns tank tops hanging outside the local post office. I took the road most visitors take when they visit Window Rock. It allows a glimpse, though not much of an immersion, into the Navajo community. After several miles of introduction to the reservation, it led past an open-air market to the political center of Window Rock, a nondescript, could-be-anywhere office park where I met Eddie Tso.

Eddie worked in a modest office with white-washed walls, a Dell desktop computer, and a number of posters and tribal teachings taped to his walls. He was a sturdy man with sunburned brown skin, thin black hair parted down the middle and receding from his forehead, and eyeglasses tinted blue. I thought maybe Eddie and Juan Olivas had secured a two-for-one deal on colored lenses. A series of three arched wrinkles curved above each eyebrow, and a wrinkle that looked like a scar jutted down from the right corner of his mouth. If the other side had had its own wrinkle, his mouth might have resembled that of a wooden doll. Eddie Tso was the program director of the Navajo Nation's Office of Diné Education.

Diné is the term Navajos usually use to describe themselves. It can be translated literally as "the people," though I had also read that another, more idiomatic translation understood the word to mean "the children of God." *Navajo*, meanwhile, came from a Spanish word for "stealer." (The community uses this name as well to refer to itself. I therefore go ahead and use it in the rest of this chapter. If it represented a centuries-old sleight, an onus of historical misrepresentation that the tribe shunned, I would abandon it.) Spanish missionaries and traders were the first Europeans to encounter the tribe in the late sixteenth century. Their "discovery" of the long-established Navajo community began a gradual, two-century demise that reached its tragic nadir in 1863 with the Long Walk. Just as the Union army was gaining the upper hand in the War Between the States 2,500 miles away, Union soldiers followed orders to kill Navajo men old enough to bear arms, and to capture the remaining women and children. The soldiers led the conquered Navajo on a three-hundred-mile forced march.

America's Navajo removal policy took its cues from the Cherokee removal policy a generation earlier. Interestingly, of all the native tribes encountered and decimated by the European, and later American, settlers, the Cherokee had been the most inclined to acculturation. The Cherokee leaders in the late eighteenth and early nineteenth centuries assumed that if the tribe became "civilized" by accepting Christianity, if the people developed a written language and drafted a constitution and established mission schools, they would then be allowed to remain on their own land. While the Cherokee leaders encouraged assimilation and Christianization, a group of Cherokee "nationalists" by 1820 had renounced their membership in the Cherokee tribe because they saw their leadership as Indian "Uncle Toms." These renegades became citizens of North Carolina and strove to see traditional home life and governance and religion survive. These were the Cherokee who remained in the area when the vast majority of the tribe was loaded onto wagons on a forced march in 1838 known today as the Trail of Tears. Nearly half of the tribe died on that march, killed by exposure to the conditions and disease. The ones who survived settled in what is today Oklahoma. God, I thought, the appeasement that seeks security at first, then ends in deportation and cultural genocide, sounded sickeningly familiar.

The Navajo, meanwhile, uprooted from traditional tribal land, exiled from their sacred landscape, had to find a way to make sense of that displacement. How to persevere as a tribe was the struggle handed to that generation's leaders and medicine men. Nearly 140 years later, Eddie Tso had made that same struggle his life's mission.

Eddie grew up on the "res." "My grandfather was a medicine man," he said. "So was my uncle. They both passed away. But I wasn't so interested then, when I was growing up."

In the 1970s, Eddie told me, the Navajo commissioned a survey to count how many medicine men remained alive and practiced their craft. Two Navajo researchers spent six months traveling around the reservation; they located two thousand men, most of whom were in their mid-to-late sixties. During 1993 and 1994, another set of Navajo researchers conducted a second survey of medicine men; this time they found only a few hundred. Traditions, rituals, sacred wisdom: they had evaporated before the community's eyes.

This wasn't accidental. The educational system developed by the Bureau of Indian Affairs, headquartered in Washington, D.C., and prevalent on the reservation since the end of World War II pushed assimilation and English study, and pulled Navajo children away from traditional values and tribal language. The customs that sustained the culture for centuries were like so many cans brought to the conversion center: used up vessels went in, something of quantifiable value was refunded. So Eddie's work was a tall task: to make traditional teaching recoverable for the contemporary Navajo, to retrieve the past while not rejecting the present, and to restore a lost balance in Navajo life.

Balance, Eddie said, is an essential, formal component of Navajo life. The Navajo are a formal culture. Not formal like duke and duchess formal, pinkies extending upward from tea cups and that impeccable British diction, hallmarks of European formality. For the Navajo, formality is different. Ceremonies performed by medicine men are regimented sequences of language and movement, primarily concerned with restoring balance. Eddie told me that each ritual, in its own way, boiled down to a transformation of illness into healing and suffering into meaning. The illness could be an individual's, he said, or it could be the community's. The purpose of ceremony was to reinforce the interrelatedness of all beings to one another, to confirm and cement one's place in the universe. In that knowledge, in the certainty that one has a place, there was healing.

"Our spirits, the sun, the moon, the earth, the air, the plants: each has a role," Eddie said. "We need all these things for life. Without air, we die. Without water, we starve. Without them, we don't exist. Life is relationship. This is the same way with our religion, the same way with our beliefs and our ceremonies. They all coexist with nature and with man."

Less than a year earlier, with Navajo religious life depending on the survival of this ceremonial knowledge, Eddie Tso had helped hatch a project to gather together the remaining medicine men—those willing and physically able—to pass on their wisdom and ritual expertise in a systematic way. Thirty practitioners and eighty apprentices had entered the program in the eleven months since its inception. "Of course we go to the young," Eddie said when I asked about his recruitment strategy, "but we have only one or two in their twenties. Most of the people are in their forties. But they don't know full Navajo. Now we're trying to put Navajo in Head Starts and elementary schools." Eddie folded his hands in front of him on his desk. He looked in that moment like an employer about to lay off a long-term employee. "These are hard times. You know, they say back then, a hundred years ago and more, those were hard times. But these are hard times, too."

Eddie's work combined a religious mission with a micro-entrepreneur's tact. When a kid came to Eddie and asked, "What's in this for me?" Eddie answered, "Survival." The Navajo needed medicine men. The community's "trust, faith, and confidence still rested with the medicine man." And presumably the future medicine men he helped recruit and train would become community leaders, appropriately paid and endowed with traditional knowledge. He was, in essence, trying to reinvest in a professional class of clergy who would find both spiritual sustenance and self-sufficiency in sacred work.

Our conversation didn't last more than an hour, but I felt such a surge of pride and melancholy in Eddie's project that our time together seemed much longer. Navajo ceremony traditionally dealt with the cycle of exile and remembrance. But whereas once the ritual had helped to resolve a spiritual disconnection, when someone lay ill or the tribe's hunt proved fruitless, these days ritual touched both the spiritual and the geographical landscapes of the Navajo. The land played an elemental role in Navajo religion. Four sacred mountains stood in the four cardinal directions. The terrain, the rain clouds, the tobacco for the peace pipe, insects, all played their role in ceremonies. Because of this umbilical link between land and ritual, exile from the land means exile from ritual, and exile from ritual means exile from order. The Navajo world became disordered as soon as the Navajo people were displaced. Navajo life depended on the memory and enacting of these ceremonies. When they went away, so too would the Navajo.

In Eddie's story, I glimpsed a sense of solidarity, something that bound the two of us together. It was a sense of shared purpose, of shared responsibility about how to make sure we remember who we are, and who we were. Neither of us had grown up gung ho about our respective traditions. Maybe that's what fueled us in our commitments now. The departure and arrival point of Eddie's quest was his community's preservation of memory. His crisis was not dissimilar from that faced by my own ancient predecessors in their own exiles. Slaughtered by a conquering army, its children orphaned, its women widowed, its sacred sites profaned, its community uprooted and led away in chains, the Hebrews in their Babylonian exile and after the Roman army's siege of Jerusalem were faced with momentous decisions about how to go on. How were they to interpret their exile in light of their relationship with the Divine? Was the sacred, which had dwelled in a particular place, transportable? Were they to remain independent as a tribe or to assimilate into the dominant culture? Were they to retain specific memory or to adopt another history as their own? For many centuries Judaism had survived because of the institutional commitment to the preservation of memory, even though and even while individual Jews chose acculturation or blending in as their means of survival.

Listening to Eddie helped clarify what faith looks like for me. Faith is believing in something not because eventual deliverance is inevitable, but because it is nearly unimaginable. Faith is the recognition that only through the efforts of your own community in your own time can the messianic era draw closer. I was suddenly struck by the usefulness of Judaism for the Navajo. One example of a successful response to exile came to mind, and there in the Navajo Nation's offices, I saw it as perfectly and immediately essential. "I don't know if you know the story of Moses," I said. He motioned for me to continue. "Maybe you know this already, but there's a great moment when Moses, with God's help, has led the Hebrews out of Egypt, out of slavery, out of amnesia about their history, over the sea, and into the wilderness. And the Bible says that Moses has something like six hundred thousand people gathered, living in tents, fending for scraps for food. And he's trying to figure it all out by himself, how to lead them. Now Moses was a prince in Egypt; he took off to a little desert community called Midian, and then, called by this voice in the burning bush to go back to Egypt, he returned. You maybe know all that. In that desert community he got married. His father-in-law was a man named Jethro. Jethro joined the Hebrews in the desert, at the very front end of the Exodus. Jethro's a priest from Midian, an elder. He's got some experience, and he's looking at Moses like, 'You got to be kidding if you think you can do this all by yourself.' So he pulls Moses aside and he says, 'What you've got to do is this: you've got to get seventy elders, and you've gotta enlist them in this whole governing and teaching thing. You've gotta teach Hebrews who are slaves how not to be slaves. How're you gonna do that? It's paradoxical, maybe. The more you delegate authority, the more you let it out of your own clutches, the more people feel like they have a piece of it. Once he realized that the task was his, but not his alone, Moses could share the burden with the others. He had to learn to delegate. And he had to get to the point where he understood that his tribe's survival, their liberation, depended on their participation."

No doubt there was a long way between scripture's example and Eddie Tso's making it happen. At a selfish level, though, I felt I could almost pat myself on the back. In this idiomatic offering of one chapter of the Exodus story, I had taken Moses and Jethro and served them up like homiletic *hors d'oeuvres*. In that moment, in the space where my Jewish knowledge became useful to a tenacious, committed Navajo, I suddenly realized that Judaism was all I needed. This didn't negate the value and need of pursuing the wisdom of other traditions. These religions were still worth studying; other people's faiths were still worth encountering. But my inquiries into other traditions, my pilgrimage to see how other people believed, had taken a Navajo shape, had become a circle. My pilgrimage returned me to myself, to a tradition that not long before I had not believed to be worth retrieving. Eddie and I walked on a parallel path, both finding our own particular ways to grow out our afros and try on our dashikis, both recovering what our predecessors had either surrendered or had taken from them. My body tingled at the thought. This is mine, I said without saying.

When I told Eddie I was Jewish, I asked if he knew anything about the tradition. He lifted both hands from his desk, and extended a few fingers on each hand from his palms, toward the ceiling. "What do you call this?" he asked.

"A *menorah*," I told him. The candelabra used during Hanukkah was, coincidentally, the symbol of a holiday that celebrated the triumph of particular over universal community, Jewish over Hellenistic identity.

"I admit I don't know much about Jewishness. The few things I know about it," Eddie said, shrugging, "I learn from television." That wasn't dissimilar to how most Jews learned of the reservation.

I clasped both of Eddie's hands as I walked out and asked him where I could go for some lunch. He suggested the open-air crafts market I had passed on my way into Window Rock.

A thin red dust floated up from the ground. People sold turquoise jewelry and Navajo rugs from the backs of bedraggled trucks. One border of the market, adjacent to the road that led the tourist into Window Rock, was lined with a row of half a dozen lunch shacks, one-room affairs constructed with plywood, aluminum siding, and corrugated cardboard. The lunch shack I entered had five or six picnic tables and benches filled with people on their lunch breaks. I heard what the three people in front of me in line ordered and once I reached the counter, asked for the same. It was a mutton and steamed corn stew with fry bread on the side. I carried my plate to a table where a shrunken, ancient man, his skin deep maroon under a black cowboy hat, sat next to two middle-aged Navajo men in button-down shirts and ties across from me. The old man nodded at me and my arrival, and I did the same, lifting my leg over the bench and under the table. He gave me another nod, and I too repeated the gesture. He did it once more and I smiled, thinking we must have looked like the partici-pants in a caricatured Japanese tea ceremony who bow themselves to ex-haustion.

"He only speaks Navajo," one of the men in a tie sitting next to him said. "Enjoy your soup." I dug in, looking up after each bite as though to assure my neighbors, all of whom I thought had me in the corner of their eyes, that I felt perfectly at home. There in that space I was acutely aware of the difference of my whiteness. It wasn't lost on me, as I chatted with the two men, both engineers on their lunch break, that it was the most Anglo-looking Navajos in the place who engaged me in conversation. They were bicultural, Navajo and Anglo, and so enjoyed a kind of medi-ator position. And I, though in a Navajo space, was only too happy to re-ceive them in my own cultural language. They rose from the table and said good-bye when I was only halfway through my meal. I noticed the small gray mutton bones that sat beside the old man's bowl. He looked up as the men touched his shoulder and slipped behind him toward the door. Then his gaze came back to me, and he squinted and smiled once more. I smiled back. I spoke only English.

Before I left the reservation I drove past a white sign for the Bible Nav-ajo Mission–Wildcat Christian Academy. Its bumper psalm read, "Way to Heaven—Turn Right—Go Straight."

I pulled in and wound up receiving a tour from the mission's white pas-tor and school principal, a long-time resident of the reservation, originally from West Virginia, named Jimmy Bowling. Jimmy walked me through the school, a few sunlit rooms of low desks and well-worn textbooks. A handmade sign rested on one of the classroom's mantles. A blue-eyed, red-lipped Jesus, his wavy shoulder-length hair parted down the middle, his neatly trimmed goatee framing his face like a chin strap, stared from the frame. In bubble-font black letters, the words that accompanied the image read, "Fall in love with Jesus." There, explicitly, as I had not seen it be-fore, was the conflation of Jesus the savior and Jesus the matinee idol.

In the New Testament the Church is described as the bride of Christ. American Evangelical Christianity had taken that metaphor literally. God had grown so human, so intimate, so like us in America, that the Messiah had become a pinup. To the right of the Jesus head shot was a picture of Jesus on the cross. Though crucified, his arms were not drained of strength but taut with exaltation. If you'd put a jersey on him, this could have been Jesus' Wheaties box cover. He was, even in his pain, an All-American God. That meant white and handsome and direct and a winner—the God who ends up with the girl and the land.

I told Pastor Bowling about my visit with Eddie Tso.

"I had a medicine man who gave his life to Christ at the age of ninety-five. Gave me his medicine bag," Jimmy said. He retained a touch of an Appalachian twang, a little bit more rough-edged than the lilt of the South. "It was his daughter that was the first girl I ever picked up on my bus route coming to a church locally. 'Course she's in my church with her husband and her children. Her dad was real sick, and God in his greatness touched him. And he lived five years after that. I took one of my Indian men and we explained to him about giving his life to Christ. And he did. But he would point up to heaven, with tears rolling down his cheeks, 'One day I'm going to live in the Big Teepee.' He couldn't say a whole lot, but he gave me his medicine bag, and he said, 'I don't need this any longer.'"

"Do you think folks see being Christian as a step up?" I asked Jimmy.

"Oh yes, definitely. I have policemen and policewomen in my church. The president of the tribe has attended my church. We have prayer with him once a month in his office. He is a very kind, gracious man who wants God's best for his people. My theology is not to take the culture or tradition away from 'em, but to put Christ into that. They'll always be an Indian, but I want them to die a Christian Indian. And that is not the mentality of a lot of people or denominations. Other folks want to make them a Nazarene or a Methodist or a Baptist. That's certainly not my mentality. Not at all. I just want them to be Christian."

The Navajo who converted, Pastor Bowling said, assumed positions of responsibility and achieved success in the Navajo community. Christianity represented a way out of the reservation's poverty and struggle. Good livings awaited Christian converts, who found both a well-established professional network through church and an ethos that equated achievement in the economic sphere with divine blessing. How the Navajo escaped their particular predicament and sprinted toward American identity was through Christianity.

Seen in this light, the Navajo predicament raised still more connections with my own Jewishness. How different was their assimilation, really, from that of my predecessors, who understandably, given their historical struggles as Jews, leapt at the chance to be Americans? In their name changes, their business successes in the yarn-dying industry, their country club memberships, and their clustering with other Jews whose predecessors had done just the same, my family came to think of themselves as majority, not minority. It wasn't that they ceased to be Jewish, but the identity they located as Americans superceded that of their tribal identity. Each of our communities had, in its own way, handed over its medicine bag at the door.

The transmission of tradition, the finding of successors—these were challenges faced by the people who introduced modern, spoken Hebrew to the world of East European Jewry at the close of the nineteenth century. Eliezer Ben-Yehuda, an early Zionist pioneer from Russia, moved to Palestine in 1881. When he and his wife had their first child, Ben-Yehuda refused to allow the boy to have contact with any language other than Hebrew. Ben-Yehuda's vision was to demonstrate that if one child could be raised who spoke Hebrew as a first language, then a community could be created that used Hebrew similarly. Ben-Yehuda and his fellow pioneers made up Hebrew words for modern inventions. As it happened, the son was to become the first native-born Hebrew speaker in more than a thousand years. Thus, from an act of single-handed commitment, he and his family paved the way for the reintroduction of Hebrew, a language that had been reserved for liturgical use for almost two millennia, into the living world. An American linguist and scholar of language revivals named Einar Haugen confirmed the point. "It appears to be almost the rule," he wrote, "that such movements can be traced back to a single devoted person." That individual's personal campaign is grafted onto a community's wider struggle, and the resuscitation of the language becomes a symbol of both individual protest and communal nostalgia. In other words, Eddie's was an awesome task, but it had precedents.

Somewhere in the intersection of Navajo and Jew, in the relationship between memory and newness, ritual and exile, was a key to understanding why I had set out seeking to learn of religion in America from strangers. The world was a web of sacred relationships, Eddie said. To the Navajo, the individual's independence exists to contribute to the fabric of the community. To the American, it is the other way around.

The sun set before I reached Albuquerque. I dropped my bags in a motel room on a strip of neon not too far from the airport I'd fly out of early the next morning. It took a few tries to rise up from the polyester bedspread. I shuffled over to the front desk and asked for directions to the nearest supermarket. I got back in the car. The supermarket glowed like a night-time construction site. It was nice to be around people doing shopping for their families. I felt like a sap, getting sentimental at so ordinary a thing. I walked up and down each aisle of the massive place, scanning the shelves before making my decisions. I made a few mental notes about which aisles I would return to: prepared bakery near the front of the store for two croissants, aisle five for grape juice, and aisle eleven for the box of tea candles on sale for a dollar. I was gathering necessary items for *Shabbat* and silently requesting some leeway from the Spirit for using croissants instead of challah, and deliberating on what kind of hoagie to buy at the Subway nearby. It took some effort to smile at the cashier. The single plastic bag felt melodramatically heavy for the few things inside it. I had to get back in the car, turn the ignition, buckle my seatbelt, switch on my headlights, signal left, stop at red. I was eye-rubbingly weary, and all of these small things seemed Herculean.

I lit the candles and braided the croissants together and broke out the grape juice and set the alarm and turned on HBO. I finished the hoagie, turned the channels, did some writing, locked the door, brushed the teeth, propped the pillows, fell asleep.

On a stopover in the Dallas–Fort Worth Airport late the next morning, I retrieved my messages from the previous three days. Three or four of them had been from my mom, telling me about the birth of my new nephew, Zack, the baby my sister had had on Thursday. I called my sister and soaked up the details as boarding was announced. And as the boarding area thinned out, I called Liz. She sounded surprised that I would call her with such good news—or if not surprised, grateful. Something about her gratitude irked me. What's there to be grateful about for doing such an obvious thing? I asked myself after we said good-bye.

Before setting out, back in late July, I had plotted Zack's birth date as a finish line for my trip. My little nephew, my sister and her husband's first baby, was a sort of destination. But given the space between an August beginning in Boston and an early November flight changeover in Dallas, I knew I still had more to hear. After learning of the Army's tolerance of Wiccan religion, and after hearing about Cora Jean and Darnell's church on the military base in San Antonio, I did a search on the Internet and realized that the Army Chaplaincy School, located in South Carolina, was a must-visit. I was scheduled to visit my friend Kim on my trip through the Smoky Mountains. I had met Harvey Lee Green in prison, and hoped to meet his mother, a pastor in coastal North Carolina. I had met *I Ching* devotee Dolores Ledbetter, and hoped to meet her Hasidic daughter in Borough Park, Brooklyn.

A chorus of dissonant voices competed for air-time in my head. While their words cohered into refrains, they also featured soloists who took center stage by dint of the nearness of my contact with them. Eddie Tso meditated about creation's oneness, how the sun and the moon, the earth and the sky complement each other. In the same way, death is balanced by life, exile by homecoming. Eddie's was a particular perspective, but it mushroomed in my mind into a commonly held conviction: that the breadth of creation, the entirety of our experiences, is part of one whole. My nephew's birth was countered by his dad's brother's death, and the thought that a family contained that wholeness, just as the larger world did, struck me then as both obvious and necessary.

Just as I had announced Robin's name during the Friday night service in Baton Rouge, so I whispered Zack's name in the little nook beside the mechanical revolving door near Gate 32 in the Delta terminal of the Dallas–Fort Worth Airport. I celebrated the words like an improvised ceremony with the wall and the ceiling, a seed I dropped to visit on future changeovers on trips toward other pilgrims. Boarding the flight from Dallas to Boston, I knew that the words I offered were my own way of acknowledging the pivot between Wedgwood Baptist and rebirth, Waco and reconstruction, my late relative Robin and my newborn nephew Zack, between condolence and consolation, Kaddish and thanksgiving. Though we are saddled with the inexplicable, we are buoyed by the inexpressible. It can't be any other way.

[31]

"We're all backpackers in this world," Kim Jones had told a crowd in Saudi Arabia a few months before her death. By the time I revisited Washington, D.C., that first week of November, I felt as though she were talking about me. Even when around my family, even when ostensibly "home," I pulled clothes from a duffle bag, slept under polyester bedspreads on the second floor of motels, and spoke on my cell phone from sidewalks and front seats and stairwells.

Following my flight from Dallas, I retrieved my car in Boston and hustled down to D.C. The damp and gray next morning I was introduced to my new nephew, Zachary Arthur Robin Kreisberg (pronounced "criseburg"; I had intermittently lobbied for the name Jesus so that the kid would be Jesus Kreisberg, but I never got far in that naming campaign). The two middle names commemorated his recently departed great-grandfather and uncle. His monogram was a vanity plate inscribed to memory.

My sister rested her baby, wrapped and puckered and ruddy, against her chest and took a bite of a take-out hamburger. She and my mom were talking about children and parents, how parents, even though they might not expect to, eventually become so wrapped up in their kids' successes and failures that they can't help but forge a significant chunk of their own identities from the lives of their children. My sister couldn't imagine that at the time, mostly because her baby was so new and malleable. My mom said it wasn't something that happened consciously or intentionally; the wins, losses, draws, and do-overs of your kids just had a way of sticking to your own skin.

Right around that moment, in the wake of their words, just as I settled into a food coma from a double burger and side of fries, I leapt up, grabbed my phone, and sprinted to the trunk of my car. The conversation about parents and children, how the lives of the latter shape and reframe the lives of the former, reminded me that I still had not arranged my meeting with Reverend Mary Gooding, Harvey Lee Green's mother. Who and what had she become in the wake of her son's crime, death sentence, and execution? How did a minister, her son murdered for his own double murder, understand the suffering he had caused and in turn endured? I had located her phone number beforehand and reached her on the second ring. She had a husky voice and a thick drawl.

"Are you callin' from a newspaper?" she asked me. "'Cause I already have been interviewed."

I told her no, that I had met her son a week before he died, and that in reading his obituary I had learned about her and her ministry. This was an overstatement. I gleaned from the obituary only that she had a *Rev.* in front of her name. Hoping to share some of my reflections about Harvey, I also wanted to hear more about her. Would she be willing to meet me for lunch two days later? She offered a wavering yes. She suggested the Hardee's in Mayville, North Carolina, on Route 17 at noon. I hung up and raised my phone as though it were a medal, holding the moment in a forearm-clenching triumph.

Later that night, in the echoing and isolated back stairwell of the American Inn in Bethesda, Maryland, I lowered my phone as though it were an iron anchor. It was Liz on the other end. I was barefoot, in sweatpants, a T-shirt, and a jacket, and against the isolated hum of incinerators and industrial-strength heaters I heard her ask me the same questions she had asked repeatedly over the past months since I had been on the road. Where were we going? What was I planning? How was I acting to ensure she and I would be, for the long term, a we? As she talked, I pulled the phone from my ear and lay it at my side. I stretched my arms in front of me, jerked my neck left, then right, all while her words piled on top of one another, like so much relationship landfill. Could I make any commitment about my future plans? Would I make any commitment to her and me? Or was my commitment only to my own future, indefinite and gauzy?

I sighed, stayed quiet. There was nothing but breathing on the other end.

"Damn Tom," she said, her voice cracking, at once brokenhearted and indignant. "Don't you have any clearer picture of what you want than you did when you started?" She paused, gathering herself. "Step up," she sighed, and there came another pause, followed by a repetition of her plea. "Just step up."

That night, I heard her plea as an order, and what she hoped for us only as an obligation placed on me. There was a sort of pilgrim's filter hanging invisibly over both of my ears. So much of what I had learned on the road had just appeared before me; as a result, there formed for me a kind of taboo against preparedness. Liz shared her sadness, her struggles with me. But when she said, "I'm drowning and I need your hand," I heard, "I'm drowning, and I want to take you down with me." I didn't hear, let's swim to shore together; I heard murder-suicide.

And yet even then, as the course for our dissolution was being hatched, as I nodded at the itemized list of reasons for our breakdowns and imminent break-up, I thought of all the ways I loved her. I thought of the way she glows when she answers the front door, or the baby-soft skin on the inside of her arms, the way she interacted with my grandfather when he was on his deathbed. I daydreamed about the way she is sexy and serious and powerful and silly and in charge and wise and beautiful and such a great dancer and a far better cook than I had ever acknowledged and as Jewishly committed as I figured I could find. And I remember thinking, even then, that I love this woman so deeply I can't reach the bottom. But in spite of those attributes and that sentiment, as though spitting in the face of some composite ideal woman I had sketched, I chose me over us that night. Each of these sessions felt like an interrogation, and they occurred with such numbing frequency over those weeks that I reached the point where ending seemed emancipating. This was how I understood what it was to be true to myself. The only way I knew how to step up was to walk out.

Liz and I broke up that night—in truth I saw it as more her choice than mine—but as I drove south late the next afternoon, feeling slightly annoyed but surprisingly grateful, I still didn't quite get the connection between our demise and the lure of the road.

PART FIVE

[All That's Holy]

[32]

Eastern North Carolina's Route 17 was a stretch of traffic lights, car deal-erships, and advertised three-piece fried chicken meals. Not far from the roadside, trees missing limbs leaned toward the asphalt like wobbly observ-ers on a parade route. They had been damaged by Hurricane Floyd two months earlier, which I remembered beginning with a drizzle as I left Har-vey Lee Green and the Raleigh prison.

I pulled into the Hardee's parking lot a few minutes after twelve. Two tables in the Muzak-filled, airy restaurant were occupied: at one, an el-derly white couple and their grandchild ate lunch, while at the other, a slightly stooped, older black man and a considerably younger black woman both had their hands folded on the empty table in front of them.

I walked toward this couple. "Reverend Gooding?" I asked the woman.

"Uh-huh," she said, and we shook hands. I introduced myself to Mary Gooding and the man with her. This was Harold Gooding, Mary's hus-band. I offered to buy them sodas. They accepted. I returned a couple of minutes later with two Pepsis and a Hawaiian Punch.

Harold Gooding, Mary's third husband, was seventy-four years old, twenty years older than Mary, who was fifty-four when we spoke. They were a somewhat unlikely pair. Mary gave the impression that she might be ten years younger than she was; Harold, that he might be ten years older than he was. Their faces offered a study in contrasts. The skin on Mary's face was smooth, lustrous, like a puddle of chocolate milk sitting on a white countertop. Harold had a thin layer of stubble above his lip and on his chin, and a constellation of dark brown moles circling his right eye. Harold's head was shaved, his hairline receding, its contours suggesting a road narrowing in the distance. Mary had thick, helmet-shaped, jaw-length black hair that framed her face like a horseshoe.

We spent fifteen minutes at Hardee's, a quarter hour, I realized while it was happening, that served as Mary Gooding's opportunity to feel me out. In the news crush both preceding and following Harvey's execution, her phone had rung with the calls of reporters and pranksters and avengers; she had received crude calls and cruel calls. Her husband Harold sat with her that afternoon at Hardee's as a precautionary measure, though I wasn't sure that if I was up to no good Harold would have been able to stop me.

Once sufficiently assured of my sincerity, Mary suggested we head back to her church. They rose from the table and I noticed the two were about the same size, five feet, seven inches, maybe. But as different as their complexions were, so were their gaits. Mary walked erect, her shoulders back. Harold's feet skimmed the ground: his steps were short, and his shoes barely rose from the pavement. They led me by car from the congestion of Route 17 to the hush of a narrow country road. The church was an ivory white building with white doors and a slanted roof that sat across from harvested tobacco fields. Mary opened the front door to the church with a key, and we walked through the shadowy, unlit sanctuary to her office.

It was, to be honest, a stroke of bittersweet good fortune that led me to Mary Gooding. My eyes had lit up when I saw Rev. in front of Mary Gooding's name in that news article, largely because I knew instantly that her perspective would make a moving coda to the story line involving Harvey. It's a little hard to say that because I hear myself as unduly opportunistic, a documentary hearse chaser. But the truth is, had I read a different obituary, a different paper's account of the execution, I might never have heard of Harvey's mother. In fact, in another piece, by another beat writer, I might have read a quote by a member of one of the victims' families who attended the execution, and been led to contact them and not Mary.

When I started to ask Mary about her church and her life, I saw these inquiries as a conversational warm-up to my questions about Harvey. I had understood Reverend Gooding to be, basically, a character in her son's story. Like the biblical Hagar, she played a supporting part in the cast of a drama that included activists and attorneys, news crews and family members, state politicians and other local clergy. All I knew of her I had gleaned from that newspaper account. The paper reported that she had spent the last day of her son's life with him at the prison. At eleven o'clock, as he was led away, she left the prison, prayed with death penalty opponents outside the penitentiary, then entered again to take her seat among those gathered to witness the execution. The next time she saw Harvey, he was strapped onto a gurney. The political appeals for clemency and the legal efforts at another stay of execution had been pursued, and denied. That was to be the last time Mary would see her son.

What I neglected to realize, foolishly, as I drove toward Reverend Gooding was that I solicited an account not only of the death of her son, but also of her own spiritual evolution. One forgets too easily when speaking to supporting players that they are themselves featured performers, albeit in dramas with different arcs and different terminals. As was Hagar, each of us is an extra, a supporting actor, and a star—anonymous, individual, and archetypal, all at the same time. I cast Mary Gooding as victim, that is, Dead Man's Mother, and in some ways as a co-conspirator, that is, Minister Who Raised Murderer, and in the process, at least in the path leading up to our meeting, almost forgot her.

But Mary Gooding's story, I learned, was as individual as her son's. Her first husband died just a few years into their marriage. Mary gave birth to Harvey when she was fifteen; by the age of twenty she had four children. For more than a decade after, she worked in a number of jobs, as a housekeeper and as a caretaker. Sometime after that she received her call from God. Her second husband, also a minister, died a few years into her ministry.

Mary said she had been the pastor at St. Stephen's African Methodist Episcopal Zion Church for four years. Ordained as a deacon in the AME Zion Church eleven years earlier, she pastored another church for seven years before taking over at St. Stephen's.

"Had you ever met a woman who was a pastor before you became one?" I asked Reverend Gooding.

"When I was coming up, in the Baptists, I never met a woman pastor. As time went by I heard of one, but I was finally grown by the time I met her, and she was so old she was ready to retire."

"When you met her did you ever think, well, that's something I might do?"

"I think I sorta did. But I had only known men preachers, and most of them were old. You know, I'm talking 'bout old."

Mary said she and her kids had joined a Methodist church because of how much closer it was to their house than the Baptist one. It wasn't a theological decision. Still, the choice seemed providential to me. The AME Zion Church was formed as an offshoot of the AME Church, one of the churches that Hollis Watkins grew up attending. The AME Zion denomination itself was organized in 1821, and before long it came to be known as the "Freedom Church," because its sanctuaries were used as way-stations on the Underground Railroad. Its clergy included impassioned advocates of abolition, and among its members were Sojourner Truth,

Harriet Tubman, and Frederick Douglass. The denomination became an
early expression of an urban, emancipated, egalitarian black community,
an identity emphasized during and after the Civil War. AME Zion missionaries marched with the Union Army into the South, adding converts
and organizing small congregations along the way. This is how the church
first reached Mary's home state of North Carolina. In 1898, the AME
Zion Church became the first American denomination to ordain women
regardless of their color. Mary was part of a long line of boundary-crossing
women.

Harold said he attended Mary's church but remained a Baptist. The reverend shook her head, a note of disdain in the way she curled her mouth.
"There are quite a few differences between the Baptists and the Methodists,"
she said, "but there's one especially that irritates me. In the Baptist church
a woman preacher is an Eldress. But in the Methodist church we are Rev-
erends. The men and the women carry the same title. My sister's Baptist,
and she's a minister; they address her Eldress Austin. When I go there they
want to call me Eldress. I tell them, 'I'm not an eldress 'cause I don't know
what that is.'" You go, Reverend Gooding. "Now they call me Reverend
Gooding. And that's fine. I see the Baptist men preachers dominating the
women. I said I could not be there 'cause I'm not going to be dominated in
the ministry." Harold was nodding his head in assent. Mary took a breath
and leaned back in her chair. "I don't get a whole lot of calls to go preach at
Baptist churches," she confessed with a sharp laugh.

I wanted to pursue this conversation, learn more about Mary's ministry
and leadership in her church. There were moments as she spoke that I
flashed back to Mother Booker, fifty years Mary's senior. Both of their accounts seemed emblematic of a larger history of Black religious institutions—
the AME churches and the Baptist denominations, and later on some of the
Pentecostal Holiness movements—initially formed as analogous institutions
to the white, established churches that resisted and rejected black congregants. Even then, separate but equal hadn't made them equal to all. Mary's
refusal to be called Eldress while visiting Baptist churches reflected a deeper
urge for liberation within the women of the black churches.

In the midst of this thought process, I reminded myself that I had arrived
to hear more about Harvey. We'd been sitting together for more than an
hour and he hadn't even come up. As Mary spoke, I listened, all the while
mustering up what felt like the requisite courage to begin my inquiry about
Harvey's crime and subsequent conversion. Be gentle, I told myself, but direct. After she's done, go ahead. Mary paused. I broke into a nervous smile.

"Umm," I started, "Do you, um—" From the corner of my eye I caught
Harold cover his mouth with a closed fist, as though tending to a burp, and

the gesture distracted me for another moment. "This is a very difficult question to answer but, uh, how do you make sense of all that's happened?"

"When I went to see him the first time in the prison," Mary said, "he told me how he got where he was. Did he tell you?" I shook my head no. "When Harvey went in the Army, he didn't come home in four years. That day, when I went to see him, he said, 'Momma, the Lord has been trying to get my attention ever since I been gone.' He was a cook in the Army, and he said there was an old lady that worked in the kitchen with him who kept telling him about the Lord. But he did not want to hear her. He said, 'So many times the Lord tried to talk to me and I turned my back.' When he confessed that night he said the jailer came by and handed him one of them little New Testaments. One newspaper article said when the word came down about his execution, that's when he started clinging to the Lord." She laughed. The notion that Harvey's was a death row conversion struck her as outlandish. "No. He started a long time ago."

This was true, but it also seemed like a bit of revisionist family history. After all, it was in prison that Harvey had been born again, on death row that he had taken a leadership role in a community of faith, the day of his death, I came to learn, that he preached a sermon to the assembled about discipline and hope. Harvey became a Christian and a better person behind bars. The journalists who reported that he groped for salvation as his execution date neared were misinformed. And yet clearly the remorse for his crimes and the prospect of his punishment had been the initial igniters of his faith journey.

I had wondered how Harvey's execution affected Mary's faith. But as the pastor spoke, I started to consider that Harvey's crime had led to two conversions: his and his mother's. If my timeline was accurate, Mary received her call after Harvey was locked up. And those conversions had initiated two ministries, his inside and hers outside. Each saw faith as an antidote—or if not an antidote, a balm—to the crime. Mary told me that when she was first mulling over her call she had dreamed of a pristine white house whose insides were filthy. Later, as she moved further along in her process to ordination, she dreamed again of the white house, and its rooms looked clean and in order. She was the house, and its straightening up, I thought, had been her own. Perhaps, both Harvey and Mary found in their faith not necessarily resolution, but possibility, a newfound opportunity to begin again. Faith was a funnel into which one could pour contrition and regret and pain, and from that mixture produce hope.

Though it was only six weeks after his death, Mary seemed surprisingly composed when talking about her son and the events of his last day, including the necessary logistics of dealing with a family death. "We are poor people. We did not have $5,000 for that funeral. So a funeral home right there in Raleigh cremated him. And I went and picked up his ashes. They're home in my closet."

"Are they on a special shelf?"

"Naw," Mary said, "they're just sittin' up there among my purses. The funeral home director said a lot of people share them with different parts of the family. So I had to ask my two daughters if they wanted some of Harvey. I told them I'm gonna get him a nice urn. They said, 'What you gonna say when people ask what that is?' I said, 'This is my son Harvey. Have you all met?'

"You know, I know people grieve in a lot of different ways, but see, I learnt a long time ago that death is coming. You ain't going to get around it. My father died before I ever even entered the world. My brother drowned. Then my older sister died. I preached my father's funeral, I preached my two former husbands' funerals." She shot a coy look over at Harold who, playing along, gave a gentle, loose tug at his collar. Mary's gallows humor was the product of a life's worth of experience with the deaths of loved ones. "I preached my brother's funeral. So I learned long ago that death is coming. Now the sad part to me is if you not ready. But with Harvey, I know how he went. I was sitting there, looking right at him. I know."

As soon as she said that, I felt a pang of guilt course through my chest and neck and head. Suddenly, I had the sense that somehow it had been wrong to come. Wasn't it wrong that I hadn't scheduled time to spend with Harvey's victims' families? They certainly would have an entirely distinct view on death. Their children, their siblings, had not been ready. Members of those families had attended the execution, too. They had sat directly in front of Mary as together they watched Harvey Lee Green die. Mary told me she was satisfied that he went that way, "instead of hearing that he died in an accident or so many ways that's more drastic. I won't have to have nightmares about them old grizzly stories they tell." But what of the nightmares of the victims' families? They didn't have the luxury, if one can even call it that, of closure, of resolution.

I wanted to humanize Harvey, a convicted murderer who died for his crimes, not lionize him. And I wanted to pay appropriately sincere respects to the mournful families, not bait them. But in that moment when Mary said Harvey had died peacefully, I realized that I really had no control over others' perceptions of what I was doing. While I could acknowledge my ambivalence, it seemed a futile effort to solicit approval from each party on a wound so raw. The two families' sadnesses weren't the same. But they both had endured sadness. The most I could do, it seemed, was be present to the one I was face-to-face with, and acknowledge the grief that was its counterweight.

"That day was the first time we ever had a contact visit," Mary told me. "I hadn't hugged him in fifteen years."

"I'm sorry," I said.

We talked a little bit longer, but by then it was late in the afternoon. I had spent four hours with the Goodings.

Mary and I embraced. She told me she hoped I would keep in touch.

I promised I would. I said I'd send them pictures I had taken of Harvey when we met.

"Oh, good!" Mary's eyes flashed.

This was the best compensation I had ever offered one of my conversation partners for taking the time to talk with me. Pictures of Harvey, I thought, in exchange for conversation might be a fair swap.

Eventually, once my pilgrimage ended, as I sat and surveyed the rolls of photographs I had taken, from the dead of summer through the middle of the fall, I came to understand as a useful metaphor the making of the pictures I took of Harvey, especially that last one, during which I had focused and refocused for half a minute or more before I left him and the prison. It was only as I turned the dial on the manual focus, only as I had Harvey in the frame, first fuzzy, then clear, then fuzzy once more through the lens, that I understood my own selfish impulse in that moment. There I was, manipulating the room, waiting for each person there to move at my own invented pace. In effect, I had paused the world, as though answering a phone while watching a movie on the VCR. Then I recalled the unfinished Via Dolorosa in San Luis, Colorado. That thirteenth sculpture, the portrait of Jesus' entombment, was conspicuously absent, and I got the feeling that the artist and I were up to the same trick. We both thought we could hover in that threshold, that sacred in-between of space, before being compelled to move forward.

[33]

I stumbled into the Oyotunji African Village in Sheldon, South Carolina, late the next morning. I was on my way to Savannah, Georgia, when I saw the sign for the site: a tall wooden plank hand painted with a figure in an African-print robe, a drum strapped to his shoulder, and a cane at his side. "African Village As Seen on TV," it said. There in the backwoods of South Carolina, down an unpaved, brutally potholed road lived a community that had attempted to re-create a West African village from the time before the slave trade began. The price of admission for adults was $5, for children, $3.50.

Inspired by the Afrocentric identity movements of the 1960s, Oyotunji was conceived in 1970 by a Detroit native who had rediscovered West African Yoruba religion and tradition. In the Yoruba language, *Oyotunji* broke down into *Oyo,* a once great, long-uninhabited city in Nigeria; and *tunji,* which meant "return." Yoruba was a polytheistic religious culture, and shrines to different gods and goddesses sat around the village on cement pedestals. There was the god of iron, circled by custom-shaped pieces of iron, and the priestess of the ocean, a cement figure with big, stylized eyes, the kind one sees in 2,500-year-old Egyptian portraits; her spindly arms held the pillars of a narrow grotto the statue sat beneath. Forty people lived in the village's small huts.

Oyotunji was the home of New World Yoruba, a religion recognized by U.S. law, and featured a marketplace of pan-African goods that was something of a South Carolina tourist trap. The day I visited, two busloads of African American teenagers from a high school in Trenton, New Jersey, were there also. It was a curious study in contrasts: the students in Knicks jerseys and Fubu jackets and hats worn sideways, the Oyotunji inhabitants in African print dresses and white head coverings. Like a field trip of time travel, the Oyotunji village tapped imprecisely into a dim, ancestral past for these kids, and it looked to the visitors as inconsistent and unremembered as revisiting photographs from your own birth. Still, it wasn't as though the Oyotunjians and the Trentonians couldn't recognize one another. Everybody was talking English. Most of the Oyotunji villagers were from the industrial Northeast and Midwest.

The Oyotunji Village concentrated these few dozen inhabitants' individual searches for their roots into its own. Oyotunji had been built from scratch. The people raised livestock and welcomed paying guests, both for everyday touristy or educational visits and for Yoruba festivals. I found myself admiring their inventiveness and their stick-to-itiveness, but sighing at the dilapidated setting and cheesy self-promotion. Oyotunji, its dusty dirt roads and mosquito-infested marketplace, felt a little like a ghost town. That they advertised this return to their vestigial African roots, their communal self-sufficiency, with "As Seen on TV" felt like they had built for themselves an infomercial in which to live. Did they feel as though they were living authentically when that essential self-sufficiency was contingent on tourism dollars?

Still, despite these misgivings, it was clear that it took a lot of guts to uproot from up North and relocate to this buggy, dusty, hand-to-mouth struggle for self-preservation. The Oyotunji villagers were black people who found common cause in their shared quest for origins. At one point or another, each of them had said, maybe while on a city bus or working at a dead-end job, "Who I am is not who I was," and asked as a follow-up, "How do I get back there?" Oyotunji, as place and as source of meaning, gave people access to return, and as I drove further south I had the tingly feeling that the village and I shared a primal restlessness.

My pleasure at this serendipitous discovery was countered by an eerie sense that finding the Oyotunji Village when I hadn't been looking for it really was not a surprise at all. Maybe it sounds weird, but I felt then, and I believe still, that I had been opening myself up to communities and people who were making conscientious responses to their loss of identity and tradition. It was as though the Oyotunji African village was a second draft of American religion for its residents, and it presented one more testimonial that for many on the American religious walk, the way forward is backward.

At the U.S. Army Chaplain Center and School, I glimpsed that for others the way forward is outward.

It was Darnell and his grandma Jean and their Catholic church on the military base in San Antonio that offered my first glimpse into the work of military chaplains. But what made me want to visit the chaplains' training facility in Columbia, South Carolina, was what had gone on with the Wiccans at Fort Hood. Though the government had come under fire from conservative Christian ministers who sought a ban of "evil witches" from military service, the Army had responded by shaking its head no. Stamped as a legitimate religious expression by the Army, Wiccan soldiers asked for and were given both a chaplain and a place to worship.

This commitment to its Wiccans ran counter to my own impressions of the Army. Though a widely respected institution and a place of maturation for the enlisted, it had, I assumed, earned its reputation as the stomping grounds of reactionary, ugly Americans. My basis for this? Pop culture. After all, for every movie that painted soldiers as heroes, there seemed to be an opposite version that portrayed the Armed Forces as armed and dangerous, a culture in which the tyranny of hierarchy made good people do bad things. For every *Glory* there came, as a rebuttal, *Platoon*.

The Army is nearly half a million enlisted men and women, stationed in the United States and all over the world. For this community and their families there are twelve hundred Army chaplains. That's one chaplain for every four hundred-plus soldiers and their families, a tall order for these clergy. The Army Chaplaincy was established in 1775 by the Second Continental Congress. The school itself was created in 1917, as the country prepared to send tens of thousands of soldiers to Europe to fight. By the time the school graduated its first class, the First World War was ending. Over the ensuing eighty years, the school bounced around army bases

across the country, from Kentucky to Michigan to Kansas to Brooklyn to
New Jersey, before laying down what look like long-term roots in South
Carolina in 1995.

The current Chaplain Center is a modern glass and red brick complex
located on the sprawling army base in Fort Jackson, South Carolina. The
base itself is the size, and bears the design consistency, of a small city: the
Chaplain Center and the market and the post office are driving distance
from one another; the base's own water tower rises above a low tree line;
and the roads and parking lots are a uniform pale gray. If soldiers and staff
did not wear fatigues, one could easily imagine oneself at the slightly worn-
down world headquarters of a former industry leader. I had made an appointment to meet Colonel Kenneth J. Leinwand in his office earlier that
week. Leinwand, I learned over the phone, was a full colonel, and an ordained rabbi, and the director of training at the Army Chaplain Center and
School, a position analogous to that of dean of students at civilian schools.

Upon entering the building, I saw banners representing different faith
traditions and denominations hanging from the first floor rafters. The
satiny material of the banners, shimmering like a line-up of prom dresses,
fluttered as doors opened and shut. The yellow-bordered white banner of
the Jewish Chaplains Council was sandwiched between a regal purple
banner from the Church of the Nazarene and some other indistinguish-
able one, composed like the American flag, with four multicolored stripes
and a red cross on a white background in the space where the fifty stars
are. Nearby, banners from the United Church of Christ and the United
Methodists and the Full Gospel Baptists and many, many more all flashed
their colors and logos. I felt like I was gliding through the United Nations
of faith. A professionally mounted photo montage of chaplains serving
troops—a priest blessing a soldier in a densely covered jungle; four men
in fatigues and camouflage face paint listening to a man, similarly turned
out, read from the Bible beside a jeep; an imam in a knit head covering
and Army jacket speaking to seated soldiers in an open field—featured
American flag bunting on its frame. It was as though a lavishly budgeted
school spirit committee had been given free rein to decorate the school in
as tasteful, respectful, collegial a way as possible.

The rabbi wore fatigues. (Sounds like the beginning of the worst hard-
boiled crime novel ever written.) His name was stitched in black block letters into his right breast pocket. The walls of his office were cream-colored,
his chair was black leather, and behind his large desk were two framed
pieces: one, his rabbinic diploma, and the other, a World War I–era poster
featuring a man in uniform calling out from the frame, a light blue star of
David on his right side, appealing to the Jewish community for wartime

support. Kenneth Leinwand has been an Army chaplain since his ordination as a Reform rabbi in 1977.

Rabbi Leinwand, forty-nine, grew up in Brooklyn, but when he was a teenager his family moved to western Canada. Despite being gone for thirty years, his New York accent was still audible. "People used to think I moved to Canada to avoid the Army, but I kept in touch with the draft board." Rabbi Leinwand went to college in Canada, and as a seminarian, had a student deferment through the end of the Vietnam War. "I was legal about the draft," he told me, "but in many ways I felt I'd got over on the government and my peers." He met his wife during his year in Israel as a rabbinical student. Though she came from a religious family, and was thereby exempt from military service, he said "she was always pro-military herself." When he raised the idea of serving as a chaplain, his classmates thought he was "absolutely nuts." Even his father, who served in the Navy during World War II, "wasn't exactly thrilled about the plan." But his wife supported him. They went in for a three-year stint. By the time he and I met, he had been a chaplain for twenty-two years and counting.

"What sort of curriculum does the Chaplain School teach?" I asked.

"All our training is designed to be battle-focused training. One of the tasks would be to perform critical incident debriefing: so, you're a captain, you're assigned to a battalion, your unit has just encountered heavy fire. Your unit has suffered 10 to 15 percent casualties. People have been killed, a lot have been wounded, you have folks that are shell-shocked. In the aftermath, you have to work with the medical people or other logistic support people who've had to tend to the wounded. Those folks need a specific form of ministry. How do you handle this?" Like other officers, chaplains train in a variety of what Rabbi Leinwand called "soldiering skills: anything from how to put on a uniform, to physical training, to road marching, to setting up a tent in a field, to land navigation. All that good stuff." They also endure some of the deprivations that privates experience, from pre-dawn physical training to a compulsively maintained daily schedule to sleeping in pup tents. "If they're going to minister to privates, they need to learn the kinds of things that they go through. They've got to be miserable a little bit," Rabbi Leinwand said, chuckling. One thing chaplains do not do is carry weapons. They are forbidden to by the Geneva Convention, so they have chaplain assistants who act as bodyguards.

Rabbi Leinwand, however, looked as though he could probably hold his own, as though he'd be the favored competitor for the over-forty division rabbinic weightlifting championship. Granted, this was not stepping out on a limb. He was a young-looking forty-nine, with broad shoulders, sandy brown hair grown longer than a crew cut and parted to the right, and a doughy-white complexion that might convince a visitor to think the rabbi had to shave only once a week.

"How does a chaplain work with troops?" I asked.

"There is a direct relationship between preparedness and doubt. The more prepared you are, the less doubt there is. There is a great term in Hebrew, *chizuk*, which means strengthening. When you go out to war against your enemy, and I'm quoting the Bible here, 'you shall be strong and have courage.' *Chizuk.*

"I was in Desert Storm. I was a major for First Armored Division, support command. In retrospect, we know we had very few casualties in that war. But I was plenty scared. I couldn't believe how many religious people I had all of a sudden. And they didn't care if I was a rabbi or the man from the moon. I was the chaplain. That's what's great about the Army. Soldiers and officers, they don't care whether you're a priest or a rabbi, imam, minister, whatever. They're looking to you as someone they can talk to, someone to give them hope.

"That's where we make our big bucks, so to speak," the chaplain continued. He crossed his hands on the table in front of him. Like his face, they were pale white and appeared soft and fleshy, like a plump toddler. I noticed, too, that his nails were well-groomed—not manicured, but longish, extending just beyond his fingertips. I sensed he hadn't been out in the field for a while. "I'm not airborne, but we got a whole bunch of chaplains who are airborne. When you're up 1,500 feet, in a C-130 or C-141, and the first one to lead off a jump is a chaplain, the other guys are gonna follow. For a soldier, that puts things in very plain terms: if the chaplain's good with God, it's gonna be okay for me, too." Just listening to the rabbi made me feel better for his soldiers. Rabbi Leinwand was an excellent spokesman and salesman. He almost had me picturing myself in fatigues.

"People don't believe this, but my XO, he's Presbyterian, my S3, he's in the Full Gospel Church." XO and S3 are military titles. I just nodded right along. "Go down the hallway," he continued, "there's a Southern Baptist; then there are a couple of Lutherans. My former XO used to be Roman Catholic. We get Heinz 57 varieties. When you think about it, here I am, a rabbi, in an organization that's 98 percent Christian, and I'm responsible on my watch, which will be a three-year watch, for all the training for the entire chaplain's corps. Where does this exist in the world? Nowhere. It's one of the strengths of our democracy, and it's certainly one of the strengths of our military."

What he stressed was, and is, amazing. America has been, and continues to be, an extraordinarily safe space for people to worship and create communities of faith. He didn't mention any Wiccans in the upper echelons of his Chaplain Corps, but the Army had made provisions for their secure worship experience. America might demand sacrifices of the past, but it also ensured that in the present, if you're inclined to retrieve something lost in the move over here, you are free to do so.

The rabbi told me that he had spent several years as chaplain for an infantry division in Germany. That in itself, serving as a rabbi for the U.S. military in Germany, was very intriguing. During that stint he was invited by the senior Protestant chaplain of the German Army on a tour of the Wiesbaden synagogue—I was surprised anything had survived—and a nearby military facility. "They asked me to talk about my role as division chaplain, and at the same time my role as rabbi, in covering a good portion of Germany. So one of the German colonels stood up and said, 'Let me get this straight. Are you the senior rabbi for all the Jewish chaplains in the division, or are you the senior chaplain for all the chaplains?'" To be the senior rabbi for all the Jewish chaplains wouldn't have been too demanding a job, as there were only two in all of Europe. "I said to him, 'No, I'm the only rabbi in the division, and I am a senior chaplain for all the twenty-one chaplains in the division.' So he said to me, 'You're telling me everybody listens to you, Protestants and Catholics?' I said, 'Yeah, it's really not an issue.' He said, 'That's amazing, because in the German Army, we have the Protestant chaplaincy and the Catholic chaplaincy. The two seem to be in separate organizations.' He said, 'Explain it to me: how is it that you get along so well?' I said, 'Gentlemen, it's very simple. All my chaplains, they're either captains or majors, and I'm a lieutenant colonel. They say to me, 'Sir,' and that solves all the problems.'" Rabbi Leinwand smirked, like the class know-it-all. "We are hierarchical. Because we have this hierarchy, we have roles that we all play, and we know what the boundaries are." He shrugged, an acknowledgment that that's the way this system works. Then he raised his hand, his palm facing me, as though to pause a follow-up question. "Within the rules of the game, though, there's actually quite a bit of freedom.

"So if there's anything I can't do," he continued, "my job is to find someone who can. When you go to war, it's time for absolution. Obviously, I don't do mass. I had to go find me a priest. That was a challenge, 'cause they were almost as rare as rabbis. I was fortunate to have a priest who came into our area once a week. Another good example: one weekend we organized Chaplain Leinwand's a capella gospel choir. When you think about it, you chuckle, but at the time I had a real problem: I had over a thousand soldiers where I was, in Saudi Arabia on the border of Iraq. My main support battalion chaplain, she had been forward deployed, 'cause there was gonna be combat operations." I made a note that the chaplain had not winked or nudged or indicated to me that he was making a special point by including a woman chaplain in this anecdote. There didn't seem to be anything extraordinary about her role, which in itself was important. "I was there in the rear. I had no other Protestant chaplain in the neighborhood. So I still had to do something for my folks. Fortunately, I had a licensed minister—he wasn't ordained, but he was licensed—who was an intelligence officer. I hooked up with him, I got a couple of my NCOs, and I said, 'All right guys, now you've got to be the choir.' Then I asked this guy if he wanted to preach for me. I said to him, 'You basically run the service. The rules say I've got to run the service, so I'll do a little scripture, then you do the sermon, have those guys sing.' We had forty or fifty soldiers show up. I had to bend a little bit, he bent a little bit, and we were able to pull this off for four Sundays until we got our chaplain back from the front." Rabbi Leinwand nodded his approval at the message of his story. "We do this all the time, and we are able to pull it off rather successfully. It comes as a real eye-opener, especially for new chaplain assistants who've never seen a rabbi. It makes people think."

Though frequently lampooned for its rigid uniformity in our individualistic time, the Army has in fact long been on the front lines of exposing America's pluribus to itself. And the chaplaincy, though only formally institutionalized on the cusp of America's entry into World War I, has helped engineer that expanding self-knowledge for far longer than these intervening eighty or ninety years. During the Civil War, President Lincoln appointed the first Jewish and black chaplains to the Union Army. It was around that time that AME Zion missionaries first brought their mission south. Rabbi Leinwand acknowledged the Wiccan community as another unique example of the Army's impulse to integrate people of disparate religious faiths more readily and effectively than any other institution in American life. In a military culture that demands homogeneity and discipline, such freedom of religious expression is all the more extraordinary. Even the fact that the Chaplain School had moved around so much, from Midwest to Great Plains to Northeast to Deep South, reflected both an itinerant impulse and a deeper organizational knowledge about what the country looks and sounds like.

Yet while the Army Chaplaincy stitches its Americanness to its sleeve, it is in other ways decidedly countercultural in the emphases it places on order, obedience, and hierarchy. For all of its emphasis on creative ministry, the Army Chaplaincy still has a job to do: readying soldiers emotionally and spiritually to follow orders, to fight, and if need be, to kill and to die. Rabbi Leinwand admitted as much. "The success of the unit ultimately depends on the fighting ability, meaning the spirit of the organization. But being technically proficient, having the ability to fire a weapon and to occupy ground, that's only part of the equation. It's the spirit of the soldier that really achieves the success. You can have all the firepower, but if you don't have the will to use it, the organization's gonna fall apart. During the Gulf War there were tankers who blew up tanks. They knew they had killed people. They may not have seen the bodies, but they know they did that." Rabbi Leinwand returned to the notion of *chizuk*, preparedness, as a response to that remorse. "Still, folks have to wrestle with the morality of what they did."

Speaking with Rabbi Leinwand confirmed for me an aphorism I had learned years earlier, in Mr. De Vito's high school religion class: there are no foxhole atheists. This, however, was a pretty superficial reading of the rabbi's observations, because in a deeper sense the point he was making was that in times of physical crisis, the spiritual borders that define and demarcate a community can dissolve. (True, these same borders can calcify during crises, too, as communities turn inward, close ranks, point fingers.) In the wake of the terrorist attacks of September 11, mourners assembled in churches and temples, their established communities of connectedness, but also in interfaith stadium services and at makeshift sidewalk shrines. A shared trauma, and a collectively felt grief, not only increased religious attendance (albeit temporarily), but also catalyzed an outpouring of interfaith handholding and arm-interlocking. There were the reports of sporadic attacks on Muslims and Sikhs and mosques, but for the most part, it seemed as though politicians and the press and everyday people had digested multiculturalism and political correctness over the prior decade; those crimes were deplored, their victims protected, their faiths uplifted. In the aftermath of those events, when the future political and military campaigns were still hazy, when the culture seemed really and wholly united in its devastation, the best we could aspire to was offering one another consolation and compassion. This, I recognized by the end of my conversation with Rabbi Leinwand, amounted to the constant prospect of turmoil that binds together the members of the military.

I had assumed that the military, in preparing its soldiers for duty and battle, leeches the particularity of their faith from them. This seemed an important ingredient in the process of building an Army of One, as its advertising campaign stressed in 1999. The armed forces have long been one of America's formative assimilating institutions. The military drills into its soldiers, though many of them had this well before they entered, a duty to country that approached a higher calling. That Friday afternoon at Fort Jackson, I saw clearly that the interfaith model I had imagined taking root in seminaries in my early student days at Harvard Divinity School was perhaps more effectively being patched together in, of all places, the U.S. Army. It is an institution that has brought Baptists and Buddhists and Mormons and Muslims and Jews and Wiccans and Catholics together under one banner.

What was true for death row is true for the U.S. Army: sometimes it's the places that seem most overlookable that have the most to teach us. I recalled the brief conversation I had with a thirty-year-old office custodian named Luis Barrientos whom I met during my time in San Francisco. It was a conversation that suggested precisely the same thing. A Guatemalan raised Catholic, Luis had left behind the faith of his upbringing when he moved to the United States in 1984. He was in high school then, and he spent some of his first years in America living the life of a mildly delinquent teenager, drinking and partying. "We liked heavy metal," he told me. "We went to Ozzy Osbourne concerts. I never listened to my parents. I liked being a rebel. I lived my life like I didn't care about no one. But one day, you know, I was coming out of a concert—it was Ozzy, Slaughter, and Megadeth—and there were these white people giving out these gospel tracts. I remember when I read that little piece of paper on the bus home, I was gonna throw it away, but I couldn't. The paper had a phone number on it. It was late, but I was like, who's this Jesus? Everybody's talking about him, Jesus here, Jesus there. This guy is popular. When I got home, while everybody was sleeping, I called the number." Within a couple hours of walking out of a heavy metal triple bill, a slightly intoxicated Luis removed his combat boots, bent down onto his knees, prayed to Jesus to forgive him his sins, and accepted Christ as his personal savior. And since that night, more than a decade earlier, Luis has been an active Pentecostal. Though he had been only a credulous teenager, Luis had found that night at the Ozzy Osbourne concert a faith that worked for his life. Pay attention to the places and people you think you have nothing to learn from, I reminded myself. They are trying to tell you something.

[34]

By the time I arrived in Waynesville, North Carolina, following a four-hour drive west from Fort Jackson and Rabbi Leinwand, the sun had been down for two hours and the small town was dark. A chill had plunked down for the evening in the Great Smoky Mountains, and Waynesville, about a half-hour east of the national park, had that crisp, mountain-fresh feeling that room deodorizer commercials try to sell you. The evening air had turned cold enough that I turned on the heater for the first time since the previ-

ous winter, and was greeted with a familiar, discontented knocking from
my dashboard. Given a built-in metronome, I kept time to my own befuddlement in discerning the correct way to reach my friend Kim's house. I retraced my path past the same gas station, on the same curve in the road,
and through the same quiet downtown three times before calling her to
concede my cluelessness. She asked if I wanted her to come retrieve me.

"That's totally embarrassing," I said. "I'd just like to know how to get
there."

I did arrive, finally, and stepped into the dim yellow light and cozy heat
of Kim's mother's kitchen. I had seen Kim a few months earlier, in Seattle, at my friend Danny's house. It had been the night I met Dolores Ledbetter. Kim was back home now, for the weekend, to see her mom, Jan, a
feisty fifty-something with puffy hair and a Dolly Parton–type Southern
accent who lived alone in the house where Kim had grown up.

A long time earlier, back in college, when I first learned that she had
grown up on the fringe of Appalachia, I had communicated to Kim a vague,
ill-informed desire to see a snake-charming church up close—you know,
the kind where the pastor uses his wiles to wield a snake as an interlocutor
from the Great Beyond, a hissing Ouija board. Five years later, that desire
remained. Once she'd heard, back in Seattle, that I was going to be down
in this part of the country in mid-November, Kim had invited me to visit
her mom's house. I made it a point not to turn down the hospitable offers
of home bases, so I had said, back then, that I'd be happy to see Kim and
her hometown.

That Friday evening marked my last Shabbat on the road. In the months
prior I had marked my observance of Shabbat in an Ohio cornfield with
Liz, in apartments in Durham and Los Angeles, at a synagogue in Baton
Rouge, and in a motel room in Albuquerque, among other more prosaic
places along the way. Shabbat had become an anchor for me, a reminder
no matter where I was of what day it was. Jan, a Methodist, asked me a
bunch of questions about Judaism and growing up in New York and this
ritual of Shabbat. It was as though she had turned on the recording equipment for her own research. Her questions were a generous expression of
her hospitality.

After Jan retired for the evening, Kim and I leaned against the kitchen
counter, talking, recapping. I told Kim about what had gone down with Liz.
She expressed her sympathies. I more than half-hoped this sympathy would
encourage her to take a step closer, hold my face in both hands, and sing
some sweet little lullaby. Is this what I have come to? I wondered—this
sending of a telepathic request for emotional, perhaps if need be carnal,
Band-aids. The answer was yes, and I was fine with it. Nevertheless, she
held her ground. I told her about Fort Jackson, then ranged back to Luis

Barrientos and the counterintuitive conclusion I had drawn that made me
think that the Army had a lesson to teach the rest of the culture about religion. She nodded, said that my morning reminded her of Vrindaban, the
city she had lived in during her first few months in India as a student on a
Fulbright Scholarship.

To the first-time visitor, Vrindaban is a dirty, grimy, disheveled city, where
obese hogs roam the streets and fresh feces steam at curbsides. It is, at the
same time, a sacred city, a pilgrimage destination devoted to the worship
of Krishna. Kim said that the city is a sty because, believers assert, that's
how Krishna wants it. Apparently the Hindu god isn't interested in the
supplications of half-hearted seekers or the dalliances of meandering spiritual tourists. Vrindaban is a city for the hard-core devoted, who learn and
savor the fact that the city's external horrors dissuade those who are blind
to the wonders of the inside from entering it. A pit on purpose, in other
words, is how devotees see the city, a place where the sacred is accessible
only to those who understand that the truth is often camouflaged in the
garbage heap, on the road side, amid the unexpected. Exactly, I thought,
smiling at Kim's useful analogy; the Army is like an American Vrindaban,
a red herring for the possibility of religious community, where faiths meet
and mesh without feeling compelled to melt into one another. The homey
smell of the kitchen, the low buzz of a time-tested refrigerator, our agreement, these small things in that domestic space had the mellowing effect
of a warm bath.

Kim and I spent that weekend tooling around western North Carolina,
visiting some of her country relatives in nearby Ironduff on Saturday afternoon, hearing bluegrass in Asheville Saturday night, failing at finding
a snake-charming church up in the rural hills on Sunday morning, and hik-
ing in the Smokies that Sunday afternoon. It was like stepping back in time,
and it was a gift.

I was still asleep that Monday morning when Kim rose before dawn to
get back to Atlanta for work. She kissed me good-bye on the forehead. I
mumbled a barely coherent thank you and good-bye. Visiting Waynesville
was like a vacation to a well-preserved archaeological site. It was a self-
contained pocket of nostalgia, and it lasted only as long as I remained.

[35]

The closer I got to New York, the fancier the cars got. On the Garden State
Parkway, a well-worn road that runs north-south through New Jersey,
and subsequently on the roads that cut into the chill of southern Con-

necticut, the highway filled with shiny SUVs, and there were noticeably fewer American cars. I shook my head. The values of this place, I snarled to myself. Don't they recognize what's important? I mean, really important? Hadn't they learned anything since I'd been away? At one of the parkway's insufferably tacky 35-cent tollbooths, I felt kind enough to allow a gold Lexus to edge in front of me. I waited for the driver's acknowledgment of my generosity. Nothing came. *No problem,* I shouted to my windshield. Why were people so damned inconsiderate? In the time I had been away I had assumed that a soul meld would take place—or more accurately said, I had pined for it—for a transfer of my values into the hearts of all others. But no: this personal fundamentalist ministry to remake the world in my own image was flawed from the beginning. Indelibly, I was being alerted, the world was still messy, the culture still greedy, people still flawed, the highway still a jungle. I seemed poised to accept everyone and anything but my glittering, flawed home.

I stopped for lunch at a pizza place just off the highway in Waterbury, Connecticut. A few women from a nearby office stood at the counter. They were, each of them, a little overweight, and dressed, it seemed, in whatever the Gap had told them to wear: matching sweater sets, pastel colors, large khakis. They stared up at the slightly elevated menu behind the register. I waited for them to order. The New Yorker in me had officially returned. *C'mon ladies, let's do it.* Then my inner Howard Stern bubbled to the surface, and I glanced at them with impatience and disdain. *Oy, like there isn't enough up there for you to eat. Choose something.* I clenched my jaw, a fusion of anger and superiority, the way my friends and I did in pictures from our high school yearbook—imitation poses of Gap ads, no doubt. Suddenly everything was a rush, everyone an obstacle.

Back in familiar surroundings, on the well-tread road between New York to Boston, I found myself catapulted into a blasé cockiness. Fat women in a Waterbury pizzeria were owed my smugness. On familiar terrain, with my trip near its end, strangers had ceased being subjects. Somehow they had recommenced as objects: of envy, of pity, of disregard. This was like shifting into behavioral cruise control. People drove too aggressively, or too meekly. They were too fat or too thin, too conventional or too flashy.

Traveling between a pilgrimage and the ho-hum, sure of my next stop but unsure of my next steps, I retreated into my personal fortress of certitude. In it, I was the jaded but seasoned arbiter of good taste, the omniscient judge of proper action. It was a safe, proven place of retreat. There I was right, and I knew it. It took me the length of the meal and forty miles of subsequent driving for me to understand why. Anxiousness upon reentry, culture shock—that's how I understood this clutching at self-satisfied isolation. But it's more than that, I thought, and less. It was arrogance, too, and in a flash somewhere north of Hartford I understood that arrogance is the Siamese twin of insecurity. They are bound at the hip, or fused in the skull. The appropriate religious—no, even more basic: human—posture lay in the recognition of one's uncertainty and insecurity about belonging. In these responses lay vulnerability, and in vulnerability, openness; in openness, honesty; and in honesty, trust. And trust is the anchor of community, the immeasurable currency that weaves us together, even when other loose strands pull us apart.

What is a homecoming when there is no home to speak of? I arrived in Boston, gathered for Shabbat with a dozen friends, then slept on a comfortable futon. Part of me hoped, even expected, that my return would be the main attraction of the evening. But many of these friends had not seen one another, let alone me, for three months, so the conversation focused on the big events going on in one another's worlds. My pilgrimage constituted only one chapter in the evening's series of discussions. I was disappointed, I guess. I had returned poised to march back onto familiar soil with the sound of cymbals and timbrels and other biblical noisemakers blaring in the background. Coming home from my time in the wilderness, I felt ready to talk about what I had found. But what I found that night was that I hadn't accurately measured the effects of what I had lost.

The evening passed, and so too the next morning and afternoon. Darkness came early. I sat at a desk in Harvard's Lamont Library late that afternoon, having flashed my expired Divinity School ID to a bored guard, and tried to think of something to write. Nothing came. In the absence of words I thought of something to do. I got back in my car, left Harvard Square, and headed to Storrow Drive. The trip to the South End took no thought. I had made it from Cambridge to Liz's place at least a hundred times the previous winter and spring. There was the curve in the road, then the skyline of downtown Boston, Boston University on the right, then the exit at Clarendon Street. I drove to the South End, past Beacon Street, past Commonwealth Avenue, past Tremont Street, until I reached Shawmut and its intersection with Hanson. Liz's old apartment. There was the spot where she had performed the Chicken Dance. There was the lamp we walked under when I told her about my column in the Nation of Islam's New York newspaper. There was her old doorway, that narrow entry, that fading wood painted blue, the spot where we dived into one another at the end of our first date. There was her *roommate*. Holy shit! It was in fact the former roommate, pushing the door open with a trundle of laundry slung over one shoulder, her hair in a ponytail, her sweatpants yellow. I caught sight of nothing else, because I pressed the gas and flew out of there like I was the designated getaway driver at a bungled bank robbery.

Oh, how ugly the thought that I might have been caught staring at her old doorway. How humiliating. How humbling. But how hopeful that I might see Liz bound out of her doorway once more.

Like all the people I had spoken with, I too longed for return. Yet there I was, my homecoming set against my enduring nostalgia for the way it used to be. Driving away from Liz's old place, retracing my route back to Cambridge, passing those familiar sights, and speeding through those timed stoplights, I knew both that I had returned and that I was still far gone.

Meanwhile, Liz called late on Thanksgiving morning. She left a message. It was the first time I'd heard her voice in a week and a half. She sounded chipper. She had just put pumpkin bread in the oven. She wished I could be there to run a taste test. She had gotten her hair cut short, just below her ears. To save the message, I heard, press one; to replay the message, press two; to delete, press three. I pressed two. An entire unspoken emotional conversation occurred between her message and my hearing, and I wanted to hear it again. But this time, syrup seeped from her voice. The sweetness sounded saccharine, an artificial substitute for the original. This time, I pressed three.

It's how someone changes after a conversion that matters. And a pilgrim knows how his journey shaped him only in its aftermath.

Most of the streets in New York City have designated times for cleaning. Along the strip of blocks near where my parents live, sanitation trucks rumble past on Monday and Thursday mornings from 8 to 11. With round, rotating brushes, the trucks sweep the curbsides. There exists in New York a bunch of on-street parking regulars, for whom these biweekly sweeps are a defining measure of time's circularity. The trick, known by all building superintendents and transmitted to the observant, is this: find a street that's been swept, pull in, and wait 'til 11. You wait with the car because police can ticket you and the fines can be big. You wait because once the time elapses, you're free. After Monday mornings, you have three days of blissful, automotive ignorance. After Thursday mornings, the ignorance expands to four days.

In the weeks following Thanksgiving, I became one of these regulars. I'd move the Altima at five to eight, then return a couple hours later to do my hour of time in the parked car on the swept street while waiting for a cue of permission to put my club on and exit the car, like the guy sitting in the car in front of me. But half a December's worth of this indigenous New York ceremony bored the crud out of me. Soon I pined again for departure. The ritual of the road—wake up, wander, find, meet, connect, depart, crash, wake up to do it again elsewhere—still swam in my bloodstream. Getting in my car to drive four blocks so I could secure a plum parking spot every third or fourth day sounded an internal warning: it was the don't-plan-on-sticking-around-here-too-long model, and it operated with the incessant frequency of an alarm clock on the fritz.

Being home amid comfortable, familiar surroundings nudged me to eye the day when I'd leave home again. Being away, amid foreign, unpredictable settings, had made my homecoming, while I was on the road, a mirage of permanence. I lived in a head-scratching, head-turning rhythm, and I posed the same questions to myself again and again: how are you supposed to make the place you live like the places you stopped? How should I locate, and if need be invent, the community on my street the way I found it in Alameda and Fort Worth and Dayton and Window Rock? How do I make home feel like away, when I'd spent the past months trying to turn away into a kind of home? Once at each destination, the next embarkation appeared gilded, the ensuing departure a climate-controlled, battery-operated, no fuss, no muss land of possibility.

In the immediate aftermath of my return, I became a curmudgeonly former pilgrim. Being in one place functioned as a general anesthetic. That I felt anesthetized in New York—a teeming world of eight million stories, where free housing and plentiful cable TV were my birthrights, where family and friends swirled through each day—was especially demoralizing. The mild, early winter proved to be no help. The mediocre New York Jets offered none either. I moved my car twice a week. I wrote every day, spent eight, ten, twelve hours a day transcribing everything I had heard and said. Still, I just missed being out there.

Anxiety crept toward me and whispered that I had not met enough people, had failed to cross off all the names on some checklist of the world's religions. This was, of course, true; this could never fail to be true. I had missed just about everybody. The thought that this umbrella of omissions was what, despite the best of intentions and efforts, I had wound up with propelled me into a spasm of activity. I made a list of all the communities I hadn't entered, all the tables I hadn't supped at, fearing that those I had encountered on my trip were a bland, homogenous bunch. In New York, and on a quick trip back north to Boston, I visited the Watchtower building in Brooklyn Heights, mission control for Jehovah's Witnesses worldwide; then the First Church of Christ Scientist in Boston's Back Bay, also known as the Mother Church because it was there that Mary Baker Eddy revealed her teachings; and then the Quakers in North Cambridge. Then, on another trip south, to Philadelphia, I met two young women—one Hindu, one Muslim—working at an Internet start-up. My list of unfinished business was filled with the exotic and the commonplace: I plotted ways to meet Zoroastrians, Baha'is, practitioners of Falun Gong, Rastafarians, Presbyterians. They were all out there. Some would be easy to find, others would be more of a struggle, but by no means was any out-of-reach. I made a laughable parody of Oskar Schindler at the close of *Schindler's List*, and I knew it: with just one more trip west I could have sat with the Plains Indians; I should have made it to the Temple in Salt Lake City; and I needed to track down that snake charmer. Just one more day, two more hours: more, more, more was what I needed.

The weeks passed. The transcribing continued. I pressed play, paused, rewound. The voices of Muslims in Dayton, Mormons in Vegas, witches in Dallas, the Army's rabbi in South Carolina; the memory of a Branch Davidian outside Waco and an imam outside Toledo; an *I Ching* devotee in Seattle; reclusive monks and Southern Baptist standard-bearers and withered evangelists—each and all paraded through my earphones, and I began to see my anxiety at the group's homogeneity as an ironic blessing. In our conversations these strangers had become familiars. I feared they had not articulated enough difference to display in Technicolor the radical variety of faith in America. Their commonality, for that extended moment after Thanksgiving, was a mark of my failure. The further I traveled in this revisiting, the less I worried. What if, I wondered, this commonality revealed something found, not something else missed?

I knew then that the pilgrimage had not ended simply because the trip had. Of course there was more to hear. I would have been a big league horse's ass if I had raised my journey like a trophy, proclaiming on the victory stand that I had gotten it all down. Commonality didn't mean sameness. Lord, no. The people I met were all over the map, and rightly so. They saw from different fields of reference, spoke from distinct sources of conviction. In their stories, though, I had begun to hear my own. Finding my faith was not—is not, since it continues—a singular, solitary experience. It depends on, and is determined by, the contours of three hundred million other paths, if not six billion more.

Failing to gauge my indebtedness to the world around and before me, I tried to go it alone. But there is no going it alone. The stories we learn about pilgrims, their years in the wilderness, their self-hermitism, persuade us—or at least they persuaded me—that such isolation is a necessary feature of the pilgrim's landscape. My soul resonated with the story of someone like Dolores Ledbetter, who had picked up and shuffled off and thought herself stronger for it. She found truth in coin tosses; I found it in turn signals. We both used the road as our means of egress and entry. And yet, to escape, and to see that escape as the locus for one's self-discovery (or self-recovery, in Dolores's case), is like trying to whip up some gourmet meal in the microwave at the Maysville, North Carolina, Hardee's. We need more ingredients than we bring with just ourselves.

Dolores Ledbetter understood this far better than I did. "A bird should not try to surpass itself and fly into the sun," she had read to me from the *I Ching*. "It should descend to the earth, where its nest is.'" Hearing these words once more through my headphones, I remembered I still had one interview left.

[36]

On a balmy Sunday morning, January 2, 2000, with Y2K-related fears and sales on electric generators and fallout-proof cans of beans as conspicuously absent from the streetscape as the snow, I descended a couple levels of nosebleed-steep escalators down to the B Line at Lexington Avenue and Sixty-Third Street. I headed east, out to Borough Park, the neighborhood in Brooklyn where Dolores Ledbetter's daughter, Jasmine Fraser, lived with her husband, Reuven, and their three kids. Borough Park is one of the centers for New York's booming Orthodox Jewish community. Yet on the street of walk-up three-story brownstones where the Frasers lived, I noticed a bumper sticker reading "I ♥ Islam," and Puerto Rican flags fluttering from window bars. Reuven and Jasmine lived on the periphery of Borough Park, blocks away from the main drag of Kosher groceries and wig shops.

I walked up a narrow stairwell to their apartment. They greeted me at the door. I shook Reuven's hand. Jasmine and I smiled at one another, our hands waving at our waists like flippers because we could not touch. While not staring, I tried to see Dolores in Jasmine. The daughter was more slender than the mother, though the faces, doughy, porcelain-like, were the same. Jasmine had inherited her dark, narrow eyes from Dolores, but not their suspiciousness. Reuven's red beard and English brogue gave him an impish, Bilbo Baggins quality. They both covered their heads in traditional Jewish covering, he with a *yarmulke* that partially camouflaged his receding hairline, she in a puffy hat that would have made her look like a chef in a French kitchen had it been white instead of navy blue.

I was grateful, and not all that surprised, to find the table set for brunch. Plates piled with herring, whitefish, and bagels crammed its surface. I had encountered similar expressions of fill-'em-up hospitality during several Shabbat dinners in the homes of Jerusalem's Ultra-Orthodox. The Frasers' three kids, none over five, it seemed, were nervous, polite, and quiet. The two oldest, both girls, wore ankle-length dresses decorated with flowers and stars. On the floor next to the table, they watched a videotape of Barney and Friends singing "It's a Small World" in Hebrew.

Jasmine and Reuven were a cute couple. Hard-hitting analysis, I know. But I liked the way they riffed off each other while telling a story, the thoughtfulness they brought to discussing Judaism, and the way they dressed their kids in a fashion half Old Order Mennonite, half hippie. They had been introduced to one another by a matchmaking rabbi about seven years earlier, and had moved to Borough Park in 1993. Both are converts to Judaism.

"I was on the subway here and I had a couple of questions: one, do you ever feel claustrophobic about the homogeneity of this community? And do you feel safer here?"

"Both," Jasmine said. She had lived on Manhattan's Upper West Side before moving to Borough Park, and she was a student of the famous rabbi and troubadour Shlomo Carlebach, a Hasidic-hippie hybrid. Hasidism, an Orthodox Jewish movement started in the first half of the eighteenth century, is at once a deeply traditional faith and a radical, almost flamboyant expression of Jewish spirituality. Hasidism teaches that all Jews are capable of a close relationship with God. Through a hyperattentiveness to the laws mandated by traditional rabbinic Judaism, the Hasid believes that he or she can transform, through prayer, even the most banal everyday words and tasks into a sanctification of life and the worship of God. Like the Amish, they dress modestly, always in simple black; yet like the Pentecostal, they pray with a fervent, emotional intensity. Of the two hundred thousand Hasids in the world, more than half live in Brooklyn. "Manhattan was a free-for-all," Jasmine said. "Borough Park gave me a taste of what it feels like to live in a small town. At Shlomo's *shul* (synagogue), women were very involved. Women aren't as involved here. When we first moved here, everybody seemed to be very different from me. I thought it was obvious to everyone. People looked at me differently. But at the same time, when I was being myself, I felt like I was being a rebel. Like just by being me I was being against the rest of the community. Moving over here last year gave me a little bit of breathing room in my head." They had only recently moved to this apartment after living first in the heart of Hasidic Borough Park.

"Of course it was all in my head to begin with. Now when people move in there and complain that the people aren't being friendly, I say, 'How can they not be? You move in and you judge them by your rules and your standards. They're living their lives.' Eventually I came to learn

that it was okay for me to be me. There are so many different Jewish people. I knew it before, but then somehow there's this lure when everybody
looks the same. The truth is, they look the same, but they're not anything
like one another. They're as different as you and me. People will ask, Are
you Reform? Do you live in Williamsburg? Do you live in Washington
Heights? Are you Conservative? Modern Orthodox? What are you?"

"But we're all *k'lal Yisrael*," Reuven said. The phrase means "the Jewish community." "And you're as much a part of it as I am."

"My father's Jewish," Jasmine said. "I don't know if Dolores told you
that. From Iran. She always told me growing up that I was Jewish. My father never mentioned it, but she did. But I didn't grow up with any Jewish
knowledge. When I was eighteen, I went to visit his father, who was also
Jewish. After that visit I was like, well, I guess I'm Jewish. Not long after
I went to the bookstore and bought everything I could about Judaism.
Then I went to the library. After that ran out, I went to the local synagogue. Then I started going to the synagogue every day. I didn't know
what I was doing." Yet the tradition was calling her. She learned about
the dietary laws of *kashrut*, which stipulated what the observant Jew
could and could not eat, and how those foods had to be prepared. She remembered that she was "constantly asking questions. But you don't have
to know everything when you convert." Jasmine paused. "It's not what
you know, it's what you commit yourself to."

I asked, "What was your mother's reaction when you became Jewish,
and when she heard you were going to marry Reuven? Did she know how
deeply immersed in this community your life was going to be?"

"I really didn't have a lot of contact with her in the years when I was
learning about Judaism. We kind of went our separate ways. I thought
her input was—" Jasmine waited to find the appropriate phrase, "not necessary at the time. My father was around. He was living in Los Angeles.
He told his whole family. They were all proud. My mother has been toler-
ant. She holds Jewish people to a very high standard. She heard that Hasidic people are very ethical and pious. So she liked that. She was concerned
that we hadn't known each other for so long, and that I had a Hebrew
name on the invitation. She was like, who is this?"

In the three months since I had met Dolores Ledbetter, I had puzzled
over the relationship between her and her Orthodox Jewish daughter. On
paper, as sports statisticians might say, this was one of the wackier pair-
ings in modern nuclear family lore. How had the one wound up in a Seattle shelter, divining with a library loan, the other in a Brooklyn *shtetl*,
davvening (praying) with her limey love? Inquiring minds wanted to
know, and on especially long, straight drives I had envisioned this meet-

ing with Jasmine and the questions I'd ask to find out. Once in Borough Park, though, grilling Jasmine about how Dolores had wandered into a shelter three thousand miles away seemed none of my business. The line dividing freelance investigative journalist and considerate guest looked then as wide as the East River.

Just as I was about to abandon the subject, though, Jasmine reflected about her path and her mother's influence. "But I can say I'm not like the people who don't follow their family traditions, because we were raised with a lot of morals. Not in a puritanical way, but in a very human way. We were held accountable for what we did from the time we were very young. Every decision I ever made in my life I take full responsibility for. Dolores really gave me that strength and freedom to be able to choose Judaism. I can say that. I should tell her."

"As much as I love my mother-in-law," Reuven said, "without being too sarcastic, she is a very straight person. Everybody has screwed up ideas in some aspects, but she's straight. She says what's on her mind, whether you like it or not. And she lets you know that whatever you've done, you've done it."

"We were given the strength to be individuals," Jasmine said. "In Judaism you have to find your own way. There is an underlying structure, but you have to plug into it. It says in *Pirke Avot*, the Ethics of the Fathers, 'You have to find yourself a rabbi.' You have to find the people that are going to guide you. There's a *midrash* (rabbinic interpretation) that says that before you're born you know the whole Torah, and then an angel touches you here," Jasmine touched the spot of her lip below the tip of her nose, "and you forget the whole Torah."

"That's where this little cleft comes from, " Reuven said.

"In this lifetime," Jasmine continued, "you'll find one or more rabbis, friends, that will teach you word for word what you knew before you were born. But it's your responsibility to find them." Amen, I thought. Amen.

The responsibility of Jewish immersion for Reuven, by contrast, lay initially not with him but with his mother. He was nine and had two siblings when his mother, "a Guinness-guzzling, party-loving English girl who used to model and do makeup" launched herself into Ultra-Orthodoxy. It wasn't a gradual thing. It happened in the span of three weeks. Without warning, she shaved her head and put on black stockings. He absorbed enough Yiddish in two weeks to get by in the insular world into which his mother had thrust him. (The Ultra-Orthodox Jewish community still speaks Yiddish, the language of pre-Holocaust Eastern European Jewry, reserving Hebrew for prayer life.) Reuven memorized the Hebrew alphabet in a day and a half.

"What brought it about?" I asked.

"Have you ever asked?" Jasmine wondered.

"Deep down inside," Reuven said, "I don't really know what made her change. Maybe I don't want to ask her, for some reason. I'm just happy that it happened." The transformation that most dramatically altered Reuven's life remained a mystery to him. His mother lived in Jerusalem. If she had come to live in the States, I no doubt would have made room for one more interview. The symmetry of a mother leading me to a daughter whose husband led me to his mother would have been neo-classical in its proportions. But it wasn't meant to be. Still, I was surprised that Reuven had not investigated the events surrounding his mother's 180-degree turn. In Christian conversions, the self before salvation is a vital piece of the testimony. Was it different in Orthodox Judaism? Was the community so homogenous that it sought to present a united front, whiting out the differences and making over all the idiosyncratic pasts that had led people there? I didn't press Reuven.

Yet clearly he had absorbed both his mother's Orthodoxy and her rebelliousness. Reuven admitted that he started "living a double life" as he grew older. "James Bond was my hero. Friday night I would stay at home, sing *zemiros* [hymns sung during the Friday evening of Shabbat], enjoy the *Shabbos* [Yiddish for "Sabbath"] meal, and later on I'd go dancing. I'd go with a plastic bag in my pocket: I'd take my hat off, take my coat off, meet a friend, and we'd go to a disco down the road when no Jews were around. Why I did that, I don't know. I was just being self-indulgent, I suppose. It's the only justification I can give anything. That led to a time when I wasn't religious."

Jasmine turned to her husband. "How long were you not religious?" she asked.

Reuven grinned, then pointed at me. "He's doing the interview." He thought I would uphold the conversation's unwritten rules.

"No, no," I said, "this is good."

He was up against it now, two against one. He shrugged and thought for a moment. "Really not religious? Just for two years." At that time he had lived with his father, who was dying from multiple sclerosis. He had made good money working as a cook and manager at a fish and chips pub.

"What brought you back?" Jasmine asked. I couldn't quite tell if she was asking because she knew both the answer and that Reuven would respond most insightfully and honestly to her voice, or if she didn't know these details herself. Earlier Reuven had told me that when they met, he had laid out his life story for Jasmine on the first date, so she could know where he was coming from and could, given his full disclosure, stay or go.

But maybe these were details he had omitted. Three weeks after they met, he had proposed. Perhaps their life together had begun so suddenly, with both feeling the need to demonstrate their faith through observance so completely, that they had focused entirely on present and future.

"I was living in a vicious circle," he said. "Going to work, drinking, meeting a friend, meeting a girl, having a drink, going back to work, meeting a friend, having a drink."

"It's hard to imagine, isn't it?" Jasmine grinned at me.

I nodded yes, though truthfully I could imagine it without too much mental strain.

"When I wasn't practicing, I met Hindus, Sikhs, Muslims, Christians, Catholics. I figured the best place to go meet people when you're coming out of a yeshiva and you don't want to be *frum* [Jewishly observant] is to go work in a bar. You meet girls. Everybody tells you their trouble because you're a naïve little idiot. Which I was. People liked that about me. I didn't know anything about anything. I was working at a very popular place in London. There was another guy working there, Ray from Ireland. Me and Ray hit it off. His nickname was Jesus 'cause he had long hair and a beard. Ray was living in a government house flat. No one lived there, but it had electricity and running water. One day a guy named Matthew came in off the street. Matthew was a yubbo, as we call them in England—a football villain. He was homeless and he didn't have anything to wear. Ray took Matthew in with him, and I took his laundry. We kinda shared chores to help him get on his feet. One day, when Ray was asleep, Matthew came in drunk and hit 'im on the head with a hammer six times. Totally deformed his face and his head. Ray went into a coma. I went to the hospital every day. Whenever I had time I would go. The regulars from the bar would come visit. Everyone was doing their own prayers, and he didn't come out of the coma.

"One day his whole family was there. I put on my *yarmulke* and *tzistzis* for the first time in two years. It felt foreign to me. I opened up a *siddur* [prayer book]. I grabbed hold of Ray's hand. I said, 'Please forgive me, Ray, I haven't done this for a long time. I don't know how good my prayers are, but I was always taught to believe that God does listen.' I finished the prayer for the sick people and I burst out in tears. Everybody in the room, including the nurse, broke down. I ran out of the room. They told me later he woke up from his coma.

"It wasn't long after that I ended up home, at my mother's house, on a Tuesday afternoon. My mother said, 'Tomorrow's Yom Kippur. Maybe you'll stay home.' I truly didn't know it was the next day. I spent the whole Yom Kippur in bed. I didn't eat, I didn't drink. I sat there and I read through Ecclesiastes. I just felt it was my life. I felt like the whole thing was written for me. Do you remember what I told you about what made it snap for me?" he asked Jasmine.

"*Havem havulim,*" she answered. "The first verse, right at the beginning."

He nodded. "Everything is nothing."

The existential crisis of a despondent Solomon, possessed of yet dissatisfied by wealth, and wisdom, and the world. In my translation, the passage begins, "Utter futility. All is futile." Ecclesiastes is the canonization of despondency. In it, demoralized ancient king and nihilistic contemporary teenager can find one another, voicing in unison the eternal question, "What's the point?" then amid their shared affliction, follow Liz's Chicken Dance in Eddie Bauer sackcloth. After all, dancing's not out of the question, despite the morose mood. It's in chapter 3 that the author tells us that there is a season set for everything, and it is this verse that Wren McCormick cites to the town council in the movie *Footloose*.

The mention of Ecclesiastes, I admit not at all bashfully, made me think of *Footloose*. It was the first movie—maybe the first story, period—that showed me, then a fourth grader already jaded by Hebrew school, the persuasiveness and utility of scripture. Wielded skillfully, scripture could shape the background and backbone of an argument, adding emphasis to an argument, heft to a request, validity to a lifestyle. When Kevin Bacon's character Wren McCormick nervously advocates to the dour town council for the graduating seniors' right to dance at their prom, he quotes Ecclesiastes to the pastor, who until now has been a foil to Wren throughout the film.

I had never put the story in those terms before, but there at that Borough Park dining room table, I understood that *Footloose* had been the first piece of my own Introduction to Biblical Interpretation curriculum. *Footloose* let me know, if not consciously, then intuitively, that religion was flexible and protean and functional in ways I had not encountered before. Before I knew who King Solomon was, I knew that Wren McCormick cited him to make a prom happen. Before Peter Gomes and Harvey Cox, before the religion department and Harvard Divinity School, there had been Kevin Bacon and Kenny Loggins. Let's hear it for the boy, indeed.

Reuven Fraser turned back toward Judaism that Yom Kippur, the day of atonement. He tries not to demonize who he was. "I shouldn't feel a total washout," he said. "Because you can beat yourself up. Nobody's better at doing that than you."

Jasmine smiled at her husband. "Nachman of Bratislav [a Hasidic master] said, 'I fall thousands of times every single day, and I'm constantly picking myself up. I do *teshuvah* [asking for repentance, turning back toward God] thousands of times a day.' It's not once a year or once a month. It's a constant thing. Any time you want to turn back to God, it's one turn. I think Judaism is much more forgiving than we are of ourselves."

Reuven brushed crumbs from the table into his hand. "I always remind myself of these things," he said. "I was a real good Hasidic boy, one of the best in my class at studies. I was trying really hard to be connected to God. In some ways I still try and seek the innocence I had then. Before I left, before my dad died. Before I came back. Innocence is a beautiful thing. Not knowing has its value. But for me, to be religious now is more than it was then. It may not be as pure as it was then. But I think it has greater value now, because I've been out in the world. I've tasted a lot of things that I really enjoyed. Like disco dancing, for example."

We picked at our plates and talked a while longer. The girls were sprawled out on the sofa in front of the television. We cleaned the table together. Then it came time for me to leave. In place of shaking her hand or giving her a hug, I gave Jasmine a little mini-bow, like I had gone to Gandhi's finishing school for interfaith greetings and departures. It just came to me. Reuven said he'd walk me out. He paused on the stoop at the base of the stairs, pulled out a soft pack of cigarettes, and lit up. He offered me one. I accepted.

"Sounds like you've had quite a trip," he said, the hint of a former bartender's banter detectible through the smoke.

"Yeah, thanks," I said. "You, too."

"You know something, your project reminds me of an old Hasidic teaching. Care to hear it?" I exhaled, nodding. "The story goes that a young man once wanted to change the world. He packs a satchel, laces up his boots, and early one morning, with the sun just rising, he sets about to change the world. He walks for a morning and an afternoon, and by evening, he realizes that the world is a very big place. A little too big. So he returns home. Now he understands that maybe he's bit off a little more than he can chew, so he says, 'Okay, forget the whole world. It is my country that needs change.' And so he repacks the satchel and heads out into his country. But the country is large, too. Smaller than the world, of course, but still big. So once again he returns and reconsiders his mission. 'I will focus my energies,' the young man says, 'on the town I have grown up in. It is there I will make my mark, there I will make my change.' He begins again, newly charged, resolved to his work." Reuven flicked ash over the banister and I noticed the corner of his lips break into the slightest, subtlest kind of grin. "But it too is big. Too big? The young man cannot say for sure, but he knows that it is bigger than he can change alone. He is a little bit disappointed by now, for the ambition he once had has, in his experience, shrunk considerably. He can, thankfully, still change his family. But he discovers that they're doing just fine, thank you very much, and that they're not especially interested in his help right now. He is left, at the end, with himself. And the beginning of this young man's wisdom arrives one morning when he realizes that he is responsible for his own change. And that *this* is a lifelong task."

Middle of a Sunday afternoon. The long B Line ride back to Manhattan. On Sunday afternoons some New York City subway cars feel like the reading room of libraries. So it was that Sunday afternoon after I left the Frasers, chewing over Reuven's last parable. I was a hundred pages through *The Grapes of Wrath* at the time, with five hundred or so more to go. In place of the hiccups and tentative beginnings I endure when starting any book, I was then, there on the B, rolling. The train doors opened and closed. The conductor announced the stops, strangers boarded and departed, and I did not notice. A soiled, balled up front page from the previous day's *New York Post* skidded by my feet. I crossed my legs.

My eyes sprinted across Steinbeck's pages. Tom Joad is marching back home after being released from jail a few days earlier. He recognizes Jim Casy, an older man—a minister, Tom recalls—who used to preach and save folks all over Oklahoma. Casy tells Tom that he has given it up. Well, he amends, not exactly all of it, but *that* particular part. The saving part, he says. It got to be too much for him, he confides, the pressure to save souls under a tent and the impulse to lay with bodies outside the tent afterward. He couldn't do both and feel right, couldn't play a part amid the crowd and subvert it under cover of scrub brush. Well? Tom as much as asks once they have arrived back home at the Joads'. They sit at the table with Mrs. Joad. What now?

> "I'm gonna be near to folks. I ain't gonna try to teach 'em nothin'. I'm gonna try to learn. Gonna learn why the folks walks in the grass, gonna hear 'em talk, gonna hear 'em sing. Gonna listen to kids eatin' mush. Gonna hear husban' an' wife a-poundin' the mattress in the night. Gonna eat with 'em an' learn." His eyes were wet and shining. "Gonna lay in the grass, open an' honest with anybody that'll have me. Gonna cuss an' swear an' hear the poetry of folks talkin'. All that's holy, all that's what I didn't understan'. All them things is the good things.'"

This I read on the B two stops before it crossed the East River and entered Manhattan. Have you ever cried on the subway? Not from discomfort or panic, but from clarity? Have you ever looked at the people who ignore you and one another, standing, sitting, bored, and restless, and looked up from the book you were reading, with eyes wet and shining, knowing well and completely that all these strangers have voices, that all these straphangers have souls, and that you need them more than you could ever make plain? Have you reached the uncontestable conclusion that strangers, when you listen to them, don't simply tell their stories but yours as well?

I looked across the aisle on that B Line, into people's faces, and I did not turn away. There I was, underground, returning to the place where my nest was, as Dolores Ledbetter had counseled in her *I Ching* reading. My mind darted to Tim Turner, then to Johnny and Ellen Lay and on to Mother Booker. And on and on still. All of them were strangers once. But I had come to carry their stories like my own.

We are, taken in sum, a congregation of small things.

[Epilogue]

Small things accompany me still.

In the early evening of an October Monday, I am heading home when the Red Line jerks its brakes and rumbles to a halt. The lights flicker, the train's electric hum shuts down, and from an unseen speaker a garbled voice announces, "Kids on the track," and the train won't move until they're cleared away. Elevated above Broadway, perched between the Wilson and Sheridan stations, the Chicago Transit Authority train acquires an unfamiliar hush, not unlike the quiet of that Manhattan-bound B Line almost three years earlier. There are only a few other people scattered throughout the car, and they read, doze off, or gaze out at the gray street below. Because I fell asleep while reading the weekly Torah portion the previous Saturday afternoon, I pull from my knapsack a paperback Bible, hoping to cover what I have missed.

"Now all the Earth was of one language," chapter 11 begins. The world's inhabitants congregate in an empty valley, and resolve to build bricks and create a city with a tower whose top reaches the heavens. God looks down at the construction site, "over the city and the tower that the humans were building," and hatches the idea to jumble the languages of the neighbors. If humans can do this with one language, God's divine logic goes, then there's no upper limit to their achievement and their ambition. God stops the project and scatters its builders across the Earth.

Only nine biblical verses long, the Tower of Babel story persists, in the minds of most biblical commentators, as a warning against human pride. As compensation for this mythic hubris, the world's peoples are fated to live in exile from one another, our words, values, and aspirations unintelligible to one another. Yet curiously the text makes no mention of the tower's razing. If God were enraged, if God wanted to teach this people a lesson, why not topple the thing? Why not destroy the tower and preserve

299

it in an abandoned heap as a warning to the proud, the ambitious, the all-too-human? Ultimately, we receive no answer. And we have no postscript, no allusion to a "Where are they now?" feature that follows. The story of Babel arrives, and just like that it is gone, never to be mentioned again. In my mind I envision the half-finished tower, frozen in a kind of urban rigor mortis, like the abandoned Soviet city that borders the Chernobyl nuclear power plant.

With the electricity shut off, the train's air conditioning stops working and the car turns not stifling hot but a cozy kind of warm. I start to feel the weight of my eyelids. I sit up in my seat and feel for my bag with the side of my foot, a paranoid tic developed while catching catnaps on New York subways and buses. I realize, for the first time, that the train is no longer stopped but is instead gliding along the tracks. The din of wheels on steel tracks gives way to a tranquil quiet, the way a marble might roll on carpet. The Chicago streetscape moves past me in slow motion. When I look left, I see the storefronts on Broadway, advertising tacos and used appliances in Spanish and English. When I turn to look out the window to the right, I see the green expanse of a vast cemetery against the backdrop of a sky the color of a pencil point. I stare and in what feels like an instant feel the snap of my head, bolting me back from a doze. I'm up now, I tell myself. I'm awake. To stay awake I should get up and take a walk along the length of the train car.

As soon as I decide to get up, I find I'm already walking along a winding sidewalk in the cemetery below. I don't quite remember arriving at a station, getting off the train, and descending to the street, but that's no matter. I am here now.

The things I notice: the buzz of a hundred crickets, the scent of newly mown grass, the faded polish of tall stone crypts. I seem to know where I'm headed, though I can't remember having visited this cemetery before. In the distance I can make out a crowd standing at the peak of a green ridge. With each of my steps the group seems to grow larger: the ranks somehow swell at the edges. Soon I stand before them, and among them, and behind us is a long table draped with a white tablecloth and held down by candles already lit and melting.

Recognizable figures step from the crowd and drift, almost as though floating, to the table. I see Mike Holton: he carries a heaping bowl of tortilla chips to the table and sets it down. I see Ellen Lay: she holds a platter of Saran-wrapped sandwiches and piles them on a tray next to the chips. I see Tim Turner: he flips a switch and the coffee begins to percolate. I see Sokha Diep: she opens her kettle of curried fish, the dinner she prepared the afternoon we spoke, and steam billows from its top. They are gathered together, all of these strangers, and they have created a banquet. Now standing next to three headstones, I hear the delicate tremor of bells. Usilinanda, sitting cross-legged in his burgundy robe, holds a chime with one hand and contributes a traditional Buddhist funeral offering. Roxanne Masni brushes past me, her head and body covered in a loose-fitting *hijab*. She kneels to the ground and with one hand shovels a bit of dirt into her other palm. She rises and in keeping with the Islamic mourning custom makes three tosses of dust onto each grave.

They have arrived here, all of these strangers, to acknowledge the deaths of those in our midst. Familiar names are etched into the granite headstones. One shows that Pastor Wallace Johnson died early in 2001, following a fall in his bathroom. The second informs us that Edna Doyle, of Axtell, Texas, and the Branch Davidian compound, died in July 2001. And the third has three names on it: Harvey Lee Green and his two victims, Sheila Marlene Bland and John Michael Edmundson.

Chaplain Colonel Rabbi Kenneth Leinwand steps forward and places a small stone at the base of each headstone. Jasmine and Reuven Fraser follow him, placing their stones on top of his. It is a Jewish tradition to place stones on a grave, a symbolic act that conveys respect to the dead and the sacred obligation of memory for the living. Others step forward, bend down, and leave an offering, each as personal as the next. Darnell Lyman unhinges a gold stud from his left ear and removes a pair of silver studs from his pocket. He places one on each headstone. As though approaching an oracle with an offering, Dolores Ledbetter holds her Altoids tin open in front of her, drops to her knees with a grunt, and positions a sacred *I Ching* penny on the growing pile at each grave. I help her to her feet, she pats me on the back and returns to the crowd. Expectant eyes look toward me. Do they want a prayer? A gesture? A homily? I have nothing prepared. I ruffle through my knapsack and see that, unexpectedly, I actually have a chapter written about each of them inside. With these offerings in one hand, I kneel to the soft turf. With a lurch my eyes open.

Again the train is moving, now at its customary speed, toward the next stop. How long had we been stopped? How long had I dozed? How much longer was the Torah portion? The scenes from the imagined gathering float in and out of my head—the remembered smells, the invented sounds. In my daydream an earring sat between a pebble and a penny, and Jews and a young Catholic and an *I Ching* devotee could mount an improvised memorial to strangers.

I wipe the side of my forehead, moist with my sweat and the condensation from the train's window. Somehow, in daydreaming about that gathering on the heels of thinking about that unfinished biblical tower, I reflect on our own fallen towers. In that moment I am struck by the thought that perhaps the Tower of Babel story reveals a God not so much affronted by the pride of humans as awed by our creative capacity. For centuries, commentators on Babel have suggested that the people's impulse to build a temple, to enshrine their own ambition, was a mockery to the Divine. And yet in that hubris is a blueprint for reconstructing a new tower from this pile of rubble. Perhaps, I think, God left the tower standing and humanity scattered, our tongues garbled, because God wanted to see if, despite our different languages and exiles, we might again learn how to work on the tower together. Perhaps it was less a punitive sentence than the issuing of a challenge. Back in Babel, when we all talked and believed the same way, the world came too easily. Let's really test these people, God might have thought: if they're really destined to build a tower that reaches the sky, they'll come back to this abandoned valley.

Once again I find myself on a train when I glimpse something marvelous. How to build a tower when we all have different blueprints? That *is* a challenge. But suddenly I understand that each humble stone, each gold stud, each dull penny in my dream was an offering, a symbol of somebody's story. Each story is a brick, I think. And perhaps all of our stories, piled together, might begin to rebuild our own tower in our own time.

In the early morning hours of September 13, 2001, before the sun rose over Perrysburg, Ohio, somebody fired a bullet from a rifle through one of the stained-glass windowpanes of the Islamic Center of Greater Toledo. When Imam Farooq abo-Elzahab arrived at work that morning, his assistant told him to check the prayer room. He found a finger-width shaft of light streaming through the shattered opening and shards of Technicolor glass scattered across the carpeted floor.

The staff at YES-FM, the Toledo Christian Rock Radio station that promises "All Jesus, All the Time," heard about the vandalism on the news. Staff members there discussed the act and considered a response. A couple of days later, a deejay at YES-FM announced over the air that the station wanted to form a human prayer circle at the mosque, to pray for the safety of and show its support for those who worshiped there. On September 18, 2001, in the late afternoon, almost two thousand people gathered and circled the mosque with arms interlocked. Together the visiting Evangelical Christians and the Muslims in their familiar space prayed and sang songs about America through wet and shining eyes, while members of the Islamic Center handed out Hershey's Kisses.

And yet feel-good episodes like this to the contrary, the world is not an after-school special. After the attacks of September 11 and throughout the dismantling of the Taliban regime and the first weeks of the war in Iraq, as the federal government froze the bank account of a Chicago-area foundation alleged to be funding Islamic extremism and arrested Muslims in Lackawanna, New York, for plotting a terrorist attack somewhere on American soil, various religious authorities and social critics crawled from the cultural woodwork and onto the nation's television sets, proclaiming the need for an alternative, or modernized, or Westernized, Islamic world. They spoke of the Muslim world's backwardness, narrowness, and extremism and neglected to look at the Muslim world as manifested here in America. They overlooked the seismic religious transformation shaking communities in places like Perrysburg, Ohio, where the imam preaches an Islam of moderation, of openness, of community with its neighbors. They forgot that just as America exports Hollywood and cheeseburgers, so too it exports a vision of religious pluralism and interfaith understanding.

At the same time, when New Yorkers could still see the smoke and smell the burning metal, when the country's terror was just beginning to give way to grief, a not altogether unexpected cultural response was happening in, of all places, film-editing rooms. A few days after the attacks, Ben Stiller, the star and screenwriter of a movie called *Zoolander,* made the decision to delete any glimpse of the Twin Towers from the film. Similar editorial alterations were made for the title sequences of TV programs set in New York, including *Friends* and *Sex and the City.* On September 14, Harvey Weinstein, cochair of Miramax Films, hired a digital editor to erase the World Trade Center from the Manhattan skyline in the movie *Serendipity.* In a statement to the media, Weinstein said, "We don't want to be reminded in our entertainment of the disaster we went through." With that, *whoosh.* The magician waved his wand, moved his mouse, and the Twin Towers, as though in a made-for-TV magic special, disappeared.

Shaken, uncertain, America sat perched in a strangely recognizable place, unsure whether to remember or wipe clean, to mourn or move forward. The culture, in reality, could choose only one path, and that, of course, was to do both at the same time.

I drove from Chicago to visit Imam Farooq in Perrysburg, Ohio, a year later, on September 18, 2002, and asked him about the event organized by YES-FM.

"It was so moving to see people hug each other who had never met," he told me. "A truck driver met a teacher who met a clergy member who met a housewife, and all just came to be together. To be together was enough. People here were concerned about their safety and the backlash. The attack was a Tuesday. Friday we had our regular service. Some mosques thought it wise to close their doors. But we kept the doors open, like a Friday as usual. We had clergy and non-Muslims come and worship with us. They sat in the lecture hall attached to the prayer room. Closing the door is not the right policy. We need to expose ourselves, not hide."

In the wake of September 11, the Islamic Center partnered with Toledo's public television station to show the interior of the mosque and of its community. At a time when self-preservation seemed to necessitate barring the doors and shuttering the windows, Imam Farooq's community responded by flinging its gates wide open. The membership at the Islamic Center of Greater Toledo grew by nearly 20 percent from September 2001 through September 2002. Other mosques and Muslim communities throughout America reported similar gains. Some non-Muslims were no doubt motivated by the explosion of available information about Islam; some non-affiliated Muslims saw anew the value of worshiping and participating in Muslim community. No matter how many caricatures of Islam surfaced in the wake of September 11, a roughly equivalent number of authentic portraits of the faith and its practitioners emerged as well.

─────────── ○ ───────────

I take the Red Line train south, past Wrigley Field, through the downtown Loop, past Chinatown, past housing projects, and past Comiskey Park, until I reach 55th Street, where I transfer to an eastbound bus into Hyde Park. The bus drops me ten minutes from home. When I reach my apartment's entryway and turn the key, I hear the sound of feet on our hardwood floor. When I open the door, I see the glowing face and open arms of Liz. She is home already.

Liz and I journeyed through a not altogether unpredictable postbreakup period: it was a cycle of disenchantment, regret, nostalgia, and possibility, not necessarily in that order. With deliberate focus I concealed from her the details of these interviews and the progress of my writing during our sporadic conversations. In this way I buttoned my shirt to the collar, exposing nothing that lay beneath. The first time I felt we might have a future together was in the midwinter following my trip, when I had returned to Boston and gotten a job. But that's not specific enough. In truth, the moment I again glimpsed us as a "we" was the first time I read to her from the initial draft of this book over the phone. In *reading to* her, I was suddenly struck by the possibility that I was *writing for* her. For all of its apparent gravity, the decision to move to Chicago to be with her, while sudden, was surprisingly simple. Strangers may have been my Meccas, but Liz, I came to realize, is my home. I asked her to marry me the following August. She said yes.

In Chicago I worked as a fundraiser at the National Interfaith Committee for Worker Justice, an organization that hosted the meeting where I first met Dolores Huerta. The organization's offices were in a Presbyterian church. I shared an office with a Catholic nun. I organized a weekly text study with a Pentecostal and a Baptist and a member of the United Church of Christ. I played pickup basketball with a member of the Nation of Islam and an aspiring Unitarian minister in the gym on the church's third floor. The Muslim, my friend Touré Muhammad, teased me when, after he sank jump shots over my outstretched fingertips, I blurted "Jesus" in fits of competitive dejection. "I made Tom find Jesus," he'd brag at lunch the next day, and our colleagues laughed. I started to attend temple on Saturday mornings, and taught an adult education class there on Wednesday nights. I wore my grandfather's old knit ties to meetings. I tried to keep my shirt as unbuttoned as decorum allowed. Instead of flitting around the perimeters of communities, I chose to become a part of a few. They weren't perfect, and better-fitting ones might soon appear on the radar screen, but they represented meaningful beginnings.

o

This is a story of how I begin to remember.

The word *genizah* is Hebrew for "hiding place." A *genizah* is a sacred burial ground, a depository for holy Hebrew books deemed, because of age or poor condition, no longer usable. The sacred, one learns through the use of a *genizah,* has a special resting place. Because they cannot be discarded, these documents, sometimes scrolls, sometimes books, sometimes fragments, are saved. Often they are buried underground, stashed in an attic, or crammed into the empty nook of an ancient wall. Judaism, I suppose, is a religion for pack rats.

Each of us knows the way to a *genizah,* a dim and dusty space in a cellar or soul that, though dormant, testifies to what was and what may yet be. Perhaps in its own way this book is a *genizah,* a resting place for a time in our shared lives before we became who we are.

Each of these words and all of these lives are holy.

ACKNOWLEDGMENTS

Thanks to my family for their love, my teachers for their encouragement, and my conversational partners for their openness.

Thanks to all those whose words are in the book, and thanks to those whose words are not included: Fred Lehman, Pastor David Riebeling, Pasquale DeVito, Mikhail Morgulis, Curtis Whitener, Patrinka Kelch, Joanne Krzywena and Michael Angelo NiCastro at the Human Kindness Ashram, Alan Medinger and Exodus International, Reverend Patricia Simpson, Pastor Chad Canipe, Dan Levitan, Wally Pegram, Charles Masicault Gandolfo and the New Orleans Voodoo Museum, Randy Malone, Shelly Wood at Betwixt and Between, Reverend Christy Harley, Bo Taylor at the Cherokee Museum, Deepak Rajegowda, Bhana Grover and Abeer Hoque at Chaitime.com, Robert Dove, Jim Noe, Emma Witmer, Iya Egunleti Adelabu at the Oyotunji Village, Robert Van Ardsdale, Nicole Kimbrough, Larce Vinson, Barbara Sonnenborn, Nella Hobson at the U.S. Army Chaplaincy and School, Sergio Sanchez and the SEIU local in Salinas, California, Robert Gauthier, Jak Kuntsler, Lawrence Ohaegbulam, Billy Bryan, Rebecca Benoit, Kelly Doyen, Charles Guilyot, Jed Mannis, the Museum of the Southern Jewish Experience, the Penn Center in Sea Islands, South Carolina, Kevin Hicks and the City Mission Group at Old Colony Correctional Complex, Steve Pomerantz, and Reverend Claudia Highbaugh. My sincere apologies, and thanks, to anyone unwittingly omitted.

My gratitude to those who opened their homes to me: Drs. Jacqueline and Elliott Kieff, Scott Kieff, Reverend Earl and Ruth Lehman, Joanne Lehman and her partner, Thor Wagner, Andy Friedman, Per Luedtke and Carolyn Hoecker, the Johnson family in West Chicago, Illinois, the Russell family in Maumee, Ohio, Michael Brown and Jessica Goldhirsch, Simon Klarfeld, my brother and sister-in-law Nick Levinson and Julia Moll, my sister and brother-in-law Lynn Levinson and Roderick Kreisberg, KinKin Min, Jan Newell, David and Christina Khoury, Chris Greene, Andy Michaelson and Juliette Dellecker, Dan Rosenberg and Carly Glassmeyer, Joel Rodriguez, Greg and Margaret Connor, Meredith Wells, Anke Vriesendorp, Ruth Blum, Cary Kramer, Dan and Meredith Schlanger, Jesse

Mencken, the Gongawares in Savannah, Georgia, Mark and Stephanie Rambler, Wesley Hogan and Bohdan Bietz.

My deep appreciation to those whose financial assistance helped me on my way: Mark Horowitz and the Uniterra Foundation, the Valeda Lea Roy Foundation, and most notably, Victor Levinson, my dad. For providing a nomad office space and computer access, my logistical thanks go out to Genesis at Brandeis University.

Special thanks to those friends who read early drafts of the book for their insight and generosity: Lynn Levinson, Elinor Renfield, Michael Donohue, Cristina Ramos, Nathan Dorn, Anthony Elia, Mark Rambler, Morgaen Donaldsen, Greg Heyman, Clio Baker III, Renee Simon, and of course, Elizabeth Kieff.

In particular, I'd like to acknowledge Professor Harvey Cox for his early enthusiasm about the project and for introducing me to Donald Cutler, an insightful critical reader and wonderful agent. Thank you to Julianna Gustafson, a terrific reader and collaborative editor, and thanks to all of her colleagues at Jossey-Bass. Thank you also to Paul O'Donnell for offering an early public forum for my writing on Beliefnet.com.

Chicago, Illinois   TOM LEVINSON
May 2003

THE AUTHOR

Tom Levinson is a graduate of Harvard Divinity School and a former student of Harvey Cox. Formerly the Development Director for the National Interfaith Committee for Worker Justice in Chicago, he has written columns for Beliefnet, the popular Internet religion magazine, and is currently attending law school at the University of Chicago.

Levinson lives with his wife in Chicago. He recently sold his 1994 Nissan to a friend.